Preface

Welcome to the Operating System Text Book! As you hold this book in your hands or view it on your screen, you are embarking on a journey into the fundamental underpinnings of modern computing. Operating Systems are the silent orchestrators behind the scenes, the unsung heroes that enable our computers and devices to perform the myriad of tasks we take for granted.This book is designed to be your guide through the intricate and often fascinating landscape of Operating Systems. Whether you are a student delving into the subject for the first time or a seasoned professional seeking to deepen your understanding, this book aims to provide you with a comprehensive and UpToDate reason.

Operating Systems are the bridge between hardware and software, the guardians of resources, and the facilitators of user experiences. They are the complex software layers that manage memory, process scheduling, file systems, networking, and so much more. Understanding how they work is crucial for anyone in the field of computer science, software engineering, or IT.

Beyond the technical aspects, Operating Systems offer a rich history, reflecting the evolution of computing itself. From the early days of batch processing and punch cards to the modern, interconnected world of cloud computing and mobile devices, the story of Operating Systems is intertwined with the story of technology and innovation.

This book is divided into several chapters, each dedicated to a specific aspect of Operating Systems. We'll start with the fundamentals, exploring the core concepts and principles that underpin all Operating Systems. From there, we'll dive into the architecture of Operating Systems, discussing topics such as process management, memory management, and file systems.We will also explore how Operating Systems have evolved over time, from the early mainframes to the rise of personal computing and the emergence of mobile and embedded systems. Additionally, we'll delve into contemporary challenges and trends, including virtualization, containerization, and the role of Operating Systems in cloud computing.

This book is intended for a diverse audience, including students, educators, professionals, and anyone curious about the inner workings of the technology that powers our digital world. Whether you are pursuing a degree in computer science, preparing for certification exams, or simply eager to deepen your knowledge, you will find valuable insights within these pages.Each chapter is structured to provide a clear and systematic exploration of its respective topic. You can read this book cover to cover or skip to specific chapters that pique your interest. Throughout the text, you will find practical examples, diagrams, and case studies to help reinforce the concepts discussed.

Table of Contents

Chapter 1 Introduction to Operating Systems

What is an Operating System?

An Operating System (OS) is a fundamental software component that serves as an intermediary between computer hardware and software applications. It provides a platform for running and managing programs, controlling hardware resources, and facilitating user interactions. The primary functions of an Operating System include:

Resource Management: The OS allocates and manages computer resources such as the central processing unit (CPU), memory (RAM), storage devices, input/output devices (e.g., keyboard, mouse, printer), and network connections. It ensures that multiple programs can run concurrently and efficiently share these resources.

Process Management: Operating Systems oversee the execution of programs or processes. They handle task scheduling, process creation, termination, and communication among processes. This ensures that programs run smoothly without interfering with each other.

Memory Management: The OS manages system memory, including RAM, to optimize its usage. This involves allocating memory to running processes, tracking available memory, and implementing virtual memory systems to expand available memory beyond physical RAM when necessary.

File System Management: Operating Systems organize and manage files and directories on storage devices (e.g., hard drives, SSDs). They provide a structured way to store and retrieve data, handle file permissions, and maintain data integrity.

Device Management: Operating Systems interact with hardware devices, such as printers, scanners, and network adapters, through device drivers. These drivers serve as intermediaries between software applications and hardware, making it easier for software to communicate with diverse hardware components.

User Interface: Operating Systems offer user interfaces to interact with the computer. This can be a commandline interface (CLI), where users enter text-based commands, or a graphical user interface (GUI), featuring visual elements like windows, icons, and menus for user-friendly interactions.

Security and Access Control: OSes incorporate security features to protect the system from unauthorized access and data breaches. They manage user authentication, access permissions, and encryption to safeguard sensitive information.

Error Handling and Recovery: Operating Systems are equipped with mechanisms to detect and handle errors, whether they are hardware failures or software issues. These mechanisms aim to minimize system downtime and data loss.

Operating Systems come in various types and are tailored for different purposes. For example, single user operating systems are designed for personal computers, while multiuser Operating Systems are used in server environments where multiple users access resources concurrently. Real Time Operating Systems (RTOS) are employed in systems with strict timing requirements, like robotics and industrial automation.

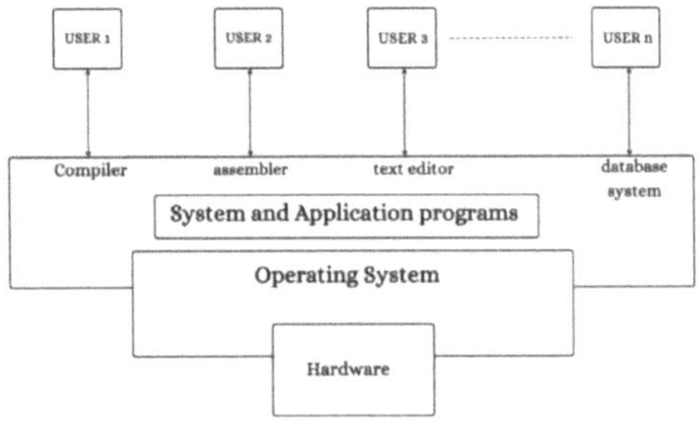

Video Link: https://youtu.be/Cqex4tLAkcs

Historical Overview

A historical overview of Operating Systems highlights the evolution of these essential software components from the early days of computing to the present:

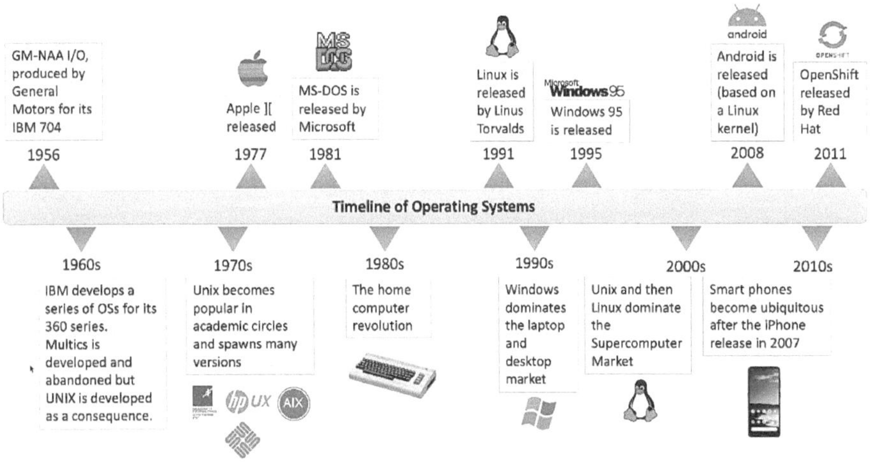

A. 1940s 1950s: PreOperating System Era

In the earliest electronic computers, there were no Operating Systems as we know them today.

Users had to manually configure and control the hardware, often through plugboards and switches.

Early machines like the ENIAC and UNIVAC were programmed using machine language.

B. 1950s 1960s: Batch Processing Systems

As computers became more widespread, batch processing systems emerged.

These systems allowed users to submit jobs in batches, which were then processed sequentially.

IBM's OS/360, introduced in the 1960s, was a notable example of a batch processing Operating System.

C. 1960s 1970s: Multiprogramming and TimeSharing

Multiprogramming allowed multiple jobs to be loaded into memory simultaneously.

Timesharing systems provided interactive access to computers, allowing multiple users to share a single systemconcurrently.

IBM's TSS/360 and CTSS (Compatible TimeSharing System) were among the early timesharing OSs.

D. 1969: UNIX

UNIX, developed at AT&T's Bell Labs by Ken Thompson, Dennis Ritchie, and others, had a significant impact on the Operating System landscape.

It introduced the concept of a modular, portable, and hierarchical file system, along with a powerful shell for commandline interaction.

UNIX's influence extended to the development of Linux and macOS.

E. 1970s 1980s: The Rise of Microcomputers

The 1970s saw the emergence of microcomputers (personal computers).

Operating Systems like CP/M, Apple DOS, and MSDOS (later evolving into Windows) were developed to support these machines.

F. 1980s 1990s: Graphical User Interfaces (GUIs)

The introduction of GUIbased Operating Systems, such as Apple's Macintosh OS and Microsoft Windows, revolutionized personal computing.

These systems made computers more accessible to a broader audience.

G. 1990s 2000s: The Internet and Networked Computing

The advent of the internet led to the development of network centricOperating Systems.

UNIX based systems, like Linux and various BSD variants, gained popularity as powerful, opensource options for servers and workstations.

H. 2000s Present: Mobile and Cloud Computing

The rise of smartphones brought mobile Operating Systems like iOS and Android.

Cloud computing platforms, like AWS and Azure, rely on specialized Operating Systems optimized for virtualization and scalability.

Modern Trends: Containers and Virtualization

Containers, driven by technologies like Docker, have become popular for application deployment and management.

Virtualization platforms, such as VMware and KVM, allow multiple virtual machines to run on a single physical host.

Security and Privacy

Operating Systems continue to evolve to address security and privacy concerns, with features like secure boot, encryption, and user data protection.

Future Directions

Emerging technologies like edge computing, quantum computing, and AI are likely to influence the development of Operating Systems in the coming years.

Throughout this history, Operating Systems have evolved to meet the changing needs of users and the rapid advancements in hardware and software technology. They remain a critical component of modern computing, enabling users to interact with computers and software in increasingly sophisticated ways.

Operating System Functions:

Operating Systems (OS) perform several essential functions to manage hardware resources and provide a stable and user-friendly environment for running software applications. These functions ensure that multiple processes can run concurrently, communicate with hardware devices, and interact with users. Here are the core functions of an Operating System:

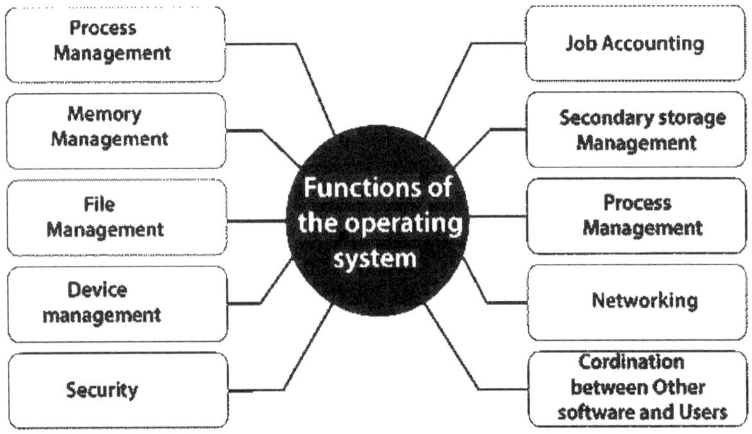

Process Management:

Process Creation: The OS initiates and manages processes, which are individual programs in execution. It creates and terminates processes as needed.

Process Scheduling: It determines the order in which processes share CPU time. Process scheduling algorithms help optimize CPU utilization and system responsiveness.

Process Communication: The OS facilitates communication and data sharing among processes, either through shared memory or interprocess communication mechanisms.

B. Memory Management:

Memory Allocation: The OS assigns memory space to processes, ensuring they have sufficient memory to execute.

Memory Protection: It enforces memory access rights to prevent one process from accessing or modifying the memory used by another, enhancing system security and stability.

Virtual Memory: Operating Systems use virtual memory techniques to efficiently manage physical RAM

and swap data between RAM and storage devices when necessary.

C. File System Management:

File Creation, Deletion, and Manipulation: The OS provides mechanisms for creating, deleting, reading, and writing files and directories.

File Access Control: It enforces access permissions to files and directories, protecting data from unauthorized access.

File System Integrity: The OS maintains the consistency and integrity of file systems, even in the event of system crashes or power failures.

D. Device Management:

Device Drivers: Operating Systems use device drivers to communicate with hardware devices, translatinghigh-level commands from software applications into low-level instructions for devices.

Input/output Operations: The OS manages input and output operations, ensuring that data flows between software and hardware devices efficiently.

E. User Interface:

Command Line Interfaces (CLIs): Some Operating Systems provide text-based interfaces where users interactwith the system by typing commands.

Graphical User Interfaces (GUIs): Others offer graphical interfaces with windows, icons, menus, and a pointer device (mouse) for more user-friendly interactions.

F. Security and Access Control:

User Authentication: The OS verifies the identity of users through login credentials (e.g., usernames and passwords).

Access Control: It enforces access policies, determining which users or processes can access specific resources.

Data Encryption: Some Operating Systems offer data encryption features to protect sensitive information.

G. Error Handling and Recovery:

The OS detects and manages errors, both hardware and software related, to minimize system downtime and data loss.

It often includes mechanisms for error logging, reporting, and recovery.

H. Networking:

Operating Systems provide networking capabilities, allowing devices to connect to and communicate with other devices over local area networks (LANs) or the internet.

Printing and Spooling:

The OS manages print jobs, spooling them to printers and ensuring efficient use of printing resources.

Backup and Restore:

Many OSs offer backup and restore utilities to protect and recover data in case of data loss or system failure.

These functions collectively make an Operating System a vital component of modern computing, enabling users to run applications, share resources, and interact with their devices effectively and securely.

Types of Operating Systems

Operating Systems (OS) come in various types, each designed for specific use cases and environments. Here are some of the common types of Operating Systems:

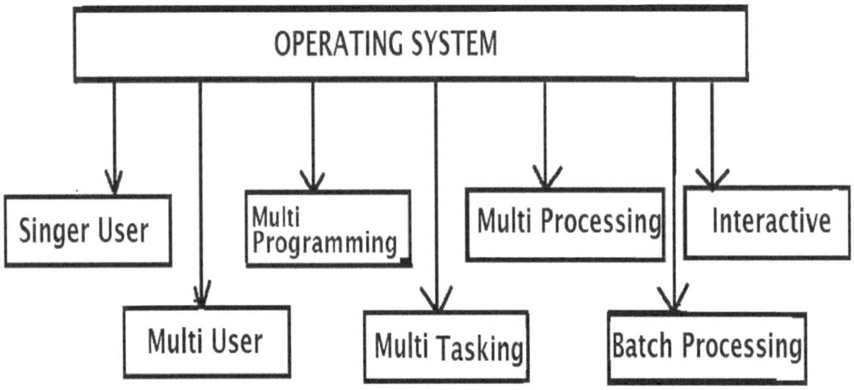

Batch Operating System:

Job Processing: Batch OS processes jobs in batches, without user interaction.

No User Interaction: It lacks direct user interaction during job execution.

Queue Management: Jobs are queued for execution, and the OS schedules and runs them sequentially.

Advantages:

High resource utilization as jobs are processed in batches.

Efficient for largescale data processing tasks.

Limitations:

Lack of interactivity; user input is limited.

Inefficient for interactive or real-time tasks.

B. Time Sharing (MultiUser) Operating System:

Multitasking: Supports multiple users running multiple tasks concurrently.

Time Slicing: Timesharing OS divides CPU time into small slices, allowing each user to have a fair share of processing time.

Interactive: Designed for interactive use, providing quick response times for user inputs.

Advantages:

Supports multiple users and concurrent tasks.

Fair resource allocation.

Suitable for interactive and multiuser environments.

Limitations:

Overhead from managing multiple users can reduce system efficiency.

C. RealTimeOperating System:

Deterministic: Realtime OS guarantees that tasks meet deadlines and respond to events within a predefined time frame.

Priority Scheduling: Tasks are often assigned priorities to ensure critical tasks are executed with minimal delay.

Predictable: Ensures predictable and consistent response times for critical applications.

Advantages:

Precise and predictable timing for critical tasks.

High Speed data processing for realtime applications.

Limitations:

Limited flexibility; may not be suitable for generalpurpose computing.

Complexity in meeting strict timing requirements.

D. Distributed Operating System:

Networked: Manages resources and tasks across multiple interconnected computers or nodes.

Transparency: Provides a transparent view of the distributed resources to users and applications.

Concurrency: Supports concurrent processing and resource sharing across a network.

Advantages:

Scalability and fault tolerance.

Resource sharing and efficient workload distribution.

Limitations:

Complex administration and maintenance.

Increased network communication overhead.

E. Single User, Single Tasking Operating System:

Single Tasking: Supports only one task or process at a time.

No Multitasking: No capability for running multiple programs simultaneously.

Simple: Designed for straightforward, single user environments.

Advantages:

Simplicity and minimal resource requirements.

Suitable for basic computing tasks.

Limitations:

Limited multitasking and user interaction.

F. Single User, MultiTaskingOperating System:

Multitasking: Allows a single user to run multiple tasks concurrently.

User Friendly: Provides a user-friendly environment with task switching capabilities.

Advantages:

Enables a single user to run multiple tasks concurrently.

Enhanced user productivity and multitasking capabilities.

Limitations:

Potential resource contention among tasks.

System responsiveness may degrade with excessive multitasking.

G. MultiUserOperating System:

Multiple Users: Supports multiple users concurrently, each with their own environment.

User Isolation: Ensures isolation between users' processes and data.

Resource Sharing: Allows multiple users to share resources like files and printers.

Advantages:

Supports multiple users simultaneously.

Enhanced resource sharing and collaboration.

Limitations:

Requires strong security measures to protect user data and privacy.

Increased complexity in managing multiple users.

H. Mobile Operating System:

Mobile Devices: Designed for smartphones, tablets, and other mobile devices.

Touch Interface: Optimized for touch screen input and mobilespecific hardware.

Power Efficiency: Focuses on power management to extend battery life.

Advantages:

Optimized for mobile devices, including smartphones and tablets.

Power efficient and designed for touch interfaces.

Limitations:

Limited versatility compared to desktop Operating Systems.

May not support all desktop software.

Network Operating System:

Network Management: Specialized for managing network resources and services.

Protocol Support: Provides network protocols and services for communication.

Security: Emphasizes network security and user access control.

Advantages:

Optimized for mobile devices, including smartphones and tablets.

Powerefficient and designed for touch interfaces

Limitations:

Limited versatility compared to desktop Operating Systems.

May not support all desktop software.

Embedded Operating System:

Resource Constrained: Tailored for embedded systems with limited resources.

Specialized: Designed for specific hardware and applications (e.g., IoT devices).

RealTime Capabilities: Often includes real-time features for control systems.

Advantages:

Tailored for specific hardware and applications.

Efficient resource usage and real-time capabilities.

Limitations:

Limited versatility; not suitable for generalpurpose computing.

Can be challenging to update and maintain.

Hypervisor/Virtualization Operating System:

Virtualization: Manages and creates virtual machines (VM's) on a physical host.

Resource Allocation: Allocates hardware resources to VM's.

Isolation: Ensures strong isolation between VM's.

Advantages:

Efficient resource utilization by running multiple virtual machines.

Isolation and security between virtual environments.

Limitations:

Overhead from virtualization can impact performance.

Requires specialized hardware support for optimal performance.

Cloud Operating System:

Cloud Management: Designed for managing cloud resources and services.

Scalability: Provides scalable infrastructure for cloud-based applications.

Resource Orchestration: Automates resource provisioning and management in cloud environments.

Advantages:

Scalable and on demand resources for cloud-based applications.

Streamlined management of cloud infrastructure.

Limitations:

Dependency on network connectivity.

Security and privacy concerns in cloud environments.

Special Purpose Operating System:

Niche Applications: Developed for specific, specialized tasks or hardware (e.g., gaming consoles, supercomputers).

Optimized Performance: Highly optimized for the intended purpose.

Limited Functionality: Typically lacks the general-purpose features of mainstream OS.

Advantages:

Highly optimized for specific tasks or hardware.

Efficient performance in dedicated applications.

Limitations:

Limited versatility; not suitable for general computing.

Lack of support for diverse applications.

Multiprocessing Operating System:

Parallel Processing: Supports execution on multiple processors or CPU cores.

Concurrency: Manages concurrent execution of multiple processes.

Resource Sharing: Handles resource synchronization and sharing among processes.

Advantages:

Efficiently utilizes multiple processors for parallel processing.

Improved system performance for multithreaded applications.

Limitations:

Complexity in managing concurrent processes.

May require specialized hardware and software support.

Multiprogramming Operating System:

Process Management: Manages multiple processes in memory simultaneously.

Efficiency: Maximizes CPU and resource utilization by swapping processes in and out of memory.

Response Time: Aims to reduce user perceived response times.

Advantages:

Maximizes CPU utilization by overlapping I/O and CPU bound tasks.

Reduces user perceived wait times.

Limitations:

Increased system complexity.

Risk of resource contention and deadlock.

Interactive Operating System:

User Interaction: Designed for real-time user interaction and responsiveness.

Quick Response: Prioritizes quick response to user inputs and interactive tasks.

Multitasking: Supports concurrent execution of interactive tasks.

Advantages:

Prioritizes quick response to user inputs.

Suitable for tasks that require real-time interaction.

Limitations:

May not be optimized for batch processing or background tasks.

Responsiveness can degrade under heavy workloads.

These are some of the primary types of Operating Systems, but there are many more specialized and niche Operating Systems designed for specific tasks and industries. The choice of OS depends on the intended use case, hardware requirements, and user needs.

Needs of Operating Systems

Operating Systems fulfil several fundamental needs in the context of computer systems. These needs are critical for ensuring efficient, reliable, and user-friendly computing experiences. Here are the key needs of Operating Systems:

Abstraction of Hardware: Operating Systems abstract the underlying hardware components (CPU, memory, storage devices, peripherals) to provide a consistent and standardized interface for applications. This abstraction shields software applications from hardwarespecific details, making it easier to develop and run programs across different hardware platforms.

Resource Management: Operating Systems efficiently manage and allocate hardware resources. They allocate CPU time, memory, and other resources to various processes and ensure fair utilization. Resource management includes process scheduling, memory allocation, and input/output (I/O) device management.

Process Management: OS supports multitasking by managing multiple processes or programs simultaneously. It schedules and controls the execution of processes, ensures proper process synchronization and communication, and facilitates process creation and termination.

Memory Management: Operating Systems are responsible for managing system memory. This includes allocating memory to processes, releasing memory when it's no longer needed, and managing virtual memory to allow efficient use of physical RAM and disk storage.

File System Management: OS provides a file system for organizing and storing data on storage devices. It enables the creation, reading, writing, and deletion of files and directories, ensuring data integrity and security.

Device Management: Operating Systems control and coordinate interactions with hardware devices, such as printers, keyboards, mice, and network adapters. Device drivers facilitate communication between the OS and specific hardware components.

Security and Access Control: OS enforces security policies, user authentication, and access control mechanisms. It ensures that only authorized users and processes can access system resources, protecting against unauthorized access and potential security threats.

User Interface: Operating Systems provide a user-friendly interface for interacting with the computer system. This interface may take the form of a Graphical User Interface (GUI) or a Command LineInterface (CLI) that allows users to execute programs and configure system settings.

Error Handling and Fault Tolerance: OS monitors system operations for errors and faults. It may attempt to recover from errors, generate error messages for diagnostic purposes, and provide mechanisms for fault tolerance and system stability.

Networking: In modern computing environments, Operating Systems support networking capabilities, enabling devices to connect to networks, communicate with other devices, and access remote resources.

Concurrency Control: Operating Systems manage and regulate concurrent access to shared resources among multiple processes or threads, ensuring data consistency and preventing conflicts.

Resource Accounting and Monitoring: OS keeps track of resource usage by processes and users, enabling administrators to monitor system performance, allocate resources efficiently, and enforce resource limits.

System Administration: OS provides tools and utilities for system administrators to configure, maintain, and troubleshoot the system effectively.

Compatibility and Portability: Operating Systems aim to maintain compatibility with a wide range of software applications and hardware platforms, promoting software portability and flexibility.

Interprocess Communication (IPC): OS facilitates communication between different processes or programs through mechanisms like pipes, sockets, and shared memory.

In summary, Operating Systems are a critical component of modern computing environments, serving as a bridge between hardware and software. They address various needs to ensure the efficient and secure operation of computer systems, making them essential for both end-users and system administrators.

Spooling and Buffering

Spooling and **buffering** are both techniques used in computing and data processing to manage and optimize input and output (I/O) operations. While they serve similar purposes in terms of improving I/O efficiency, they have distinct characteristics and advantages and disadvantages.

Spooling (Simultaneous Peripheral Operation On Line):

Spooling involves temporarily storing data from I/O operations in a spool or a queue, typically on a secondary storage device like a disk, before it is processed by the associated input or output device. Spooling is commonly used for tasks like printing, where there may be a significant mismatch between the speed of data generation and the speed at which the peripheral device (e.g., printer) can process the data. Here are its characteristics and advantages and disadvantages:

Advantages of Spooling:

Concurrency: Spooling allows multiple I/O operations to occur concurrently. While one operation is in the spool, others can continue, improving overall system efficiency and user productivity.

Resource Management: Spooling effectively manages system resources. It prevents resource contention, ensuring that one process's slow I/O operation doesn't impact the performance of others.

Fault Tolerance: Data is stored in the spool, reducing the risk of data loss in case of device failures or system crashes. The system can retry sending data to the device later, if an error occurs during the initial attempt.

User Transparency: Users can initiate I/O operations without needing to understand or manage the complexities of the underlying devices. Spooling provides a seamless and user-friendly experience.

Optimized Device Utilization: Spooling allows devices with varying speeds to operate at their own pace. For example, a fast CPU can generate print jobs quickly, and the spooling system manages the output to the slower printer.

Disadvantages of Spooling:

Disk Space Usage: Spooling may consume disk space to store the spooled data. Large spooled files can lead to significant disk space usage.

Access Delay: There may be a delay in accessing the spooled data because it is stored on disk. This delay can impact the responsiveness of I/O operations.

Management Overhead: Spooling requires additional management overhead to maintain the spool, manage queues, and ensure proper data flow to and from devices.

Buffering:

Buffering involves using a memory buffer (temporary storage area) to hold data temporarily during I/O operations. Data is read from or written to the buffer, which can be in RAM, before being transferred to or from the actual I/O device. Buffering is employed to overcome speed disparities between the CPU and I/O devices, reduce the frequency of I/O operations, and improve system performance. Here are its characteristics and advantages and disadvantages:

Advantages of Buffering:

Speed Matching: Buffering helps match the speeds of devices with different data transfer rates, reducing idle time for the CPU and peripherals.

Reduced I/O Operations: By batching data into blocks in the buffer, the number of actual I/O operations is reduced, which can be more efficient.

Improved Responsiveness: Buffering can improve system responsiveness by reducing wait times associated with I/O operations.

Data Integrity: Buffering can help ensure data integrity by temporarily holding data until it is successfully transferred to or from the device.

Disadvantages of Buffering:

Memory Usage: Buffering consumes memory resources. Large buffers can lead to increased RAM usage.

Complexity: Managing buffers and ensuring data consistency can add complexity to software development and maintenance.

Overhead: Buffering introduces some overhead in terms of copying data between the buffer and the device.

In summary, Spooling and Buffering are techniques used in I/O management to improve system efficiency and user experience. Spooling is particularly useful for managing large, time consuming I/O operations, while buffering focuses on optimizing data transfer between the CPU and devices. The choice between them depends on the specific requirements of the system and the nature of the I/O operations being performed.

Spooling Over Buffering

Spooling and Buffering are both techniques used in computing to optimize input and output (I/O) operations, but they have distinct characteristics and offer different advantages and disadvantages. Let's compare the advantages and disadvantages of spooling over buffering:

Advantages of Spooling Over Buffering:

Concurrency: Spooling allows multiple I/O operations to occur concurrently. While one operation is in the spool, others can continue, improving overall system efficiency and user productivity. Buffering may not provide the same level of concurrency.

Resource Management: Spooling effectively manages system resources. It prevents resource contention, ensuring that one process's slow I/O operation doesn't impact the performance of others. Buffering primarily focuses on matching speeds between the CPU and devices but may not provide the same level of resource management.

Fault Tolerance: Data is stored in the spool, reducing the risk of data loss in case of device failures or system crashes. The system can retry sending data to the device later if an error occurs during the initial attempt. Buffering may not offer the same level of fault tolerance, as it typically doesn't involve persistent storage of data.

User Transparency: Spooling provides a transparent experience for users. They can initiate I/O operations without needing to understand or manage the complexities of the underlying devices. Buffering may require more explicit management of buffers and data flow by the application or system.

Optimized Device Utilization: Spooling allows devices with varying speeds to operate at their own pace. For example, a fast CPU can generate print jobs quickly, and the spooling system manages the output to the slower printer. Buffering focuses primarily on optimizing data transfer between the CPU and devices but may not offer the same degree of device optimization.

Disadvantages of Spooling Over Buffering:

Disk Space Usage: Spooling may consume disk space to store the spooled data. Large spooled files can lead to significant disk space usage. Buffering primarily uses memory (RAM), which may be more limited than disk space but is generally faster.

Access Delay: There may be a delay in accessing the spooled data because it is stored on disk. This delay can impact the responsiveness of I/O operations. Buffering, being primarily in memory, typically offers faster access times.

Management Overhead: Spooling requires additional management overhead to maintain the spool, manage queues, and ensure proper data flow to and from devices. Buffering, while not without complexity, may involve fewer management overhead considerations.

In summary, spooling is advantageous when dealing with large, timeconsuming I/O operations, ensuring concurrency, fault tolerance, and user transparency. However, it may introduce delays due to disk access and consume significant disk space. Buffering, on the other hand, excels at matching speeds between the CPU and devices and reducing the frequency of I/O operations, but it may not provide the same level of concurrency and fault tolerance as spooling. The choice between these techniques depends on the specific requirements of the system and the nature of the I/O operations being performed.

Objective of Operating System

The primary objectives of an Operating System (OS) are to provide a convenient, efficient, and secure environment for both users and software applications. Operating Systems serve as an intermediary between the computer hardware and the software running on it, and they aim to fulfil several key objectives:

Resource Management:

Efficiently allocate and manage hardware resources such as CPU time, memory, storage, and input/output (I/O) devices.

Ensure fair resource sharing among multiple users or processes.

B. Process and Task Management:

Enable the execution of multiple processes or tasks concurrently, allowing for multitasking and efficient utilization of the CPU.

Provide mechanisms for process creation, scheduling, termination, and synchronization.

C. File System Management:

Manage files and directories on storage devices.

Provide file access, organization, and protection mechanisms.

Ensure data integrity and reliability.

D. Device Management:

Control and coordinate interactions with input and output devices such as keyboards, displays, printers, and storage devices.

Provide device drivers and abstractions to facilitate device communication.

E. User Interface:

Provide a user-friendly interface for interacting with the computer system, which can include commandline interfaces (CLI) or graphical user interfaces (GUI).

Support user input and output operations.

F. Security and Access Control:

Enforce access control mechanisms to protect system resources and user data.

Ensure user authentication and authorization.

Implement security features to defend against unauthorized access and malicious activities.

G. Error Handling and Recovery:

Detect and handle hardware and software errors gracefully.

Provide mechanisms for fault tolerance, error reporting, and system recovery.

H. Resource Optimization:

Maximize system performance and resource utilization.

Implement scheduling algorithms and optimization techniques to minimize idle time and improve system responsiveness.

Abstraction:

Present hardware resources to applications and users through abstractions, making it easier to write software that runs on different hardware configurations.

Hide lowlevel hardware details from users and applications.

Interprocess Communication (IPC):

Facilitate communication and data sharing between processes and tasks.

Support mechanisms like pipes, sockets, and shared memory.

Networking (in network aware OSes):

Enable network communication and protocols.

Manage network connections and data transmission.

Scalability and Extensibility:

Support the addition of new hardware, software, and services.

Allow the system to scale and adapt to changing requirements and technologies.

Virtualization and Cloud Computing (in modern OSes):

Provide virtualization capabilities to run multiple Operating Systems or instances on a single physical server.

Support cloud computing environments with resource provisioning and management.

The specific objectives of an Operating System can vary depending on its type and use cases. For example, realtimeOperating Systems prioritize predictable and timely execution for critical tasks, while mobile Operating Systems focus on power efficiency and user experience. Regardless of the specific goals, an Operating System aims to create a stable, efficient, and secure environment for users and software applications to operate effectively.

Previous Years Solved Questions

Q 1. A. Whatisan Operating System? (RU BCA 2022, RTU B. Tech. Feb 2021)

Ans: An Operating System (OS) is a crucial software component that acts as an intermediary between a computer's hardware and its users or applications. Its primary purpose is to manage and coordinate various hardware resources like the CPU, memory, storage devices, and input/output devices, ensuring they work together efficiently. The OS provides essential services, such as process management (running and controlling programs), memory management (allocating and managing system memory), and file system management (organizing and accessing data on storage media). It also offers a user interface, which can be graphical or text-based, allowing users to interact with the computer.Additionally, an OS plays a pivotal role in security, implementing access controls and user authentication to safeguard the system and data. It facilitates network communication, enabling devices to connect and share information. Operating Systems are essential for nearly all computing devices, from personal computers and servers to mobile phones and embedded systems, as they create a stable and consistent platform for running software applications.

Q 1. B. WhatisBatch System? (RU BCA 2022, RTU B. Tech. Feb 2021)

Ans: An Operating System(OS)is basically a collection of software that manages computer hardware resources and provides common services for computer programs.Operating System is a crucial component of the system software in a computer system.

Batch Operating System is one of the important type of Operating System.

The users who using a batch Operating System donot interact with the computer directly.Each user prepares its job on an off-line device like punch cards and submits it to the computer operator.To speed up the processing, jobs with similar needs are batched together andrun as a group. The programmers exit their programs withthe operator and the operator then sorts the programs with similar requirements into batches.

The problems that occurs with fetch Systems areas follows:

There is a lack of interaction between the user and the job.
CPU is being often idle, because the speed of the mechanical I/O devices is slower than the CPU.
It is difficult to provide the desired priority.

Q 2. What is Multi-Programming System?(RU BCA 2022)

Ans:A Multi-Programming System is an Operating System that allows multiple programs to run concurrently on a computer system. It enhances the utilization of CPU and system resources by efficiently switching between different programs, providing the illusion of parallel execution. In a multi-programming environment, when one program is waiting for I/O or other resources, the Operating System can quickly switch to executing another program, keeping the CPU busy and improving overall system throughput.

Key features of multi-programming systems include process scheduling, memory management, and resource allocation. These systems also employ techniques like time-sharing and interrupt handling to ensure fair and efficient utilization of resources among multiple programs. Multi-programming is particularly useful in scenarios where multiple users or tasks need to be accommodated simultaneously, such as in mainframes, servers, and multi-user systems.

Overall, Multi-Programming Systems enhance system efficiency, reduce idle time, and improve user responsiveness by allowing several programs to share and utilize system resources concurrently.

Q 3. What is Direct Access Memory Buffering?(RU BCA 2022)

Ans: Direct Access Memory Buffering, often referred to as DAMB or simply memory buffering, is a technique used in computer systems to enhance data transfer speed between two devices, typically between slower peripheral devices (like hard drives or network cards) and faster central processing units (CPUs) or memory.

Here's how it works:

Data Buffer: A buffer, or a small, fast-access memory area, is placed between the slower peripheral device and the CPU/memory. This buffer temporarily stores data as it's transferred between the two.

Parallelism: While the peripheral device is reading or writing data to the buffer, the CPU can perform other tasks concurrently, increasing system throughput and efficiency. This is especially beneficial when the CPU is faster than the peripheral device.

Efficiency: DAMB minimizes data transfer delays because the CPU doesn't need to wait for the slower peripheral device to complete its operation before continuing with other tasks. It can continue processing data from or to the buffer while the peripheral device catches up.

Optimization: The buffer can be optimized to match the specific characteristics of the peripheral device and the CPU, helping to smooth out data transfer rates and reduce bottlenecks.

Error Handling: DAMB can also help with error handling by allowing the CPU to verify data integrity before it's transferred to or from the slower device, reducing the chances of data corruption.

Overall, direct access memory buffering is a vital technique for improving the overall system performance by reducing data transfer latency, improving CPU utilization, and ensuring efficient data flow between various system components. It's commonly used in storage devices like hard drives and solid-state drives to optimize data transfer rates.

Q 4. What is the difference between Job and Process?(RU BCA 2019)

Ans: In the Context of Operating Systems, "Job" and "Process" are related but distinct concepts. They both represent a program in execution, but they are used in slightly different contexts, and their characteristics differ.

Job:

Submission Unit: A Job is typically used as a submission unit. It represents a complete program or a batch of tasks submitted by a user or an application. Jobs are often submitted to a batch processing system, where they are placed in a queue and executed one by one.

Independence: Jobs are generally independent of each other. They can be entirely separate programs or tasks that don't share memory or resources. Each job runs in its own address space.

Longer Lifespan: Jobs often have a longer lifespan. They may include tasks or processes that can take a considerable amount of time to complete.

Resource Allocation: Resource allocation for jobs is typically done at the job level. This includes allocating CPU time, memory, and other resources for the entire job.

Process:

Execution Unit: A Process is an execution unit within a job. It represents an individual program or task that is currently running on the system. In a multitasking Operating System, multiple processes can run concurrently.

Resource Sharing: Processes within a job may share resources, including memory, files, and other system resources. They can communicate with each other, and they may be interdependent.

Shorter Lifespan: Processes are typically shorter-lived than jobs. They start, perform their tasks, and terminate, and new processes can be created dynamically.

Resource Allocation: Resource allocation for processes is done at the process level. Each process may have its own allocation of CPU time, memory, and other resources.

In summary, a Job is a higher-level concept that represents a collection of one or more processes or tasks submitted for execution, often as a batch. Processes, on the other hand, are individual units of execution that run concurrently within a job or independently. Jobs are typically used in batch processing environments, while processes are the fundamental units of execution in multitasking and multiprocessing Operating Systems.

Q 5. Enlist the various service provided by the Operating System?(RU BCA 2017)

Ans: Following are some of important functions of an Operating System.

Memory Management

Processor Management

Device Management

File Management

Security

Control over System Performance

Job Accounting

Error detecting aids

Coordination between other Software and Users

Q 6. Explain the features of Operating System.(RTU B. Tech. Jan 2022)

Ans: Operating Systems (OS) are complex software systems that provide an interface between the hardware and user applications. They offer a wide range of features and functionalities to manage and control computer resources efficiently. Here are the key features of an Operating System:

1.Process Management:

Process Creation: The OS allows the creation of processes or programs, each with its own memory space and resources.

Scheduling: It schedules processes to run on the CPU, allocating time slices to each process.

Synchronization: OS provides mechanisms for processes to synchronize and communicate with one another to avoid conflicts.

2.Memory Management:

Virtual Memory: The OS abstracts physical memory, allowing multiple processes to run, even if they do not fit entirely in RAM.

Memory Protection: It ensures that processes do not interfere with each other's memory, preventing unauthorized access.

Allocation and Deallocation: The OS manages memory allocation and deallocation for processes and ensures efficient use of available memory.

3. File System Management:

File Creation and Deletion: The OS allows the creation, deletion, and organization of files and directories.

Access Control: It enforces file permissions and access control to protect data.

-File I/O: Provides functions for reading from and writing to files, ensuring data persistence.

4.Device Management:

Device Drivers: The OS manages hardware devices by using device drivers. It abstracts hardware details from user applications.

I/O Scheduling: It manages I/O requests to devices, optimizing data transfer and reducing latency.

Error Handling: The OS handles device errors and can recover from failures when possible.

User Interface:

Command-Line Interface (CLI): Offers text-based interaction for advanced users.

Graphical User Interface (GUI): Provides a visual environment for easier user interaction.

APIs: Enables application developers to access OS services through defined interfaces.

Security and Access Control:

User Authentication: OS authenticates users and controls their access to resources.

File and Data Security: Enforces file and data protection to prevent unauthorized access.

Firewalls and Security Protocols: Manages network security and access controls to protect against external threats.

Networking:

Network Protocols: The OS supports network protocols for communication over local and wide-area networks.

Socket Management: Provides APIs for application-level network communication.

Routing and Packet Forwarding: Manages network traffic and routing.

Error Handling:

-Error Reporting: The OS detects and reports hardware and software errors to prevent system crashes.

Fault Tolerance: Implements strategies to continue operation even in the presence of errors or hardware failures.

Task Scheduling:

CPU Scheduling: The OS allocates CPU time to processes, ensuring fair and efficient resource utilization.

Priority Management: Assigns priorities to processes and handles their execution accordingly.

Inter-Process Communication (IPC):

Provides mechanisms for processes to communicate and share data, such as message queues, semaphores, and shared memory.

System Utility Programs:

Includes various utility programs for tasks like system monitoring, file management, and system configuration.

Resource Management:

Manages system resources such as CPU, memory, and I/O devices, ensuring efficient utilization and preventing resource contention.

Backup and Recovery:

Implements backup and recovery mechanisms to safeguard data and recover from system failures or data loss.

Localization and Internationalization:

Supports multiple languages, character encodings, and cultural preferences for a global user base.

Software Updates and Maintenance:

Allows for software updates, patches, and system maintenance to enhance security and performance.

These features collectively enable the OS to provide a stable, efficient, and secure environment for users and applications to run on computer systems. The specifics of these features may vary depending on the type of Operating System (e.g., Windows, Linux, macOS) and its intended use (desktop, server, embedded systems).

Q 7. What is file management? Explain its types and structures.(RU B. Tech. Jan 2022)

Ans: File Management in an Operating System refers to the organization, manipulation, storage, and access of files and directories on a computer's storage devices, such as hard drives, SSDs, and network storage. It is a critical component of any modern Operating System and plays a crucial role in managing data for both users and applications. Here are some

key aspects of file management in Operating Systems:

File Structure: The Operating System provides a structure for organizing files and directories. This structure typically forms a hierarchical tree, with directories (folders) containing files and subdirectories. The top-level directory is often referred to as the root directory.

File Operations: File Management Systems enable users and applications to perform various file operations, such as creating, opening, reading, writing, deleting, copying, and moving files. These operations are performed through System Calls or application programming interfaces (APIs).

File Attributes: Each file in a file system has associated attributes, including a filename, file size, permissions, owner, creation date, modification date, and file type. These attributes help determine how files are accessed and manipulated.

Directories: Directories are used to organize and group related files. They provide a convenient way to categorize and locate files. Users can navigate the directory structure to find the files they need.

File Access Control: File Management Systems enforce access control to restrict who can read, write, execute, or delete files. This is achieved through file permissions and ownership settings.

File Storage: Files are stored on storage devices, and file management involves allocating and managing storage space, tracking file locations, and ensuring data integrity. The file system manages the physical locations of files on the storage media.

File Naming Conventions: File Systems often have rules and conventions for file naming, including valid characters, maximum filename lengths, and case sensitivity (or insensitivity).

File System Types: Various file system types exist, including FAT (File Allocation Table), NTFS (New Technology File System), HFS+ (Hierarchical File System Plus), ext4 (Fourth Extended File System), and more. Each File System has its own features and capabilities.

File Backup and Recovery: File Management Systems may offer backup and recovery mechanisms to protect data in case of accidental deletion or hardware failures.

File Metadata: Many File Systems store additional metadata about files, such as file tags, extended attributes, and indexing information, to facilitate searching and organization.

File Compression and Encryption: File Management Systems can offer features for file compression to reduce storage space and file encryption to secure sensitive data.

File Management is a fundamental component of any Operating System, and it plays a crucial role in providing users and applications with a structured and organized way to create, access, and manage data. Different Operating Systems may use different file systems and offer varying sets of file management features, but the core principles of file organization and manipulation remain consistent.

Q 8. Explain introduction of Parallel Processing with example.(RU B. Tech. Jan 2022)

Ans: Parallel Processing is a computer processing technique that involves the execution of multiple tasks or processes simultaneously, typically with the goal of improving performance, throughput, and overall efficiency. In an Operating System, parallel processing can be implemented through various mechanisms to make the most efficient use of available hardware resources, such as multiple CPU cores.

Here's an introduction to parallel processing in Operating Systems with an example:

Introduction to Parallel Processing:

In traditional computing, a single processor executes instructions sequentially, one after the other. This can limit the system's ability to handle large workloads efficiently. Parallel processing aims to overcome this limitation by allowing multiple tasks to be executed concurrently. It can be achieved at different levels:

Instruction-level parallelism (ILP): This involves breaking down individual instructions into smaller tasks and executing them in parallel. Modern CPUs use techniques like pipelining and out-of-order execution to exploit ILP.

Task-level parallelism: In this approach, multiple tasks or processes run simultaneously on multiple CPU cores or processors. Each core works on a different task, allowing for improved performance.

Example of Parallel Processing in Operating Systems:

Consider a scenario where an Operating System is responsible for managing a web server. Multiple users are accessing web pages hosted on the server, and their requests are processed concurrently. In this example, parallel processing can be implemented at different levels:

Task-Level Parallelism:

The Operating System assigns multiple threads to handle incoming web requests. Each thread can handle one request independently.

These threads run concurrently on multiple CPU cores or processors.

As each thread processes a web request, it can handle tasks such as fetching data from a database, generating dynamic content, and delivering the response to the client.

Instruction-Level Parallelism:

Within each thread, the CPU can exploit instruction-level parallelism to execute instructions more efficiently. For instance, when generating a web page, the CPU can pipeline tasks like fetching data, rendering HTML, and compressing images.

Benefits of Parallel Processing in this Example:

Improved Performance: With multiple threads handling web requests simultaneously, the server can respond to more users and process requests more quickly.

Enhanced Throughput: The server can efficiently utilize available CPU cores, leading to a higher throughput of processed requests.

Responsiveness: Users experience reduced wait times, leading to a more responsive web service.

It's important to note that effective Parallel Processing in an Operating System requires proper synchronization and coordination mechanisms to manage shared resources and prevent conflicts between parallel tasks. Additionally, the degree of parallelism depends on the available hardware resources and the design of the software system.

Q 9. What do you mean by Palm OS?(RTU B. Tech.)

Ans: Palm OS is an Operating System designed for Personal Digital Assistants (PDAs) and handheld devices. It was developed by Palm, Inc., which was originally part of 3Com, and later became Palm Source, a subsidiary of ACCESS Co., Ltd. Palm OS was widely used in the late 1990s and early 2000s and played a significant role in the early PDA and handheld computing market.

Key characteristics and features of Palm OS include:

Graphical User Interface (GUI): Palm OS featured a simple and intuitive graphical user interface that made it easy to navigate using a stylus or a finger. It included elements like icons, menus, and a digital input area for text and handwriting recognition.

Synchronization: Palm OS devices were known for their synchronization capabilities. Users could easily synchronize their PDAs with desktop computers (often running Windows or Mac OS) to exchange data, such as contacts, calendars, and notes.

Palm Graffiti: Palm OS included a handwriting recognition System Called Graffiti, which allowed users to input text by writing characters in a specific, easy-to-learn script. This was especially useful for quick note-taking on the small screens of early Palm devices.

Third-Party Apps: Palm OS had a thriving ecosystem of third-party developers who created a wide range of applications and games for the platform. Many popular apps and utilities were available for Palm OS devices.

Expansion Cards: Many Palm devices supported expansion cards, such as Secure Digital (SD) or CompactFlash (CF) cards, which allowed users to add storage capacity and functionality to their devices.

Customization: Users could customize their Palm devices with various software and hardware accessories, such as cases, screen protectors, and additional memory.

Stylus Input: Palm OS devices relied on stylus-based input and touchscreens, making them suitable for tasks like note-taking, calendaring, and contact management.

Multitasking: Palm OS was designed for multitasking, allowing multiple applications to run simultaneously.

Built-in Apps: Palm OS included built-in applications like a calendar, address book, to-do list, memo pad, and calculator.

Palm Desktop: A desktop software application, known as Palm Desktop, was used to manage and synchronize data between the Palm device and a computer.

Palm OS enjoyed significant popularity in its prime, especially with devices like the Palm Pilot and Handspring Visor. However, with the advent of smartphones and the dominance of platforms like iOS and Android, Palm OS gradually declined and was eventually discontinued. Palm, Inc. was later acquired by Hewlett-Packard (HP), and webOS, a different mobile Operating System, was developed for Palm's later devices.

Q 10. What is meant by Batch Systems? (RTU MCA 22)

Ans: Batch Systems are a type of computing environment where tasks are grouped together and executed in batches, rather than being processed in real-time. In this setup, multiple jobs or tasks are collected and scheduled to run at a specific time or in a specific sequence. This approach is particularly useful for optimizing resource utilization and efficiency, as it allows for the efficient processing of large volumes of data without the need for constant human intervention.

In a batch system, users submit their jobs to a queue, and the system processes them in the order they are received. This contrasts with interactive systems, where users interact with the computer in real-time. Batch processing is commonly used in scenarios where tasks can be automated and don't require immediate user input, such as large-scale data processing, scientific simulations, or routine maintenance jobs.

Q 11. What are the advantages of Multiprogramming? (RTU MCA 2022)

Ans: Multiprogramming offers several advantages in a computing environment:

Increased CPU Utilization: Multiprogramming allows for better utilization of the CPU by keeping it busy with tasks from different programs. This helps in reducing idle time and maximizing the efficiency of the system.

Improved Throughput: With multiple programs running concurrently, the overall throughput of the system increases. This is because the CPU can switch between programs, executing instructions from one while others are waiting for I/O operations or other resources.

Enhanced Response Time: Multiprogramming provides quicker response times to users. Since multiple programs are in the queue, even if one program is waiting for I/O or other resources, the CPU can switch to another program, giving the illusion of simultaneous execution.

Resource Sharing: Multiprogramming facilitates efficient resource sharing. Different programs can share resources such as memory, input/output devices, and CPU time without interfering with each other, leading to optimal resource utilization.

Cost Efficiency: By keeping the CPU busy with various tasks, multiprogramming helps in achieving cost efficiency. It allows organizations to make the most of their computing resources, avoiding unnecessary idle time and improving overall system performance.

Better System Responsiveness: Users experience a more responsive system since tasks are interleaved, and the system can quickly switch between programs. This is crucial in interactive computing environments where users expect timely responses.

Overall, multiprogramming is a key strategy for optimizing system performance and resource utilization in modern computing environments.

Q 12. Define the essential properties of the following types of Operating Systems: (IGNOU Dec 2010)

(i) Batch

(ii) Time sharing

(iii) Real time

(iv) Distributed

Ans: (i) Batch Operating System:

Essential Properties:

No User Interaction During Execution: In a batch Operating System, users submit jobs to be processed without direct interaction during execution. Jobs are executed one after another without user intervention.

Efficient Resource Utilization: Batch Systems aim to maximize resource utilization by executing multiple jobs sequentially, allowing the CPU and other resources to be continuously utilized.

Job Scheduling: Jobs are typically scheduled based on criteria such as priority, deadlines, or arrival time. The Operating System's scheduler manages the execution of jobs in the system.

Limited Interactivity: Batch Systems lack interactivity as users submit jobs and wait for the results without the ability to interact with the system during job execution.

Optimized for Batch Processing: Batch Systems are designed for processing large volumes of data efficiently, making them suitable for tasks such as batch processing, data processing, and automated tasks.

(ii) Time Sharing Operating System (Multiprogramming):

Essential Properties:

Interactive Environment: Time-sharing Operating Systems provide an interactive environment where multiple users can interact with the system concurrently. Users can run programs, execute commands, and access resources simultaneously.

Fair Resource Allocation: Time-sharing Systems allocate CPU time and other resources fairly among multiple users and processes. Time slices are allocated to each process, allowing them to execute for a short duration before switching to another process.

Support for Multitasking: Time-sharing Systems support multitasking, enabling multiple processes to execute concurrently. Each process receives a fair share of CPU time, enhancing system responsiveness and efficiency.

Process Scheduling: Time-sharing Systems employ preemptive scheduling algorithms, such as round-robin or priority scheduling, to manage the execution of processes. The scheduler determines which process to execute next based on predefined criteria.

Terminal Handling: Time-sharing Systems provide terminal handling capabilities to facilitate user interaction. Terminals allow users to input commands, receive output, and interact with the system in real-time.

(iii) Real-Time Operating System:

Essential Properties:

Predictable Response Times: Real-time Operating Systems prioritize tasks based on their deadlines and ensure timely completion to meet stringent timing requirements. Tasks must execute within specified time constraints to guarantee correct system behavior.

Deterministic Behavior: Real-Time Systems exhibit deterministic behavior, where the timing and outcome of tasks are predictable and consistent. This property is critical for systems deployed in time-critical applications such as aerospace, automotive, and industrial control.

Task Scheduling: Real-Time Systems employ scheduling algorithms optimized for deterministic behavior, such as rate-monotonic or earliest deadline first (EDF) scheduling. These algorithms ensure that tasks with higher priority or tighter deadlines are executed first.

Hard and Soft Real-Time: Real-Time Systems can be classified into hard real-time, where missing deadlines can lead to catastrophic consequences, and soft real-time, where occasional missed deadlines are acceptable but degrade system performance.

Concurrency Control: Real-Time Systems may incorporate mechanisms for managing concurrency and resource sharing to prevent conflicts and ensure consistent task execution. Techniques such as priority inheritance and priority ceiling protocols are commonly used.

(iv) Distributed Operating System:

Essential Properties:

Resource Sharing: Distributed Operating Systems enable resource sharing across multiple interconnected computers or nodes in a network. Resources such as files, printers, and computational power are shared transparently to users.

Transparency: Distributed Systems provide transparency to users, hiding the complexities of distributed computing and network communication. Users perceive the distributed system as a single integrated environment.

Fault Tolerance: Distributed Systems are designed to tolerate failures of individual nodes or components. Redundancy, replication, and fault detection mechanisms are employed to ensure system reliability and availability.

Concurrency Control: Distributed Systems manage concurrent access to shared resources to prevent conflicts and ensure data consistency. Techniques such as distributed locking, transaction management, and concurrency control protocols are used.

Communication: Distributed Systems rely on network communication for inter-process communication and coordination. Communication protocols, middleware, and distributed algorithms facilitate efficient communication and coordination among distributed entities.

Q 13. Mention the advantages and limitations of Multi-user Operating Systems. (IGNOU June 2013)

Ans: Multi-user Operating Systems offer several advantages, but they also come with certain limitations:

Advantages:

Resource Sharing: Multi-user Operating Systems facilitate efficient sharing of hardware resources such as CPU, memory, and peripherals among multiple users. This leads to better resource utilization and cost-effectiveness.

Increased Productivity: By allowing multiple users to interact with the system simultaneously, multi-user Operating Systems enhance productivity. Users can run multiple applications, collaborate on projects, and access shared resources concurrently.

Cost Efficiency: Multi-user Systems allow organizations to maximize the utilization of their hardware resources, reducing the need for additional hardware investments. This can result in cost savings for businesses and institutions.

Centralized Administration: Multi-user Operating Systems typically offer centralized administration tools, making it easier for system administrators to manage user accounts, access permissions, security settings, and system configurations from a central location.

Security: Multi-user Systems often incorporate robust security features such as user authentication, access control mechanisms, and file permissions. This helps protect sensitive data and resources from unauthorized access and malicious activities.

Limitations:

Resource Contention: In Multi-user Systems, resource contention may occur when multiple users simultaneously compete for access to shared resources such as CPU, memory, and I/O devices. This can lead to performance degradation and reduced responsiveness for users.

Complexity: Managing a Multi-user Operating System can be complex, especially in large-scale environments with numerous users and diverse computing needs. System administrators must handle user management, resource allocation, security policies, and system maintenance tasks effectively.

Security Risks: Multi-user Systems are vulnerable to security risks such as unauthorized access, data breaches, malware infections, and insider threats. Ensuring robust security measures, regular updates, and user education is essential to mitigate these risks.

Performance Overhead: Supporting multiple users concurrently can impose overhead on system resources, particularly in terms of CPU and memory usage. Context switching between different user processes and managing user sessions can affect system performance.

Dependency on Network: Some Multi-user Systems rely on network connectivity to provide remote access and collaboration features. Network failures or disruptions can impact user accessibility and productivity, highlighting the importance of reliable network infrastructure.

Overall, while Multi-user Operating Systems offer numerous benefits in terms of resource sharing, productivity, and centralized administration, they also pose challenges related to resource contention, complexity, security, performance, and network dependency. Effective management and proactive measures are essential to maximize the benefits and mitigate the limitations of multi-user systems.

Q 14. What are the objective of Operating Systems? (Anna University 2017)

Ans: The objectives of Operating Systems revolve around providing an efficient, secure, and user-friendly environment for managing hardware resources and executing software applications. Here are the primary objectives:

Resource Management:

Efficiently manage hardware resources such as CPU, memory, disk storage, and I/O devices to ensure optimal utilization.

Allocate resources to different processes or users based on priority, fairness, and resource availability.

Control access to resources to prevent conflicts and ensure data integrity.

Process Management:

Manage and control the execution of multiple processes concurrently, facilitating multitasking and parallelism.

Provide mechanisms for process creation, termination, suspension, and synchronization to coordinate the execution of programs effectively.

Memory Management:

Manage system memory to allocate and deallocate memory space for processes, ensuring efficient utilization and avoiding memory fragmentation.

Implement memory protection mechanisms to prevent unauthorized access to memory regions and ensure data security.

File System Management:

Organize and manage file systems to store and retrieve data efficiently, supporting file creation, deletion, and manipulation operations.

Implement file access controls, permissions, and security mechanisms to protect sensitive data from unauthorized access or modification.

Device Management:

Manage communication with peripheral devices such as printers, keyboards, monitors, and network interfaces.

Handle device I/O operations, device driver management, and interrupt handling to ensure smooth interaction between software and hardware components.

User Interface:

Provide a user-friendly Interface for interacting with the Operating System and executing applications.

Support Graphical User Interfaces (GUIs), Command-Line Interfaces (CLIs), and other user interaction methods to accommodate diverse user preferences and requirements.

Security and Protection:

Ensure the Security and Integrity of system resources, data, and user accounts by implementing authentication, access control, and encryption mechanisms.

Protect the system from malware, viruses, and other security threats through proactive measures such as antivirus software and firewall protection.

Error Handling and Fault Tolerance:

Detect and handle errors, exceptions, and system failures gracefully to prevent system crashes and data loss.

Implement fault-tolerant mechanisms such as backup systems, redundancy, and recovery procedures to ensure system reliability and availability.

Performance Optimization:

Optimize system performance by minimizing resource contention, reducing overhead, and improving response times for user requests.

Employ performance monitoring and tuning techniques to identify bottlenecks, optimize system configuration, and enhance overall system efficiency.

Overall, the objectives of Operating Systems aim to provide a stable, efficient, and secure computing environment that meets the needs of users, applications, and hardware components while ensuring reliable operation and optimal performance.

Q 15. What is Operating System? Explain evolution of Operating System. (RU BCA 2022)

Ans: An Operating System (OS) is a software program that manages computer hardware and software resources and provides common services for computer programs. It acts as an intermediary between users and the computer hardware, facilitating communication and coordination between various software applications and the hardware components.

The evolution of Operating Systems can be traced back to the early days of computing, where the concept of an Operating System was virtually non-existent. Here's a brief overview of its evolution:

Batch Processing Systems: In the early days of computing, programmers had to manually load programs and data into the computer's memory, execute them, and then unload them. Batch processing systems were developed to automate this process, allowing users to submit jobs to be executed in batches. IBM's OS/360 is a notable example from this era.

Time-Sharing Systems: Time-Sharing Systems were developed to allow multiple users to interact with a computer simultaneously. These systems allowed users to share the resources of the computer, such as the CPU and memory, by dividing them into time slots. Unix, developed by Bell Labs in the late 1960s, is one of the earliest examples of a time-sharing Operating System.

Personal Computer Operating Systems: With the advent of personal computers in the 1970s and 1980s, Operating Systems evolved to meet the needs of individual users. Operating Systems such as MS-DOS, developed by Microsoft, and Apple's Macintosh System Software provided users with a Graphical User Interface (GUI) and simplified the interaction with the computer.

Network Operating Systems: As computer networks became more prevalent, Operating Systems evolved to support network communication and resource sharing. Novell NetWare and Microsoft Windows NT are examples of network Operating Systems that emerged during this period.

Mobile Operating Systems: The rise of mobile computing in the late 20th and early 21st centuries led to the development of Operating Systems specifically designed for mobile devices. Operating Systems such as Android, developed by Google, and iOS, developed by Apple, are optimized for touch-based interfaces and provide features such as app stores and cloud integration.

Distributed Systems: In recent years, Operating Systems have evolved to support distributed computing environments, where resources are spread across multiple machines connected by a network. Operating Systems such as Linux and Windows Server are used to manage clusters of servers and provide services such as load balancing and fault tolerance.

Overall, the evolution of Operating Systems has been driven by advances in hardware technology, changes in computing paradigms, and the evolving needs of users and businesses. From simple batch processing systems to complex distributed environments, Operating Systems have played a crucial role in enabling the development and use of computer technology.

Q 16. Explain types of Operating Systems with example? (RU BCA 2022)

Ans: Operating Systems can be categorized into several types based on their intended use, architecture, and target devices. Here are some common types along with examples:

Single-User, Single-Tasking Operating Systems: These Operating Systems are designed to manage the resources of a single user and allow only one task to be executed at a time. Examples include MS-DOS (Microsoft Disk Operating System) and early versions of Apple's Macintosh System Software.

Single-User, Multi-Tasking Operating Systems: These Operating Systems allow a single user to run multiple programs simultaneously, with the Operating System managing the scheduling of tasks. Examples include Microsoft Windows, macOS (formerly OS X), and various flavors of Linux distributions like Ubuntu and Fedora.

Multi-User Operating Systems: Multi-user Operating Systems allow multiple users to interact with the computer simultaneously. These systems manage resources such as CPU time, memory, and peripherals to ensure fair and efficient usage among users. Examples include Unix-based systems like Linux distributions, FreeBSD, and Solaris.

Real-Time Operating Systems (RTOS): RTOS are designed to handle tasks with strict timing requirements, where the correctness of the system's operation depends on meeting deadlines. These Operating Systems are commonly used in embedded systems, industrial automation, and other time-sensitive applications. Examples include FreeRTOS, VxWorks, and QNX.

Network Operating Systems (NOS): Network Operating Systems are specifically designed to support network communication and resource sharing among multiple computers. They provide features such as file and print sharing, user authentication, and centralized administration. Examples include Novell NetWare, Windows Server, and Linux-based server distributions like CentOS and Debian.

Mobile Operating Systems: Mobile Operating Systems are designed for smartphones, tablets, and other mobile devices. They typically feature touch-based interfaces, support for mobile apps, and integration with cloud services. Examples include Android (developed by Google), iOS (developed by Apple), and Windows Phone (developed by Microsoft, now discontinued).

Embedded Operating Systems: Embedded Operating Systems are optimized for use in embedded systems, which are specialized computing devices designed for specific functions. These Operating Systems are often lightweight and tailored to the hardware they run on. Examples include Embedded Linux, Windows Embedded Compact, and RTOS like FreeRTOS and eCos.

Each type of Operating System serves specific purposes and has unique characteristics tailored to the needs of its intended users and devices.

Q 17. Explain following (RU BCA 2019)

Time Sharing OS

Multi Programming OS

Real Time OS

Ans:

Time Sharing OS: Time-Sharing Operating Systems allow multiple users to interact with a computer system concurrently by dividing the CPU time into small time slots, typically milliseconds or microseconds. Each user gets a small portion of CPU time during these time slices to execute their tasks. Time-sharing OS ensures that all users get a fair share of CPU resources and provides the illusion of simultaneous execution to users. Examples of time-sharing Operating Systems include Unix, Linux, and modern versions of Microsoft Windows.

Multi-Programming OS: Multi-Programming Operating Systems take advantage of idle CPU time by allowing multiple programs to reside in memory simultaneously. These systems keep several programs loaded in memory and switch between them when one program is waiting for I/O operations to complete. This overlapping of CPU and I/O operations increases overall system efficiency and throughput. Multi-programming OS aims to maximize CPU utilization and keep the system busy with productive tasks. Examples of multi-programming Operating Systems include early versions of Unix, MS-DOS, and IBM's OS/360.

Real-Time OS: Real-Time Operating Systems are designed to handle tasks with strict timing constraints, where the correctness and timeliness of task execution are critical. These systems guarantee that tasks are completed within specified time frames, known as deadlines, to ensure proper functioning of real-time applications. Real-time OSes are commonly used in embedded systems, industrial automation, robotics, and other time-sensitive applications. Examples of real-time Operating Systems include FreeRTOS, VxWorks, and QNX.

Q 18. What do you mean by an Operating System? (RU BCA 2017)

Ans:"Operating System" refers to a crucial software component that serves as an interface between computer hardware and user applications. It manages computer hardware resources such as CPU, memory, storage devices, and peripherals, providing a platform for software programs to run efficiently. Additionally, the Operating System facilitates communication between hardware components and software applications, ensuring proper coordination and resource allocation.

In essence, an Operating System acts as a mediator, allowing users to interact with the computer system without needing to understand the intricate details of hardware operations. It provides essential services such as process management, memory management, file system management, device management, and user interface management.

Overall, the Operating System plays a vital role in enabling the effective and efficient use of computer systems, enhancing user productivity and providing a stable and reliable computing environment.

Q 19. What is Multiprogramming System? (RU BCA 2017)

Ans: Multiprogramming is a computing technique where multiple programs are loaded into memory simultaneously and executed concurrently. In a multiprogramming system, the CPU is kept busy by switching between different programs, allowing them to progress concurrently even though only one program is actively executing at any given moment. This technique aims to maximize CPU utilization and improve overall system throughput.

In a multiprogramming system, when one program is waiting for I/O operations (such as reading from or writing to a disk), the CPU switches to another program that is ready to execute. This overlapping of CPU and I/O operations helps to minimize the idle time of the CPU, thereby increasing system efficiency.

Multiprogramming systems typically employ scheduling algorithms to determine the order in which programs are executed and how CPU time is allocated among them. Examples of multiprogramming Operating Systems include early versions of Unix, MS-DOS, and IBM's OS/360.

Overall, multiprogramming systems enhance system performance by allowing multiple programs to make progress simultaneously, leading to better resource utilization and improved user experience.

Q 20. Give Brief introduction of four advanced Operating System. (RTU 2016)

Ans: Here's a brief introduction to four advanced Operating Systems:

Linux: Linux is a powerful and widely-used open-source Operating System kernel originally created by Linus Torvalds in 1991. It is based on Unix principles and is known for its stability, security, and flexibility. Linux is highly customizable and is used in a wide range of devices, from servers and supercomputers to embedded systems and smartphones. Its popularity stems from its open-source nature, which allows users to modify and distribute the source code freely.

macOS: macOS is the Operating System developed by Apple Inc. for its line of Macintosh computers. It is based on Unix and features a user-friendly interface known for its elegance and ease of use. macOS offers seamless integration with other Apple devices and services, such as iCloud and iOS devices. It is known for its stability, security, and performance, making it a popular choice among creative professionals and everyday users alike.

Windows Server: Windows Server is a series of Operating Systems developed by Microsoft designed for server-based computing. It provides a range of features tailored for server deployment, including support for networking, virtualization, cloud integration, and enterprise-level security. Windows Server is widely used in businesses and organizations of all sizes to host websites, manage databases, and run enterprise applications.

Android: Android is a mobile Operating System developed by Google based on the Linux kernel. It is designed primarily for touchscreen mobile devices such as smartphones and tablets. Android is known for its openness, allowing device manufacturers to customize and modify the Operating System to suit their hardware. It has a vast ecosystem of apps available through the Google Play Store and is the most widely-used mobile Operating System globally.

Each of these advanced Operating Systems offers unique features and capabilities tailored to different computing environments and user needs.

Exercise

Exercise 1 – MCQ

1. Which of the following is NOT a function of an Operating System?

a) Memory Management

b) Process Scheduling

c) File Encryption

d) Device Management

2. Which type of Operating System is designed for systems with strict timing requirements, such as robotics and industrial automation?

a) MultiUser OS

b) RealTime OS (RTOS)

c) SingleUser, MultiTasking OS

d) Network OS

3. Which of the following is a primary objective of an Operating System concerning process management?

a) Maximizing CPU utilization

b) Minimizing disk space usage

c) Maximizing printer efficiency

d) Minimizing network latency

4. What is the main goal of memory management in an Operating System?

a) Minimizing the number of processes

b) Maximizing the usage of secondary storage

c) Ensuring each process has enough CPU time

d) Efficiently allocating and deallocating memory resources

5. What is the primary purpose of file system management in an Operating System?

a) Reducing network traffic

b) Ensuring efficient use of CPU

c) Managing and organizing data on storage devices

d) Minimizing the number of running processes

6. What is a key distinction between spooling and buffering in the context of Operating Systems?

a) Spooling is used for temporary storage of data, while buffering is used for permanent storage.

b) Spooling is a technique for parallel processing, while buffering is focused on sequential processing.

c) Spooling involves the use of a secondary storage device, while buffering uses temporary storage in RAM.

d) Spooling is primarily applied to graphics processing, while buffering is related to input/output operations.

7. What is a notable advantage of spooling over buffering in Operating Systems?

a) Spooling reduces the need for secondary storage.

b) Spooling improves system performance by parallelizing tasks.

c) Spooling eliminates the need for RAM.

d) Spooling simplifies the input/output operations.

8. In the context of Operating Systems, what is the primary purpose of buffering?

a) To store intermediate results during data processing.

b) To provide a permanent storage solution for critical system files.

c) To manage the execution of parallel tasks.

d) To control the flow of data between the CPU and peripheral devices.

9. What is the primary purpose of the "Scheduler" function in an Operating System?

a) To manage memory allocation and deallocation.

b) To control the flow of data between the CPU and peripheral devices.

c) To prioritize and schedule processes for execution.

d) To provide a user interface for interaction with the system.

10. Which function of the Operating System is responsible for managing the distribution of system resources such as CPU time, memory space, and peripheral devices among various tasks?

a) File Management

b) Security and Protection

c) Resource Allocation and Management

d) Communication Management

Exercise 2 – True/ False

1. An Operating System manages the allocation of physical hardware resources such as CPU, memory, and storage.

2. Operating Systems are responsible for the creation and development of software applications.

3. The primary function of an Operating System's "File Management" is to ensure the physical storage and retrieval of data on secondary storage devices.

4. The "Security and Protection" function of an Operating System is primarily concerned with optimizing the performance of the system.

5. Spooling is a technique primarily used for temporary storage of data, while buffering is focused on permanent storage.

6. Spooling involves the use of a secondary storage device, whereas buffering relies on temporary storage in RAM.

7. One of the advantages of spooling over buffering in Operating Systems is that spooling eliminates the need for RAM.

8. One of the primary objectives of an Operating System is to maximize the usage of secondary storage.

9. Efficiently allocating and deallocating memory resources is a key goal of an Operating System concerning memory management.

10. A primary objective of an Operating System in process management is to minimize network latency.

Exercise 3 – Fill in the blanks

1. A ___________ Operating System is optimized for smartphones, tablets, and other mobile devices.

2. RealTimeOperating Systems (RTOS) are designed for systems with strict ___________ requirements, such as robotics and industrial automation.

Exercise 4 – Match case

Column A

1. Process Management
2. Memory Management
3. File System Management
4. Device Management
5. Security and Access Control

Column B

a. Allocates and tracks system memory, ensuring utilization and preventing conflicts.

b. Enforces user authentication, access permissions, and safeguards data from unauthorized access.

c. Controls the execution of programs and manages task scheduling.

d. Organizes and controls data storage, including file creation, deletion, and access.

e. Manages hardware components and interacts with device drivers to facilitate communication with peripherals.

Exercise 5 – One-word

1. What is an OS?
2. What does BIOS stand for?

Exercise 6 – Small answer

1. What is the primary function of an Operating System?
2. What is the purpose of a device driver in an Operating System?

Exercise 7 – Long answer

1. How does the memory management function of an Operating System work, and why is it crucial for efficient system operation?

2. How does the memory management subsystem of an Operating System work, and what are its key components and functions?

Answer

Exercise 1 – MCQ

Ans: 1 c, 2 b, 3 a, 4 d, 5 c, 6 c, 7 b, 8 a, 9 c, 10 c

Exercise 2 – True/False

Ans: 1 True, 2 False, 3 True, 4 False, 5 False, 6 True, 7 False, 8 False, 9 True, 10 False

Exercise 3 – Fill in The Blanks

Ans: 1 Mobile, 2 Timing or time sensitive

Exercise 4 – Match Case

Ans: 1 c, 2 a,3 d, 4 e, 5 b,

Exercise 5 – One-word

Ans: 1 Software, 2 Basic Input/Output System

Online Resources

Videos:

MCQ Link:https://youtu.be/4itQGrApfok

QR Code:

True/False Link: https://youtu.be/05qfk4TVhVY

QR Code:

Online Test Paper: https://forms.office.com/r/mTEacgxzEt

QR Code:

Chapter 2 Computer System Structures

Computer Hardware Overview

In the context of an Operating System, a "Computer Hardware Overview" typically refers to a high-level description or abstraction of the computer's physical components and how the Operating System interacts with them. This overview is essential for understanding the role of an Operating System in managing and controlling the hardware resources of a computer system. Here's a brief computer hardware overview within the context of an Operating System:

Computer Hardware Overview

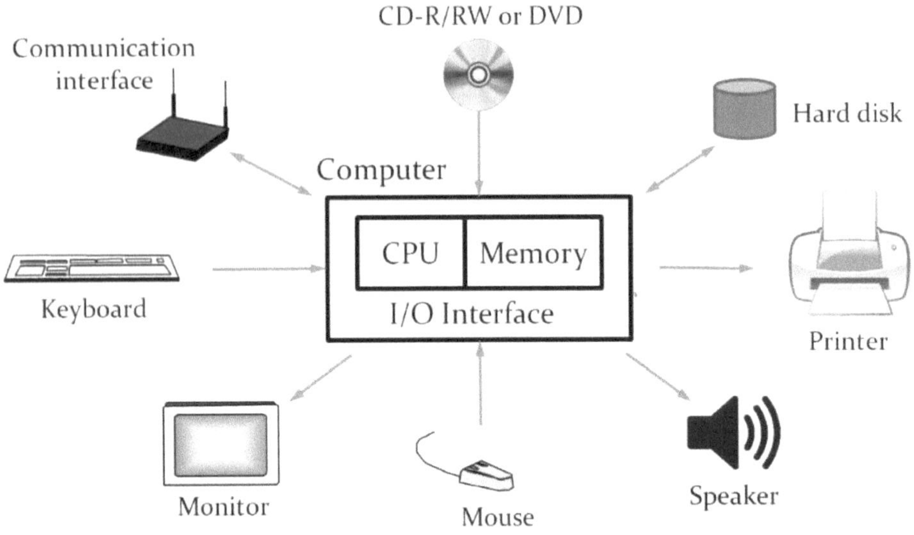

Computer Hardware constitutes the physical components of a computing system. These components can be broadly categorized into the following major categories:

A. Central Processing Unit (CPU):

The CPU is the brain of the computer, responsible for executing instructions and performing calculations. The Operating System interacts closely with the CPU to manage processes, allocate CPU time, and ensure efficient execution.

B. Memory (RAM):

Random Access Memory (RAM) is where the computer stores data and programs that are actively in use. The Operating System manages memory allocation, ensuring that processes have the necessary memory space to run.

C. Storage Devices:

Storage devices like hard drives (HDDs) and solid-state drives (SSDs) provide long-term data storage.

The OS manages file systems and storage access, enabling users and programs to read and write data.

D. Input/Output (I/O) Devices:

These include peripherals such as keyboards, mice, monitors, printers, and networking equipment.

The Operating System facilitates communication between these devices and user applications.

E. Motherboard:

The motherboard is the main circuit board that connects and interconnects all hardware components.

The OS interacts with motherboard components like the BIOS (Basic Input/Output System) to facilitate hardware initialization.

F. System Bus:

The system bus is a communication pathway that allows data to flow between CPU, memory, and peripheral devices.

The OS manages data transfer on the system bus to ensure efficient operation.

G. Power Management:

Modern Operating Systems incorporate power management features to optimize energy consumption.

This includes features like sleep mode and CPU throttling to reduce power usage during periods of inactivity.

H. Security Features:

Operating Systems play a vital role in hardware security, managing user access, encryption, and firewall configurations.

They work with hardware security features like Trusted Platform Modules (TPMs) for enhanced security.

I. Device Drivers:

Device drivers are software components that facilitate communication between the OS and specific hardware devices.

They allow the OS to control and utilize hardware effectively.

Interrupts:

Interrupts are signals generated by hardware devices to request the CPU's attention.

The OS handles interrupts, prioritizing them and ensuring that critical tasks are executed promptly.

In summary, an Operating System serves as the intermediary between software and hardware, managing hardware resources, and providing a stable platform for running applications. Understanding this computer hardware overview is fundamental to grasping how an Operating System functions and how it optimally utilizes and safeguards the underlying hardware.

Operating System Services

Operating SystemServices are fundamental functionalities and resources provided by an Operating System (OS) to enable the efficient execution of computer programs and the management of hardware resources. These services play a crucial role in abstracting and managing the underlying hardware, providing a consistent and user-friendly interface to software applications. Here are some essential Operating System services:

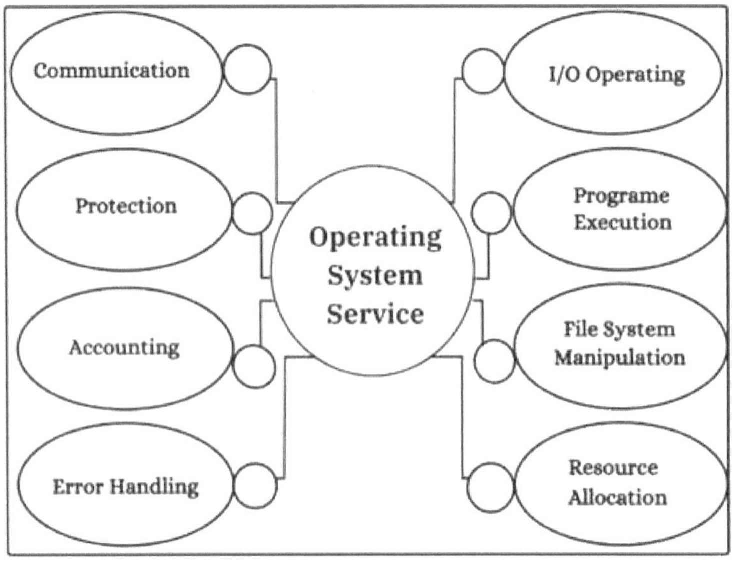

Program Execution: The OS loads programs into memory and schedules their execution on the CPU. It manages the execution of multiple programs, known as multitasking or multiprocessing.

I/O Operations: The OS provides mechanisms for input and output operations, allowing programs to read from and write to devices such as keyboards, displays, disks, and network interfaces.

File System Manipulation: It offers services for creating, reading, writing, and deleting files and directories. It also manages file access permissions and maintains metadata like file size and modification times.

Error Detection and Handling: The OS detects and handles hardware and software errors, aiming to keep the system stable and prevent crashes or data corruption.

Resource Allocation: It manages hardware resources like CPU time, memory, and I/O devices. This involves task scheduling to ensure fair and efficient resource utilization.

Security and Access Control: The OS enforces security policies, authenticates users, and controls access to system resources. This includes user authentication, file permissions, and encryption.

Networking: For systems connected to a network, the OS provides networking services, including protocols for communication and managing network interfaces.

User Interface: The OS provides user interfaces, which can be command line interfaces (CLI) or graphical user interfaces (GUI), to interact with the system and run applications.

Interprocess Communication (IPC): It enables processes to communicate with each other, either within the same computer or over a network. IPC mechanisms include message passing, shared memory, and sockets.

Device Management: The OS manages various hardware devices by providing device drivers, which are software components that allow the OS to communicate with and control hardware devices.

System Monitoring and Performance Analysis: It includes tools and services for monitoring system resource usage, performance analysis, and debugging.

Virtual Memory Management: Many modern OS's use Virtual Memory to manage physical memory efficiently. This service involves swapping data in and out of RAM to disk and memory allocation for processes.

Time Keeping: The OS provides accurate timekeeping services, which are essential for various system functions, such as scheduling tasks, logging events, and network communication.

Backup and Recovery: Some OSs offer backup and recovery services, helping users and administrators create and restore system backups to protect against data loss.

Printing Services: The OS manages printers and provides services for queuing print jobs, handling print requests from applications, and configuring printer settings.

These Operating System services collectively form the foundation of a computer's software environment, allowing users and applications to interact with hardware resources in a controlled and efficientmanner. Different Operating Systems may offer varying implementations and additional services tailored to their specific purposes and user requirements.

System Calls

System Calls are a fundamental mechanism in an Operating System that enables userlevel processes to request services and functionality from the kernel, the core part of the Operating System. They provide a controlled interface for applications to interact with the hardware and access various Operating System services. Here are some common System Calls found in most Operating Systems:

A. Process Control:

`fork()`: Create a new process (child) that is a copy of the calling process (parent).

`exec()`: Replace the current process image with a new process image.

B. File Management:

`open()`: Open a file or create a new one.

`read()`: Read data from a file.

`write()`: Write data to a file.

`close()`: Close a file.

`lseek()`: Move the file pointer to a specific position within a file.

C. Device Management:

`ioctl()`: Perform I/O control operations on devices, like configuring device settings.

`read()` and `write()`: Can also be used for device input and output.

D. Information Maintenance:

`getpid()`: Get the process ID of the calling process.

`getuid()` and `getgid()`: Get the user and group IDs of the calling process.

`getcwd()`: Get the current working directory.

E. Communication:

`pipe()`: Create a communication pipe between two processes.

`socket()`, `bind()`, `connect()`, `send()`, and `recv()`: Functions for network communication.

F. Thread Control:

`pthread_create()`: Create a new thread.

`pthread_exit()`: Exit a thread.

`pthread_join()`: Wait for a thread to terminate.

G. Synchronization:

`mutex_lock()`, `mutex_unlock()`: Functions for managing mutex locks.

`sem_wait()`, `sem_post()`: Functions for managing semaphores.

H. Memory Management:

`malloc()`, `free()`: Functions for dynamic memory allocation and deallocation.

`mmap()`: Map a file or device into memory.

I. Time:

`gettimeofday()`: Get the current time and date.

`sleep()`: Suspend the calling process for a specified number of seconds.

H. File and Directory Operations:

`mkdir()`: Create a new directory.

`rmdir()`: Remove a directory.

`rename()`: Rename a file or directory.

These are just some examples of System Calls. The specific System Calls available can vary between Operating Systems and are typically documented in the Operating System's API (Application

Programming Interface) documentation. Application developers use these System Calls to interact with the Operating System and perform tasks like file I/O, process management, and memory allocation in a controlled and secure manner.

System Programs

System Programs, also known as System Software or Utility Programs, are software applications that are designed to perform specific tasks related to the management and operation of a computer system. These programs work in conjunction with the Operating System to provide various services, utilities, and tools for both users and system administrators. Here are some common categories of system programs found in Operating Systems:

File Management Programs:

File Explorer/File Manager: Allows users to browse, create, delete, and manipulate files and directories.

Disk Clean-up: Helps users remove unnecessary files to free up disk space.

Disk Defragmenter: Reorganizes data on a hard drive to optimize disk performance.

Text Editors and Viewers:

Text Editors: Programs like Notepad on Windows and nano/vi on Unix based systems for creating and editing text files.

PDF Readers: Applications like Adobe Acrobat Reader for viewing PDF files.

Compression and Archiving Utilities:

ZIP and RAR Utilities: Programs for compressing and decompressing files and folders.

Tar and gzip: Unix based utilities for creating and extracting compressed archive files.

Backup and Restore Tools:

Backup Software: Allows users to create backup copies of their data for recovery in case of data loss.

System Restore: Allows users to revert the system to a previous state.4ex

Disk Partitioning and Formatting Tools:

Disk Management: Programs to create, delete, resize, and format disk partitions.

fdisk and mkfs:UNIX based utilities for partitioning and formatting disks.

Security and Antivirus Software:

Antivirus Programs: Protect the system from malware, viruses, and other security threats.

Firewalls: Control network traffic and protect against unauthorized access.

System Information and Monitoring Tools:

Task Manager: Provides information about running processes and allows users to manage them.

System Information Utilities: Display detailed system hardware and software information.

Network Configuration and Diagnostic Tools:

Network Configuration Wizards: Assist users in setting up network connections.

Ping and Traceroute: Utilities to test network connectivity and diagnose network issues.

Text Processing and Printing Utilities:

Print Spooler: Manages print jobs and printer queues.

Text Formatting Tools: Tools like `awk` and `sed` in Unix for text processing.

Command Interpreters (Shells):

Command Prompt (cmd.exe) on Windows.

Bash, Zsh, and others:UNIX basedcommand line shells for interacting with the system.

Performance Monitoring and Tuning Utilities:

Performance Monitor (Windows) and `top` (Unix): Monitor system performance and resource usage.

Task Scheduler (Windows) and `cron` (Unix): Schedule tasks to run at specific times.

Device Drivers:

These are not traditional user facing programs but are essential for enabling communication between the Operating System and hardware devices.

Installation and Update Managers:

Software like Windows Update on Windows and package managers like `apt` and `yum` on Linux for installing and updating software packages.

System Configuration Tools:

Programs like `sysconfig` in Unix for configuring system settings.

System Programs enhance the functionality of the Operating System and simplify various system related tasks for users and administrators. They are an integral part of the software ecosystem, helping users manage files, troubleshoot issues, optimize system performance, and interact with the hardware effectively.

Operating System Structure

The structure of an Operating System (OS) can vary depending on its design and purpose, but most modern Operating Systems share some common structural components. Here, I'll describe a typical layered structure of an Operating System, which helps in organizing and managing the various functionalities of the OS:

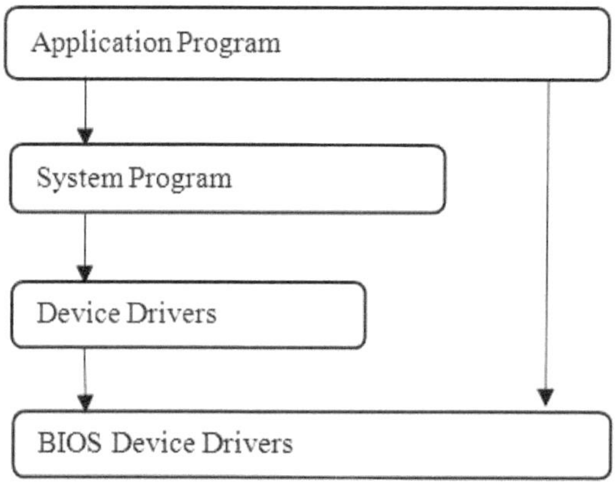

Kernel:

At the core of the Operating System is the kernel. The kernel is responsible for the most fundamental tasks of the OS, including process management, memory management, hardware abstraction, and System Call handling.

It provides the essential services that all other parts of the OS and userlevel programs rely on.

Device Drivers:

Device drivers are a crucial part of the OS that allows it to communicate with hardware devices, such as hard drives, keyboards, mice, printers, and network interfaces.

These drivers serve as intermediaries between the kernel and hardware, translating high-level OS requests into low-level hardwarespecific commands.

System Libraries:

System libraries are collections of precompiled code that provide standard functions and procedures to applications and other parts of the OS.

These libraries abstract many low-level details, making it easier for software developers to interact with the OS and hardware.

Common system libraries include the C Standard Library (libc) on Unix like systems and the Windows API on Windows.

System Services:

Above the kernel, there are various system services responsible for managing specific aspects of the Operating System. These services include:

Process Management: Services that handle process creation, scheduling, and termination.

File System Management: Services for creating, reading, writing, and managing files and directories.

Memory Management: Services that manage memory allocation and deallocation.

Device Management: Services for managing hardware devices.

Security and Access Control: Services that enforce security policies and permissions.

Networking: Services for managing network connections and protocols.

E. User Interface:

The user interface component provides a way for users to interact with the Operating System. There are typically two types of user interfaces:

CommandLine Interface (CLI): Users interact with the system by typing commands at a text prompt (e.g., the Unix shell).

Graphical User Interface (GUI): Users interact with the system through graphical elements like windows, icons, menus, and buttons (e.g., Windows, macOS, Linux desktop environments).

Applications:

Applications are userlevel programs and software that run on top of the Operating System.

These include word processors, web browsers, media players, games, and other software that users run to perform specific tasks.

Utilities:

Utilities are small programs and tools that provide various services and functionalities for both users and system administrators.

Examples include file management utilities, system monitoring tools, backup utilities, and networking tools.

Shell:

The shell is a command line interface that allows users to interact with the Operating System by typing commands.

It interprets user commands and communicates with the kernel to execute those commands.

This layered structure helps in organizing and modularizing the components of an Operating System, making it more maintainable, extensible, and understandable. Different Operating Systems may have variations in their structure, especially when considering specialized or embedded systems, but the core principles of managing hardware and providing services to user level programs remain consistent.

Virtual Machines

Virtual Machines (VM's) in the context of Operating Systems refer to the creation and management of multiple virtual instances of an Operating System running on a single physical machine. Each virtual machine operates as if it were an independent computer with its own dedicated resources, including CPU, memory, storage, and network interfaces. This technology has several use cases and advantages:

Isolation: VM's provide strong isolation between different virtual machines on the same physical host. Each VM operates independently, with its own dedicated resources, preventing one VM from impacting the performance or stability of others. This isolation is crucial for security and stability.

Resource Optimization: VM's allow for efficient utilization of hardware resources. Multiple VM's can run on a single physical server, making better use of available CPU, memory, and storage capacity. This consolidation can lead to cost savings in terms of hardware procurement and maintenance.

Hardware Independence: VM's abstract the underlying hardware, allowing virtual machines to run on different physical servers with varying hardware configurations. This flexibility enables workload mobility and makes it easier to migrate VM's between hosts.

Snapshot and Rollback: VM's often support snapshot functionality, which allows you to capture the current state of a virtual machine. This is valuable for backup and recovery purposes, as well as for testing and development since you can easily roll back to a previous state, if needed.

Easy Deployment: VM's are portable and can be deployed quickly. You can create a VM image, configure it with the necessary software and settings, and then replicate it across multiple virtual machines. This simplifies the deployment of new services or applications.

Resource Isolation: VM's allow you to allocate specific amounts of CPU, memory, and storage to each virtual machine. This fine-grained resource allocation ensures that one VM cannot consume all available resources, preventing resource contention.

Compatibility: VM's can run a wide range of Operating Systems, making them versatile for running different types of applications. This is particularly useful for legacy applications that may require older or specialized Operating Systems.

Security: VM's can enhance security by isolating workloads. If one VM is compromised, it is more challenging for an attacker to move laterally to other VM's on the same host, compared to running multiple services on a single Operating System.

Testing and Development: VM's are valuable for creating isolated test environments. Developers and testers can have their own VM's to work on, allowing them to experiment without affecting production systems.

Scalability: VM's can be easily scaled up or down to meet changing workload demands. You can provision additional VM's as needed, making it easier to accommodate increased traffic or workloads.

Management and Automation: Virtualization platforms often come with management tools that facilitate the automation of tasks such as VM provisioning, monitoring, and resource management.

Disaster Recovery: VM snapshots and replication can be used for disaster recovery purposes. In the event of a failure, VM's can be quickly restored to a previous state on another host.

Green Computing: By consolidating multiple workloads onto fewer physical servers, virtualization can lead to reduced power consumption and a smaller data center footprint, contributing to environmentalsustainability.

Resource Consolidation: VM's allow multiple Operating Systems to run on a single physical machine, maximizing resource utilization. This can lead to cost savings in terms of hardware and energy consumption.

Legacy Software Support: VM's can run older or legacy software that may not be compatible with the host Operating System or modern hardware. This can be essential for maintaining older systems and applications.

Server Virtualization: In data centers, server virtualization is commonly used to run multiple virtual servers on a single physical server. This helps in efficient resource utilization and dynamic allocation of resources based on demand.

Here are some key components and concepts related to virtual machines in Operating Systems:

Hypervisor: A Hypervisor (also known as a Virtual Machine Monitor or VMM) is the software or hardware layer that manages and allocates physical resources to virtual machines. It sits between the physical hardware and the VM's, ensuring that each VM operates in isolation and with dedicated resources.

Guest OS: Each Virtual Machine runs its own guest Operating System. This can be the same or different from the host Operating System.

Virtualization Types: There are two primary types of virtualization:

Full Virtualization: In Full Virtualization, the guest Operating System is unaware that it is running in a virtualized environment. This type requires a hypervisor that emulates the hardware, providing a high level of isolation and compatibility.

Paravirtualization: In Paravirtualization, the guest Operating System is modified to be aware of the virtualization layer, which allows for better performance and efficiency, but may require modifications to the guest OS.

Snapshots: VM snapshots are point Intime copies of a VM's state, including its disk and memory. Snapshots are used for backup, recovery, and creating restore points.

Live Migration: Some Virtualization Technologies support live migration, which allows VM's to be moved from one physical host to another without downtime, ensuring high availability.

Popular virtualization platforms and technologies include VMware vSphere/ESXi, Microsoft Hyper-V, Oracle VirtualBox, and opensource solutions like KVM (Kernel based Virtual Machine) for Linux.

Overall, Virtual Machines in Operating Systems provide a flexible and efficient way to manage and utilize computing resources, making them a fundamental component of modern data centers and computing environments.

Virtual machines (VM's) offer numerous advantages in various computing scenarios.

Here are some of the key advantages of using Virtual Machines:

Isolation: VM's provide strong isolation between different virtual machines running on the same physical host. Each VM operates independently, with its own dedicated resources, preventing one VM from impacting the performance or stability of others. This isolation is crucial for security and stability.

Resource Optimization: VM's allow for efficient utilization of hardware resources. Multiple VM's can run on a single physical server, making better use of available CPU, memory, and storage capacity. This consolidation can lead to cost savings in terms of hardware procurement and maintenance.

Hardware Independence: VM's abstract the underlying hardware, allowing virtual machines to run on different physical servers with varying hardware configurations. This flexibility enables workload mobility and makes it easier to migrate VM's between hosts.

Snapshot and Rollback: VM's often support snapshot functionality, allowing you to capture the current state of a virtual machine. This is valuable for backup and recovery purposes, as well as for testing and development since you can easily roll back to a previous state, if needed.

Easy Deployment: VM's are portable and can be deployed quickly. You can create a VM image, configure it with the necessary software and settings, and then replicate it across multiple virtual machines. This simplifies the deployment of new services or applications.

Resource Isolation: VM's allow you to allocate specific amounts of CPU, memory, and storage to each virtual machine. This fine-grained resource allocation ensures that one VM cannot consume all available resources, preventing resource contention.

Compatibility: VM's can run a wide range of Operating Systems, making them versatile for running different types of applications. This is particularly useful for legacy applications that may require older or specialized Operating Systems.

Security: VM's can enhance security by isolating workloads. If one VM is compromised, it is more challenging for an attacker to move laterally to other VM's on the same host, compared to running multiple services on a single Operating System.

Testing and Development: VM's are valuable for creating isolated test environments. Developers and testers can have their own VM's to work on, allowing them to experiment without affecting production systems.

Scalability: VM's can be easily scaled up or down to meet changing workload demands. You can provision additional VM's as needed, making it easier to accommodate increased traffic or workloads.
Management and Automation: Virtualization platforms often come with management tools that facilitate the automation of tasks such as VM provisioning, monitoring, and resource management.
Disaster Recovery: VM snapshots and replication can be used for disaster recovery purposes. In the event of a failure, VM's can be quickly restored to a previous state on another host.
Green Computing: By consolidating multiple workloads onto fewer physical servers, virtualization can lead to reduced power consumption and a smaller data center footprint, contributing to environmental sustainability.

While virtual machines offer numerous advantages, it's essential to consider the specific requirements and constraints of your use case when deciding whether VM's are the right solution or if alternatives like containers or serverless computing might be more appropriate.

Previous Years Solved Questions

Q 1. Explain dynamic memory for data structure with example. (RU BCA 2022)

Ans: Memory Allocation is the process of setting aside sections of memory in a program to be used to store variables, and instances of structures and classes.

There are two types of memory allocations possible in C:

Compile-Time or Static Allocation.

Run-time or Dynamic Allocation (using pointers).

Compile-time or Static allocation

Static memory allocation allocated by the compiler. Exact size and type of memory must be known at compile time.

int x, y;

float a[5];

When the first statement is encountered, the compiler will allocate two bytes to each variables x and y. The second statement results into the allocation of 20 bytes to the array a (54, where there are five elements and each element of float type tales four bytes). Note that as there is no bound checking in C for array boundaries, i.e., if you have declared an array of five elements, as above and by mistake you are intending to read more than five values in the array a, it will still work without error. For example you are reading the above array as follows:

for (i = 0; i< 10; i++)

```
{
Scanf("%d", &a[i]);
}
```

Run-Time or Dynamic Allocation

Dynamic Memory Allocation is when an executing program requests that the Operating System give it block of main memory. The program then uses this memory for some purpose. Usually the purpose is to add a node to a data structure. In Object-Oriented Languages, Dynamic Memory Allocation is used to get the memory for a new object.

The main memory comes from above the static part of the data segment. Programs may request memory and also return previously dynamically allocated memory. Memory may be returned whenever it is no longer needed. Memory can be returned whenever it is no longer needed. Memory can be returned in any order without any relation to the order in which it was allocated. The heap may develop "holes" where previously allocated memory has been returned between blocks of memory still in use.

A new dynamic request for memory might return a range of address out of one of the holes. But it might not use up all the hole, so further dynamic requests might be satisfies out of the original hole.

Q 2. Describe fork ( ) System Call. (RTU B. Tech.)

Ans: The **fork()**System Call is a fundamental and important operation in Unix-based Operating Systems. It is used for creating new processes, and it works by duplicating the current process, resulting in two identical processes, often referred to as the parent process and the child process. The **fork()**System Call is the foundation for process creation and multiprocessing in Unix-like systems. Here's an overview of the **fork()**System Call and how it works:

Process Duplication:

When a program calls the **fork()**System Call, the Operating System creates a copy of the current process. This copy is known as the child process.

The child process is nearly identical to the parent process. It has its own memory space, its own copy of the parent process's code and data, and its own program counter. Both the parent and child processes start executing after the **fork()** call, with the same program counter value.

Return Values:

The **fork()**System Call returns a value to both the parent and child processes. In the parent process, it returns the process ID (PID) of the newly created child process. In the child process, it returns 0. This return value is used to differentiate between the parent and child processes.

Usage:

Typically, the return value of **fork()** in the parent process is checked to determine whether the fork operation was successful and to decide whether the process should follow the parent or child branch of execution.

The child process can be used for various tasks, such as running a different program or performing some computation in parallel with the parent process.

Use Cases:

Fork() is a fundamental building block for creating multiple processes in Unix-like Operating Systems. It is commonly used in various scenarios, including concurrent programming, parallel processing, and implementing certain types of servers.

Caveats:

While the child process is nearly identical to the parent process, changes made by one process to its memory do not affect the other process. Modifications to data in one process's memory are not reflected in the other process.

In summary, the **fork()**System Call is essential for process creation in Unix-based Operating Systems. It allows a process to create a copy of itself, resulting in two separate processes that can execute in parallel, each with its own memory and execution context. The return value of **fork()** helps distinguish between the parent and child processes.

Q 3. What is System Programs? (RU MCA 2022)

Ans: System Programs are a set of software applications that manage and control the operation of a computer system. Unlike application programs, which are designed to solve specific user problems, system programs are responsible for ensuring the proper functioning of the entire computer system. These programs act as intermediaries between the hardware and the application software, providing essential services and maintaining the overall integrity of the system.

Some common types of system programs include:

Operating System (OS): The core system program that manages hardware resources, provides a user interface, and facilitates the execution of application programs. Examples include Windows, macOS, and Linux.

Device Drivers: Programs that enable communication between the Operating System and hardware devices, ensuring proper functioning of peripherals such as printers, graphics cards, and storage devices.

Utilities: Additional programs that perform specific system-related tasks, such as disk clean-up, file compression, and system maintenance. Examples include antivirus software, disk management tools, and backup utilities.

Compiler and Assembler: Tools that translate high-level programming languages or assembly language into machine code that the computer's central processing unit (CPU) can execute.

Loader and Linker: Programs that handle the process of loading and linking executable files into the computer's memory for execution.

Shell: The interface between the user and the Operating System, allowing users to interact with the system through commands or a graphical user interface (GUI).

System Programs collectively ensure the efficient utilization of hardware resources, provide a stable and secure environment for application programs, and facilitate a seamless user experience. They play a critical role in managing the complexity of modern computer systems and maintaining their reliability.

Q 4. What is Kernel? (RTU MCA 2022)

Ans: The Kernel is the core component of an Operating System that acts as an intermediary between the hardware and the software applications. It is a fundamental part of the Operating System responsible for managing system resources and providing essential services for the execution of processes. The kernel plays a crucial role in ensuring the stability, security, and efficiency of the entire Operating System.

Key functions of the kernel include:

Process Management: The kernel oversees the creation, scheduling, and termination of processes. It allocates CPU time, manages process states, and facilitates communication between processes.

Memory Management: It is responsible for managing the computer's memory, including allocating and deallocating memory space for processes, implementing virtual memory, and handling memory protection.

File System Management: The kernel manages file operations, including reading, writing, and organizing data on storage devices. It provides an interface for file access and ensures data integrity.

Device Drivers: The kernel contains device drivers that allow communication between the Operating System and hardware devices. These drivers enable the OS to interact with peripherals such as printers, keyboards, and network adapters.

System Calls: The kernel provides a set of System Calls, which are interfaces that allow user-level applications to request services from the Operating System. Examples include opening files, creating processes, and managing network connections.

Security and Access Control: The kernel enforces security policies, controls access to system resources, and protects against unauthorized actions. It manages user permissions and ensures the integrity of the overall system.

Interrupt Handling: The kernel handles hardware and software interrupts, ensuring that critical tasks are executed in response to external events, such as input from devices or errors.

In essence, the kernel is the core "brain" of the Operating System, coordinating and managing the interactions between software and hardware components. It provides a stable and secure platform for running applications and enables the efficient use of computer resources.

Q 5. Describe what is Virtual Machine and what are the advantages of Virtual Machine. (Anna University 2017)

Ans:A Virtual Machine (VM) is a software emulation of a physical computer system that runs on a host machine. It allows multiple Operating Systems (OS) to run concurrently on a single physical hardware platform. Each virtual machine behaves like a separate computer with its own CPU, memory, storage, and network interfaces, even though they are sharing the underlying physical resources.

Virtual Machines are created and managed by a hypervisor, which is a layer of software that sits between the hardware and the virtual machines. The hypervisor allocates and manages the resources of the physical hardware, enabling multiple virtual machines to run independently.

Advantages of Virtual Machines:

Resource Optimization: Virtualization allows for better utilization of physical hardware resources by running multiple virtual machines on a single physical server. This reduces hardware costs and energy consumption.

Isolation: Each Virtual Machine is isolated from other virtual machines running on the same host, providing a secure environment for running different applications and Operating Systems.

Flexibility and Portability: Virtual Machines can be easily moved and migrated between different physical servers without requiring significant downtime. This provides flexibility in managing workloads and facilitates disaster recovery and business continuity planning.

Consolidation: Virtualization enables server consolidation by running multiple virtual machines on a single physical server. This reduces the number of physical servers needed, leading to cost savings on hardware, maintenance, and management.

Testing and Development: Virtual Machines are ideal for software testing and development, allowing developers to create and test applications in isolated environments without affecting production systems.

Legacy Application Support: Virtualization enables organizations to run legacy applications that may require older Operating Systems or hardware configurations on modern infrastructure, extending the lifespan of legacy systems and applications.
Scalability: Virtualization allows for easy scaling of resources by adding or removing virtual machines based on workload demands. This provides agility in adapting to changing business requirements.

Overall, Virtual Machines offer numerous benefits including resource optimization, isolation, flexibility, and scalability, making them a popular choice for deploying and managing computing environments in both enterprise and cloud computing environments.

Q 7. What are System Calls? Explain different categories of System Calls with example. (RU BCA 2019)
Ans: System Calls are the interface between user-level processes and the Operating System kernel. They allow user-level programs to request services from the Operating System, such as accessing hardware devices, managing files, and performing various system-related tasks. When a program makes a System Call, it transfers control to the Operating System kernel, which then performs the requested operation on behalf of the program.

There are several categories of System Calls, each serving a specific purpose. Here are some common categories with examples:

Process Control:
fork: Creates a new process identical to the calling process.
exec: Loads and executes a new program in the current process.
exit: Terminates the calling process and returns its resources to the system.

File Management:
open: Opens a file for reading, writing, or both.
read: Reads data from an open file into a buffer.
write: Writes data from a buffer to an open file.
close: Closes a previously opened file.

Device Management:
ioctl: Performs I/O control operations on devices, such as setting device parameters.
read: Reads data from a device into a buffer.

write: Writes data from a buffer to a device.

Information Maintenance:
getpid: Retrieves the process ID (PID) of the calling process.
getuid: Retrieves the user ID (UID) of the calling process.
gettimeofday: Retrieves the current system time.

Communication:
socket: Creates a communication endpoint for network communication.
connect: Establishes a connection to a remote socket.
send: Sends data over a connected socket.
recv: Receives data from a connected socket.

Memory Management:
brk: Adjusts the end of the data segment to allocate more memory to the calling process.
mmap: Maps files or devices into memory.
munmap: Unmaps previously mapped memory regions.

Security:
chmod: Changes the permissions of a file.
chown: Changes the ownership of a file.
setuid: Sets the effective user ID of the calling process.

These are just a few examples of System Calls, and the specific System Calls available may vary depending on the Operating System. System Calls provide a crucial interface for user programs to interact with the underlying Operating System, enabling a wide range of functionalities and services.

Q 8. What is System Call? (RU BCA 2017)
Ans:A System Call is a mechanism provided by an Operating System that allows user-level processes or programs to request services or operations from the Operating System kernel. These services typically involve interactions with hardware devices, managing resources, or performing privileged operations that require kernel-level access.
When a program needs to perform a task that requires the assistance of the Operating System, such as reading from a file, creating a new process, or allocating memory, it makes a System Call. This action

transitions the program's execution from user mode to kernel mode, where the Operating System kernel can perform the requested operation on behalf of the program.

System Calls provide an interface between user-level applications and the underlying Operating System, abstracting away the complexities of hardware access and resource management. They enable programs to interact with hardware devices, manage system resources, and perform various tasks in a controlled and secure manner.

Examples of common System Calls include opening and closing files, reading from and writing to files, creating and terminating processes, managing memory, and performing network operations. Each Operating System provides a set of System Calls that applications can use to access its services and functionality.

Overall, System Calls are a fundamental component of the interaction between user-level programs and the Operating System, enabling applications to utilize the full capabilities of the underlying hardware and Operating System environment.

Exercise

Exercise 1 – MCQ

1. What is the primary purpose of system cells in an Operating System?
a) To store user data and application programs
b) To manage and control hardware resources
c) To provide a graphical user interface (GUI)
d) To execute user commands
2. Which of the following functions is typically NOT performed by system cells in an Operating System?
a) Process scheduling
b) File management
c) User authentication
d) Graphic rendering
3. What is the primary function of the CPU (Central Processing Unit) in a computer system?
a) Managing storage devices
b) Executing instructions and performing calculations
c) Handling network communications
d) Displaying graphics on the monitor
4. Which of the following is a volatile memory used for temporarily storing data that the CPU is currently working with?

a) Hard disk drive (HDD)

b) Solid-state drive (SSD)

c) Random Access Memory (RAM)

d) Read-Only Memory (ROM)

5.Which of the following is NOT considered one of the primary services provided by an Operating System?

a) Process management

b) File management

c) Network management

d) Keyboard input management

6. What is the primary purpose of a System Call in an Operating System?

a)To provide a user interface for the Operating System

b)To facilitate communication between hardware and software

c)To manage files and directories

d)To control the flow of the program

7. Which of the following is a primary function of system programs in an Operating System?

a) Providing a graphical user interface

b) Managing user accounts and permissions

c) Enhancing the performance of application programs

d) Generating random numbers for application use

8. In a layered Operating System structure, what is the main advantage of dividing the system into layers?

a) Simplifies debugging and maintenance

b) Increases overall system performance

c) Reduces the need for device drivers

d) Enhances user interface design

9. What is the purpose of the Kernel in the microkernel architecture of an Operating System?

a) Provides a user interface for applications

b) Manages device drivers

c) Handles only the essential functions like process management and memory management

d) Performs complex computations for user programs

10. What is the primary purpose of a Virtual Machine (VM) in the context of Operating Systems?

a) Enhancing graphics performance

b) Simulating the behavior of physical hardware on a software layer

c) Managing network connections

d) Optimizing file system operations

Exercise 2 – True/ False

1. Virtual Machines (VM's) allow multiple operating systems to run concurrently on the same physical hardware.
2. Virtual Machines can only be used for development and testing purposes, not for production environments.
3. The BIOS (Basic Input/output System) is a type of non-volatile memory that stores firmware for the computer's start-up process.
4. A GPU (Graphics Processing Unit) is responsible for managing the computer's file system and data storage.
5. Memory Management is a crucial service provided by an operating system to allocate and deallocate memory space for programs.
6. System Calls provide an interface for higher-level software to request services from the operating system's kernel.
7. System Programs are primarily responsible for interacting with the computer hardware to execute user applications.
8. The monolithic operating system structure combines all operating system functionalities into a single layer.
9. Virtual Machines allow multiple operating systems to run on a single physical machine concurrently.
10. A key advantage of using Virtual Machines is that they always offer better performance compared to running operating systems directly on physical hardware.

Exercise 3 – Fill in the blanks

1. In the operating system structure, the ____________ is responsible for managing and scheduling tasks or processes.
2. The ____________ provides a user-friendly interface for interacting with the operating system and its resources.

Answer

Exercise 1 – MCQ

Ans: 1 b, 2 c, 3 b, 4 c, 5 c, 6 b, 7 b, 8 a, 9 c, 10 b

Exercise 2 – True/False

Ans: 1 True, 2 False, 3 True, 4 False, 5 True, 6 True, 7 False, 8 True, 9 True, 10 False

Exercise 3 – Fill in The Blanks

Ans: 1 kernel, 2 shell

Online Resources

Videos:

MCQ Link: https://youtu.be/aRpWJ2mN-UM

QR Code:

True/False Link: https://youtu.be/RS_6hrCIh4w

QR Code:

Online Test Paper: https://forms.office.com/r/6sCn21WFb9

QR Code:

Chapter 3 Process Management

Processes and Threads

Processes and threads are fundamental concepts in Operating Systems, and they play crucial roles in managing the execution of programs and tasks. Here's a brief overview of processes and threads:

Processes:

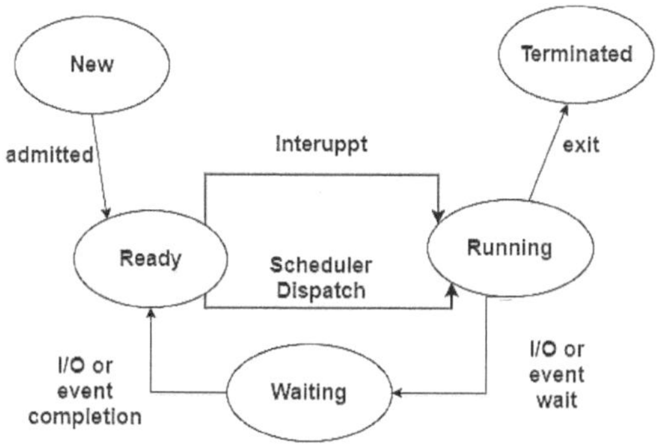

Definition: A process is an independent, self-contained unit of execution in an Operating System. It consists of its own memory space, program code, data, and system resources.

Isolation: Processes are isolated from each other, meaning one process cannot directly access the memory or resources of another process without going through Operating System mechanisms.

Resource Management: Each process has its own set of system resources, such as file handles, open sockets, and CPU time. The Operating System is responsible for allocating and managing these resources.

Multitasking: Operating Systems use process scheduling to allow multiple processes to run concurrently on a single processor or multiple processors.

Fault Tolerance: Processes provide fault isolation. If one process crashes, it generally does not affect other processes.

Threads:

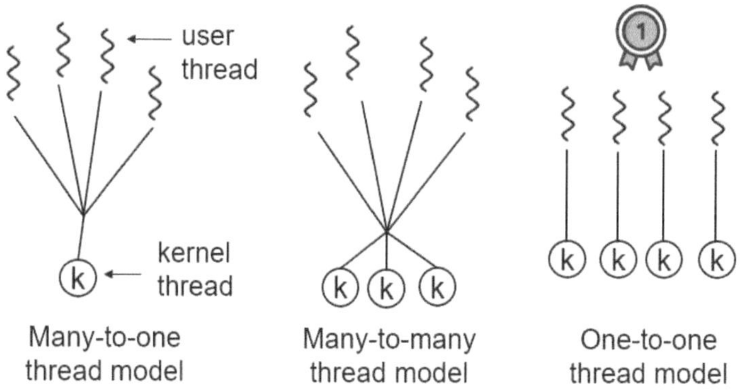

Definition: A thread is the smallest unit of execution within a process. Threads within the same process share the same memory space and resources.

Lightweight: Threads are more lightweight compared to processes because they share resources with other threads within the same process.

Concurrency: Multiple threads within a single process can execute concurrently, enabling better utilization of multicore processors.

Communication: Threads within the same process can easily communicate and share data since they share the same memory space.

Efficiency: Creating and managing threads is generally more efficient than creating and managing processes, as threads have lower overhead.

Fault Impact: Since threads within the same process share resources, a bug or crash in one thread can potentially affect other threads in the same process.

In summary, processes and threads are essential components of an Operating System's structure, providing the foundation for multitasking, resource management, and concurrency in modern computing environments. Processes offer isolation and robustness, while threads provide efficiency and easy communication within a single process. Understanding these concepts is crucial for designing and optimizing software in Operating Systems.

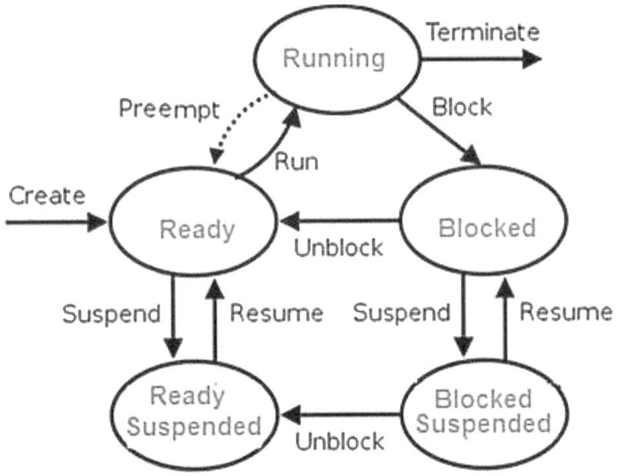

Process States

In an Operating System, a process can exist in several states as it progresses through its lifecycle. The primary process states are as follows:

New: In this state, a process is being created but has not yet been allocated system resources or entered into the scheduling queue. It is essentially being initialized.

Ready: A process in the **"Ready"** state is prepared to execute and is waiting for the CPU to be allocated. It has been loaded into the memory and is awaiting its turn for execution.

Running: When a process is in the **"Running"** state, it is actively executing its instructions on the CPU. At any given moment, only one process can be in the running state on a single processor core (in a uniprocessor system).

Blocked (or Waiting): A process enters the **"Blocked"** state when it is unable to proceed due to some event or condition, such as waiting for user input, file I/O, or a resource to become available. It is temporarily suspended until the event occurs.

Terminated (or Exit): The **"Terminated"** state represents the end of a process's lifecycle. It occurs when a process has completed its execution or has been explicitly terminated. Resources associated with the process are released, and its entry in the process table is removed.

Suspended (optional): Some Operating Systems have an additional **"Suspended"** state. Processes in this state are not actively executing but are not terminated either. They may be swapped out to disk to free up memory, or they could be explicitly suspended by the system or a user.

Ready/Suspend and Blocked/Suspend (optional): In systems with process suspension, processes in the **"Ready"** or **"Blocked"** state may also have suspended variants, denoted as **"Ready/Suspend"** and **"Blocked/Suspend."** These processes are in a suspended state but are ready to resume execution when explicitly awakened.

Processes can transition between these states based on various events and scheduling decisions made by the Operating System's scheduler. The goal of process management is to efficiently allocate CPU time and system resources to ensure that processes run effectively and concurrently in a multitasking environment.

Process Scheduling

Process Scheduling is a crucial aspect of operating system management, responsible for determining which process should run on the CPU at any given time. The primary goal of process scheduling is to make the most efficient use of the CPU, ensuring that processes are executed fairly and in a manner that minimizes delays. Here's an overview of process scheduling in an operating system:

Scheduling Queue: Processes that are ready to execute but are waiting for CPU time are placed in a scheduling queue. This queue typically uses scheduling algorithms to determine the order in which processes will be executed.

Dispatcher: The dispatcher is a component of the operating system responsible for selecting the next process from the scheduling queue and allocating CPU time to it. It is a context switcher that saves the state of the currently running process and loads the state of the next process to be executed.

Scheduling Algorithms: Various scheduling algorithms are employed to decide which process should run next. These algorithms include:

FirstCome, FirstServed (FCFS): Processes are executed in the order they arrive in the scheduling queue. It is non-preemptive, meaning a process runs until it completes or voluntarily yields the CPU.

Shortest Job Next (SJN) or Shortest Job First (SJF): The process with the shortest expected execution time is selected next. It minimizes average waiting time and is non-preemptive.

Round Robin (RR): Each process is given a fixed time slice (quantum) to execute, and then it is moved to the back of the queue. This ensures fairness but may not be optimal for all scenarios.

Priority Scheduling: Each process is assigned a priority, and the process with the highest priority runs next. Preemptive priority scheduling may lead to starvation, if lowerpriority processes are never executed.

Multilevel Queue Scheduling: Processes are divided into multiple queues based on their priority or other characteristics. Each queue may have its scheduling algorithm.

Multilevel Feedback Queue Scheduling: Similar to multilevel queue scheduling, but processes can move between queues based on their behavior, allowing for dynamic priority adjustment.

Pre-emption: Pre-emptive scheduling allows the Operating System to interrupt a running process and move it back to the scheduling queue based on predefined criteria (e.g., time quantum expiration or higher priority process arrival). This ensures fairness and responsiveness.

Aging: In priority-based scheduling, aging is used to prevent starvation. Over time, the priority of waiting processes may be increased, ensuring that even lowpriority processes eventually get a chance to execute.

Scheduling Criteria: Scheduling decisions can be based on various criteria, such as minimizing turnaround time, minimizing waiting time, or maximizing throughput, depending on the specific goals of the system.

Efficient process scheduling is critical for optimizing system performance and resource utilization in an Operating System, particularly in multiuser and multitasking environments. The choice of scheduling algorithm depends on the specific requirements and characteristics of the system and the trade-offs between fairness, responsiveness, and efficiency.

Inter-Process Communication

Inter-Process Communication (IPC) is a fundamental concept in operating systems that allows processes to exchange data and information with each other. IPC mechanisms enable cooperation and coordination among processes running concurrently on a computer system. There are several IPC methods available, each suited to different communication scenarios:

Shared Memory:

Description: Processes can create a shared memory segment in which they can read from and write to, allowing for fast data exchange.

Pros: It is very fast and efficient since processes can directly access shared memory.

Cons: Care must be taken to synchronize access to shared memory to avoid conflicts.

Message Passing:

Description: Processes communicate by sending and receiving messages. This can be implemented through either direct or indirect message passing.

Direct Message Passing: Processes explicitly name each other and send messages directly.

Indirect Message Passing: Messages are sent to and received from mailboxes or message queues, which can be identified by unique IDs.

Pros: Simplifies communication between processes and reduces the risk of data conflicts.

Cons: Slower than shared memory due to message copying, and the complexity of naming and managing mailboxes.

Sockets (Network Communication):

Description: Processes can communicate over a network using sockets, which are endpoints for sending and receiving data.

Pros: Enables communication between processes on different machines, making it ideal for distributed systems.

Cons: Overhead associated with network communication and potential issues like network failures.

Pipes and FIFOs (Named Pipes):

Description: Processes can establish communication through pipes, which are unidirectional or bidirectional data channels.

Pipes: Typically used for communication between parent and child processes.

FIFOs (Named Pipes): Allow processes to communicate even, if they are not related.

Pros: Simple and efficient for stream-based communication.

Cons: Unidirectional nature of pipes might require additional mechanisms for bidirectional communication.

Semaphores:

Description: Semaphores are synchronization objects used to coordinate access to shared resources or protect critical sections.

Pros: Effective for managing access to resources in a multiprocess environment.

Cons: Must be carefully designed to prevent deadlocks or race conditions.

Signals:

Description: Processes can send signals to each other to notify about specific events or to request specific actions.

Pros: Useful for process management and handling events like interrupts.

Cons: Limited in the amount of data that can be transmitted.

Remote Procedure Calls (RPC) and Remote Method Invocation (RMI):

Description: Allows processes to invoke functions or methods in remote processes, as if they were local.

Pros: Makes remote communication transparent, often used in distributed systems.

Cons: Complexity in handling remote failures and ensuring data consistency.

The choice of IPC mechanism depends on the specific requirements of the processes involved, including factors such as performance, data sharing needs, security, and network topology (in the case of distributed systems). Properly implemented IPC is essential for maintaining the integrity and functionality of concurrent processes in an operating system.

Process Synchronization

Process Synchronization is a critical concept in operating systems, especially in multiprocess or multithreaded environments. It involves managing and coordinating the execution of concurrent processes to ensure they access shared resources in an orderly and controlled manner. The primary goals of process synchronization are to prevent race conditions, avoid data inconsistencies, and ensure that processes or threads cooperate effectively. Here are some key mechanisms and techniques used for process synchronization:

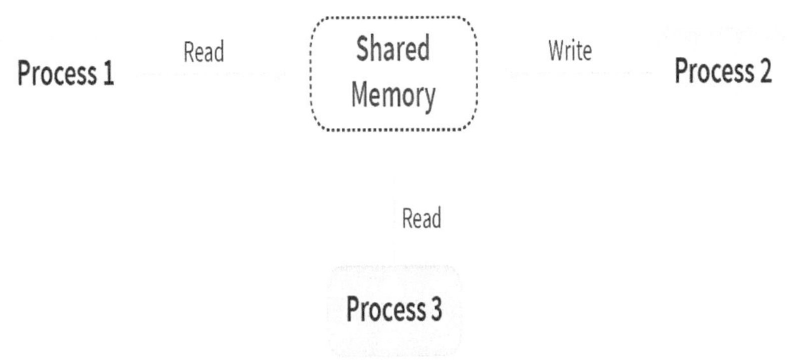

Mutex (Mutual Exclusion):

Description: Mutex is a synchronization primitive that allows only one process or thread to access a shared resource at a time. It acts as a lock that must be acquired before accessing the resource.

Pros: Simple and effective for protecting critical sections.

Cons: Care must be taken to avoid deadlocks and contention.

Semaphore:

Description: Semaphores are integer-based synchronization mechanisms that can be used to control access to shared resources or limit the number of processes in a critical section.

Binary Semaphore: Actsas a mutex with two values (0 and 1).

Counting Semaphore: Allows multiple processes to access a resource simultaneously but within a specified limit.

Pros: Versatile for a wide range of synchronization scenarios.

Cons: Requires careful management to prevent deadlocks and resource leaks.

Condition Variables:

Description: Condition variables are used for signaling and waiting in synchronization. They allow processes or threads to wait for a certain condition to be met before proceeding.

Pros: Useful for scenarios where processes need to coordinate based on specific conditions.

Cons: Typically used in conjunction with mutexes, which can be complex.

Barrier:

Description: A barrier is a synchronization point that forces a set of processes or threads to wait until all have reached the barrier before any of them can proceed.

Pros: Ensures that a group of processes or threads reach a certain point before proceeding, useful for parallel processing.

Cons: May introduce delays if not used carefully.

Readers Writers Problem:

Description: In this scenario, multiple processes want to access a shared resource for reading (simultaneous access allowed) or writing (exclusive access required).

Readers Priority: Allow multiple readers concurrently but give priority to writers.

Writers Priority: Give priority to writers, allowing them to proceed ahead of readers.

Pros: Balances access to shared resources between reading and writing processes.

Cons: Requires careful design to avoid starvation or priority inversion.

Mutex with Condition Variables:

Description: A combination of mutexes and condition variables can be used for complex synchronization scenarios, where processes need to coordinate based on certain conditions.

Pros: Provides fine-grained control over synchronization.

Cons: Complexity increases, making it more prone to errors, if not designed carefully.

Atomic Operations:

Description: Some hardware and programming languages provide atomic operations that can be used to perform certain actions without the need for locks.

Pros: Efficient for simple synchronization requirements.

Cons: Limited to specific operations and may not cover all synchronization needs.

Monitor:

Description: A monitor is a high-level synchronization construct that combines data and procedures into a single unit. It ensures that only one process can execute the monitor's procedures at a time.

Pros: Simplifies synchronization and encapsulates data and synchronization logic.

Cons: Limited to programming languages or libraries that support monitors.

Process synchronization is a critical component of concurrent programming, and the choice of synchronization mechanism depends on the specific requirements of the application or system. Careful design and implementation are essential to avoid issues such as deadlocks, lovelocks, and race conditions.

Peterson's Algorithm in Process Synchronization

Peterson's Algorithm is a classic algorithm used in concurrent programming and operating systems to provide a solution to the critical section problem, which is the problem of coordinating multiple processes or threads to ensure that they do not access shared resources simultaneously, thereby preventing data corruption or race conditions. Developed by Gary L. Peterson in 1981, Peterson's Algorithm is designed for two processes and is often used for educational purposes to demonstrate the concept of mutual exclusion.

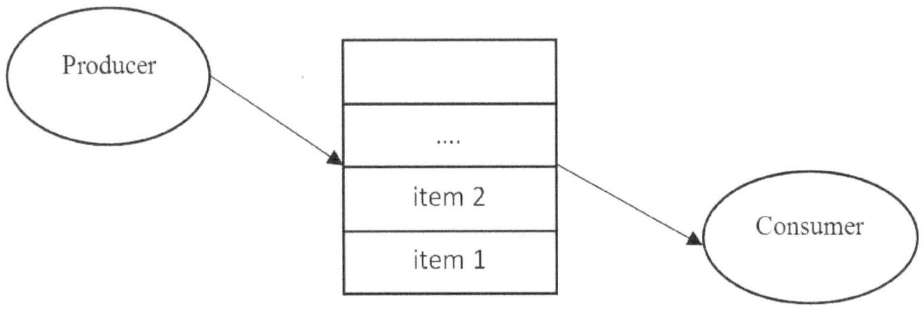

Buffer

The algorithm uses two shared variables and an array of flags to achieve mutual exclusion:

int turn: This variable indicates whose turn it is to enter the critical section. It alternates between the two processes, typically represented as 0 and 1.

Boolean flag[2]: An array of flags, one for each process. These flags signal the intention of each process to enter the critical section. When a process wants to enter the critical section, it sets its flag to true.

Key points to note about Peterson's Algorithm:

Both processes set their respective flags to indicate their intention to enter the critical section.

The variable `turn` indicates whose turn it is to enter the critical section. The other process must wait until it is its turn.

A process must busy-wait in a loop while the other process is in the critical section and it's not its turn.

When a process exits the critical section, it sets its flag to false to indicate that it is no longer interested in entering the critical section.

Advantages:

Simplicity: Peterson's Algorithm is relatively simple to understand and implement.

Mutual Exclusion: It guarantees that only one process can be in the critical section at any given time.

Fairness: The algorithm ensures fairness by alternately allowing each process to enter the critical section.

Disadvantages:

Limited to Two Processes: Peterson's Algorithm is designed for two processes and cannot be easily extended to handle more processes.

Busy-Waiting: The algorithm employs busy-waiting, which can be inefficient and consume CPU resources.

Not Suitable for Modern Systems: For modern multi-core systems or systems with more than two processes, more efficient synchronization primitives like mutexes or semaphores are typically used.

While Peterson's Algorithm is a valuable learning tool for understanding mutual exclusion, in practical applications, modern synchronization constructs provided by operating systems and programming languages are preferred due to their efficiency and scalability.

Semaphores

Semaphores are synchronization mechanisms used in operating systems and concurrent programming to control access to shared resources and coordinate the execution of multiple processes or threads. They were introduced by Dutch computer scientist EdsgerDijkstra in 1965 and have become a fundamental tool for managing concurrency. Semaphores are typically implemented as integer variables with two primary operations: `wait` and `signal`.

Here's a detailed explanation of Semaphores in Operating Systems:

Semaphore Operations:

`wait` Operation (also known as "P" or "down"): When a process or thread executes a **`wait`** operation on a semaphore, it attempts to decrement the semaphore's value by 1. If the resulting value is zero or positive, the `wait` operation proceeds without blocking, and the process can continue its execution. If the resulting value is negative, indicating that resources are currently unavailable, the `wait` operation blocks the process, effectively putting it to sleep until the semaphore's value becomes non-negative.

`signal` Operation (also known as "V" or "up"): The **`signal`** operation increments the semaphore's value by 1. If there are processes or threads blocked on this semaphore due to previous `wait` operations, one of them is awakened, allowing it to continue its execution. The `signal` operation is typically used when a process releases a resource, signaling that it is now available for other processes or threads to use.

Binary Semaphore vs. Counting Semaphore:

Binary Semaphore: A Binary Semaphore can have only two values, typically 0 and 1. It is often used for scenarios where mutual exclusion is required, meaning only one process or thread can access a critical section of code at a time. Binary semaphores are useful for simple synchronization tasks, such as protecting shared data from concurrent access.

Counting Semaphore: A Counting Semaphore can take on a range of non-negative integer values. It is used to manage multiple identical resources. Processes or threads can increment and decrement the semaphore to represent the availability of multiple resources. Counting semaphores are valuable for managing resource pools with a fixed capacity.

Applications of Semaphores:

Mutexes (Mutual Exclusion): Binary Semaphores are often used to implement mutual exclusion, ensuring that only one process or thread can access a critical section of code at a time. Mutexes are a common use case for binary semaphores and help prevent data corruption and race conditions.

Resource Allocation: Counting Semaphores are employed to control access to a limited pool of resources, such as database connections, file handles, or printing resources.

Producer-Consumer Problem: Semaphores can solve synchronization problems, such as the producer-consumer problem, by regulating interactions between producer and consumer processes or threads.

Readers-Writers Problem: Semaphores can address concurrency issues in the readers-writers problem, where multiple readers and writers access shared data.

Thread Synchronization: In Multi-Threaded Programs, Semaphores are used to synchronize threads, ensuring controlled execution and avoiding race conditions.

Task Synchronization in Real-Time Systems: Real-Time Operating Systems use Semaphores to coordinate the execution of real-time tasks, ensuring that they meet deadlines.

Semaphore Characteristics:

Atomicity: The operations `wait` and `signal` on semaphores are typically atomic, meaning that they are executed without interruption. This atomicity is essential for synchronization.

Blocking and Unblocking: Semaphores can block processes or threads (via `wait`) when resources are not available, and they can unblock waiting processes (via `signal`) when resources become available.

Concurrency Control: Semaphores provide a means to control the level of concurrency in a system. By regulating access to resources, semaphores help avoid contention and data corruption.

Deadlock Prevention: Careful management of semaphores is required to prevent deadlocks, where processes or threads wait indefinitely for resources. Proper resource allocation and release are critical to deadlock prevention.

Semaphores are a versatile synchronization tool, but they require careful design and usage to ensure correct and efficient synchronization. Misuse or improper management of semaphores can lead to issues like deadlocks and priority inversion. Therefore, they are often used alongside other synchronization mechanisms and locking strategies to build robust concurrent systems.

Types of Semaphores:

Semaphores are synchronization mechanisms that come in several types, each designed to address specific synchronization requirements and scenarios. The primary types of semaphores include:

Binary Semaphore (Mutex):

Values: 0 or 1.

Purpose: Used for mutual exclusion, allowing only one process or thread to access a critical section at a time. Often referred to as mutex (short for "mutual exclusion").

Operations: `wait` (P) and `signal` (V).

Use Cases: Protecting shared resources from concurrent access, preventing race conditions.

Counting Semaphore:

Values: Non-negative integer.

Purpose: Used for managing multiple identical resources or controlling access to a resource pool with a fixed capacity.

Operations: `wait` (P) and `signal` (V).

Use Cases: Resource allocation, controlling access to resource pools (e.g., managing connections, file handles).

Mutex Semaphore (Mutex):

Values: Typically, binary (0 or 1) but can be extended to support more complex scenarios.

Purpose: Provides mutual exclusion like a binary semaphore, but can be extended to handle more complex locking scenarios.

Operations: `wait` (P) and `signal` (V).

Use Cases: More complex synchronization scenarios where binary semaphores are insufficient.

Counting Semaphore with Upper Bound:

Values: Non-negative integer with an upper bound (maximum count).

Purpose: Similar to a counting semaphore but with a constraint on the maximum value, ensuring that the count does not exceed a specified limit.

Operations: `wait` (P) and `signal` (V).

Use Cases: Limiting the number of resources that can be allocated.

Priority Semaphore:

Values: Non-negative integer with priority levels.

Purpose: Assigns priorities to processes or threads, allowing higher-priority tasks to access resources first.

Operations: `wait` (P) and `signal` (V).

Use Cases: Real-Time Systems and situations where certain tasks must be prioritized.

Readers-Writers Semaphore:

Values: Typically, binary (0 or 1).

Purpose: Solves the readers-writers problem, where multiple readers and writers access shared data. Ensures that multiple readers can access the data simultaneously, but only one writer can access it at a time.

Operations: `wait` (P) and `signal` (V).

Use Cases: Protecting shared data in scenarios where multiple readers and writers coexist.

Barrier Semaphore:

Values: Typically, binary (0 or 1).

Purpose: Coordinates the synchronization of multiple processes or threads, making them wait until a specified number of processes reach a common point before proceeding.

Operations: `wait` (P) and `signal` (V).

Use Cases: Synchronizing parallel tasks in parallel computing or parallel algorithms.

Mutex with Priority Inheritance (Priority Mutex):

Values: Typically, binary (0 or 1).

Purpose: Extends the basic mutex to prevent priority inversion, where a lower-priority task holds a mutex needed by a higher-priority task. Priority inheritance temporarily boosts the priority of the lower-priority task holding the mutex.

Operations: `wait` (P) and `signal` (V).

Use Cases: Real-Time Systems and scenarios wherepriority inversion must be avoided.

Dining Philosophers Semaphore:

Values: Typically, binary (0 or 1).

Purpose: Solves the dining philosophers problem, a classic synchronization problem where philosophers (processes) share forks (resources) for dining. Ensures that philosophers can pick up two forks to eat.

Operations: `wait` (P) and `signal` (V).

Use Cases: Teaching synchronization concepts and solving resource allocation problems.

The choice of semaphore type depends on the specific synchronization requirements of the system or application. Different semaphore types offer flexibility in addressing various synchronization challenges and resource allocation scenarios.

Producer Consumer Problem using Semaphores

The Producer-Consumer Problem is a classic synchronization problem used to illustrate challenges related to sharing data and coordinating the activities of two types of processes or threads: producers and consumers. In this problem, producers generate data items, while consumers consume or process those data items. To ensure proper coordination and avoid issues like data corruption or deadlock, semaphores are commonly used. Let's explain the **Producer-Consumer Problem usingsemaphores:**

Problem Statement:

There is a shared buffer or queue that can hold a limited number of data items.

Producers produce data items and place them into the buffer.

Consumers consume data items from the buffer.

Multiple producers and consumers may be operating concurrently.

Producers should not produce data, if the buffer is full.

Consumers should not consume data, if the buffer is empty.

Solution using Semaphores:

A. Initialization:

Initialize a counting semaphore `empty` to represent the number of empty slots in the buffer. Initially, it is set to the maximum buffer size.

Initialize a counting semaphore `full` to represent the number of filled slots in the buffer. Initially, it is set to 0.

Use a mutex semaphore (binary semaphore) to protect access to the buffer when producers and consumers are modifying it.

Initialize the buffer itself, which is a shared data structure.

B. Producer Code:

"Python"

```
produce_item()  # Generate a new data item

wait(empty)    # Wait for an empty slot in the buffer
wait(mutex)    # Enter the critical section
add_item_to_buffer()  # Add the item to the buffer
signal(mutex)  # Exit the critical section
signal(full)   # Signal that a slot in the buffer is now filled
```

C. Consumer Code:

"Python"

```
wait(full)     # Wait for a filled slot in the buffer
wait(mutex)    # Enter the critical section
remove_item_from_buffer()  # Remove an item from the buffer
signal(mutex)  # Exit the critical section
signal(empty)  # Signal that a slot in the buffer is now empty
consume_item()  # Process or consume the data item
```

Explanation:

The `empty` semaphore tracks the number of available slots in the buffer, initially set to the maximum buffer size. It is decremented by producers when they add items to the buffer and incremented by consumers when they consume items.

The `full` semaphore tracks the number of filled slots in the buffer, initially set to 0. It is incremented by producers when they add items to the buffer and decremented by consumers when they consume items.

The mutex semaphore (`mutex`) is used to protect access to the buffer during insertion and removal operations. It ensures that only one producer or consumer can access the buffer at a time, preventing race conditions.

Producers and consumers use the `wait` operation on the `empty` and `full` semaphores to block or unblock themselves based on the availability of slots in the buffer.

Producers and consumers also use the `wait` and `signal` operations on the `mutex` semaphore to enter and exit the critical section when accessing the buffer, ensuring mutual exclusion.

By using semaphores, the Producer-Consumer Problem can be effectively solved, ensuring that producers and consumers cooperate to maintain the integrity of the shared buffer and avoid issues such as overfilling or emptying the buffer. This synchronization approach ensures that producers wait when the buffer is full and consumers wait when the buffer is empty, allowing for efficient data sharing and coordination between the two types of processes.

Previous Year Solved Questions

Q 1. What is Synchronization? (RU BCA 2022)

Ans: When two or more process cooperates with each other, their order of execution must be preserved otherwise there can be conflicts in their execution and inappropriate outputs can be produced.

A cooperative process is the one whichcan affected the execution ofother processorcan beaffected by theexecution of other process. Such processes need to besynchronized so thattheir order of execution can be guaranteed.

The procedure involved in preserving the appropriate order of execution of cooperative processes is known as Process Synchronization.

Q 2. What is deadlock? Explain with example? (RU BCA 2022)

Ans: Deadlock is a situation in which two or more processes in a computer system are unable to proceed with their execution because they are each waiting for a resource that is held by another process within the same group. Essentially, it's a state of mutual waiting, where processes prevent each other from completing their tasks.

Here's an example to illustrate deadlock:

Consider a simplified scenario with two processes, P1 and P2, and two resources, R1 and R2.

Initial State:

P1 holds R1 and requests R2.

P2 holds R2 and requests R1.

Execution:

P1 executes and gets R1.

P2 executes and gets R2.

Stalemate:

Now, P1 needs R2 to complete its task, but cannot proceed because P2 is holding R2. Similarly, P2 needs R1 but can't proceed because P1 is holding R1. Both processes are waiting for a resource held by the other, and neither can make progress.

This state of affairs is a deadlock. In a real-world computer system, this can lead to the system becoming unresponsive and requiring intervention, such as restarting or forcibly terminating one of the processes involved.

Deadlocks can occur in multi-process/multi-threaded systems where processes or threads contend for shared resources and can't reach a consensus on resource allocation. To manage and prevent deadlocks, various synchronization mechanisms and algorithms, such as mutex locks and deadlock detection, are used in Operating Systems and programming languages.

Q 3. What is Priority of Scheduling? Explain with example.(RU BCA 2022)

Ans: Priority Scheduling is a process scheduling algorithm used in computer Operating Systems to determine the order in which processes or threads are executed based on their assigned priorities. Each process is given a priority value, and the scheduler selects the process with the highest priority to run first. Priority scheduling can be either pre-emptive or non-pre-emptive, depending on whether a higher-priority process can interrupt the execution of a lower-priority one.

Here's an explanation with an example:

Consider three processes, P1, P2, and P3, with the following priority values:

P1: Priority 1

P2: Priority 2

P3: Priority 3

In a non-pre-emptive priority scheduling algorithm, the process with the highest priority is allowed to run until it completes or enters a waiting state. Let's say P3 arrives first, followed by P2 and then P1.

P3 starts executing because it has the highest priority.

P2 waits for P3 to finish.

P1 waits for both P3 and P2 to finish.

The execution order would be: P3 → P2 → P1. In this case, processes are executed in decreasing order of priority, with lower-priority processes waiting until higher-priority ones are completed.

In a pre-emptive priority scheduling algorithm, a higher-priority process can interrupt the execution of a lower-priority one if it becomes available. For example, if P1 has a higher priority than P2 and P3, it can pre-emptively interrupt the execution of P2 or P3 if it becomes ready to run.

Priority Scheduling is useful in scenarios where some processes are more critical or time-sensitive than others. However, it can lead to starvation if lower-priority processes never get a chance to execute. To mitigate this, some systems implement aging mechanisms to gradually increase the priority of waiting processes.

Q 4. What is Process? Draw and explain process state diagram?(RU BCA 2019, RU B. Tech Feb 2021)

Ans:A **process** in an Operating System is an independent program in execution. It consists of the program code, data, and resources (e.g., memory, CPU registers) that are required for its execution. A process is the basic unit of execution, and the Operating System manages and schedules processes to ensure efficient and concurrent execution of multiple tasks.

Process State Diagram:

A Process State Diagram is a visual representation of the different states a process can go through during its lifecycle in an Operating System. These states typically include:

New: In the "New" state, the process is being created but has not yet started execution. It may involve tasks such as loading the program into memory and setting up data structures.

Ready: In the "Ready" state, the process is prepared to run but is waiting for its turn to execute. Processes in this state are typically placed in a queue or a ready list, awaiting their CPU time slice.

Running: The "Running" state indicates that the process is actively executing on the CPU. Only one process can be in this state on a single CPU core at a given time. The process can transition back to the "Ready" state when its time slice expires or when it voluntarily yields the CPU.

Blocked (or Waiting): A process enters the "Blocked" state when it cannot continue execution because it is waiting for some event, such as I/O completion, a signal, or a resource allocation. While in this state, the process is not using CPU time.

Terminated: The "Terminated" state represents the end of a process's execution. This can happen when the program finishes or when it is terminated due to an error or user request. After termination, resources held by the process are released, and the process is removed from the system.

Here's a simplified process state diagram:

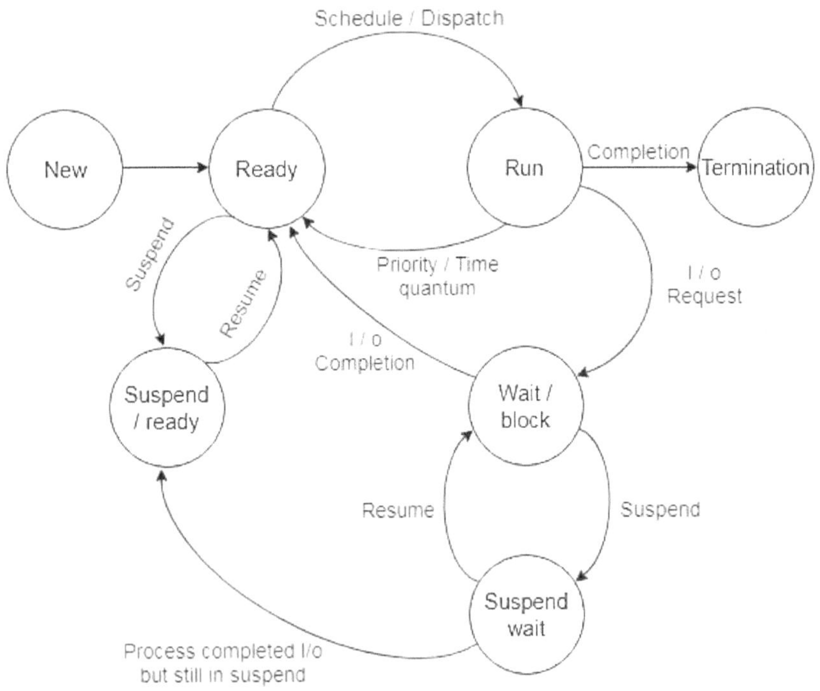

Transitions between States:

A process can transition from "New" to "Ready" when it is loaded into memory and ready to be scheduled for execution.

The transition from "Ready" to "Running" occurs when the Operating System selects the process to run and allocates CPU time to it.

When a process is waiting for I/O or some other event, it moves from "Running" to "Blocked" (or "Waiting").

When the waiting event is satisfied, the process moves from "Blocked" to "Ready," and it may eventually return to "Running" if it is the highest-priority process in the ready queue.

A process reaches the "Terminated" state when it completes execution or is forcibly terminated.

The process state diagram illustrates how processes move through various states, and the Operating System's task is to manage these transitions to maximize system throughput, efficiency, and responsiveness. Proper process scheduling and management are crucial for effective multitasking in modern Operating Systems.

Q 5. Write the method of recovery from deadlock?(RU BCA 2017)

Ans: Deadlock is a situation in which two computer programs sharing the same resource are effectively preventing each other from accessing the resource, resulting in both programs ceasing to function,

Deadlock Recovery: Traditional Operating System such as Windows doesn't deal with deadlock recovery as it is time and space consuming process. Real time Operating Systems use Deadlock recovery.

Recovery method

Killing the process:

killing all the process involved in deadlock. Killing process one by one. After killing each Process check for deadlock again keep repeating Process till system recover from deadlock.

Resource Pre-emption

Resources are pre-empted from the processes involved in deadlock, pre-empted resources are allocated to other processes, so that there is a possibility of recovering the system from deadlock. In this case system goes into starvation.

Q 6. What is deadlock?(RU B. Tech Jan 2022)

Ans: Deadlock is a specific condition that can occur in a multitasking Operating System when two or more processes (or threads) become unable to proceed because each is waiting for the other to release a resource. In a deadlock situation, the involved processes or threads may remain stuck indefinitely, and the system cannot make progress. Deadlocks are undesirable and need to be avoided or resolved. Here's a detailed explanation of deadlock in the context of Operating Systems:

Necessary Conditions for Deadlock:

Four necessary conditions must be met for a deadlock to occur. These conditions are often referred to as the Coffman **Conditions, named after computer scientist Edward G. Coffman:**

Mutual Exclusion: At least one resource must be held in a non-shareable mode, meaning only one process can use it at a time.

Hold and Wait: Processes must be holding resources while waiting for additional resources.

No Pre-emption: Resources cannot be pre-empted from processes; they must be released voluntarily by the holding process.

Circular Wait: A circular chain of processes exists, where each process is waiting for a resource held by the next process in the chain.

Deadlock Examples:

Common examples of deadlock occur in various scenarios, such as in database systems (two transactions locking tables), printer queues (multiple print jobs waiting for the same printer), and resource allocation in Operating Systems (processes waiting for memory, file locks, or I/O devices).

Detection and Resolution:

There are several approaches to deal with deadlocks:

Detection: Detecting deadlocks when they occur, and then takingaction to resolve them. This approach involves periodically checking the system's state and identifying deadlocks.

Prevention: Designing the system in a way that prevents at least one of the necessary conditions from ever occurring. This can be achieved by careful resource allocation and management.

Avoidance: Employing algorithms to allocate resources dynamically, ensuring that the system remains in a safe state, where no deadlock can occur.

Recovery: Restarting affected processes or releasing resources to break the deadlock, but this approach can be complex and may result in data loss.

Resource Allocation Graph:

One common method for modeling and visualizing deadlocks is the Resource Allocation Graph. In this graph, processes are represented as nodes, resources as resource types, and resource instances as edges. By analyzing this graph, it is possible to identify the presence of a cycle, which is indicative of a deadlock.

Implications of Deadlocks:

Deadlocks can lead to system resource wastage and reduced system throughput. In extreme cases, they can result in system crashes or unresponsiveness.

Prevention Strategies:

To prevent deadlocks, strategies include careful resource allocation, ensuring that resources are never pre-allocated together, using timeouts, and employing appropriate resource management techniques.

Real-world Applications:

Deadlocks are a concern in numerous applications, including operating systems, database management systems, distributed systems, and concurrent programming. Various protocols and algorithms have been developed to address deadlock issues in these domains.

In conclusion, deadlock is a challenging and undesirable situation that can occur in operating systems and other distributed environments. Understanding the conditions that lead to deadlocks and implementing appropriate prevention, detection, or resolution mechanisms is crucial for maintaining system stability and reliability.

Q 7. What are the necessary conditions for deadlock? Explain resource graph model and safe-unsafe states with a suitable example.(RU B. Tech Jan 2022)

Ans:Deadlock is a state in which two or more processes are unable to proceed because each is waiting for the other to release resources. Deadlocks occur in systems where processes compete for resources, and to avoid or resolve deadlocks, certain necessary conditions must be met. These conditions are often referred to as the "Four Coffman Conditions," named after computer scientist Edward G. Coffman. The necessary conditions for deadlock are:

Mutual Exclusion: At least one resource must be non-shareable, meaning that only one process can use the resource at a time. This condition ensures that no two or more processes can simultaneously hold a resource.

Hold and Wait: Processes must hold resources while waiting for additional ones. In other words, a process that has already acquired some resources can request additional ones without releasing its current resources. This condition can lead to a situation where processes are waiting indefinitely for resources.

No Pre-emption: Resources cannot be pre-empted or forcibly taken away from a process. If a process holds a resource and needs another resource, it cannot have the second resource allocated to another process, even temporarily.

Circular Wait: There must be a circular chain of two or more processes, each waiting for a resource held by the next process in the chain. In other words, Process A is waiting for a resource held by Process B, Process B is waiting for a resource held by Process C, and so on, with the last process waiting for a resource held by Process A.

The **Resource Graph Model** is a graphical representation used to analyze and detect deadlocks in a system. It consists of two types of nodes:

Process Nodes: Each process in the system is represented as a node in the resource graph.

Resource Nodes: Each resource type is represented as a node in the resource graph. If there are multiple instances of a resource type, there will be multiple nodes of that type.

The Edges in the graph represent two types of relationships:

Request Edge: A directed edge from a process node to a resource node indicates that the process is requesting the resource.

Assignment Edge: A directed edge from a resource node to a process node indicates that the resource is currently allocated to the process.

Safe and Unsafe States:

In the context of deadlock detection and avoidance, states of a system can be classified as "safe" or "unsafe."

Safe State: A state in which there exists a sequence of process allocations (resource assignments and releases) that will allow all processes to complete their execution without resulting in a deadlock. In a safe state, there is no circular wait.

Unsafe State: A state in which deadlock is possible. There is a potential for a circular wait, meaning that processes may enter a deadlock if resource allocations continue.

Example:

Consider a simplified example with two processes (P1 and P2), two resource types (A and B), and a single instance of each resource. The processes request and release resources as follows:

P1 requests resource A, gets it, and then requests resource B.

P2 requests resource B, gets it, and then requests resource A.

Initially, both processes have one resource each (P1 has A, and P2 has B). In the resource graph:

P1 has an assignment edge from A to P1.

P2 has an assignment edge from B to P2.

P1 has a request edge from P1 to B (P1 requests B).

P2 has a request edge from P2 to A (P2 requests A).

This state is **unsafe** because there is a circular wait:

P1 is waiting for B.

P2 is waiting for A.

If resources continue to be allocated this way, a deadlock can occur. A safe state, on the other hand, would be one where all processes can complete without the potential for a circular wait, **such as:**

P1 requests A, gets it, releases A.

P2 requests B, gets it, releases B.

This example illustrates the concept of safe and unsafe states and how they can be detected using the resource graph model in the context of the necessary conditions for deadlock.

Q 8. Define Process. (RTU MCA 2022)

Ans: In the context of an Operating System, a process refers to an independent and self-contained program in execution. It represents the dynamic state of a program, including the program counter, registers, and variables, as it runs on a computer's central processing unit (CPU). A process is the unit of work in a system, and multiple processes can run concurrently, allowing for multitasking and parallel execution.

Key characteristics of a process include:

Program Counter (PC): The program counter keeps track of the address of the next instruction to be executed within the program.

Registers: Processes have their own set of registers, including the accumulator, index registers, and stack pointer, which are used for temporary storage and execution of instructions.

Memory Space: Each process has its own memory space, containing the code, data, and stack segments. This isolation prevents one process from directly accessing the memory of another, ensuring data integrity and security.

State: A process can be in one of several states, such as "ready," "running," "waiting," or "terminated." The Operating System manages the transitions between these states based on events and scheduling decisions.

Resources: Processes may require various system resources, including CPU time, memory, I/O devices, and files. The Operating System allocates and manages these resources to ensure fair and efficient execution.

Processes are fundamental to achieving multitasking, allowing users to run multiple programs simultaneously. The Operating System's process management capabilities coordinate the execution of processes, allocate resources, and facilitate communication between different processes.

In summary, a process in an Operating System is an instance of a program in execution, characterized by its program counter, registers, memory space, and state. It represents the dynamic aspect of a program and is managed by the Operating System to achieve efficient and concurrent execution of multiple tasks.

Q 9. What is meant by Binary Semaphore? (RTU MCA 2022)

Ans:A Binary Semaphore is a synchronization primitive in computer science and Operating Systems that can take on only two integer values, typically 0 and 1. It is used to control access to a shared resource or coordinate the execution of processes by signalling whether the resource is available or not.

Key characteristics of a binary semaphore:

Values: The binary semaphore can only have two values—0 and 1. The value 0 usually indicates that the resource is unavailable or in use, while the value 1 indicates that the resource is available or unoccupied.

Operations:

Wait (P) Operation: If the binary semaphore's value is 1,then it decrements the value to 0, allowing the process to proceed. If the value is already 0, the process is blocked until the semaphore becomes 1.

Signal (V) Operation: Increments the binary semaphore's value from 0 to 1. If there are processes waiting (blocked) due to a previous Wait operation, one of them is allowed to proceed.

Binary Semaphores are often used for mutual exclusion, where only one process can access a critical section of code or a shared resource at a time. They help prevent race conditions and ensure that conflicting operations do not occur simultaneously.

While Binary Semaphores are effective for basic synchronization, more advanced synchronization mechanisms, such as mutexes or monitors, are often used in modern programming to provide additional features and flexibility in managing concurrency.

Q 10. What is a semaphore? Give a solution to 'Readers Writers' problem using semaphore. Explain the steps. (IGNOU 2010)

Ans:A Semaphore is a synchronization mechanism used in concurrent programming to control access to shared resources. It is essentially an integer variable that can only be accessed through two atomic operations: wait (P) and signal (V). Semaphores can be used to coordinate access to shared resources among multiple threads or processes.

The Readers-Writers problem is a classic synchronization problem where multiple readers and writers access a shared resource, such as a file or database, simultaneously.

The problem can be summarized as follows:

Multiple readers can access the shared resource simultaneously without any issues.

Only one writer can access the shared resource at a time, and no other reader or writer can access it while a writer is writing.

Writers have higher priority than readers to prevent starvation.

To solve the Readers-Writers problem using semaphores, we can use two semaphores: a mutex semaphore to ensure mutual exclusion for writers and a semaphore to keep track of the number of readers currently accessing the resource. Here's a high-level solution:

Initialize two Semaphores: Mutex (initialized to 1) and ReaderCount (initialized to 0).

Writers' Solution:

A writer waits on the Mutex semaphore to acquire exclusive access to the resource.

After acquiring the mutex, the writer checks, if any readers are currently accessing the resource. If there are readers, it waits.

Once no readers are accessing the resource, the writer performs its write operation.

After completing the write operation, the writer signals the mutex, allowing other writers or readers to access the resource.

Readers' solution:

A reader waits on the Mutex semaphore to acquire exclusive access to the resource.

After acquiring the mutex, the reader increments the ReaderCountSemaphore to indicate that it is accessing the resource.

If the ReaderCount is 1 (i.e., this is the first reader),then the reader waits on the mutex semaphore to prevent writers from accessing the resource.

After completing its read operation, the reader decrements the ReaderCountSemaphore.

If the ReaderCount becomes 0 (i.e., this is the last reader), the reader signals the mutex semaphore to allow writers to access the resource.

Finally, the reader releases the Mutex Semaphore.

By using semaphores to control access to the shared resource, we ensure that writers have exclusive access to the resource and readers can access it concurrently without interference from writers. This solution prevents race conditions and ensures mutual exclusion and synchronization in accessing the shared resource.

Q 11. Explain multistage switch-basedsystem in Multi-Processor System. (IGNOU 2010)

Ans: In a Multiprocessor System, a multistage switch-based system is a method used for interconnecting multiple processors and memory modules to facilitate efficient communication and data transfer between them. This architecture is commonly used in large-scale parallel processing systems to achieve high throughput and scalability.

A multistage switch-based system consists of multiple stages of switches interconnected in a hierarchical or mesh topology. Each switch connects multiple input ports to multiple output ports, allowing data packets to be routed from source processors to destination processors through multiple stages of switches.

The key components of a multistage switch-based system include:

Switches: Each Switch in the system has multiple input ports and output ports, allowing it to route data packets from any input port to any output port based on routing algorithms and control signals.

Interconnection Network: The switches are Interconnected to form a network topology that enables communication between processors and memory modules. Common topologies include crossbar, mesh, torus, and hypercube.

Control Logic: The Control Logic is responsible for determining the routing paths for data packets through the network, based on the destination address of the packets and the current network congestion.

Routing Algorithms: Routing Algorithms determine the paths taken by data packets through the network to reach their destination efficiently. Examples of routing algorithms include deterministic algorithms (such as dimension-order routing) and adaptive algorithms (such as least congested path routing).

Advantages of a multistage switch-based system in a multiprocessor system include:

Scalability: The modular nature of multistage switches allows for easy scalability by adding more switches or stages to the system as the number of processors increases.
High Throughput: By providing multiple paths for data packets to traverse through the network, multistage switch-based systems can achieve high throughput and reduce communication bottlenecks.
Fault Tolerance: The redundant paths available in the network topology can provide fault tolerance by allowing data packets to be rerouted in the event of switch or link failures.
Load Balancing: Multistage switch-based systems can dynamically balance the load across different paths in the network, optimizing resource utilization and reducing congestion.

Overall, multistage switch-based systems are an effective solution for interconnecting processors and memory modules in multiprocessor systems, providing high throughput, scalability, fault tolerance, and load balancing capabilities.

Q 12. What is a Semaphore? Give solution to producer consumer problem using semaphores, explain the solution.(IGNOU 2010)
Ans:A Semaphore is a synchronization mechanism used in concurrent programming to control access to shared resources. It is essentially an integer variable that can only be accessed through two atomic operations: wait (P) and signal (V). Semaphores can be used to coordinate access to shared resources among multiple threads or processes.

The Producer-Consumer problem is a classic synchronization problem where multiple producers produce data items and put them into a shared buffer, and multiple consumers consume these data items from the buffer. The problem can be summarized as follows:

Producers must wait if the buffer is full before they can produce new items.
Consumers must wait if the buffer is empty before they can consume items.
To solve the Producer-Consumer problem using semaphores, we typically use three semaphores: empty, full, and mutex. **Here's a High-Level Solution:**

Initialize three semaphores: empty (initialized to the size of the buffer), full (initialized to 0), and mutex (initialized to 1).
Producers' solution:

A producer waits on the empty semaphore to ensure there is space in the buffer to produce new items.

After acquiring the empty semaphore, the producer waits on the mutex semaphore to acquire exclusive access to the buffer.

Once the producer acquires the mutex, it adds a new item to the buffer.

After adding the item, the producer signals the mutex semaphore to release the buffer and increments the full semaphore to indicate that the buffer is no longer empty.

Consumers' Solution:

A Consumer waits on the full semaphore to ensure there are items available in the buffer to consume.

After acquiring the full semaphore, the consumer waits on the mutex semaphore to acquire exclusive access to the buffer.

Once the consumer acquires the mutex, it removes an item from the buffer.

After consuming the item, the consumer signals the mutex semaphore to release the buffer and decrements the full semaphore to indicate that the buffer may be empty now.

Finally, the empty, full, and mutex semaphores must be properly initialized and cleaned up.

This solution ensures that producers and consumers can safely access the shared buffer without race conditions or deadlock. The empty semaphore tracks the available space in the buffer, the full semaphore tracks the number of items in the buffer, and the mutex semaphore ensures mutual exclusion to prevent multiple producers or consumers from accessing the buffer simultaneously.

Q 13. What are the essential conditions for Deadlock to occur? Explain Deadlock Avoidance Algorithm with an example. (IGNOU 2010)

Ans: Deadlock is a situation in concurrent systems where two or more processes are unable to proceed because each is waiting for the other to release a resource, resulting in a cyclic dependency and none of the processes being able to make progress.

Deadlock can occur if the following four conditions hold simultaneously:

Mutual Exclusion: At least one resource must be held in a non-sharable mode, meaning only one process can use the resource at a time.

Hold and Wait: Processes must hold resources already allocated to them while waiting to acquire additional resources that are currently held by other processes.

No Pre-emption: Resources cannot be forcibly taken away from a process; they can only be released voluntarily by the process holding them.

Circular Wait: There must exist a circular chain of two or more processes, each of which is waiting for a resource held by the next process in the chain.

Deadlock AvoidanceAlgorithms aim to prevent the occurrence of deadlock by ensuring that at least one of the essential conditions for deadlock cannot hold. One such algorithm is the Banker's Algorithm.

Banker's Algorithm is a deadlock avoidance algorithm used in resource allocation systems, where processes request resources from a finite pool of available resources. The algorithm dynamically determines whether granting a request for resources will leave the system in a safe state, i.e., whether deadlock can be avoided.

Here's an explanation of the Banker's algorithm with an example:

Consider a system with 3 types of resources (A, B, and C) and 5 processes (P0, P1, P2, P3, and P4). The maximum demand and current allocation of resources for each process are as follows:

	Max	Allocation
	A B C	A B C
P0	7 5 3	0 1 0
P1	3 2 2	2 0 0
P2	9 0 2	3 0 2
P3	2 2 2	2 1 1
P4	4 3 3	0 0 2

We also have the available resources in the system: (3, 3, 2).

The Banker's algorithm works as follows:

When a process requests resources, the system checks whether granting the request will lead to a safe state. If so, the resources are allocated; otherwise, the process must wait.

To determine, if a state is safe, the algorithm simulates the execution of processes and checks whether there exists a safe sequence of processes that can finish without deadlock.

If a safe sequence exists, then the requested resources are allocated, and the process can proceed. Otherwise, the process must wait until the requested resources become available.

For example, if process P1 requests (0, 2, 0) resources, the system checks if the state (3, 1, 0) (current allocation plus request) is safe. It simulates the execution of processes in a way that ensures they can finish without deadlock, considering the available resources and maximum demands of processes.

If the state is safe, the resources are allocated; otherwise, the process must wait until the requested resources become available. By ensuring that resources are allocated in a way that does not lead to deadlock, Banker's algorithm effectively avoids the occurrence of deadlock in resource allocation systems.

Q 14. What are the necessary conditions to hold a deadlock in a system? Explain the Resource Allocation Graph algorithm to deal with deadlock problem. What are the limitations of this approach? (IGNOU 2015)

Ans: Deadlock is a state in a concurrent system where two or more processes are unable to proceed because each is waiting for a resource that is held by another process. Deadlock can occur if the following four necessary conditions hold simultaneously:

Mutual Exclusion: At least one resource must be held in a non-sharable mode, meaning only one process can use the resource at a time.

Hold and Wait: Processes must hold resources already allocated to them while waiting to acquire additional resources that are currently held by other processes.

No Pre-emption: Resources cannot be forcibly taken away from a process; they can only be released voluntarily by the process holding them.

Circular Wait: There must exist a circular chain of two or more processes, each of which is waiting for a resource held by the next process in the chain.

To deal with the deadlock problem, various deadlock avoidance and deadlock detection algorithms have been developed. One such algorithm is the Resource Allocation Graph (RAG) algorithm, which is used for deadlock detection.

The Resource Allocation Graph algorithm works as follows:

Construct a Resource Allocation Graph representing the allocation of resources to processes and the dependencies between them.

Nodes in the graph represent processes and resources, and edges represent resource allocation and resource request relationships.

Apply the following two rules to detect cycles in the graph:

Rule 1 (Resource-Request Edge): If a process requests a resource that is currently held by another process, then add a request edge from the requesting process to the resource node.

Rule 2 (Resource-Allocation Edge): If a process is holding a resource and waiting for another resource, then add an allocation edge from the process to the resource it holds.
If a cycle is detected in the graph, deadlock is present in the system. The processes involved in the cycle are deadlocked, and appropriate actions must be taken to resolve the deadlock.

Limitations of the Resource Allocation Graph algorithm include:

State Explosion: The graph can become complex and large in systems with a large number of processes and resources, making it difficult to analyze and detect deadlock efficiently.
Assumption of Single Instance Resources: The algorithm assumes that resources are allocated one at a time, which may not hold true in systems with multiple instances of resources.
Overhead: Constructing and maintaining the Resource Allocation Graph incurs overhead in terms of computation and memory, especially in large-scale systems.

Despite these limitations, the Resource Allocation Graph algorithm provides a useful framework for detecting deadlock in concurrent systems and can be augmented with additional techniques to address its shortcomings.

Q 15. Explain the concept of a Critical Section. What is mutual exclusion and how does it solve the problems of a critical section? Explain Dekker's algorithm for mutual exclusion. (IGNOU Dec 2010)
Ans:A Critical Section is a section of code within a concurrent program that accesses shared resources or variables that must be accessed in a mutually exclusive manner. In other words, only one thread or process should execute the code within the critical section at any given time to prevent race conditions and maintain data consistency.
Mutual exclusion is a synchronization technique used to ensure that only one thread or process can execute a critical section at a time. It prevents concurrent access to shared resources by multiple threads, thereby avoiding data corruption and inconsistency.
Mutual exclusion solves the problems of a critical section by guaranteeing that only one thread can execute the critical section at any given time, regardless of the number of threads attempting to access it concurrently. This ensures that shared resources are accessed in a coordinated and consistent manner, preventing race conditions, data corruption, and other concurrency-related issues.
Dekker's Algorithm is a classic mutual exclusion algorithm that allows two processes to share a single resource in a mutually exclusive manner. It was one of the first algorithms to achieve mutual exclusion without using hardware support for atomic operations.

Here's an explanation of Dekker's Algorithm:

Each process maintains a flag variable indicating whether it wants to enter the critical section. Initially, both flags are set to false.
Each process takes turns entering the critical section based on the value of the other process's flag.
Process 1 sets its flag to true and checks if Process 2's flag is true. If it is, Process 1 resets its flag and waits until Process 2's flag becomes false.
Once Process 2's flag is false, Process 1 enters the critical section and sets its turn variable to indicate that it is Process 1's turn to enter the critical section.
Process 1 performs its critical section operations and then sets its flag to false, indicating that it has exited the critical section.
Process 2 follows the same steps, but with the roles reversed.

Dekker's Algorithm ensures mutual exclusion by ensuring that only one process can enter the critical section at a time, and it avoids deadlock by allowing processes to take turns accessing the critical section.

However, Dekker's Algorithm suffers from the following limitations:

It is not scalable and does not generalize well to more than two processes sharing a resource.
It does not guarantee progress if both processes simultaneously attempt to enter the critical section.
It may suffer from race conditions and synchronization issues in certain scenarios, especially in modern multi-core and distributed systems.

Overall, while Dekker's Algorithm was a significant contribution to the field of mutual exclusion, it has limitations that make it less suitable for use in modern concurrent programming environments.

Q 16. What is a Semaphore? Give solution to sleeping barber problem with the help of semaphore. (IGNOU June 2011)

Ans:A Semaphore is a synchronization primitive used in concurrent programming to control access to shared resources or coordinate the execution of multiple threads or processes. It is essentially an integer variable that can only be accessed through two atomic operations: wait (P) and signal (V). Semaphores are commonly used to implement mutual exclusion, where only one process can access a shared resource at a time, and to implement synchronization between multiple processes.

The sleeping barber problem is a classic synchronization problem that illustrates the challenges of coordinating access to a shared resource among multiple processes. In this problem, there is a barber who runs a barbershop with a limited number of chairs for waiting customers. When a customer arrives at the barbershop and finds all chairs occupied, they either leave the shop or wait until a chair becomes available. Meanwhile, the barber either serves a waiting customer (if any) or goes to sleep if no customers are waiting.

Here's a solution to the sleeping barber problem using semaphores:

Initialize two semaphores: customers (initialized to 0) and barber (initialized to 0).
Initialize a mutex semaphore (mutex) to ensure mutual exclusion.
The customers semaphore represents the number of waiting customers, and the barber semaphore represents whether the barber is available or not.
When a customer arrives:
Wait on the mutex semaphore to acquire exclusive access to the shared variables.
If there are no available chairs (i.e., the number of waiting customers equals the number of chairs), release the mutex semaphore and leave the shop.
Increment the customers semaphore to indicate that a customer is waiting.
Signal the barber semaphore to wake up the barber (if asleep).
Release the mutex semaphore.
When the barber wakes up:
Wait on the customers semaphore to check if there are any waiting customers.
Serve a customer by decrementing the customers semaphore.
Signal the barber semaphore to indicate that the barber is available again.
The barber repeats the process of serving customers until there are no more waiting customers, then goes back to sleep.
Repeat the process indefinitely.
This solution ensures that the barber serves waiting customers one at a time and goes to sleep, if no customers are waiting. The use of semaphores provides synchronization and mutual exclusion to prevent race conditions and ensure correct behavior in the sleeping barber problem.

Q 17. Explain Havender's Algorithm for deadlock prevention. Give a suitable example to explain the algorithm. (IGNOU June 2011)

Ans: Havender's Algorithm is a deadlock prevention algorithm used in resource allocation systems to ensure that deadlock cannot occur by dynamically granting resource requests based on the current state of the system. It is based on the notion of resource allocation graphs and utilizes a concept called "safe states" to determine whether a resource allocation request can be granted without leading to deadlock.

The algorithm works as follows:

Initialize a state vector representing the current allocation and available resources in the system.
Construct a resource allocation graph representing the current allocation of resources to processes and the dependencies between them.
Apply the following steps to check for safe states:
Find a process that can finish execution and release all its resources without causing a deadlock.
Simulate the execution of the process and release its resources.
Check if the system enters a safe state after releasing the resources. If so, the requested resource can be granted without leading to deadlock.
If a safe state is reached, grant the resource request; otherwise, deny the request and put the process in a waiting state until the requested resources become available.
Repeat the process for subsequent resource allocation requests.

Here's an example to illustrate Havender's Algorithm:

Consider a system with three processes (P1, P2, and P3) and three types of resources (A, B, and C). The maximum resource needs and current allocation of resources for each process are as follows:

	Maximum	Allocation	Available
	A B C	A B C	A B C
P1	3 2 2	0 1 0	1 0 1
P2	6 1 3	1 0 0	
P3	3 1 4	1 1 0	

In this example, let's assume that process P1 requests one unit of resource B. We can use Havender's Algorithm to determine if this resource request can be granted without leading to deadlock:

We construct a resource allocation graph representing the current allocation of resources and dependencies between processes.

We check if there is a process that can finish execution and release all its resources without causing a deadlock. In this case, process P2 can finish execution and release its resources.
We simulate the execution of process P2 and release its resources. After releasing the resources, the system enters a safe state where all processes can finish execution without deadlock.
Since a safe state is reached after releasing the resources, we can grant the resource request of process P1 for one unit of resource B.

This example illustrates how Havender's Algorithm dynamically prevents deadlock by granting resource requests based on the current state of the system and ensuring that deadlock cannot occur.

Q 18. What is the difference between process and thread? Explain the steps in Process Switching and Thread Switching. (IGNOU June 2012)
Ans: The main difference between a process and a thread lies in their execution context and resource allocation:

Process:
A process is an independent unit of execution in a computer system. It has its own memory space, program code, data, and system resources.
Processes are managed by the Operating System kernel and can execute multiple tasks concurrently.
Each process runs in its own address space and is isolated from other processes, providing a high level of security and fault tolerance.
Processes communicate with each other through inter-process communication (IPC) mechanisms, such as pipes, sockets, and shared memory.

Thread:
A thread is a lightweight unit of execution within a process. It shares the same memory space and resources as other threads within the same process.
Threads are managed by the Operating System or a thread library (e.g., POSIX threads or Windows threads) and can execute independently within the context of a process.
Threads within the same process can communicate directly with each other and share data, making communication between threads more efficient than between processes.
Threads are typically used to perform concurrent tasks within a single process, such as handling user input, processing data, or performing I/O operations.

Now, let's explain the steps involved in Process Switching and Thread Switching:

Process Switching:

Save the current state of the running process, including the program counter, registers, and other CPU state, to its process control block (PCB).

Choose a new process to run from the ready queue or scheduling queue.

Load the state of the selected process from its PCB into the CPU, including the program counter, registers, and other CPU state.

Update the memory management unit (MMU) to map the virtual memory of the new process to physical memory.

Resume execution of the new process from where it left off, effectively switching to the context of the new process.

Thread Switching:

Save the current state of the running thread, including the program counter, registers, and other CPU state, to its thread control block (TCB).

Choose a new thread to run within the same process from the thread pool or scheduling queue.

Load the state of the selected thread from its TCB into the CPU, including the program counter, registers, and other CPU state.

Since threads share the same memory space, there is no need to update the MMU or perform memory mapping.

Resume execution of the new thread from where it left off, effectively switching to the context of the new thread within the same process.

In summary, process switching involves saving and restoring the state of entire processes, including memory mappings, while thread switching involves saving and restoring the state of individual threads within the same process. Thread switching is typically faster and more efficient than process switching due to the shared memory space and resources within a process.

Q 19. Calculate the average waiting time, average turnaround time for the processes given. Processes arrived at the same time and processing time is given in the following tables: (IGNOU June 2012)

Process	Processing Time
P1	06
P2	08
P3	07
P4	03

Ans: To calculate the average waiting time and average turnaround time for the given processes, we can use the First Come First Serve (FCFS) scheduling algorithm. In FCFS, processes are executed in the order of their arrival.

Let's calculate:

Waiting Time (WT): The waiting time for a process is the total time the process waits in the ready queue before getting executed.

Turnaround Time (TAT): The turnaround time for a process is the total time taken by the process from its arrival to its completion.

Given:

P1: Processing Time = 6

P2: Processing Time = 8

P3: Processing Time = 7

P4: Processing Time = 3

Here's the breakdown:

Arrival Time for all processes: 0 (as all processes arrive at the same time).

Waiting Time (WT):

P1: 0 (no waiting time as it starts execution immediately)

P2: 6 (waiting for P1 to finish)

P3: 14 (waiting for P1 and P2 to finish)

P4: 21 (waiting for P1, P2, and P3 to finish)

Turnaround Time (TAT):

P1: 6 (6 units of processing time)

P2: 14 (6 units of processing time + 8 units of waiting time)

P3: 21 (6 units of processing time + 7 units of waiting time)

P4: 24 (3 units of processing time + 21 units of waiting time)

Average Waiting Time:

(0 + 6 + 14 + 21) / 4 = 10.25 units

Average Turnaround Time:

(6 + 14 + 21 + 24) / 4 = 16.25 units

So, the average waiting time is 10.25 units and the average turnaround time is 16.25 units for the given processes.

Q 20. What is Mutual Exclusion? Explain Dekker's solution for mutual exclusion. (IGNOU June 2012)

Ans: Mutual Exclusion is a fundamental concept in concurrent programming that ensures only one process or thread can access a shared resource at a time. It prevents multiple processes from simultaneously accessing or modifying the shared resource, thereby avoiding race conditions and maintaining data consistency.

Dekker's solution is one of the earliest algorithms proposed for achieving mutual exclusion without relying on hardware support for atomic operations. It allows two processes to share a single resource in a mutually exclusive manner. Here's an explanation of Dekker's solution:

Initialization: Initialize two flag variables, **flag[0]** and **flag[1]**, to indicate whether each process wants to enter the critical section. Also, initialize a variable **turn** to indicate whose turn it is to enter the critical section. Initially, both flags are set to false, and **turn** is set to 0 or 1.

Process 0's Turn:

Process 0 sets **flag[0]** to true to indicate its intention to enter the critical section.

Process 0 sets **turn** to 1 to indicate that it is now Process 1's turn.

Process 0 enters a loop where it checks if Process 1 wants to enter the critical section (**flag[1]** is true) and it is Process 1's turn (**turn == 1**). If both conditions are true, Process 0 resets **flag[0]** to false and waits until it is Process 0's turn (**turn == 0**).

Once it is Process 0's turn, it enters the critical section to access the shared resource.

After completing the critical section, Process 0 resets **flag[0]** to false to indicate it is no longer interested in entering the critical section.

Process 1's Turn:

Process 1 sets **flag[1]** to true to indicate its intention to enter the critical section.

Process 1 sets **turn** to 0 to indicate that it is now Process 0's turn.

Process 1 enters a loop where it checks if Process 0 wants to enter the critical section (**flag[0]** is true) and it is Process 0's turn (**turn == 0**). If both conditions are true, Process 1 resets **flag[1]** to false and waits until it is Process 1's turn (**turn == 1**).

Once it is Process 1's turn, it enters the critical section to access the shared resource.

After completing the critical section, Process 1 resets **flag[1]** to false to indicate it is no longer interested in entering the critical section.

Dekker's solution ensures mutual exclusion by allowing processes to take turns accessing the critical section based on their **turn** variable. However, it suffers from certain limitations, such as being susceptible to race conditions and starvation in certain scenarios. Despite these limitations, Dekker's algorithm laid the groundwork for more sophisticated mutual exclusion algorithms in concurrent programming.

Q 21. What is necessary and sufficient conditions 10 for the occurrence of the deadlock? Explain with a suitable example. (IGNOU June 2012)

Ans: The occurrence of deadlock in a concurrent system is governed by necessary and sufficient conditions. Let's break down these conditions:

Necessary Conditions:

Mutual Exclusion: At least one resource must be held in a non-sharable mode, meaning only one process can use the resource at a time.

Hold and Wait: Processes must hold resources already allocated to them while waiting to acquire additional resources that are currently held by other processes.

No Pre-emption: Resources cannot be forcibly taken away from a process; they can only be released voluntarily by the process holding them.

Circular Wait: There must exist a circular chain of two or more processes, each of which is waiting for a resource held by the next process in the chain.

Sufficient Condition:

The four necessary conditions must hold simultaneously for deadlock to occur.

Now, let's explain these conditions with a suitable example:

Consider a system with two printers (Printer A and Printer B) and two processes (Process 1 and Process 2), where each process needs access to both printers to complete its task. The processes are assigned the following resource acquisition sequence:

Process 1: Acquires Printer A, then waits for Printer B.

Process 2: Acquires Printer B, then waits for Printer A.

Here's how the necessary and sufficient conditions for deadlock apply:

Mutual Exclusion: Each printer can only be used by one process at a time (non-sharable resource).

Hold and Wait: Both processes hold onto one printer while waiting for the other, creating a situation where resources are held while waiting for additional resources.

No Pre-emption: The system does not support pre-emptive resource release; processes cannot be forced to release resources.

Circular Wait: There exists a circular dependency between Process 1 and Process 2: Process 1 is waiting for Printer B, which is held by Process 2, and Process 2 is waiting for Printer A, which is held by Process 1.

Since all four necessary conditions are satisfied simultaneously, deadlock occurs in this system. Neither Process 1 nor Process 2 can proceed because they are both waiting for resources held by the other process, resulting in a deadlock situation. This example demonstrates how the necessary and sufficient conditions for deadlock manifest in a real-world scenario, leading to system-wide inactivity and resource wastage.

Previous years Unsolved Questions

Q 1. Write the algorithm for the bounded buffer 10 problem using semaphore. (IGNOU Dec 2012)

Q 2. What is a Remote Procedure Call (RPC) How is it implemented? (IGNOU Dec 2012)

Q 3. Using semaphore, write an algorithm that 10 solves the producer/consumers problem with a bounded buffer. How is it different from the unbounded buffer algorithm? Explain. (IGNOU June 2013)

Q 4. List and explain the four necessary 10 conditions that must hold simultaneously for a deadlock to occur. Explain different ways to avoid deadlock. (IGNOU June 2013)

Q 5. What is semaphores? (RU BCA 2019)

Q 6. Explain various types of process scheduling techniques? (RU BCA 2019)

Q 7. What is deadlock? What are the necessary condition for deadlock? (RU BCA 2019)

Q 8. Write the definition of process? (RU BCA 2017)

Q 9. Enlist the various states of process? (RU BCA 2017)

Q 10. What is thread? (RU BCA 2017)

Q 11. Explain following: (RTU 2016)

Three Synchronization Problems

Producer-Consumer Problem

The Readers-Writers Problem

The Dining Philosophers Problem

Time Stamping

Exercise

Exercise 1 – MCQ

1. What is the primary difference between a process and a thread in an Operating System?

a) A process is lighter than a thread.

b) A thread is an independent program, while a process is a subset of a program.

c) A process has its own memory space, while threads share the same memory space.

d) A thread can exist without a process.

2. In the context of processes and threads, what is a context switch?

a) The process of switching between different programs.

b) The process of switching between different threads within the same process.

c) The process of switching between different processes.

d) The process of switching between user mode and kernel mode.

3. What is the initial state of a process when it is first created in an Operating System?

a) Running

b) Ready

c) Blocked

d) New

4. In the context of process states, what does it mean when a process is in the "Blocked" state?

a) The process has terminated.

b) The process is waiting for a specific event to occur.

c) The process is actively executing its instructions.

d) The process is waiting for CPU time.

5. What is the primary goal of process scheduling in an Operating System?

a) To maximize CPU utilization

b) To minimize the number of processes

c) To maximize the number of I/O operations

d) To minimize the size of the process queue

6. Which of the following is a mechanism used for Inter Process Communication (IPC) in an Operating System?

a) Multithreading

b) Semaphore

c) Round Robin Scheduling

d) File System

7. What is the purpose of synchronization in Operating SystemProcesses?

a) To speed up the execution of processes

b) To ensure that processes execute in a random order

c) To coordinate the execution of concurrent processes and avoid conflicts

d) To minimize the number of processes in the system

8. Which of the following is a synchronization primitive used for mutual exclusion in Operating Systems?

a) Barrier

b) Semaphore

c) Spinlock

d) Message Queue

9. What is Peterson's Algorithm primarily used for in process synchronization in an Operating System?

a) Memory management

b) Deadlock prevention

c) Process scheduling

d) Mutual exclusion

10. What is the purpose of a semaphore in Operating SystemProcess Synchronization?

a) To manage memory allocation

b) To control access to the CPU

c) To synchronize the execution of concurrent processes

d) To allocate file descriptors

Exercise 2 – True/ False

1. Each process in an Operating System has its own copy of the code and data.
2. Threads within the same process share the same resources, such as file descriptors and memory space.
3. A process in the "Ready" state is actively utilizing the CPU.
4. A process transitions from the "Running" state to the "Blocked" state when it voluntarily releases the CPU.
5. Message Passing is a form of interprocess communication where processes directly share their memory space.
6. Priority-based scheduling always ensures fairness in the execution of processes.
7. Deadlock can occur when processes are not properly synchronized in accessing shared resources.
8. A critical section is a segment of code that can be executed by multiple processes simultaneously without causing conflicts.
9. Peterson's Algorithm guarantees progress in process synchronization by preventing starvation.
10. A binary semaphore can take on an unlimited number of states.

Exercise 3 – Fill in the blanks

1. In the Operating System structure, the ____________ is responsible for managing and scheduling tasks or processes.

2. The ____________ provides a user-friendly interface for interacting with the Operating System and its resources.

Answer

Exercise 1 – MCQ

Ans: 1 c, 2 c, 3d, 4 b, 5 a, 6 b, 7 c, 8 b, 9 d, 10 c

Exercise 2 – True/False

Ans: 1 True, 2 True, 3 False, 4 False, 5 False, 6 False, 7 True, 8 False, 9 False, 10 False

Exercise 3 – Fill in The Blanks

Ans: 1 kernel, 2 shell

Online Resources

Videos:

MCQ Link: https://youtu.be/TqUkRrNbaco

QR Code:

True/False Link: https://youtu.be/k_Sh96zOnhE

QR Code:

Online Test Paper: https://forms.office.com/r/7c6uDe3HHU

QR Code:

Chapter 4 Memory Management

Memory Hierarchy

The Memory Hierarchy in an Operating Systemreferring to the organization and management of different types of memory in a computer system, ranging from the fastest and most expensive (registers and cache) to slower and larger capacity memory (main memory and secondary storage). The memory hierarchy plays a crucial role in ensuring efficient data access and system performance.

Here are the main levels of the memory hierarchy in an Operating System:

Registers: Registers are the fastest and smallest storage locations within the CPU. They are used to store data that the CPU is actively processing. Registers have the lowest access time and are directly accessible by the CPU's instruction set. They are typically used for storing variables, intermediate results, and pointers.

Cache Memory: Cache Memory is a small, highspeed memory that sits between the CPU and the main memory (RAM). Its purpose is to store frequently used data and instructions to reduce the latency of accessing data from the slower main memory. Cache memory is organized into multiple levels (L1, L2, and sometimes L3), with L1 being the smallest and fastest and L3 being larger but slower.

Main Memory (RAM): RAM (Random Access Memory) is the primary memory of a computer and serves as a bridge between the CPU and secondary storage devices like hard drives or SSDs. It stores both data and instructions that are actively being used by running processes and applications. Access times in RAM are slower than in cache but significantly faster than secondary storage.

Secondary Storage: Secondary Storage includes hard disk drives (HDDs), solid-state drives (SSDs), optical drives, and other storage devices. These provide non-volatile storage for data and programs that are not currently in use. Data in secondary storage is persistent and remains intact even when the computer is turned off.

Tertiary Storage: Tertiary Storage refers to archival storage systems such as tape drives and network attached storage (NAS). These are used for long-term backup and data archival purposes. Access times for tertiary storage are considerably slower compared to primary and secondary storage.

Virtual Memory: Virtual Memory is a memory management technique used by the Operating System to make efficient use of physical memory (RAM) and secondary storage. It allows the OS to use disk space as an extension of RAM when physical memory becomes insufficient to hold all active processes and data. Virtual memory allows for more extensive multitasking and prevents programs from running out of memory.

The memory hierarchy is designed to balance the trade-offs between speed, cost, and capacity. Faster memory types (e.g., registers and cache) are more expensive and have limited capacity, while slower memory types (e.g., main memory and secondary storage) are less expensive and offer greater capacity. The goal of the memory hierarchy is to ensure that frequently accessed data is kept in faster, smaller, and more expensive memory levels, while less frequently accessed data is stored in slower, larger, and more costeffective memory levels.

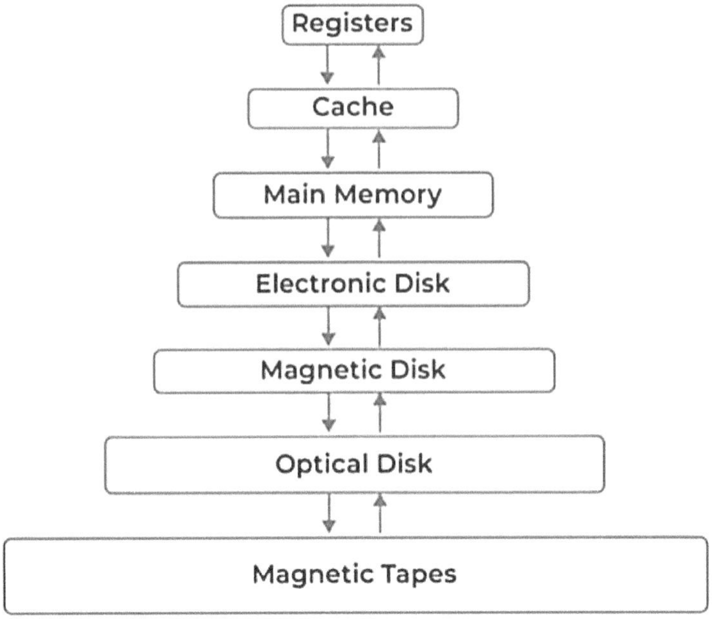

Main Memory

Main Memory, often referred to simply as "RAM" (Random Access Memory), is a critical component in computer systems, and it plays a central role in the operation of an Operating System. Main memory serves as a temporary storage area for data and programs that are actively being used by the CPU and running processes.

Here are some key aspects of main memory in an Operating System:

Primary Storage: Main Memory is the primary form of volatile storage in a computer system. It is used to store data and instructions that are currently in use by the Operating System, running applications, and active processes. Data stored in main memory can be quickly accessed by the CPU.

Random Access: RAM is called "Random Access Memory" because data can be read from or written to any location in memory with roughly equal access times. This random-access property makes it suitable for the dynamic and unpredictable needs of running programs.

Size and Capacity: The size and capacity of main memory can vary widely depending on the computer system. Modern computers typically have several gigabytes (GB) or even terabytes (TB) of RAM. The amount of RAM influences system performance and the number of programs and processes that can be run simultaneously.

Speed: Access times to main memory are relatively fast compared to other storage devices like hard drives or SSDs. This speed is crucial for the efficient execution of programs and the responsiveness of the Operating System.

Volatility: Main Memory is volatile, meaning that its contents are erased when the computer is powered off or restarted. This is in contrast to secondary storage devices like hard drives or SSDs, which provide nonvolatile storage.

Resource Management: The Operating System manages main memory resources, allocating portions of memory to different processes and ensuring that they do not interfere with each other. This memory management includes tasks like memory allocation, deallocation, and protection to prevent unauthorized access.

Virtual Memory: Many modern Operating Systems implement virtual memory, which allows the OS to use a portion of the computer's secondary storage (e.g., hard drive or SSD) as an extension of RAM. This technique enables more extensive multitasking and prevents processes from running out of memory, even when physical RAM is limited.

Page File (Swap Space): In virtual Memory systems, the Operating System may use a portion of the secondary storage as a page file or swap space. This file is used to store data that has been moved out of RAM temporarily to free up space for other processes. When needed, the OS can swap data between RAM and the page file.

Cache Hierarchy: The Operating System manages the interaction between main memory and CPU caches (e.g., L1, L2, L3 caches). Cache management is crucial for optimizing the speed of data access and minimizing the time the CPU spends waiting for data from main memory.

Overall, main memory is a crucial component of computer systems and is tightly integrated with the Operating System to provide the necessary resources for running applications and managing system processes efficiently. Effective memory management by the Operating System is essential for ensuring system stability and performance.

Virtual Memory

Virtual Memory is a memory management technique used by Operating Systems to provide an illusion of larger and more continuous memory to applications and processes than the physical RAM (Random Access Memory) available in the computer system. It allows for efficient and flexible memory utilization, even when physical RAM is limited.

Here are the key concepts and components of virtual memory in an Operating System:

Address Space: In Virtual Memory systems, each process has its own virtual address space. This address space represents the range of memory addresses that the process can use. It typically extends from 0 to the maximum address available in the system.

Physical Memory (RAM): Physical memory, or RAM, is the actual physical hardware memory installed in the computer. It has a finite capacity and is typically smaller than the total memory space needed by all running processes.

Page Table: The Page Table is a data structure used by the Operating System to map virtual addresses to physical addresses. Each process has its own page table, which is used to translate virtual memory addresses to physical memory addresses.

Page Size: Virtual Memory is divided into fixedsize blocks called "pages." Similarly, physical memory is divided into correspondingsized blocks called "frames." The size of pages and frames is determined by the Operating System and hardware.

Page Fault: A Page Fault occurs when a process tries to access a page of virtual memory that is not currently in physical memory. This triggers the Operating System to bring the required page into physical memory from secondary storage (usually a hard drive or SSD).

Swap Space/Page File: The Operating System uses a portion of secondary storage (e.g., a dedicated disk partition or a page file) as swap space to store pages of memory that are not currently in use. When a page fault occurs, the required page is swapped in from this swap space.

Page Replacement: In cases where physical memory is fully occupied, the Operating System must choose which pages to remove from physical memory to make room for new pages. Page Replacement Algorithms, such as Least Recently Used (LRU) or FIFO (FirstInFirstOut), are used to determine which pages should be evicted.

Demand Paging: Virtual Memory systems typically use demand paging, which means that pages are loaded into physical memory only when they are accessed by a process. This minimizes the amount of data that needs to be loaded into RAM at process start-up.

Page Sharing: Some Operating Systems support Page Sharing or copyonwrite techniques, allowing multiple processes to share the same physical page if they have identical memory contents. This reduces memory usage and improves efficiency.

Memory Protection: Virtual Memory systems provide memory protection mechanisms to isolate processes from each other. Unauthorized access attempts to another process's memory result in a segmentation fault or memory access violation.**Expanding Addressable Memory:** Virtual Memory allows for the expansion of the addressable memory space beyond the physical limits of the computer. This is particularly useful for 32bit systems that have a limited addressable memory range.

In summary, Virtual Memory is a crucial memory management technique that allows Operating Systems to efficiently use available physical memory while providing processes with the illusion of a large and contiguous address space. It enhances system stability, enables multitasking, and allows processes to run without being constrained by the physical memory capacity of the computer.

Memory Allocation Strategies

Memory Allocation Strategies in an Operating System referring to the methods and algorithms used to allocate and manage memory resources for processes and programs running on a computer system. These strategies aim to make efficient use of the available memory while ensuring the isolation and protection of processes. There are several memory allocation techniques, including:

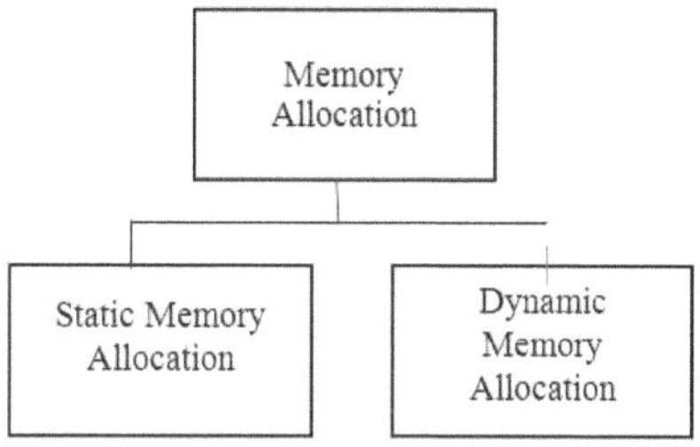

Contiguous Memory Allocation:

Single Partition Allocation: In this strategy, the entire memory is allocated to a single process. It is simple but inefficient as it does not allow for multitasking.

Fixed Partition Allocation: The memory is divided into fixedsize partitions, and each partition is allocated to a process. This strategy is more flexible than single partition allocation but can lead to memory fragmentation.

Variable Partition Allocation: Memory is divided into variablesized partitions, allowing for more efficient memory utilization. However, it still suffers from fragmentation issues.

Dynamic Partition Allocation (Paging and Segmentation):

Paging: Memory is divided into fixedsized blocks called "pages." Processes are divided into fixedsized blocks called "frames." Pages can be allocated to frames in a non-contiguous manner. Paging reduces fragmentation but may lead to page table overhead.

Segmentation: Memory is divided into segments, each representing a logical unit of a program (e.g., code segment, data segment). Segments can grow or shrink dynamically. Segmentation allows for more flexible memory allocation.

Virtual Memory Allocation:

Demand Paging: Virtual memory systems use demand paging to bring pages into physical memory only when they are accessed by a process. This minimizes the initial loading of pages into memory and optimizes resource usage.

Page Replacement Algorithms: When physical memory is full, the Operating System uses Page Replacement Algorithms (e.g., LRU, FIFO) to determine which pages should be evicted from memory to make room for new pages.

Buddy System:

In the Buddy System, memory is divided into fixedsized blocks. When a process requests memory, the system allocates a block that is a power of 2 in size. If the requested size is not available, the system allocates the next larger available block and splits it into two "buddy" blocks. This technique minimizes fragmentation.

Slab Allocation:

Slab Allocation is often used in the Linux kernel to efficiently allocate and deallocate memory for data structures of similar sizes. Memory is reallocated and organized into "slabs" for different object types. Slabs are maintained with free lists, making allocation and deallocation fast.

Best Fit, First Fit, and Worst Fit

These are memory allocation algorithms used in dynamic partition allocation. "Best Fit" allocates the smallest available partition that can accommodate the process. "First Fit" allocates the first available partition that meets the size requirement. "Worst Fit" allocates the largest available partition.

Memory Compaction:

Memory Compaction is a technique used to reduce fragmentation. It involves moving memory blocks and rearranging them to create larger contiguous free memory regions. This helps in allocating larger memory blocks to processes.

Memory Overcommitment:

Some Operating Systems allow Memory Overcommitment, where more memory is allocated to processes than physically available. It relies on mechanisms like paging and swapping to handle situations where actual memory usage exceeds physical limits.

The choice of memory allocation strategy depends on various factors, including the system's hardware architecture, memory management goals, and the specific requirements of the processes and applications running on the system. Modern Operating Systems often use a combination of these strategies to optimize memory usage and performance.

Page Replacement Algorithms

Page Replacement Algorithms are used in Operating Systems to decide which page to replace in physical memory (RAM) when a new page needs to be loaded and there is no free space available. These algorithms aim to minimize the number of page faults and optimize overall system performance.

Here are some common Page Replacement Algorithms:

FIFO (FirstInFirstOut):

Description: In the FIFO algorithm, the page that was loaded into memory first is the one selected for replacement. It treats the page frames as a queue, and the oldest page (the one at the front of the queue) is the one replaced.

FIFO (FirstInFirstOut) is one of the simplest Page Replacement Algorithms used in Operating Systems to manage memory pages. In FIFO page replacement, the page that has been in memory the longest is the one selected for replacement when a page fault occurs. Here's an explanation of FIFO page replacement with an example:

Example Scenario:

Let's assume we have a computer system with a physical memory that can hold a maximum of three pages. There are five pages of a process (A, B, C, D, and E) that need to be loaded into memory. The memory initially contains pages A, B, and C. We'll track page replacements as the process runs.

Step-by-step Explanation:

Initial Memory State: Memory contains pages A, B, and C.

Page Request (1st Page Fault): The process requests page D, which is not in memory. Since there's a page fault, the Operating System needs to replace a page to accommodate page D. In FIFO, the oldest page is replaced. In this case, page A, which has been in memory the longest, is replaced.

Memory State: B, C, D

Page Request (2nd Page Fault): The process now requests page E, which is also not in memory. Another page fault occurs, and the oldest page remaining in memory, which is page B, is replaced.

Memory State: C, D, E

Page Request (3rd Page Fault): The process now requests page A again. Since page A is not in memory, a page fault occurs. In FIFO, we replace the oldest page, which is page C.

Memory State: D, E, A

Page Request (4th Page Fault): The process requests page B. A page fault occurs, and the oldest page, which is page D, is replaced.

Memory State: E, A, B

Page Request (5th Page Fault): Finally, the process requests page C, which is not in memory. A page fault occurs, and the oldest page remaining in memory, which is page E, is replaced.

Memory State: A, B, C

The process continues running, and if any more page faults occur, the pattern repeats, with the oldest page in memory being replaced.

FIFO page replacement is straightforward to implement but has some disadvantages. In certain scenarios, it may lead to the "Belady's Anomaly," where increasing the number of page frames does not necessarily reduce page faults. Additionally, it may not always make efficient use of memory since it doesn't consider the actual usage or relevance of pages. Other Page Replacement Algorithms like LRU (Least Recently Used) and OPT (Optimal) attempt to address these limitations by making more informed decisions about which pages to replace.

Page reference 1, 3, 0, 3, 5, 6, 3

Total Page Fault = 6

Advantages: Simple to implement.

Disadvantages: May suffer from the "Belady's Anomaly," where increasing the number of page frames does not necessarily decrease the number of page faults.

LRU (Least Recently Used):

Description: The LRU algorithm replaces the page that has not been used for the longest time. It keeps track of the usage history of each page and selects the page with the oldest access time.

LRU, or "Least Recently Used," is a page replacement algorithm used in Operating Systems to manage memory pages. It selects the page for replacement that has not been used for the longest period of time. In other words, it assumes that the page that has not been referenced recently is the least likely to be used in the near future. Here's an explanation of LRU with an example:

Example Scenario:

Let's consider a computer system with a physical memory that can hold a maximum of three pages. There are five pages of a process (A, B, C, D, and E) that need to be loaded into memory. The memory initially contains pages A, B, and C. We'll track page replacements as the process runs.

Step-by-step Explanation:

Initial Memory State: Memory contains pages A, B, and C.

Page Request (1st Page Fault): The process requests page D, which is not in memory. Since there's a page fault, the Operating System needs to replace a page to accommodate page D. In LRU, we select the page that has not been used for the longest time. In this case, page A is the least recently used, so it's replaced.

Memory State: B, C, D

Page Request (2nd Page Fault): The process now requests page E, which is also not in memory. Another page fault occurs, and the least recently used page, which is page B, is replaced.

Memory State: C, D, E

Page Request (3rd Page Fault): The process now requests page A again. Since page A is not in memory, a page fault occurs. In LRU, we replace the least recently used page, which is page C.

Memory State: D, E, A

Page Request (4th Page Fault): The process requests page B. A page fault occurs, and the least recently used page remaining in memory, which is page D, is replaced.

Memory State: E, A, B

Page Request (5th Page Fault): Finally, the process requests page C, which is not in memory. A page fault occurs, and the least recently used page remaining in memory, which is page E, is replaced.

Memory State: A, B, C

The process continues running, and if any more page faults occur, the pattern repeats, with the least recently used page in memory being replaced.

LRU page replacement is effective in minimizing page faults in scenarios where programs exhibit good temporal locality, meaning they tend to reference the same pages they've used recently. However, it can be challenging to implement efficiently, especially in hardware, as it requires maintaining and updating a record of when each page was last used. There are variations and approximations of LRU that aim to strike a balance between accuracy and complexity.

Least Recently Used (LRU)

Well, OPT is not possible…..

Replace the page that has not been used for the longest period of time.

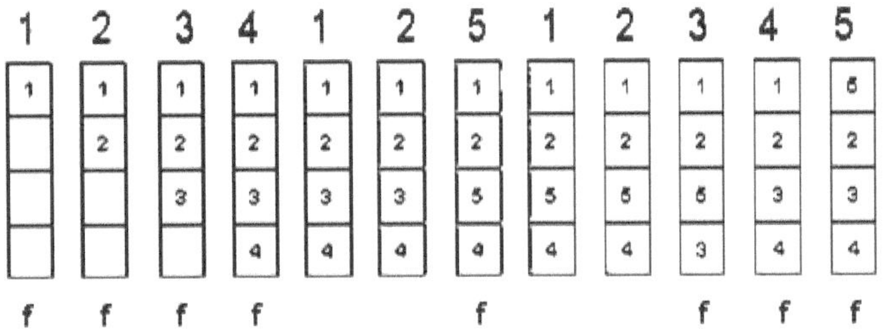

Advantages: Effective in reducing page faults in many scenarios, especially when access patterns exhibit temporal locality.

Disadvantages: Can be complex to implement efficiently. Requires maintaining a usage history for each page, which can be resourceintensive.

Optimal Page Replacement (OPT or MIN):

Description: The Optimal Page Replacement Algorithm selects the page that will not be used for the longest time in the future. It is used as a theoretical benchmark because it achieves the lowest possible number of page faults.

The Optimal Page Replacement Algorithm, also known as the "OPT" algorithm, is an idealized page replacement algorithm used in Operating Systems. It selects the page for replacement that will not be used for the longest time in the future. While OPT is considered the most efficient page replacement algorithm in terms of minimizing page faults, it is not practical to implement in real systems because it requires knowledge of future page references, which is impossible to predict accurately. Here's an explanation of OPT with an example:

Example Scenario:

Consider a computer system with a physical memory that can hold a maximum of three pages. There are five pages of a process (A, B, C, D, and E) that need to be loaded into memory. The memory initially contains pages A, B, and C. We'll track page replacements as the process runs.

Step-by-step Explanation:

Initial Memory State: Memory contains pages A, B, and C.

Page Request (1st Page Fault): The process requests page D, which is not in memory. Since there's a page fault, the Operating System needs to replace a page to accommodate page D. In the OPT algorithm, we would need to know the future page references to make an optimal decision. Let's assume we have perfect knowledge of the future references and know that pages B and C will be referenced before A. Therefore, we replace page A.

Memory State: B, C, D

Page Request (2nd Page Fault): The process now requests page E, which is also not in memory. Another page fault occurs, and the optimal replacement decision would be based on future references. Assuming we know that pages B, C, and D will be referenced before A, we replace page A.

Memory State: C, D, E

Page Request (3rd Page Fault): The process now requests page A again. Since page A is not in memory, a page fault occurs. In the OPT algorithm, the optimal decision would be based on future references. If we knew the future references, we would replace the page that will not be used for the longest time in the future, which in this case is page C.

Memory State: D, E, A

Page Request (4th Page Fault): The process requests page B. A page fault occurs, and the optimal decision would consider future references. If we knew that pages D, E, and A would be referenced before C, we would replace page C.

Memory State: E, A, B

Page Request (5th Page Fault): Finally, the process requests page C, which is not in memory. A page fault occurs, and the optimal decision based on future references would be to replace page E.

Memory State: A, B, C

The process continues running, and if any more page faults occur, the pattern repeats, with the page that will not be used for the longest time in the future being replaced.

The OPT algorithm is used as a theoretical benchmark to measure the performance of other page replacement algorithms. While it provides the lowest possible number of page faults, it's impractical to implement in real systems due to the requirement of knowing future page references. Other algorithms like LRU (Least Recently Used) and FIFO (FirstInFirstOut) are used in practice, striking a balance between efficiency and feasibility.

7	0	1	2	0	3	0	4	2	3	0	3	2	3
			2	2	2	2	2	2	2	2	2	2	2
		1	1	1	1	1	4	4	4	4	4	4	4
	0	0	0	0	0	0	0	0	0	0	0	0	0
7	7	7	7	7	3	3	3	3	3	3	3	3	3
Miss	Miss	Miss	Miss	Hit	Miss	Hit	Miss	Hit	Hit	Hit	Hit	Hit	Hit

Total Page Fault = 6

Advantages: Provides the best possible performance in terms of page faults.

Disadvantages: Not practical for implementation because it requires knowledge of future page accesses, which is impossible to obtain in a real system.

LRU Approximation Algorithms:

LRU (Least Recently Used) Approximation Algorithms are Page Replacement Algorithms used in Operating Systems to manage memory pages when implementing LRU exactly (i.e., tracking the exact order of page accesses) is too computationally expensive. These algorithms aim to approximate LRU's behavior while being more practical to implement. One common LRU approximation algorithm is the "CountBased LRU." Here's an explanation of this approximation algorithm with an example:

Example Scenario:

Let's consider a computer system with a physical memory that can hold a maximum of three pages. There are five pages of a process (A, B, C, D, and E) that need to be loaded into memory. The memory initially contains pages A, B, and C. We'll use the CountBased LRU approximation algorithm to track page replacements as the process runs.

Step-by-step Explanation:

Initial Memory State: Memory contains pages A, B, and C.

Page Request (1st Page Fault): The process requests page D, which is not in memory. Since there's a page fault, the Operating System needs to decide which page to replace based on the CountBased LRU approximation. In this approximation, each page has a counter associated with it, and this counter is incremented every time the page is accessed. In this case, since page A, B, and C have the same counters (all 0 initially), we can select the page that arrived earliest, which is page A.

Memory State: B, C, D

Page Request (2nd Page Fault): The process now requests page E, which is also not in memory. Another page fault occurs, and the CountBased LRU approximation helps determine the page to be replaced. Assuming the counters for page B and C are both 1 (indicating they've been accessed since the last replacement), and the counter for page A is 0, we replace page A, which is considered the least recently used.

Memory State: C, D, E

Page Request (3rd Page Fault): The process requests page A again. Since page A is not in memory, a page fault occurs. According to the CountBased LRU approximation, we update the counters for pages C and D to 1 (they were accessed last), and the counter for page E becomes 0 (it hasn't been accessed since it was loaded). So, page E is replaced.

Memory State: C, D, A

Page Request (4th Page Fault): The process requests page B. A page fault occurs, and the CountBased LRU approximation suggests that page E should be replaced since its counter is now 0, while the counters for pages C, D, and A are 1.

Memory State: D, A, B

Page Request (5th Page Fault): Finally, the process requests page C, which is not in memory. A page fault occurs, and the CountBased LRU approximation indicates that page B should be replaced because its counter is 0.

Memory State: A, C, D

The process continues running, and if any more page faults occur, the CountBased LRU approximation helps decide which page to replace based on the counters.

Count Based LRU Approximation Algorithms use counters to approximate the LRU behavior by keeping track of page accesses. While not as accurate as true LRU, they are more practical to implement and still provide reasonable page replacement decisions based on recent page accesses.

Clock Algorithm: The Clock Algorithm (also known as the Second Chance algorithm) maintains a circular list of pages in memory. When a page is referenced, its "use" bit is set. When a page needs to be replaced, the algorithm searches for the first page with a "use" bit unset (indicating it has not been used recently) and selects it for replacement.

LFU (Least Frequently Used): LFU replaces the page that has been referenced the least number of times. It requires maintaining a usage count for each page.

MFU (Most Frequently Used): MFU replaces the page that has been referenced themost number of times. Like LFU, it requires maintaining a usage count for each page.

Random Page Replacement:

Description: In this algorithm, a random page is selected for replacement. While it is not an effective page replacement strategy, it can be used as a baseline for comparison with other algorithms.

Random Page Replacement is a page replacement algorithm used in Operating Systems where the page to be replaced is selected randomly, without considering the usage history or patterns of the pages. It's one of the simplest page replacement algorithms and is often used for illustrative or benchmarking purposes. However, it is not efficient in minimizing page faults and does not make informed decisions based on page access patterns. Here's an explanation of Random Page Replacement with an example:

Example Scenario:

Consider a computer system with a physical memory that can hold a maximum of three pages. There are five pages of a process (A, B, C, D, and E) that need to be loaded into memory. The memory initially contains pages A, B, and C. We'll use the Random Page Replacement algorithm to track page replacements as the process runs.

Step-by-step Explanation:

Initial Memory State: Memory contains pages A, B, and C.

Page Request (1st Page Fault): The process requests page D, which is not in memory. Since there's a page fault, the Random Page Replacement Algorithm randomly selects one of the pages in memory to be replaced. Let's assume it selects page A randomly.

Memory State: B, C, D

Page Request (2nd Page Fault): The process now requests page E, which is also not in memory. Another page fault occurs, and, again, the Random Page Replacement algorithm randomly selects one of the pages in memory to be replaced. Let's assume it selects page B randomly.

Memory State: C, D, E

Page Request (3rd Page Fault): The process now requests page A again. Since page A is not in memory, a page fault occurs. Once more, the Random Page Replacement algorithm randomly selects one of the pages in memory to be replaced. Let's assume it selects page C randomly.

Memory State: D, E, A

Page Request (4th Page Fault): The process requests page B. A page fault occurs, and the Random Page Replacement Algorithm randomly selects one of the pages in memory to be replaced. Let's assume it selects page D randomly.

Memory State: E, A, B

Page Request (5th Page Fault): Finally, the process requests page C, which is not in memory. A page fault occurs, and, as before, the Random Page Replacement Algorithm randomly selects one of the pages in memory to be replaced. Let's assume it selects page B randomly.

Memory State: A, C, D

The process continues running, and if any more page faults occur, the Random Page Replacement Algorithm continues to select pages to be replaced randomly.

Random Page Replacement is a simple page replacement algorithm that selects pages to be replaced entirely at random. While it's straightforward to implement, it doesn't make any intelligent decisions based on page access patterns and is unlikely to minimize page faults effectively. Other Page Replacement Algorithms like LRU (Least Recently Used) and OPT (Optimal) are used in practice to make more informed decisions about which pages to replace.

Advantages: Simple to implement and may perform surprisingly well in some cases.

Disadvantages: Offers no optimization for page replacement and does not consider page access patterns.

Working Set Page Replacement:

Description: The working set algorithm tries to maintain a process's working set in memory by monitoring the page usage. It uses a window of time called the "working set window" to keep track of the pages referenced within that time frame.

The Working Set Page Replacement Algorithm is a memory management technique used in Operating Systems to improve the efficiency of page replacement in Virtual Memory Systems. It is primarily designed to reduce page thrashing by ensuring that a process has its working set of pages in memory. The working set represents the subset of pages that a process is actively using at any given moment. Here's an explanation of the Working Set Page Replacement algorithm:

Key Concepts:

Working Set (WS): The working set of a process is defined as the set of pages that the process has accessed recently. It represents the temporal locality of a process's memory access patterns.

Working Set Size (Δ): The working set size, denoted as Δ, is a parameter that specifies the number of pages that should be in a process's working set. It represents the window of time over which a process's memory access behavior is observed.

Page Fault: A page fault occurs when a process attempts to access a page that is not currently in memory. The page replacement algorithm is invoked to select a page to be replaced.

Working Set Page Replacement Algorithm:

The Working Set Page Replacement Algorithm aims to ensure that a process's working set (Δ) is always in memory. It does this by periodically monitoring a process's memory access behavior and adjusting the working set as needed. Here are the steps:

Monitoring the Working Set:

The Operating System periodically checks a process's memory access patterns to identify which pages it has accessed recently.

It maintains a record of the pages accessed by the process during the last Δ time units.

Checking for Adequate Memory:

The Operating System verifies whether the working set (pages accessed in the last Δ time units) can fit entirely in the available physical memory.

If there is enough memory to accommodate the working set, no page replacement is necessary, and the process continues execution.

Page Replacement (If Necessary):

If the working set is larger than the available memory, the Operating System must select pages to be removed from memory to make space for the working set.

Pages that are not part of the current working set are good candidates for replacement.

Adjusting the Working Set:

After a page replacement, the working set may change. The Operating System continues monitoring the process's memory access behavior and adjusts the working set accordingly.

Benefits:

The Working Set Page Replacement Algorithm helps prevent page thrashing by ensuring that the most actively used pages of a process are always in memory.

It can improve system performance by reducing the number of page faults and maintaining a balance between processes' memory needs.

Challenges:

Determining the appropriate value of Δ (working set size) can be challenging as it depends on the specific behavior of each process.

Frequent monitoring of page accesses and working set adjustments can introduce overhead.

In summary, the Working Set Page Replacement Algorithm is a proactive approach to memory management that aims to minimize page thrashing and improve system performance by keeping a process's working set in memory. It's a useful technique in virtual memory systems where memory is shared among multiple processes.

Advantages: Effective in preventing thrashing by ensuring that the most relevant pages are kept in memory.

Disadvantages: Requires parameters to define the working set window, and its implementation can be complex.

The choice of a Page Replacement Algorithm depends on factors such as the system's memory constraints, workload characteristics, and performance requirements. Different algorithms may perform better in specific scenarios, and the selection of the most suitable algorithm can significantly impact system performance. Operating Systems often use a combination of these algorithms or implement variants to balance complexity and efficiency.

Previous Years Solved Questions

Q 1. Explain Primary Memory. (RU BCA 2022)

Ans: Primary m=Memory is computer memory that a processor or computer accesses first or directly. It allows a processor to access running execution applications and services that are temporarily stored in a specific memory location. Primary memory is also known as primarystorage or main memory. Primary memory is a computer system's volatile storage mechanism. It may be random access memory(RAM). Cache memory or data buses. But is primarily associated with RAM. As soon as a computer starts, primary memory loads all running applications including the base Operating System(OS). User interface and any user-installed and running software utility. A program/application that is opened in primary memory interacts with the system processor to perform all application-specific tasks. Primary memory is considered faster than secondary memory.

Q 2. What is Swapping? (RU BCA 2022)

Ans: Swapping is a memory management technique used by Operating Systems to efficiently manage limited physical memory (RAM) when it becomes insufficient for the running processes and tasks. When a system runs out of available RAM due to the concurrent execution of multiple programs, the OS may move some portions of inactive or less frequently used processes and their associated data from RAM to a designated space on the computer's storage device, typically the hard disk or solid-state drive. This process is known as swapping or paging.Swapping allows the Operating System to free up valuable RAM for actively running processes, preventing system slowdowns or crashes due to memory exhaustion. When a swapped-out process is needed again, it can be swapped back into RAM from the storage device. While swapping improves system stability, it can introduce performance overhead since reading from and writing to disk is significantly slower than accessing RAM. To mitigate this, modern Operating Systems employ various algorithms and optimizations to make swapping as efficient as possible, such as using paging, virtual memory, and predictive algorithms to determine which data to swap.

Q 3. Write Short Note: (IGNOU MCA Dec 2016)

A. Primary Memory

B. Virtual Memory

C. Shared Memory

Ans:

a. Primary Memory:-Primary memory is computer memory that a processor or computer accesses first or directly. It allows a processor to computer access first or directly. It allows a processor to access running execution applications and services that are temporarily stored in a specific memory location.

Primary memory is also known as primary storage or main memory. Primary memory is a computer system's volatile storage mechanism. It may be random access memory (RAM), cache memory or data buses, but is primarily associated with RAM.

As soon as a computer starts, primary memory loads allrunning applications, including the base Operating System

(OS), user interface arid any user-installed and runningsoftware utility. A program/application that is opened inprimary memory interacts with the system processor toperform all application-specific tasks.Primary memory is considered faster than secondarymemory.

b. Virtual Memory: - Virtual memory is a memorymanagement technique where secondary memory can be useas if it were a part of the main memory. Virtual memory is acommon technique used in a computer's Operating System (OS). Virtual memory uses both hardware and software toenable a computer to compensate for physical memoryshortages, temporarily transferring data from random accessmemory (RAM) to disk storage. Mapping chunks of memoryto disk files enables a computer to treat secondary memory asthough it were main memory.

Today, most personal computers (PCs) come at least8 GB (gigabytes) ofRAM. But, sometimes, this is not enough to run several programs at one time. This is where virtualmemory comes in. Virtual memory frees up RAM by swappingdata that has not been used recently over to a storagesuch as a hard drive or solid-state drive (SSD).

Virtual memory is important for improving systemperformance, multitasking and using large programs.However, users should not overly rely on virtual memory,since it is considerably slower than RAM. If the OS has toswap data between virtual memory and RAM too often, thecomputer will begin to slow down — this is called thrashing.

Virtual memory was developed at a time when physicalmemory — also referenced as RAM — was expensive.Computers have a finite amount of RAM, so memory willeventually run out when multiple programs run at the sametime. A system using virtual memory uses a section of the hard drive to emulate RAM. With virtual memory, a system can load larger or multiple programs running at the same time, enabling each one to operate as if it has more space without having to purchase more RAM.

c. Shared Memory: -Shared Memory is a method of interprocess communication (IPC) in computer systems, where multiple processes or threads can access a common, shared area of memory. In shared memory, two or more processes can read from and write to a single shared region of memory, as if it were part of their own private address space. This allows processes to communicate and share data efficiently and quickly. Here are some key points about shared memory:

Efficiency: Shared Memory is one of the most efficient IPC mechanisms because it allows processes to exchange data without the overhead of data copying. Processes can read and write to shared memory locations directly, reducing data transfer latency.

Speed: Sharing Memory among processes is extremely fast because they can access the data directly without the need for data transfer through System Calls or other communication mechanisms.

Synchronization: Shared Memory requires explicit synchronization mechanisms, such as semaphores, mutexes, or other locking mechanisms, to prevent data races and ensure that multiple processes do not simultaneously access and modify shared data in an unsafe manner.

Communication: Shared Memory is often used for high-speed communication between processes. It is particularly valuable for processes that need to exchange large amounts of data or perform frequent data updates.

Complexity: Implementing shared memory can be more complex compared to other IPC mechanisms like message passing, as developers must manage synchronization and data consistency. Careful design and coding practices are required to avoid race conditions and other synchronization issues.

Multiprocessing: Shared Memory is commonly used in multiprocessing systems where multiple CPUs or cores work in parallel. Each CPU or core can access the shared memory, allowing processes running on different processors to communicate and coordinate their actions efficiently.

Distributed Systems: In distributed computing, shared memory is often simulated using network-based shared memory systems. These systems provide the illusion of shared memory across networked nodes, allowing processes on different machines to interact as if they were sharing memory.

Operating System Support: Shared Memory is a feature provided by the Operating System. It offers System Calls and libraries for creating, attaching, detaching, and managing shared memory segments.

Use Cases: Shared Memory is employed in various applications, including parallel computing, Real-Time Systems, databases, and multimedia processing, where efficient data sharing and communication between processes are essential.

Security and Isolation: Care must be taken to ensure the security and isolation of shared memory segments. Proper access control mechanisms are needed to prevent unauthorized access to sensitive data.

In summary, Shared Memory is a powerful method for enabling interprocess communication in computer systems. It offers high efficiency and speed but requires careful management of data and synchronization to ensure the safe and correct operation of multiple processes that share a common memory region.

Q 4. Discuss various criteria for measuring the performance of Scheduling Mechanism? (RU BCA 2017)

Ans: Different CPU scheduling algorithms have differentproperties and may favor one class of processes overanother. In choosing which algorithm to use in aparticular situation, we must consider the differentproperties of the various algorithms.

CPU utilization: We want to keep the CPU as busy as possible. CPU utilization may range from 0 to 100 percent. In a real system, it should range from 40 percent (for a lightly loaded system) to 90 percent (for a heavily used system).

Throughput: If the CPU is busy executing process, then work is being done. One measure of work is the number of processes that are completed per time unit, called throughput. For long processes, this rate may be one process per hour; for short transactions, throughput might be 10 processes per second.

Turnaround time: From the point of view of a particular process, the important criterion is how long it takes to execute that process. The interval from the time of submission of a process to the time of completion is the turnaround time. Turnaround time is the sum of the periods spent waiting to get into memory, waiting in the ready queue, executing on the CPU, and doing I/O.

Waiting Time: The CPU Scheduling Algorithm does not affect the amount of time during which a process executes or does I/O it affects only the amount of time that a process spends waiting in the readyqueue.Waiting time is the sum of the periods spent waiting in the ready queue.

Response time: In an interactive system, turnaround time may not be the best criterion, Often, a process can produce some output fairly easy, and can continue computing new results While previous results are being output to the user. Thus, another measure is the time from the submission of a request until the first response is produced. This measure, called Response Time, is the time that it takes to start responding, but not the time that it takes to output that response. The turnaround time is generally limited by the speed of output device.

Q 5. Define Logical and Physical Address. (RU B. Tech. Jan 2022)

Ans: Logical Address:A logical Address, also known as a Virtual Address, is an address generated by a CPU (Central Processing Unit) during program execution. It represents a location in the virtual memory space of a process and is used by the CPU and the program to access data and instructions. Logical addresses provide an abstraction layer that isolates processes from the actual physical hardware.

Physical Address:

A Physical Address, also known as a Real Address, is the location in the actual physical memory (RAM) of a computer system's hardware. Physical addresses correspond to the physical storage cells in RAM chips. These addresses are used by the computer's memory management unit (MMU) to access the actual data in memory chips.

Here's a more detailed explanation of logical and physical addresses in the context of Operating Systems:

Logical Address:

Abstraction: Logical Addresses provide a level of abstraction to processes, allowing them to work with memory in a way that doesn't require knowledge of the underlying physical memory layout.

Virtual Memory: Logical Addresses are used in the concept of virtual memory, where a process's memory is divided into pages or segments. The CPU generates logical addresses to access these pages.

Process Isolation: Logical Addresses ensure that each process has its own isolated memory space, even if the physical memory is shared among multiple processes.

Security: Logical Addresses help improve system security by preventing processes from accessing memory locations of other processes, thereby preventing unauthorized data access.

Memory Protection: Logical Addresses can be used to implement memory protection mechanisms. Unauthorized access or modification of memory locations can be detected and prevented.

Dynamic Allocation: Logical Addresses allow for dynamic memory allocation and deallocation. Processes can request and release memory without needing to know the exact physical location.

Address Translation: The mapping between logical addresses and physical addresses is managed by the Operating System's memory management unit (MMU). The MMU performs address translation, converting logical addresses to physical addresses.

Physical Address:

Direct Mapping: Physical addresses directly correspond to the location of data in physical memory chips. The MMU uses these addresses to fetch data from RAM.

Limited by Hardware: The number of available physical addresses is limited by the capacity of the physical RAM in the system. The actual amount of physical memory sets the upper bound for physical addresses.

Hardware Access: Physical Addresses are used by the hardware components, such as the memory controller and RAM chips, to access data.

Static Allocation: Physical Memory is statically allocated during system boot, and it remains fixed throughout the computer's operation. Processes have no direct control over physical memory allocation.

Hardware Protection: Hardware mechanisms are used to protect memory. For example, read-only and read-write access to physical memory can be enforced by memory management hardware.

Direct Hardware Interaction: Operating Systems typically restrict direct interaction with physical addresses to prevent unauthorized or harmful access to the physical memory.

In summary, logical addresses are used at the software level to abstract the underlying physical memory and provide process isolation and security, while physical addresses represent the actual locations in the physical memory hardware. The translation from logical to physical addresses is managed by the MMU, which allows processes to work with virtual memory while the Operating System ensures the proper mapping to physical memory.

Q 6. Differentiate between Pager and Swapper. (RU B. Tech. Jan 2022)

Ans: Pager and Swapper are two key components of memory management in Operating Systems, and they serve different purposes in managing memory resources. Here, we'll differentiate between pager and swapper, providing a detailed explanation of their roles and functionalities:

Pager:

Role and Functionality:

A pager is a component responsible for implementing paging in a virtual memory system. Paging is a memory management technique that allows a process's physical memory to be divided into fixed-size blocks or frames. Logical memory in a process is divided into blocks of the same size, known as pages. The pager is responsible for mapping logical pages to physical frames.

Granularity:

Pager operates at the level of individual memory pages. It is concerned with the mapping of each page of a process's logical memory to a frame in physical memory.

Responsibilities:

The primary responsibilities of a pager include:

Mapping logical pages to physical frames by using a data structure known as the page table.

Handling page faults, which occur when a process accesses a page that is not currently in physical memory. The pager is responsible for bringing the required page into memory (page-in) and, if necessary, selecting a page to evict (page-out) to make room for the new page.

Managing page replacement policies, which determine how pages are selected for eviction in case of page faults. Common policies include Least Recently Used (LRU), First-In-First-Out (FIFO), and various variations.

Involvement in Swapping:

A pager is typically not directly responsible for the process of swapping pages or entire processes in and out of secondary storage (e.g., disk). It focuses on page-level memory management within physical memory.

Swapper:

Role and Functionality:

A swapper, also known as a Swap Manager, is responsible for the process of swapping in a virtual memory system. Swapping involves moving entire processes or large sections of memory (e.g., segments or address spaces) between physical memory and secondary storage (e.g., disk). Swapping allows for more processes to be active than can fit into physical memory simultaneously.

Granularity:

Swapper operates at a higher level than the pager. It deals with the entire process address space or a significant portion of it.

Responsibilities:

The primary responsibilities of a swapper include:

Managing the swapping of entire processes between physical memory and secondary storage, either for performance optimization or to free up memory for other processes.

Ensuring that swapped processes or sections of memory are stored efficiently in secondary storage and can be brought back into physical memory when needed.

Determining when a process or a section of memory should be swapped in or out based on system-wide memory management policies and priorities.

Interaction with Pager:

Swapper interacts with the pager when a process is swapped out or in. The pager is responsible for managing individual pages within the swapped process's address space as they are brought in and out of memory.

Resource Management:

Swapper contributes to overall memory resource management by controlling which processes are kept in physical memory and which are temporarily stored on secondary storage. This helps ensure that the system can efficiently manage memory despite limitations in physical RAM.

In summary, pagers and swappers are key components of virtual memory management in an Operating System. Pagers focus on the finer-grained management of individual memory pages within physical memory, while swappers deal with the high-level management of entire processes or large sections of memory, including their movement between physical memory and secondary storage. Both components work together to provide efficient and flexible memory management in modern Operating Systems.

Q 7. What are Frames? (RU B. Tech. Jan 2022)

Ans: In the context of Operating Systems and memory management, a frame refers to a fixed-size block of physical memory or RAM. Frames are used in conjunction with paging or segmentation memory management schemes to divide physical memory into manageable units. Here's a detailed explanation of frames in Operating Systems:

Frame Basics:

A Frame is a contiguous block of physical memory, typically consisting of a fixed number of bytes or words. The size of a frame is determined by the hardware architecture or the memory management scheme used by the Operating System. Common frame sizes are 4 KB, 8 KB, or 16 KB.

Division of Physical Memory:

Physical memory is divided into these fixed-size frames to provide structure and organization for memory management. The Operating System allocates and manages memory in terms of frames.

Frame Numbering:

Frames are often numbered or indexed for easy reference. These numbers are used to uniquely identify and access each frame. The first frame may be assigned frame number 0, the second frame frame number 1, and so on.

Memory Allocation:

When a process or program is loaded into memory, it is divided into smaller units called pages in the context of paging or segments in the context of segmentation. Each page or segment corresponds to one or more frames in physical memory. The Operating System tracks the allocation of frames to these pages or segments.

Page-Frame Mapping:

The OS maintains a data structure called a page table or segment table to keep track of the mapping between pages or segments and the corresponding frames in physical memory. This table allows the OS to determine where each part of a process is located in physical memory.

Virtual Memory:

In Virtual Memory systems, frames are used in conjunction with pages to implement virtual memory addressing. When a process uses virtual memory, its logical address space is mapped to physical frames. If a required page is not present in physical memory (a page fault occurs), then the Operating System brings the page from secondary storage (e.g., a hard disk) into an available frame.

Resource Management:

Frames play a crucial role in the efficient management of physical memory resources. The Operating System must keep track of which frames are allocated to which processes, handle page replacement (swapping pages in and out of frames), and ensure processes do not access memory outside their allocated frames.

Contiguous Allocation:

In systems using Contiguous Allocation (e.g., early versions of MS-DOS), a process is loaded into a set of contiguous frames. The number of frames allocated to a process depends on the size of the process and the availability of free frames in physical memory.

Segmentation:

In Segmentation memory management, frames are used in the context of segments, where each segment represents a logical unit of a program (e.g., code, data, stack). Segments are mapped to one or more frames in physical memory.

Protection and Isolation:

Frames help enforce memory protection and process isolation. They ensure that processes do not overwrite memory in other frames, providing security and isolation between processes.

Page Replacement:

When physical memory becomes scarce, the Operating System may need to replace one or more pages in frames with pages from secondary storage. The choice of which pages to replace is based on page replacement algorithms (e.g., LRU, FIFO).

In summary, frames are a fundamental concept in memory management, providing a structured way to allocate, track, and manage physical memory in an Operating System. They are essential for implementing memory management techniques like paging, segmentation, and virtual memory, which allow multiple processes to share physical memory resources efficiently.

Q 8. What is Thrashing? (RU B. Tech. Jan 2022)

Ans: Thrashing is a critical issue in Operating Systems, especially those that implement virtual memory, and it occurs when the system spends an excessive amount of time swapping data between main memory (RAM) and secondary storage (usually a hard disk or SSD). Thrashing severely degrades system performance and can render it nearly unresponsive.

Here's a detailed explanation of thrashing in the context of Operating Systems:

Causes of Thrashing:

Thrashing typically occurs when the system is overwhelmed by a high demand for physical memory, and there is not enough RAM to accommodate all the active processes. The main causes of thrashing include:

Overcommitment of Memory: When the sum of the virtual memory allocations for running processes exceeds the physical RAM available.

Poor process scheduling: Scheduling policies that do not efficiently utilize available CPU time and memory.

Memory leaks: Programs that do not release memory properly, causing a gradual increase in memory consumption.

Large working sets: Processes with large working sets (active memory) that cannot fit in physical memory.

Symptoms of Thrashing:

The following symptoms are indicative of thrashing:

Excessive Disk Activity: The system constantly swaps pages between RAM and secondary storage, leading to high disk I/O.

Sluggish Performance: The system becomes unresponsive, and task execution becomes extremely slow.

High CPU Utilization: The CPU spends a significant portion of its time managing memory, limiting its capacity to execute user processes.

Low Memory Utilization: Paradoxically, despite a high demand for memory, the memory utilization rate is low as pages are continually being swapped in and out.

Mitigating Thrashing:

To address thrashing and restore system performance, the following strategies can be employed:

Process Prioritization: Prioritize essential or interactive processes over background or lower-priority processes to ensure their working sets are in RAM.

Page Replacement Algorithms: Employ efficient Page Replacement Algorithms (e.g., LRU - Least Recently Used) to decide which pages to swap in and out. Good algorithms reduce the thrashing effect.

Optimizing Virtual Memory: Adjust Virtual Memory settings, such as page file or swap space size, to better accommodate memory demands.

Resource Management: Ensure that system resources (CPU and memory) are allocated and managed efficiently by the scheduler.

Resource Monitoring: Use performance monitoring tools to detect thrashing early and take corrective measures.

Prevention:

The best approach to handle thrashing is Prevention. Techniques for preventing thrashing include:

Proper Sizing: Ensure that the system has an adequate amount of physical RAM to handle the expected workloads.

Page Fault Rate Monitoring: Monitor the page fault rate and allocate additional resources (e.g., RAM) before thrashing occurs.

Limiting Overcommitment: Be cautious about overcommitting memory to processes, and use mechanisms to limit memory allocation.

Efficient Process Scheduling: Use scheduling policies that make optimal use of available resources.

Real-World Applications:

Thrashing can occur in any system that implements Virtual Memory, including general-purpose desktop and server Operating Systems. Proper Resource Management and system configuration are crucial to preventing and addressing thrashing.

In summary, Thrashing is a detrimental condition in Operating Systems where excessive swapping of data between RAM and secondary storage leads to severe performance degradation. It results from overcommitment of memory, poor scheduling, and high demand for memory by active processes.

Effective prevention and mitigation strategies, along with efficient memory management, are essential to address thrashing and ensure the smooth operation of a computer system.

Q 9. Explain 'valid' and 'invalid' bit in page table? (RU B. Tech. Jan 2022)

Ans: In the context of Virtual Memory Management, the **valid** and **invalid** bits are used in a page table entry to determine whether a particular page or page frame in physical memory is valid and can be accessed by a process. These bits play a critical role in ensuring memory protection and efficient operation of virtual memory systems. Here's a detailed explanation of the valid and invalid bits in a page table:

Valid Bit:

The valid bit, when set to 1, indicates that the page or page frame referenced by this page table entry is valid and contains actual data. In other words, the page has been loaded into physical memory (RAM) and can be safely accessed by the process. The valid bit is set when a page is loaded into physical memory.

Invalid Bit:

The invalid bit, when set to 0, signifies that the page or page frame is not valid, and there is no valid data present in that memory location. Attempting to access an invalid page results in a page fault, which triggers the Operating System to bring the required page into physical memory from secondary storage (e.g., a hard disk or SSD).

Purpose and Use:

These bits are essential for memory protection and efficient use of physical memory. Here's how they are used:

When a process requests memory, the CPU generates a logical address, which is used to access the page table. The page table entry for that address contains the valid bit.

If the valid bit is set (1), it means the page is already in physical memory, and the CPU can proceed with the memory access.

If the valid bit is not set (0), indicating that the page is not in physical memory (page fault), the Operating System must intervene. It fetches the required page from secondary storage, updates the page table to set the valid bit, and then allows the CPU to access the data.

If a process tries to access an invalid page, the Operating System can terminate the process, generate an error, or take other actions to prevent unauthorized or erroneous memory access.

Benefits:

The valid and invalid bits offer several advantages:

Memory Protection: They prevent unauthorized access to memory locations that are not allocated to a process, enhancing system security.

Efficient Use of Physical Memory: Pages are only loaded into physical memory when needed, saving RAM for active processes and reducing unnecessary page swaps.

Page Fault Handling:

When a page fault occurs, the Operating System must handle it by bringing the required page into physical memory, updating the page table, and allowing the process to continue. The invalid bit indicates that this page fault resolution is needed.

Example:

Suppose a process attempts to access a memory address, and the corresponding page table entry's valid bit is set to 0. This access triggers a page fault. The Operating System then loads the required page from secondary storage into physical memory and sets the valid bit to 1 in the page table entry, making the page accessible.

In summary, the **valid** and **invalid** bits in a page table entry are used to indicate whether a particular page is valid and can be accessed in physical memory. These bits are crucial for memory protection, efficient use of physical memory, and the handling of page faults in virtual memory systems. They help ensure that processes can access only the memory locations they are authorized to use.

Q 10. What do you mean by Demand Paging? Explain Virtual Memory and Page Fault Concept in detail. (RU B. Tech. Jan 2022)

Ans: Demand Paging is a Memory Management Scheme used in Operating Systems to efficiently manage the allocation and deallocation of memory for running processes. The basic idea behind demand paging is to load only the necessary portions of a program into main memory (RAM) when they are needed, rather than loading the entire program at once. This approach helps optimize memory utilization and improves overall system performance.

Here's how demand paging works:

Virtual Memory: In a system that uses demand paging, the Operating System creates a virtual address space for each process. This virtual address space is typically larger than the physical RAM available in the system. Each process "thinks" it has access to a large and contiguous block of memory.

Page Table: The virtual address space is divided into fixed-size blocks called pages. The physical memory (RAM) is also divided into fixed-size blocks called frames. The Operating System maintains a data structure called a Page Table for each process, which keeps track of the mapping between virtual pages and physical frames.

Page Faults: When a process tries to access a portion of memory that is not currently in RAM, a page fault occurs. The Operating System intercepts the page fault and takes appropriate action.

Page Replacement: In response to a page fault, the Operating System needs to decide which page to bring into RAM to satisfy the request. It may choose to swap out an existing page, if all the frames are in use. Various page replacement algorithms, such as the Least Recently Used (LRU) Algorithm or the Second Chance Algorithm, are used to make this decision.

Loading Pages: The Operating System loads the required page from secondary storage (usually a hard disk) into an available frame in RAM.

Resuming Execution: Once the required page is in RAM, the process can resume its execution, as if nothing happened. The page table is updated to reflect the new mapping.

Demand Paging has several advantages:

It allows efficient use of physical memory since only the required portions of a program are loaded, conserving memory resources.

It enables the execution of processes that are larger than the available physical memory.

It provides better system responsiveness as it avoids the need to load the entire program into memory before execution begins.

However, Demand Paging can also lead to performance issues if not managed properly. Excessive Page Faults, especially when the working set of a process doesn't fit in RAM, can result in a phenomenon known as "thrashing," where the system spends more time swapping pages in and out of memory than executing useful work. Therefore, effective Page Replacement Algorithms and Memory Management Strategies are crucial for the success of demand paging in an Operating System.Virtual Memory and Page Faults are key concepts in modern Operating Systems that facilitate efficient memory management and the illusion of having more physical memory (RAM) than actually exists.

Virtual Memory:

Virtual memory is a memory management technique that uses a combination of physical RAM and secondary storage (usually a hard disk) to provide the appearance of a vast and contiguous address space to each process running on the system. Here's how it works:

Virtual Address Space: Each process is allocated a Virtual Address space, which is a large and contiguous range of memory addresses. This address space is divided into fixed-size blocks called pages. The size of a page is typically 4KB or 8KB, but it can vary.

Physical RAM: The Physical RAM is also divided into fixed-size blocks called frames, which correspond in size to pages. The goal of Virtual Memory is to ensure that not all pages of a process need to be loaded into RAM simultaneously.

Page Table: The Operating System maintains a data structure called a Page Table for each process. The page table maps virtual pages to physical frames. When a process accesses a specific virtual address, the page table is consulted to determine the corresponding physical location in RAM.

Swapping: If a page needed by a process is not in RAM, a page fault occurs. To resolve this, the Operating System swaps out a page from RAM to the secondary storage (paging file) to make room for the new page. The page table is updated to reflect the new mapping. When the swapped-out page is needed again, it will be brought back into RAM.

Virtual Memory provides several benefits:

It allows running processes to have the illusion of a large and contiguous address space, even if physical RAM is limited.

It enables the efficient sharing of physical memory among multiple processes.

It provides a mechanism for isolating processes from one another, ensuring that one process cannot access the memory of another process.

Page Fault:

A Page Fault is an exception that occurs when a process attempts to access a memory page that is not currently present in the physical RAM. Here's how the page fault concept works in detail:

Page Access: When a process tries to read from or write to a memory address, the processor checks the page table to find page fault.

Page Fault Handling: When a page fault occurs, the Operating System takes control. It follows a series of steps to resolve the page fault:

The Operating System looks up the page that caused the fault in the process's page table to find out where it should be in RAM.

If the page is on secondary storage,then the Operating System will schedule a disk I/O operation to load the required page into an available frame in RAM.

The page table is updated to reflect the new mapping between the virtual page and the physical frame.

The process is then allowed to continue its execution, as if nothing happened, but now the page is in RAM and accessible.

Page faults are a crucial part of virtual memory management, allowing the Operating System to transparently manage memory between RAM and secondary storage while providing the illusion of a large, contiguous address space to processes. Effective page fault handling and page replacement algorithms are essential to ensure system performance and responsiveness.

Q 11. What is Memory Management Unit (MMU)? Explain Best Fit, Worst Fit and Quick Fit Algorithms in detail. (RU B. Tech. Jan 2022)

Ans:A Memory Management Unit (MMU) is a hardware component in a computer's central processing unit (CPU) that plays a crucial role in the management of memory. The primary purpose of the MMU is to translate virtual addresses used by programs and Operating Systems into physical addresses in the computer's RAM (Random Access Memory) or other memory storage devices. The MMU ensures that programs can run with the illusion of having their own dedicated memory, even if the physical memory is limited or shared among multiple processes. Here are key functions and concepts associated with the Memory Management Unit:

Virtual Memory: The MMU enables the use of virtual memory, a memory management technique that provides an extended address space beyond the actual physical memory. This allows multiple processes to run simultaneously and ensures that each process has a separate address space.

Address Translation: When a program running on the CPU accesses a memory address, the MMU translates the virtual address (used by the program) to the corresponding physical address in RAM. This translation process is transparent to the program and the Operating System.

Page Tables: To facilitate address translation, the MMU uses data structures called page tables. A page table is a data structure that maps virtual page numbers to physical page frame numbers. When a program accesses a virtual address, the MMU consults the page table to find the corresponding physical address.

Protection and Security: The MMU enforces memory protection and access control. It checks the access rights specified in the page table to ensure that a program only accesses memory regions it is authorized to use. This helps prevent unauthorized memory access and protects the integrity of the Operating System.

Memory Allocation: The MMU plays a role in memory allocation and deallocation. It allows the Operating System to manage the allocation of memory to processes and ensures that each process operates within its allocated memory space.

Demand Paging: The MMU is often used in conjunction with demand paging. When a program accesses a portion of memory that is not currently in RAM, a page fault occurs. The MMU, in coordination with the Operating System, fetches the required page from secondary storage into RAM.

Memory Protection Rings: Some CPUs with an MMU support multiple privilege levels or protection rings. These allow the Operating System to run in a more privileged mode, with access to all system resources, while user programs run in a less privileged mode with restricted access.

Cache Control: The MMU may also control the use of memory caches, such as the Translation Lookaside Buffer (TLB), which can improve the speed of address translation by storing frequently accessed address mappings.

The MMU is a critical component in modern Operating Systems and CPUs, as it enables efficient use of memory resources, isolation between processes, and security in memory access. Different CPU architectures and Operating Systems may have variations in how the MMU is implemented, but the core functionality remains consistent.

Memory allocation algorithms, such as Best Fit, Worst Fit, and Quick Fit, are used in Operating Systems to manage the allocation of memory to processes in a way that optimizes memory utilization and minimizes fragmentation. Here, we'll explain each of these memory allocation algorithms in detail:

Best Fit:

The Best Fit Memory Allocation algorithm aims to allocate the smallest available block of memory from the free memory pool that is just large enough to accommodate the incoming process. This method helps minimize wasted memory but can lead to more frequent memory fragmentation. Here's how it works:

When a new process requests memory allocation, the Operating System scans the list of free memory blocks and selects the one that is the smallest among all the blocks large enough to hold the process. This ensures that memory utilization is optimized, as the process occupies only as much memory as needed.

The main advantage of Best Fit is that it reduces memory wastage, which can be critical in systems with limited memory resources. The corresponding physical frame, if the page is not in RAM (a page not present in RAM), then a page fault is generated.

However, the frequent allocation and deallocation of memory using the Best Fit algorithm can lead to memory fragmentation. The smaller free memory blocks created by this algorithm are more susceptible to becoming unusable due to fragmentation.

Worst Fit:

The Worst Fit Memory Allocation algorithm allocates the largest available block of memory from the free memory pool to the incoming process. This approach may lead to more efficient memory utilization in the short term but can result in increased fragmentation over time. Here's how it works:

When a process requests memory allocation, the Operating System looks for the largest free memory block available and assigns that block to the process.

Worst Fit aims to reduce fragmentation by ensuring that large memory blocks remain available for future use. However, this may lead to underutilization of memory, as the allocated block is often larger than what the requesting process needs.
As the Worst Fit algorithm allocates the largest available block, it can lead to memory fragmentation, with many small, unusable memory holes scattered throughout the memory space.

Quick Fit:
Quick Fit is a Dynamic Memory Allocation Algorithm that uses a set of fixed-size lists to manage memory blocks of specific sizes. Each list corresponds to a particular memory block size, and the lists are maintained in increasing order of block size. Here's how it works:
When a process requests memory allocation, the Operating System checks the Quick Fit lists to find the list whose block size is closest to the size requested by the process. It then allocates a block from that list.
Quick Fit is designed to strike a balance between Best Fit and Worst Fit. It minimizes fragmentation by allocating memory blocks close to the requested size, thus reducing memory wastage and fragmentation.
However, maintaining multiple lists and dynamically managing them can introduce some overhead, especially in terms of bookkeeping and searching for the appropriate list.
Quick Fit is commonly used in systems with variable-sized memory block requests, as it provides a compromise between minimizing fragmentation and optimizing memory usage.

In summary, the choice of a memory allocation algorithm, whether it's Best Fit, Worst Fit, Quick Fit, or another, depends on the specific requirements and constraints of a system. Each algorithm has its trade-offs in terms of memory utilization and fragmentation, and the choice should be based on the system's priorities and usage patterns.

Q 12. For the following set of process, find the average waiting time and turnaround time using Gantt Chart for: (RU B. Tech. Jan 2022)
SJF
Priority scheduling process
Ans: To calculate the average waiting time and turnaround time for a set of processes using Gantt Chart, we'll need the burst times (execution times) of the processes and, for priority scheduling, their priorities.
Since you provided the scheduling algorithms (SJF and Priority), I'll demonstrate the process for both of them using a hypothetical set of processes and their burst times. We'll assume that lower priority values indicate higher priority for the priority scheduling.
Set of Processes:

Process	Burst Time	Priority
P1	4	3
P2	2	2
P3	5	1
P4	1	4
P5	6	2

Let's calculate the average waiting time and turnaround time for both SJF and Priority scheduling:

SJF (Shortest Job First):

Arrange the processes in increasing order of burst time: P4, P2, P1, P3, P5

Create a Gantt Chart and calculate the completion times for each process:

Gantt Chart:

0---P4---1---P2---3---P1---7---P3---12---P5---18

Calculate the turnaround time for each process (completion time - arrival time):

Turnaround time for P1: 7 - 0 = 7

Turnaround time for P2: 3 - 0 = 3

Turnaround time for P3: 12 - 0 = 12

Turnaround time for P4: 1 - 0 = 1

Turnaround time for P5: 18 - 0 = 18

Calculate the waiting time for each process (turnaround time - burst time):

Waiting time for P1: 7 - 4 = 3

Waiting time for P2: 3 - 2 = 1

Waiting time for P3: 12 - 5 = 7

Waiting time for P4: 1 - 1 = 0

Waiting time for P5: 18 - 6 = 12

Calculate the average turnaround time and average waiting time:

Average Turnaround Time = (7 + 3 + 12 + 1 + 18) / 5 = 8.2

Average Waiting Time = (3 + 1 + 7 + 0 + 12) / 5 = 4.6

Priority Scheduling:

Arrange the processes in order of priority (lower number indicates higher priority): P3, P5, P2, P1, P4

Create a Gantt Chart and calculate the completion times for each process:

Gantt Chart:

0---P3---5---P5---11---P2---13---P1---17---P4---18

Calculate the turnaround time for each process (completion time - arrival time):

Turnaround time for P1: 17 - 0 = 17

Turnaround time for P2: 13 - 0 = 13

Turnaround time for P3: 5 - 0 = 5

Turnaround time for P4: 18 - 0 = 18

Turnaround time for P5: 11 - 0 = 11

Calculate the waiting time for each process (turnaround time - burst time):

Waiting time for P1: 17 - 4 = 13

Waiting time for P2: 13 - 2 = 11

Waiting time for P3: 5 - 5 = 0

Waiting time for P4: 18 - 1 = 17

Waiting time for P5: 11 - 6 = 5

Calculate the average turnaround time and average waiting time:

Average Turnaround Time = (17 + 13 + 5 + 18 + 11) / 5 = 12.8

Average Waiting Time = (13 + 11 + 0 + 17 + 5) / 5 = 9.2

These are the average waiting time and turnaround time values for the given set of processes using SJF and Priority scheduling. The values may vary depending on the specific processes and their characteristics.

Q 13. Suppose a disk drive has 200 cylinders. The drive is initially at cylinder position 98. The queue with request from I/O to blocks on cylinders: 86, 147, 91, 177, 94, 150, 102, 175, 130

What is the total head movement needed to satisfy the request for SCAN and C-SCAN scheduling algorithm? (RU B. Tech. Jan 2022)

Ans: To calculate the total head movement needed to satisfy the given I/O request queue for the SCAN and C-SCAN scheduling algorithms, we will use the initial position of the disk head at cylinder 98. We'll also assume that the disk arm moves towards the higher-numbered cylinders (outward) first and then reverses its direction. Here's how you can calculate it:

Given:

Total number of cylinders on the disk drive = 200

Initial position of the disk head = 98

I/O request queue: 86, 147, 91, 177, 94, 150, 102, 175, 130

SCAN (Elevator) Scheduling:

Sort the I/O request queue in ascending order: 86, 91, 94, 102, 130, 147, 150, 175, 177

The head moves towards higher cylinder numbers (outward) until the last requested cylinder.

After reaching the last requested cylinder, the head reverses direction and moves towards lower cylinder numbers (inward).

Calculate the total head movement:

Head moves from 98 to 102 (4 cylinders).

Head moves from 102 to 130 (28 cylinders).

Head moves from 130 to 147 (17 cylinders).

Head moves from 147 to 150 (3 cylinders).

Head moves from 150 to 175 (25 cylinders).

Head moves from 175 to 177 (2 cylinders).

Head moves from 177 to 200 (23 cylinders).

Head moves from 200 to 94 (106 cylinders).

Head moves from 94 to 91 (3 cylinders).

Head moves from 91 to 86 (5 cylinders).

Total head movement = 4 + 28 + 17 + 3 + 25 + 2 + 23 + 106 + 3 + 5 = 216 cylinders.

C-SCAN (Circular SCAN) Scheduling:

C-SCAN is similar to SCAN but, after reaching the last requested cylinder, the head immediately returns to the beginning of the disk without serving requests in between.

Sort the I/O request queue in ascending order: 86, 91, 94, 102, 130, 147, 150, 175, 177

The head moves towards higher cylinder numbers (outward) until the last requested cylinder.

After reaching the last requested cylinder, the head moves to the beginning cylinder (cylinder 0) without serving any requests in between.

Calculate the total head movement:

Head moves from 98 to 102 (4 cylinders).

Head moves from 102 to 130 (28 cylinders).

Head moves from 130 to 147 (17 cylinders).

Head moves from 147 to 150 (3 cylinders).

Head moves from 150 to 175 (25 cylinders).

Head moves from 175 to 177 (2 cylinders).

Head moves from 177 to 200 (23 cylinders).

Head moves from 200 to 0 (200 cylinders).

Head moves from 0 to 86 (86 cylinders).

Head moves from 86 to 91 (5 cylinders).

Head moves from 91 to 94 (3 cylinders).

Total head movement = 4 + 28 + 17 + 3 + 25 + 2 + 23 + 200 + 86 + 5 + 3 = 396 cylinders.

So, the total head movement needed to satisfy the request for the SCAN scheduling algorithm is 216 cylinders, and for the C-SCAN scheduling algorithm, it is 396 cylinders.

Q 14. Explains the followings: (RU B. Tech. Jan 2022)

A. Data Structure of Bankers algorithm

B. Segmentation

C. File Security

Ans:a) Data Structure of Banker's Algorithm:

The Banker's Algorithm is a resource allocation and deadlock avoidance algorithm used in Operating Systems to determine if granting a set of resource requests from processes will lead to a safe state or potentially cause a deadlock. To perform this analysis, the Banker's Algorithm uses several data structures:

Available Resources (vector): This is an array that represents the number of available instances of each resource type in the system at any given time. It is typically denoted as **Available**.

Maximum Demand Matrix: This Matrix specifies, for each process, the maximum number of instances of each resource type it may need during its execution. Denoted as **Max**.

Allocation Matrix: This Matrix describes how many instances of each resource type are currently allocated to each process. Denoted as **Allocation**.

Need Matrix: The Need Matrixis derived from the Maximum and Allocation matrices and represents the additional instances of each resource type that each process still needs to complete its execution. Denoted as **Need**.

These data structures allow the algorithm to determine, if a request from a process can be safely granted without causing a potential deadlock. It checks if the request can be satisfied by comparing the **Need** matrix with the **Available** vector. If the request is granted and the system remains in a safe state, then the resources are allocated to the process. Otherwise, the request is denied, and the system's state remains unchanged.

b) Segmentation:

Segmentation is a Memory Management Technique used in Operating Systems to divide the primary memory (RAM) into segments or logical address spaces. Each segment represents a part of a program or data and can vary in size. Segmentation offers several benefits:

Protection: Segmentation provides memory protection by isolating segments from each other. This prevents unauthorized access to the memory of one segment by another, enhancing security.

Sharing: Multiple processes or programs can share segments that contain shared libraries or data, reducing memory usage and improving efficiency.

Dynamic Memory Allocation: Segmentation allows for dynamic memory allocation, enabling processes to request memory as needed without fixed-size memory blocks.

Simplifies Addressing: Segmentation simplifies memory addressing by using a combination of a segment identifier and an offset within the segment to access memory. This is more flexible than traditional contiguous memory allocation.

Virtual Memory: Segmentation is often used as a basis for implementing virtual memory systems, where segments can be swapped in and out of secondary storage as needed.

One common downside of segmentation is fragmentation, both internal (within a segment) and external (in the memory space between segments). Proper memory management strategies are needed to address these issues.

c) File Security:

File Security in an Operating System involves mechanisms and policies for protecting files from unauthorized access, modification, or deletion. Key concepts related to file security include:

Access Control Lists (ACLs): ACLs are lists associated with each file or directory that specify which users or groups are allowed to perform specific actions, such as read, write, execute, or delete. ACLs provide fine-grained control over file access.

Permissions: Files and directories have permission settings, including read, write, and execute permissions for the owner, the group, and others. These permissions determine who can perform specific actions on a file or directory.

User Authentication: Access to files is often controlled through user authentication, such as usernames and passwords. Only authorized users who can provide valid credentials are allowed to access files.

File Ownership: Each file is associated with an owner, and the owner often has more control over the file's permissions. Owners can typically change permissions and grant access to others.

Encryption: File Encryption is a method to secure file contents. Encrypted files can only be accessed by users who possess the decryption key or passphrase.

Audit Trails: Some Operating Systems provide auditing features to track file access and modification. This is essential for security monitoring and forensic analysis.

Role-Based Access Control (RBAC): RBAC assigns users or processes to roles and then assigns permissions to those roles. This approach simplifies access control for large organizations.

File security is a critical aspect of Operating System design and administration, as it helps protect sensitive data, maintain data integrity, and ensure that only authorized users can access and manipulate files.

Q 15. Explain the Disk Scheduling Algorithm in brief. (RTU 2017, Dec 2013)

OR

Discuss the following Disk Scheduling Algorithm:

Shortest Seek Time First

First Come First Served

SCAN

C-Look

Ans: Disk Scheduling Algorithms are used in Operating Systems to optimize the order in which disk I/O requests are processed, aiming to reduce seek time and improve overall disk performance. Here's a brief explanation of each mentioned algorithm:

(i)Shortest Seek Time First (SSTF):

SSTF selects the I/O request that requires the shortest seek time from the current head position.

It aims to minimize the total distance the disk arm moves, thereby reducing the average seek time.

This algorithm may lead to starvation of some requests that are located far from the current head position, if there's a continuous stream of requests near the head.

(ii) First Come First Served (FCFS):

FCFS processes I/O requests in the order they arrive.

It's a simple scheduling algorithm but doesn't consider the location of the requested data on the disk.

FCFS may result in longer seek times, especially if there are frequent requests to distant locations on the disk.

(iii) SCAN:

SCAN, also known as elevator algorithm, scans the disk in a specific direction, servicing all requests along the path until reaching the end, then reverses direction.

It reduces the average response time by avoiding unnecessary movement of the disk arm.

SCAN prevents starvation of requests located at one end of the disk, but may cause delays for requests in the opposite direction of the initial scan.

(iv) C-Look:

C-Look is a variation of the SCAN algorithm that doesn't scan to the end of the disk in both directions.

Instead, it only scans to the last request in the current direction and then jumps back to the beginning of the requests in that direction.

C-Look aims to reduce the time spent on the outer tracks of the disk, where seek times are typically longer.

This algorithm may not serve requests located towards the end of the disk unless they were already in the path of the initial scan.

Each disk scheduling algorithm has its advantages and disadvantages, and the choice depends on factors such as the workload characteristics and performance requirements of the system.

Q 16. What is meant by Demand Paging? (RTU MCA 2022)

Ans: Demand Paging is a memory management scheme used in Operating Systems where pages of a process are not loaded into main memory (RAM) until they are explicitly demanded by the program during execution. Instead of loading the entire program into memory at the start, only the portions needed for the current execution are brought into RAM as and when required.

Key features of Demand Paging:

Lazy Loading: With Demand Paging, only the necessary pages of a program are loaded into memory when they are accessed. This approach minimizes the initial loading time and conserves memory resources.

Page Faults: When a program attempts to access a page that is not currently in memory, a page fault occurs. The Operating System then brings the required page from the secondary storage (usually the hard disk) into the main memory.

Efficient Use of Memory: Demand Paging allows for the efficient use of memory as only the actively used portions of a program are resident in RAM. Less frequently used pages remain on disk until needed, reducing memory footprint.

Faster Program Start-Up: Since only the essential pages are loaded initially, programs can start more quickly, improving overall system responsiveness.

Flexibility in Memory Management: Demand Paging provides flexibility in managing memory resources, allowing the Operating System to adapt to varying program memory requirements dynamically.

Optimized Page Replacement: In case the available memory is insufficient, the Operating System may need to replace a page in memory with one from the secondary storage. Demand Paging Algorithms help determine which page to swap out based on factors like page usage history.

Demand Paging is commonly used in modern Operating Systems to efficiently utilize memory resources and enhance the overall performance of systems with limited RAM. It is a part of the virtual memory system, enabling the illusion of a larger memory space than physically available.

Q 17. Explain various types of Memory Management Strategies? (RU BCA 2019)

Ans: Memory Management Strategies are techniques used by Operating Systems to efficiently allocate and manage memory resources in a computer system. These strategies ensure that each process has access to the memory it requires while optimizing memory utilization and minimizing fragmentation. Here are various types of memory management strategies:

Single Partition Allocation:

In this strategy, the entire memory is allocated to a single process.

Only one process can run at a time, and all resources are dedicated to that process.

Simple to implement but inefficient since it does not allow for multitasking or efficient utilization of memory resources.

Fixed Partition Allocation:

Memory is divided into fixed-size partitions, and each partition can accommodate one process.

Partitions are allocated to processes based on their size, and processes cannot exceed the size of the partition.

Allows for multitasking but suffers from fragmentation issues, especially if partitions are not fully utilized.

Dynamic Partition Allocation:

Memory is divided into variable-sized partitions, and each partition can accommodate a process of corresponding size.

Partitions are allocated and deallocated dynamically as processes request and release memory.

Requires efficient Memory Management Algorithms to handle fragmentation and optimize memory allocation.

Buddy System Allocation:

Memory is divided into fixed-size blocks, and allocation is done in powers of 2 (e.g., 1KB, 2KB, 4KB).

When a process requests memory, the system allocates a block that is the closest power of 2 larger than the requested size.

Efficient for managing memory with varying sizes of requests but may suffer from internal fragmentation.

Paging:

Memory is divided into fixed-size blocks called pages, and processes are divided into fixed-size blocks called page frames.

Pages are loaded into and swapped out of page frames as needed, allowing for efficient memory utilization and virtual memory management.

Reduces external fragmentation and allows for more efficient use of memory resources.

Segmentation:

Memory is divided into variable-sized segments, each representing a logical unit of a process (e.g., code, data, stack).

Each segment is allocated and managed independently, allowing for more flexible memory allocation and protection.

Helps in organizing and managing memory for complex programs with multiple segments.

Virtual Memory:

Virtual Memory extends the available physical memory by using disk space as an extension of RAM.

Portions of the program's address space are temporarily transferred between RAM and disk, allowing processes to run larger than physical memory size.

Provides efficient memory management and allows for multitasking without requiring all processes to fit in physical memory simultaneously.

These Memory Management Strategies vary in complexity and efficiency and are chosen based on the specific requirements and constraints of the system. Effective memory management is crucial for ensuring optimal system performance and resource utilization.

Q 18. What is Virtual Memory? How is it implemented? (RU BCA 2019)

Ans: Virtual Memory is a memory management technique that provides an illusion of a larger address space to processes than the physical memory (RAM) available in a computer system. It allows programs to execute as if they have more memory than is physically available by using disk space as an extension of RAM. Virtual memory enables efficient multitasking, memory sharing, and protection, and it is a fundamental component of modern Operating Systems. Here's how virtual memory is implemented:

Address Translation:

Virtual Memory operates by mapping virtual addresses used by processes to physical addresses in RAM.

Each process has its own virtual address space, starting from address 0 and extending up to the maximum addressable memory size.

The Virtual Memory manager maintains a page table for each process, which maps virtual addresses to physical addresses.

Page Tables:

The Page Table is a data structure used by the Operating System to translate virtual addresses to physical addresses.

It consists of entries, each containing a virtual page number and its corresponding physical page frame number.

When a process accesses a virtual address, the processor uses the page table to look up the corresponding Physical Address.

Page Faults:

When a process attempts to access a virtual address that is not currently mapped to a physical address in RAM, a page fault occurs.

The Operating System handles page faults by loading the required page from disk into an available physical page frame in RAM.

If all physical page frames are in use, the Operating System may need to select a page to evict (remove from RAM) to make space for the new page.

Page Replacement:

Page Replacement Algorithms are used to select which page to evict when a page fault occurs and all physical page frames are in use.

Common Page Replacement Algorithms include Least Recently Used (LRU), First-In-First-Out (FIFO), and Optimal.

These algorithms aim to minimize page faults and optimize overall system performance by selecting pages that are least likely to be accessed in the near future for eviction.

Demand Paging:

Demand paging is a Virtual Memory management technique where pages are loaded into RAM only when they are needed.

Instead of loading the entire program into memory at once, only the pages required for the current execution are brought into RAM.

This reduces the amount of memory required to run a program and improves memory utilization.

Page Size:

The size of pages used in virtual memory systems can vary, commonly ranging from 4KB to 8KB.

Smaller page sizes result in more fine-grained memory management but may increase overhead due to larger page tables.

Larger page sizes reduce the overhead of page tables but may lead to more internal fragmentation.

Overall, Virtual Memory provides several benefits, including efficient memory utilization, multitasking support, and protection between processes. By using disk space as an extension of RAM, virtual memory enables systems to run larger and more complex programs than would be possible with physical memory alone.

Previous Years Unsolved Questions

Q 1. A system contains 10 units of resource R1. 10 The resource requirement of 3 user processes P1, P2, P3 can be summarised as:

P1 P2P3

Max. Requirement 7 4 5

Current Allocation 3 2 3

Is the current allocation state feasible and safe? (IGNOU 2010)

Q 2. Apply Banker's Algorithm to check it. If a new request of (2, 1, 0) arises, check whether it will be granted or not using Banker's Algorithm?(IGNOU 2010)

Q 3. Explain what causes the thrashing? Suggest 5 the mechanism to avoid the thrashing. (IGNOU 2010)

Q 4. Discuss Lamport's Algorithm in distributed system. Estimate the cost of communication of Lamport'sAlgorithm.(IGNOU 2010)

Q 5. With the help of diagrams, explain the 4 concept of demand paging and demand segmentation. (IGNOU 2010)

Q 6. For a page Reference string as:

10 0, 1, 2, 6, 9, 4, 5, 0, 2, 6, 3, 8 and with 3 memory frames, calculate the no. of page faults using:

OPT LRU Page replacement algorithms.(IGNOU 2010)

Q 7. Explain the concept of Virtual Memory in OS.(IGNOU 2010)

Q 8. What is segmentation? Explain with an example.(IGNOU June 2010)

Q 9. Explain paging address translation by:

Direct Mapping.

Associative Mapping.

Give suitable diagrams and examples also. (IGNOU June 2011)

Q 10. What is Thrashing? Explain the working 10 set model to avoid the thrashing. (IGNOU June 2012)

Q 11. Explain the concept of Virtual Memory system.(IGNOU Dec 2012)

Q 12. Obtain the total page fault using FIFO, LRIJ and OPT page replacement algorithm for the following sequence of pages. Consider total 3 frames in memory. 1, 2, 3, 1, 4, 2, 5, 1, 3, 4, 5. (IGNOU Dec 2012)

Q 13. Explain segmented paging and paged segmentation.(IGNOU Dec 2012)

Q 14. Compare the merits and demerits of various disk scheduling algorithms.(IGNOU June 2013)

Q15. Explain the hardware support for paging. Briefly explain the three-page address translation technique. (IGNOU June 2013)

Q 16. What do you mean by 'Thrashing'?(Anna University 2013)

Q 17. With a neat sketch, explain how logical address is translated into physical address using paging mechanism. (Anna University 2013)

Q 18. Consider the following page reference string 1, 2, 3, 4, 5, 3, 4, 1, 6, 8, 7, 8, 9, 7, 8, 9, 5, 4, 4, 5, 3. How many page faults would occur for the following replacement algorithms? Assume four frames and all frames are initially empty.(Anna University 2013)

LRU replacement

FIFO replacement.

Optimal replacement.

Exercise

Exercise 1 – MCQ

1. What is the primary purpose of Memory Hierarchy in an Operating System?

a) To minimize the cost of memory devices

b) To organize memory in a hierarchical structure for efficient data access

c) To prevent unauthorized access to system memory

d) To manage process scheduling

2. Which memory type in the Memory Hierarchy has the fastest access speed?

a) Secondary Memory

b) Cache Memory

c) RAM (Random Access Memory)

d) Hard Disk Drive

3. Which memory level in the hierarchy has the fastest access time?

a) Cache memory

b) Main memory (RAM)

c) Secondary storage (Hard Disk)

d) Registers

4. What is the purpose of Virtual Memory in the Memory Hierarchy?

a) To provide additional physical RAM

b) To allow the use of secondary storage as if it were additional RAM

c) To speed up cache memory access

d) To eliminate the need for primary storage

5. Which cache mapping technique uses a direct mapping with a set-associative approach?

a) Fully Associative Mapping

b) Direct Mapping

c) Set-Associative Mapping

d) Block Mapping

6. Which algorithm follows the principle of replacing the page that will not be used for the longest period?

a) FIFO (First-In-First-Out)

b) LRU (Least Recently Used)

c) Optimal Page Replacement

d) Clock Page Replacement

7. In the context of page replacement algorithms, what does "Belady's Anomaly" refer to?

a) Increased page faults with more frames

b) Decreased page faults with more frames

c) Stability in page faults regardless of the number of frames

d) Predictable pattern of page faults

8. Which Page Replacement Algorithm requires the knowledge of future page references and is considered impractical for real-world implementations?

a) FIFO (First-In-First-Out)

b) LRU (Least Recently Used)

c) Optimal Page Replacement

d) Clock Page Replacement

9. What is the main drawback of the FIFO (First-In-First-Out) Page Replacement Algorithm?

a) It may suffer from Belady's Anomaly

b) It requires knowledge of future page references

c) It is too complex for implementation

d) It doesn't consider the order of recent page accesses

10. What is the primary purpose of Virtual Memory in an Operating System?

a) To provide additional physical RAM

b) To eliminate the need for secondary storage

c) To allow the use of secondary storage as if it were additional RAM

d) To increase the speed of cache memory

Exercise 2 – True/ False

1. Virtual Memory is a part of the memory hierarchy that directly interacts with the CPU.

2. The Memory Hierarchy helps in achieving a balance between speed, cost, and storage capacity.

3. Cache Memory is faster than main memory (RAM).

4. Virtual Memory allows programs to execute even, if the total RAM required exceeds the physical RAM available.

5. Registers are part of the main memory (RAM).

6. The Memory Hierarchy is designed to solely increase the overall size of the computer's memory.

7. The Optimal Page Replacement Algorithm is practical for implementation in real-time Operating Systems.

8. Clock Page Replacement is an approximation of the LRU (Least Recently Used) algorithm.

9. Page Replacement Algorithms are crucial for managing limited physical memory efficiently.

10. FIFO (First-In-First-Out) always results in the same number of page faults regardless of the reference pattern.

Exercise 3 – Fill in the blanks

1. In ____________ memory allocation, each process is loaded into a single, contiguous block of memory.

2. The primary goal of a memory ___________ algorithm is to decide which page or frame should be replaced when a page fault occurs.

Exercise 4 – Match case

Column A

1. FIFO
2. LRU (Least Recently Used)
3. Optimal
4. LFU (Least Frequently Used)
5. LRUK

Column B

a. Replaces the page that has not been used for the longest time.
b. May suffer from the Belady's Anomaly.
c. Requires knowledge of future page references.
d. Replaces the page with the lowest usage frequency.
e. Utilizes a fixed size page reference history to make replacement decisions.

Exercise 5 – One-word

1.What is the primary purpose of Virtual Memory?

2. What is the term for a region of disk space used to temporarily store data that doesn't fit in physical RAM?

Exercise 6 – Small answer

1.What is the primary goal of Memory Hierarchy in an Operating System?

2.What is the main purpose of main memory (RAM) in an Operating System?

Exercise 7 – Long answer

1. Explain in detail what Virtual Memory is, how it works, and its significance in modern Operating Systems?

2.How do page replacement algorithms work in Operating Systems, and what are the key factors that influence their effectiveness and performance?

Answer

Exercise 1 – MCQ
Ans: 1 b, 2 b, 3 d, 4 b, 5 c, 6 b, 7 a, 8 c, 9 a, 10 c

Exercise 2 – True/False
Ans: 1 False, 2 True, 3 True, 4 True, 5 True, 6 False, 7 False, 8 False, 9 True, 10 True

Exercise 3 – Fill in The Blanks
Ans: 1 Contiguous, 2 replacement

Exercise 4 – Match Case
Ans: 1 b, 2 a,3 c, 4 d, 5 e,

Exercise 5 – One-word
Ans: 1 Efficiency, 2 Swap

Online Resources

Videos:

MCQ Link: https://youtu.be/Q1C21rABDyU

QR Code:

True/False Link: https://youtu.be/7smah4Egr3Q

QR Code:

Online Test Paper: https://forms.office.com/r/8aEyuWqjA9

QR Code:

Chapter 5 File Systems

File Concept

In an Operating System, a file is a fundamental concept used to organize and store data on a storage device, such as a hard drive, solidstate drive (SSD), or other types of storage media. Files are essential for managing data, enabling data persistence, and facilitating data manipulation by user applications and the Operating System itself. Here are the key components and characteristics of files in Operating Systems:

File Structure: A file typically has a structure that includes data organized in a specific format. This structure can be simple, like a sequence of characters in a text file, or complex, such as the format used for executable programs, images, videos, or database files.

File Attributes: Files have associated attributes or metadata that provide information about the file. Common file attributes include the file name, size, creation date, modification date, and permissions that control who can access and manipulate the file.

File Types: Files can have various types, each associated with a specific format or purpose. Common file types include text files, binary files, executable files, directories (folders), and special files like device files used for hardware communication.

File Operations: Operating Systems provide a set of file operations or System Calls that allow users and programs to interact with files. These operations typically include creating, reading, writing, deleting, opening, closing, and renaming files.

File Naming: Files are identified by unique names within a directory. Filenames may be casesensitive or caseinsensitive, depending on the file system and the Operating System's conventions.

File Paths: Files are organized in a hierarchical directory structure, forming paths to locate and access them. A file's path specifies its location within the directory tree, starting from the root directory.

File Permissions: Operating Systems use file permissions to control access to files and directories. Permissions define who can read, write, execute, and modify files and directories. Permissions are typically assigned to file owners, group members, and others.

File Systems: Files are managed by the file system, which is responsible for storing, organizing, and retrieving data on storage devices. Common file systems include NTFS (New Technology File System), FAT (File Allocation Table), ext4, HFS+ (Hierarchical File System Plus), and more.

File Access Modes: Files can be opened in different access modes, such as read-only, write-only, or read-write, depending on the needs of the application. These access modes are specified when a file is opened.

File Sizes: Files have sizes that indicate the amount of data they contain. The size of a file may change as data is added or removed from it.

File Attributes and Metadata: In addition to basic attributes like size and permissions, files can have additional metadata or extended attributes that provide further information about the file, such as authorship, keywords, or version history.

File Compression and Encryption: Some file systems support file compression and encryption to reduce storage space and enhance data security. These features can be applied to individual files or directories.

File Locking: File Locking mechanisms are used to prevent multiple processes or users from simultaneously modifying the same file, ensuring data consistency and preventing conflicts.

Files are a fundamental part of the computing experience, enabling the storage and retrieval of data for various applications and services. The management and organization of files are critical functions of an Operating System, which provides a user-friendly interface and System Calls for working with files efficiently and securely.

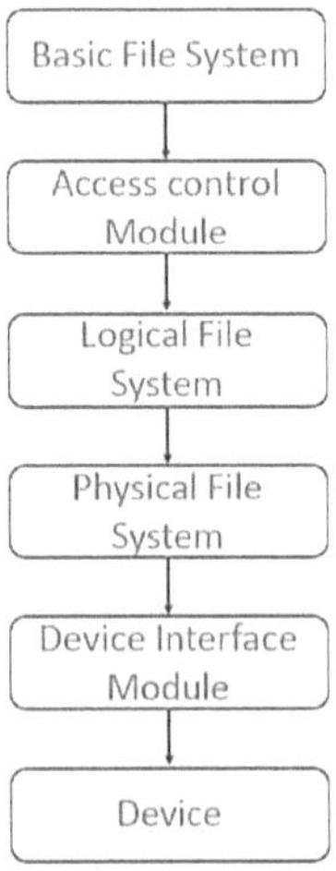

File Operations

File Operations in an Operating System are a set of fundamental functions or System Calls that allow users, applications, and the Operating System itself to interact with files. These operations enable the creation, reading, writing, deletion, and manipulation of files and directories. File operations in an Operating System refer to the actions or tasks performed on files, which are collections of data stored on secondary storage devices such as hard drives, solidstate drives, or network storage. Operating Systems provide a set of standard file operations that allow users and programs to interact with files.

File operations in an Operating System are essential functions for managing data stored on storage devices. They include creating, reading, writing, deleting, and modifying files. "Create" generates new files, while "read" retrieves data from existing ones. "Write" modifies or appends data to files, and "delete" removes them. Additionally, "rename" alters file names, and "move" relocates files within the file system. These operations are vital for user interactions, application functionality, and efficient data management, allowing users and programs to store, access, and manipulate files securely and efficiently within the Operating System environment. Here are some common file operations in Operating Systems:

Creating a File (`create` or `open`): This operation creates a new file with a specified name and file attributes. If the file already exists, it may be opened for reading and writing.

Opening a File (`open`): Opening a file allows a process to access its contents. The process can specify the desired access mode, such as read-only, write-only, or read-write, and the file is associated with a file descriptor, which is used for subsequent operations.

Reading from a File (`read`): Reading from a file allows a process to retrieve data from the file into a specified buffer. The number of bytes to read and the position from which to read can be specified.

Writing to a File (`write`): Writing to a file enables a process to add or modify data in the file. The process specifies the data to be written and the location at which to write it.

Seeking in a File (`seek` or `lseek`): Seeking in a file allows a process to change the current position (offset) within the file. This is useful for reading or writing data at specific locations within the file.

Closing a File (`close`): Closing a file operation releases the resources associated with a file descriptor and ensures that any changes made to the file are saved or flushed. Once closed, the file descriptor cannot be used for further operations on the file.

Deleting a File (`unlink` or `remove`): Deleting a file operation permanently removes a file from the file system. After deletion, the file can no longer be accessed.

Renaming a File (`rename`): Renaming a file operation changes the name of a file while keeping its content intact. This operation is useful for file management and organization.

Listing Directory Contents (`readdir` or `listdir`): Listing directory contents operation allows a process to retrieve a list of files and subdirectories within a specified directory.

Creating a Directory (`mkdir`): Creating a directory operation creates a new directory with a specified name within an existing directory.

Deleting a Directory (`rmdir`): Deleting a directory operation removes an empty directory from the file system. If the directory is not empty, it cannot be deleted without first removing its contents.

Changing File Permissions (`chmod`): Changing file permissions operation allows the owner or an administrator to modify the access permissions of a file, specifying who can read, write, or execute the file.

Changing File Ownership (`chown`): Changing file ownership operation allows the owner of a file to transfer ownership to another user or group.

File Locking (`flock` or `fcntl`): File locking operations enable processes to acquire and release locks on files to prevent concurrent access by multiple processes. Locks can be used to ensure data integrity and avoid race conditions.

File Truncation (`truncate`): File truncation operation changes the size of a file by removing or adding bytes, typically used for resizing files.

Getting File Information (`stat` or `fstat`): Getting file information operation retrieves metadata and attributes of a file, such as size, permissions, and timestamps.

These file operations provide the foundation for file management in an Operating System, enabling users and applications to work with data stored in files and directories. Operating Systems offer System Calls and libraries to make these operations accessible to developers and users through commandline tools or application interfaces.

File System Structure

The File System Structure in an Operating System refers to the organization and hierarchy of files and directories (also known as folders) on storage devices, such as hard drives, solidstate drives, or other storage media. The file system structure provides a systematic way to manage and organize data efficiently. Here are the key components and characteristics of a typical file system structure:

Root Directory: The root directory is the top-level directory in the file system hierarchy. It serves as the starting point for navigating the file system. In UNIX likeOperating Systems, it is denoted by a forward slash (/), while in Windows, it is denoted by a backslash (\).

Directories (Folders): Directories are containers that can hold files and other directories. They are used to organize and group related files. Directories can be nested within each other to create a hierarchical structure. The root directory is the first directory in the hierarchy.

Files: Files are individual data objects that can store various types of information, such as text, programs, documents, images, and more. Files are stored within directories and can be organized based on their content or purpose.

File Paths: File paths are used to specify the location of a file or directory within the file system structure. Absolute paths start from the root directory, while relative paths are specified with respect to the current working directory.

File Extensions: File extensions are typically used in some Operating Systems (e.g., Windows) to indicate the type of data stored in a file. For example, ".txt" indicates a text file, ".jpg" denotes an image file, and ".exe" signifies an executable program file.

File Attributes and Metadata: Each file and directory in the file system structure has associated metadata, which includes information such as the file's name, size, creation date, modification date, permissions, and owner.

Access Control: File systems implement access control mechanisms to determine who can read, write, execute, or modify files and directories. Permissions are typically defined for file owners, groups, and others.

File System Operations: Users and applications can perform various file system operations, such as creating, reading, writing, deleting, moving, and renaming files and directories. These operations are typically accomplished using System Calls or file system APIs.

File System Types: Different Operating Systems support various file system types, such as NTFS (New Technology File System), FAT (File Allocation Table), ext4, HFS+ (Hierarchical File System Plus), and more. Each file system type has its own features, limitations, and compatibility.

Partitioning: Storage devices can be divided into partitions, each of which can have its own file system structure. Partitioning allows for better organization and management of data.

Mount Points: In some Operating Systems, partitions or directories from different storage devices can be "mounted" into the file system structure at specific locations. This allows access to data stored on different devices as if they were part of the same file system.

File System Utilities: Operating Systems provide file system utilities and commands for managing files and directories, such as "ls" (list files), "mkdir" (create directory), "cp" (copy files), "mv" (move or rename files), and "rm" (remove files).

File System Check and Repair: File systems may include utilities for checking and repairing file system integrity, such as "fsck" in Unix like systems or "chkdsk" in Windows.

The specific structure and organization of the file system can vary between Operating Systems and file system types. Each Operating System has its own conventions and naming conventions for directories and files. Understanding the file system structure is essential for efficient data management and navigation in a computer system.

File System Implementation

File System Implementation in an Operating System refers to the process of creating and managing the data structures, algorithms, and mechanisms necessary to organize and access files and directories on storage devices. The implementation of a file system is a complex task that involves various components and considerations. Here are the key aspects of file system implementation:

Data Structures: File Systems use Data Structures to represent files, directories, and their associated attributes. Common data structures include I node structures (used in Unixlike file systems) and file control blocks (used in FAT file systems). These structures store metadata such as file size, permissions, timestamps, and pointers to data blocks.

Allocation Methods: File systems must allocate storage space on storage devices for files and directories. Common allocation methods include:

Contiguous Allocation: Files are stored as contiguous blocks on the storage medium. This method offers simple access but can lead to fragmentation.

Linked Allocation: Each block contains a pointer to the next block in the file. This method eliminates fragmentation but can be inefficient for random access.

Indexed Allocation: An index block contains pointers to data blocks. This method allows for efficient random access but may require extra space for the index.

Cluster Allocation: Used in FAT file systems, clusters are groups of blocks that are allocated together, reducing fragmentation and enabling efficient file access.

Directory Structure: The File System must maintain a Directory Structure to organize and locate files and directories. Directories typically contain entries with filenames and pointers to their respective I nodes or file control blocks.

File Operations: The implementation of File System Operations (e.g., create, read, write, delete) requires functions or System Calls to manipulate files and directories. These operations interact with data structures and storage allocation methods to manage data on storage devices.

File System Utilities: The Operating System provides utilities and commands for users to interact with the file system, such as creating, copying, moving, renaming, and deleting files and directories.

Access Control: File Systems implement access control mechanisms to ensure that only authorized users and processes can access and modify files and directories. This includes permissions, ownership, and ACLs (Access Control Lists).

File System Drivers: Operating Systems typically include file system drivers that communicate with storage devices and manage data transfer between the file system and storage media. These drivers handle lowlevel I/O operations and ensure data integrity.

Error Handling and Recovery: File Systems must incorporate error detection and recovery mechanisms to handle issues such as disk errors, power failures, and crashes. Journaling file systems, like ext4 and NTFS, maintain transaction logs to facilitate recovery.

File System Maintenance: Regular maintenance is required to optimize file system performance and prevent issues like fragmentation. Defragmentation tools may be provided to reorganize data blocks on the storage medium.

File System Security: Implementing security measures to protect data integrity and confidentiality is crucial. This includes encryption, secure deletion, and access control.

File System Features: Different file systems offer various features, such as snapshots, compression, deduplication, and quotas. Implementing these features requires additional complexity in the file system design.

File System Compatibility: Some Operating Systems support multiple file system types. Implementing compatibility layers or translators allows different file systems to coexist on the same storage device.

File System Optimization: File Systems may employ optimization techniques, such as caching, pre-fetching, and readahead, to enhance performance and minimize I/O operations.

File System implementation is a critical part of an Operating System, as it directly impacts data organization, access speed, data integrity, and overall system performance. Different Operating Systems use different file systems, each tailored to meet specific requirements and use cases, from highperformance servers to embedded devices.

Directory and Disk Structure

Directory and Disk Structures are fundamental components of an Operating System's file system, responsible for organizing and managing files and directories on storage devices, such as hard drives and SSDs. These structures play a crucial role in data storage, retrieval, and organization. Here's an overview of directory and disk structures:

Directory Structure:

Root Directory: The root directory is the top-level directory in a file system hierarchy. It serves as the starting point for all file and directory navigation. In Unixlike Operating Systems, it is represented by a forward slash (/), while in Windows, it is represented by a backslash (\).

Directories (Folders): Directories are containers used to group and organize files and other directories. They form a hierarchical treelike structure, with each directory having a parent directory and potentially containing one or more subdirectories.

Subdirectories: Subdirectories are directories located within other directories. They allow for the organization of files and directories into a structured hierarchy. Subdirectories can, in turn, contain their own files and subdirectories.

Directory Names: Directory names are used to uniquely identify directories within the file system. These names are part of the file system's path, allowing users and applications to navigate to specific directories.

Directory Operations: Operating Systems provide a set of directory operations, including creating directories, deleting directories, renaming directories, and listing the contents of directories.

Path Names: Path names are used to specify the location of a file or directory within the directory structure. There are two types of path names: absolute paths (starting from the root directory) and relative paths (specified with respect to the current working directory).

Directory Access Control: Directory Access Control mechanisms determine who can read, write, create, delete, or modify files and subdirectories within a directory. Permissions are typically set for the directory itself and may apply recursively to its contents.

Disk Structure:

Partitioning: Storage devices, such as hard drives, can be divided into partitions. Each partition is treated as a separate logical storage unit with its own file system. Partitioning allows for better organization and management of data.

File System: A File System is a method of organizing and managing files and directories on a storage device. Common file system types include NTFS, FAT, ext4, HFS+, and more. Each file system has its own structure and features.

Boot Sector (Master Boot Record MBR or GUID Partition Table GPT): The boot sector contains essential information about the disk and the file system. It includes the partition table, bootloader code, and other metadata required for the disk to be bootable.

File System Metadata: File Systems maintain metadata about files and directories, including information about file size, permissions, timestamps, and file allocation. This metadata is stored in data structures like I nodes (Unixlike file systems) or file control blocks (FAT file systems).

File Allocation Methods: Different file systems use various methods to allocate space on the storage device for files. Common methods include contiguous allocation, linked allocation, indexed allocation, and cluster allocation (used in FAT file systems).

File System Journal: Some file systems implement journaling to record changes made to the file system. Journaling helps maintain file system consistency and recover from crashes or power failures.

Disk Blocks/Clusters: Data on the storage device is organized into blocks or clusters, each with a fixed size. These blocks or clusters are the smallest units of data storage and retrieval.

Free Space Management: File systems keep track of available free space on the disk. This information is crucial for efficient file allocation and preventing disk fragmentation.

Directory and Disk Structures work together to provide a hierarchical organization for files and directories within a file system while managing the storage space and optimizing data access on the underlying storage device. The specific structures and mechanisms used may vary depending on the file system type and the Operating System in use.

File Security and Permissions

File Security and Permissions in an Operating System are crucial mechanisms for controlling access to files and directories, ensuring data integrity, and protecting sensitive information. They define who can perform specific actions on files and directories, such as reading, writing, executing, or modifying them. Here's an overview of file security and permissions:

Access Control List (ACL): ACLs are an extension to standard Unix/Linux file permissions. They provide finegrained control over file and directory access by allowing administrators to define multiple users and groups with varying levels of access. Windows Operating Systems often use ACLs extensively.

Ownership: Every file and directory in an Operating System has an owner. The owner is typically the user who created the file or directory. Ownership can be changed by a superuser (e.g., root in Unixlike systems) or the current owner.

User Permissions: File systems typically assign three types of permissions to each file or directory for the owner:

Read Permission: Allows the owner to view the contents of a file or list the contents of a directory.

Write Permission: Allows the owner to modify the file's contents or create/delete files within a directory.

Execute Permission: For files, it allows the owner to execute the file as a program. For directories, it allows the owner to access and list the contents of the directory.

Group Permissions: Files and directories can be associated with one or more groups, and permissions can be set for each group. Group permissions often mirror user permissions, including read, write, and execute.

Other (World) Permissions: Permissions can also be set for all other users who are not the owner or part of the group. These permissions are sometimes referred to as "world" permissions.

Numeric Permissions: Some systems represent permissions as numeric values, with each digit representing a set of permissions (e.g., 644 for read and write permissions for the owner and readonly permissions for others). Numeric permissions provide a more compact representation.

Superuser (Root): The superuser, often referred to as "root" in Unixlike systems, has full control over the file system. Root can read, write, execute, or modify any file or directory, regardless of its permissions.

Access Control Matrix (ACM): An ACM is a comprehensive table that lists users, objects (files or directories), and the permissions associated with each user's access to each object. ACMs are used in access control systems to define and manage access rights.

Special Permissions:

SetUID: When a program has the setUID permission, it runs with the privileges of the file's owner, not the user executing it. This is often used for system utilities that require elevated privileges.

SetGID: Similar to setUID but applies to groups. When a program has the setGID permission, it runs with the group's privileges rather than the user's.

Sticky Bit: When the sticky bit is set on a directory, only the owner of a file within that directory can delete or rename that file. This is commonly used on shared directories (e.g., /tmp).
Effective Permissions: The actual permissions a user has for a file or directory are determined by a combination of their individual permissions, group permissions, and other permissions. Effective permissions are calculated based on the most restrictive set of permissions.

File Security and Permissions are essential for maintaining the confidentiality, integrity, and availability of data in a multiuser Operating System environment. Properly configuring permissions ensures that sensitive data is protected from unauthorized access, modification, or deletion while allowing legitimate users to perform their tasks. It's crucial for administrators to understand and manage these permissions effectively to maintain system security.

Previous Years Solved Questions

Q 1. Explain Directory File System. (RU BCA 2022)
Ans:A Directory File System, also known as a hierarchical file system, is a method of organizing and structuring files and folders within a computer's storage system. It is the most common approach used in modern Operating Systems like Windows, Linux, and macOS.
In a Directory File System:
Hierarchy: Files and folders are organized in a tree-like structure, where each folder (or directory) can contain both files and subfolders. This hierarchical organization allows for easy navigation and management of data.
Directories: Directories serve as containers for files and subdirectories. They provide a way to group related files and folders together. Directories can also be nested within other directories, creating a parent-child relationship.
Paths: Files and directories are identified by their paths, which specify their location within the directory tree. Paths consist of a series of directory names, separated by slashes (e.g., "C:\Users\John\Documents" in Windows or "/home/john/documents" in Linux).
Navigation: Users can navigate through the directory structure using commands like "cd" (change directory) in command-line interfaces or by clicking through folders in graphical file managers.
Organization: Directory systems help users organize their data logically, making it easier to find and manage files. They also enable access control and permissions to restrict or grant access to specific files and folders.

Directory File Systems are fundamental to modern computing, as they provide an efficient and organized way to store, access, and manage digital information on a computer or network. Different Operating Systems may use varying directory structures and naming conventions, but the underlying concept of hierarchical organization remains consistent.

Q 2. Explain the various file types operations? (RU BCA 2019)

Ans: File operations refer to the actions performed on files in a computer system. There are several types of file operations, each serving different purposes and functionalities. Here's an explanation of various file types operations:

Open: The Open operation is used to open an existing file or create a new file, if it does not exist. When a file is opened, the Operating System allocates resources and establishes a connection between the file and the executing program, allowing subsequent read and write operations.

Close: The Close operation is used to close an opened file and release the associated resources. Closing a file ensures that all pending write operations are completed and that the file is no longer accessible to the program.

Read: The Read operation is used to retrieve data from an opened file. It reads a specified number of bytes from the file and stores them in a buffer or memory location provided by the program.

Write: The Write operation is used to write data to an opened file. It writes a specified number of bytes from a buffer or memory location provided by the program to the file, overwriting existing data if necessary.

Append: The Append operation is used to add new data to the end of an existing file. It positions the file pointer at the end of the file and writes the specified data, effectively extending the file size.

Seek: The Seek operation is used to move the file pointer to a specific position within the file. It allows random access to different parts of the file, enabling efficient read and write operations at specific locations.

Delete: The Delete operation is used to remove an existing file from the file system. Once deleted, the file is permanently removed from the storage device and cannot be recovered.

Rename: The Rename operation is used to change the name of an existing file. It updates the file's metadata to reflect the new name while preserving its content and attributes.

Copy: The Copy operation is used to create a duplicate copy of an existing file. It reads the contents of the original file and writes them to a new file with a different name or location.

Move: The Move operation is used to relocate an existing file from one location to another within the file system. It updates the file's metadata to reflect the new location while preserving its content and attributes.

These file operations provide essential functionalities for managing files and interacting with the file system in a computer environment. They enable programs to create, read, write, and manipulate files according to the application's requirements.

Previous Years Unsolved Questions

Q 1. Describe the following methods for allocating disk space: (IGNOU Jan 2015)

Linked Allocation

Contiguous Allocation.

Exercise

Exercise 1 – MCQ

1. What is a file in the context of an Operating System?

a) A hardware component for data storage

b) A collection of directories

c) A logical unit for storing and organizing data

d) A system process for file management

2. Which of the following is not a file access method?

a) Sequential access

b) Direct access

c) Random access

d) Circular access

3. Which of the following is not a basic file operation in an Operating System?

a) Read

b) Write

c) Copy

d) Execute

4. What is the purpose of the "rename" file operation in an Operating System?

a) To change the content of a file

b) To delete a file

c) To change the name or location of a file

d) To create a new file

5. What is the purpose of the "File Control Block (FCB)" in the file system structure?

a) It contains information about the file, such as its name and type.

b) It is a data structure used by the file system to manage files.

c) It is a hardware component responsible for file storage.

d) It is used for file encryption and security.

6. In a hierarchical file system structure, which component is responsible for grouping files into directories?

a) File Allocation Table (FAT)

b) Inode

c) Directory Entry

d) Superblock

7. What is the purpose of a file allocation table (FAT) in file system implementation?

a) To store the actual data of files

b) To track the allocation status of disk blocks

c) To manage file permissions

d) To store file metadata

8. In file system implementation, what role does a journaling file system play?

a) It provides a log of file accesses for auditing purposes.

b) It ensures that all changes to the file system are recorded before they are applied, improving consistency.

c) It compresses files to save storage space.

d) It encrypts file data for security.

9. What is the purpose of a File Control Block (FCB) in the context of directories in an Operating System?

a) It contains information about the file, such as its name and type.

b) It is used for file encryption and security.

c) It is a data structure that manages the directory structure.

d) It stores the actual data of files.

10. What is the primary function of the Master File Table (MFT) in NTFS (New Technology File System)?

a) To store the actual data of files

b) To manage file permissions

c) To track the allocation status of disk blocks

d) To maintain metadata about all files and directories on a volume

Exercise 2 – True/ False

1. In Unix-like Operating Systems, everything is considered a file.

2. File systems are responsible for managing both the physical and logical aspects of data storage on a computer.

3. The "seek" operation in file handling is used to position the file pointer to a specific location within the file.

4. File operations, such as reading and writing, are performed using System Calls provided by the Operating System.

5. In a file system, the Inode contains metadata about a file, such as its permissions, size, and ownership.

6. A Superblock in a file system structure is responsible for maintaining the mapping between logical and physical block addresses.

7. The concept of "inode" is typically associated with file systems that use index nodes to store file metadata.

8. Fragmentation is a common issue in file system implementation, leading to inefficient disk space utilization.

9. In a file system, a hard link allows a file to exist in multiple directories simultaneously.

10. Disk formatting is the process of creating a file system on a disk, and it erases all data on the disk.

Exercise 3 – Fill in the blanks

1. In a file system, the ___________ is a hierarchical structure that organizes files and subdirectories.

2. A ____________ is a contiguous block of data on a disk, and it is the smallest unit that can be read or written.

Exercise 4 – Match case

Column A

1. Create
2. Read
3. Write
4. Delete
5. Append

Column B

A. Allows the creation of a new file.

B. Retrieves data from an existing file.

C. Modifies the content of an existing file.

D. Permits the removal of a file from the file system.

E. Adds data to the end of an existing file.

Exercise 5 –One-word

1.What are file permissions in an Operating System, and how do they contribute to file security?

2. What is the term for a region of disk space used to temporarily store data that doesn't fit in physical RAM?

Exercise 6 – Small answer

1.What is the primary goal of memory hierarchy in an Operating System?

2.What is a file in the context of an Operating System, and how does it differ from a directory?

Exercise 7 – Long answer

1.Can you explain the importance of directory and disk structure in an Operating System, detailing how they organize and manage files and data on storage devices?

2.How do file security and permissions work in an Operating System, and what mechanisms are in place to control and protect access to files and directories?

Answer

Exercise 1 – MCQ

Ans: 1 c, 2 d, 3 c, 4 c, 5 b, 6 c, 7 b, 8 b, 9 a, 10 d

Exercise 2 – True/False

Ans: 1 True, 2 True, 3 True, 4 True, 5 True, 6 False, 7 True, 8 True, 9 True, 10 True

Exercise 3 – Fill in The Blanks

Ans: 1directory, 2 sector

Exercise 4 – Match Case

Ans: 1 c, 2 d,3 e, 4 a, 5 b

Exercise 4 – One-word

Ans: 1 Efficiency, 2 Swap

Online Resources

Videos:

MCQ Link:https://youtu.be/yMnx89ob5DY

QR Code:

True/False Link:https://youtu.be/ams0Mgbi1rA

QR Code:

Online Test Paper: https://forms.office.com/r/B1an8u7vbK

QR Code:

Chapter 6 I/O Systems

I/O Hardware

I/O (Input/Output) hardware in an Operating System plays a critical role in facilitating communication between the computer's central processing unit (CPU) and external devices. I/O hardware includes various components and devices that allow data to be transferred into and out of the computer system. Here are some key components and aspects of I/O hardware:

Input Devices:

Keyboards: Keyboards are one of the most common input devices. They allow users to enter text, commands, and other data into the computer.

Mice and Pointing Devices: Mice, touchpads, and other pointing devices provide a graphical interface for users to interact with the computer's graphical user interface (GUI).

Scanners: Scanners are used to convert physical documents or images into digital format.

Barcode Readers: Barcode readers are used to scan and interpret barcodes, commonly found on products and inventory items.

B. Output Devices:

Monitors and Displays: Monitors and displays are used to present visual information to users. This includes text, graphics, images, and video.

Printers: Printers produce hard copies of documents and graphics on paper or other media.

Speakers and Audio Output: Speakers provide audio output, allowing users to hear sound, music, and other audio content.

Projectors: Projectors are used to display computergenerated content on larger screens or surfaces.

Storage Devices:

Hard Disk Drives (HDDs): HDDs are used for longterm storage of data, software, and Operating Systems.

SolidState Drives (SSDs): SSDs provide highspeed storage and are commonly used for improving system performance.

Optical Drives: Optical drives, such as CD/DVD drives, are used for reading and writing optical discs.

USB Drives and Memory Cards: These portable storage devices are used for data transfer and backup.

Network Interfaces:

Network Interface Cards (NICs): NICs enable computers to connect to local area networks (LANs) and the internet. They support wired (Ethernet) and wireless (WiFi) connections.

Modems: Modems are used for connecting to the internet over telephone lines (DSL or dialup) or cable (cable modems).

Human Interface Devices (HID):

Game Controllers: Game controllers are used for gaming and interactive applications.

Webcams: Webcams capture video for video conferencing, streaming, and recording.

Microphones: Microphones capture audio input for voice recognition, audio recording, and communication.

Storage Controllers:

Disk Controllers: Disk controllers manage the read and write operations between the CPU and storage devices (HDDs and SSDs).

RAID Controllers: RAID controllers enable data redundancy and performance improvement through RAID configurations.

I/O Ports and Interfaces:

USB Ports: Universal Serial Bus (USB) ports are versatile interfaces used for connecting a wide range of devices, including keyboards, mice, printers, and storage devices.

FireWire (IEEE 1394): FireWire ports are used for highspeed data transfer, particularly in audio and video applications.

Serial and Parallel Ports: These older interfaces were used for connecting devices like serial printers and external modems.

PCIe Slots: Peripheral Component Interconnect Express (PCIe) slots are used for adding expansion cards, such as graphics cards, network cards, and storage controllers.

Interrupt Controllers:

Interrupt controllers manage hardware interrupts generated by I/O devices. They ensure that the CPU responds to important events, such as keyboard input or data arriving from a network card.

DMA (Direct Memory Access) Controllers:

DMA controllers allow I/O devices to transfer data directly to and from memory without CPU intervention, enhancing data transfer efficiency.

BIOS and Device Drivers:

The BIOS (Basic Input/output System) and device drivers provide the necessary software interfaces to communicate with and control I/O hardware.

Operating Systems manage I/O hardware by providing device drivers, interrupt handling, and I/O scheduling mechanisms. They ensure efficient and orderly data transfer between applications and I/O devices, allowing users to interact with computers and external devices seamlessly.

Principles of I/O Software

I/O (Input/Output) software in an Operating System is responsible for managing the communication between applications or processes and I/O devices such as keyboards, displays, disks, network interfaces, and more. It plays a critical role in providing a reliable and efficient interface for I/O operations. The principles of I/O software in an Operating System include:

Device Independence: I/O software abstracts the details of specific I/O devices, making it possible for applications to interact with devices without needing to know their specific characteristics. This abstraction allows applications to be deviceindependent, simplifying the development and portability of software.

Uniform Interface: I/O software provides a uniform and consistent interface for accessing various types of devices. This uniformity allows applications to use a standard set of I/O functions (e.g., read(), write()) regardless of the underlying hardware.

Buffering: To improve I/O efficiency, I/O software often employs buffering mechanisms. Data is read from or written to memory buffers before being transferred to or from devices. Buffering reduces the number of I/O operations and minimizes the impact of device latency.

Caching: Caching involves temporarily storing frequently accessed data in memory to reduce the need for repeated I/O operations. Caches can be implemented at various levels, including file system caching and application level caching.

Concurrency Control: I/O software must handle multiple I/O requests from different processes or threads concurrently. Concurrency control mechanisms ensure that data remains consistent and that concurrent access does not lead to conflicts.

Error Handling: Robust Error Handling is crucial in I/O software to handle device failures, data corruption, and other unexpected issues. Error codes, exception handling, and recovery mechanisms are used to manage errors gracefully.

Asynchronous I/O: Asynchronous I/O allows applications to initiate an I/O operation and continue executing other tasks without waiting for the operation to complete. Call-backs or notifications are used to inform the application when the I/O operation is finished.

I/O Synchronization: I/O software provides Synchronization Mechanisms to ensure data consistency and prevent race conditions when multiple processes or threads access the same device or file simultaneously.

I/O Request Queues: Many Operating Systems use queues to manage I/O requests. I/O Request Queues allow the Operating System to schedule and prioritize pending I/O requests, optimizing device utilization and reducing contention.

File System Abstraction: I/O software includes file system components that abstract the organization of files and directories, providing a logical structure for data storage and retrieval. The file system manages file metadata, permissions, and access control.

Device Drivers: Device drivers are specialized software components responsible for interfacing with specific hardware devices. They translate higher level I/O requests into device specific commands and handle low level device operations.

I/O Scheduling: In systems with multiple I/O devices or heavy I/O workloads, I/O scheduling algorithms determine the order in which I/O requests are serviced. These algorithms aim to minimize response times, maximize throughput, and ensure fair access to resources.

J. Power Management: Modern Operating Systems include power management features that allow the system to conserve energy by controlling the power state of I/O devices when they are not in use.

Security: I/O software enforces security policies and access control mechanisms to protect sensitive data and prevent unauthorized access to I/O devices and files.

Logging and Monitoring: I/O operations and device status are often logged for diagnostic and auditing purposes. Monitoring tools can provide insights into I/O performance and system health.

Effective I/O software design and implementation are critical for achieving optimal system performance, reliability, and usability while providing a seamless interface between applications and a wide range of I/O devices.

Disk Structure and Management

Disk Structure and Management in an Operating System are essential for efficient and reliable storage of data on hard disk drives (HDDs) and solid-state drives (SSDs). The disk structure refers to how data is organized and stored on these storage devices, while disk management encompasses various tasks related to disk maintenance, optimization, and data protection.

Here are key aspects of disk structure and management:

Disk Partitioning:

Partition: A Partition is a logically isolated section of a disk that appears as a separate storage unit. Disk partitioning divides a physical disk into multiple partitions, each with its file system.

Primary and Extended Partitions: Disk Partitions can be primary (limited to four per disk) or extended, with extended partitions further divided into logical partitions.

Master Boot Record (MBR) and GUID Partition Table (GPT): These are two common methods used to manage disk partitions and boot information. GPT is more modern and supports larger disk sizes and more partitions.

File Systems:

File System: A File System defines how data is organized and stored on a disk, including file structures, metadata, and access methods.

Common File Systems: Popular File Systems include NTFS (Windows), ext4 (Linux), HFS+ (macOS), and FAT32 (cross platform).

Formatting: Formatting creates a file system on a partition, preparing it for data storage. Quick and full formats differ in terms of data erasure and time taken.

Disk Structures:

Clusters or Blocks: Data on disks is organized into clusters (FAT file systems) or blocks (ext4, NTFS). These are the smallest units of storage allocation.

File Allocation Table (FAT): Used in older Windows systems (e.g., FAT16, FAT32) to manage file allocation.

Inode Structure: Used in Unix like systems (e.g., ext4) to store metadata and pointers to data blocks.

Disk Optimization:

Defragmentation: Defragmentation rearranges fragmented data on a disk to improve data access times. It is more relevant to HDDs than SSDs.

Trim: SSDs use trim commands to mark unused data blocks as available for new data, which helps maintain performance.

Disk Management:

Partition Resizing: Disk Management tools allow users to resize partitions, creating new ones or expanding existing ones.

Disk Cloning: Cloning tools replicate the contents of one disk to another, useful for backup and migration.

Bad Sector Handling: Disk utilities can mark bad sectors as unusable to prevent data corruption.

RAID (Redundant Array of Independent Disks):

RAID Levels: RAID configurations provide redundancy and performance improvements. Common levels include RAID 0 (striping), RAID 1 (mirroring), and RAID 5 (striping with parity).

HotSwapping: Some RAID configurations support hot swappable disks for easy replacement without shutting down the system.

Disk Encryption:

Full Disk Encryption (FDE): FDE encrypts the entire disk to protect data from unauthorized access. BitLocker (Windows), File Vault (macOS), and LUKS (Linux) are examples.

File Level Encryption: This approach encrypts individual files or directories rather than the entire disk.

H. Disk Monitoring and SMART (Self-Monitoring, Analysis, and Reporting Technology):

SMART: SMART is a technology that monitors a disk's health and predicts potential failures.

Monitoring Tools: Operating Systems and third-party tools provide disk monitoring and diagnostic utilities.

Disk Backup and Recovery:

Backup: Regular data backup is essential for data protection. Backup tools and strategies include full backups, incremental backups, and differential backups.

Recovery: Disk recovery tools help retrieve data from damaged or corrupted disks.

Effective Disk Structure and Management are critical for maintaining data integrity, optimizing storage performance, and ensuring the reliability of storage devices. Proper disk management practices can help prevent data loss and enhance overall system stability.

Disk Scheduling Algorithms

Disk Scheduling Algorithms are essential in an Operating System to determine the order in which pending disk I/O requests are serviced. The goal of these algorithms is to minimize disk head movement, reduce seek time, and optimize disk I/O performance.Disk Scheduling Algorithms are used in Operating Systems to determine the order in which pending disk I/O requests are serviced to optimize data access on a storage device. These algorithms aim to minimize seek time and maximize disk throughput. Common algorithms include FCFS (FirstComeFirstServed), SSTF (Shortest Seek Time First), SCAN (Elevator), CSCAN (Circular SCAN), LOOK, and CLOOK. FCFS services requests in the order they arrive, while SSTF prioritizes the closest request. SCAN and CSCAN move the disk arm in one direction, servicing requests along the way, while LOOK and CLOOK adjust their direction based on pending requests. These algorithms help improve disk I/O efficiency in multitasking environments. Here are some commonly used disk scheduling algorithms:

First Come, FirstServed (FCFS):

In FCFS, the I/O requests are serviced in the order they arrive in the request queue. It's simple to implement, but can lead to poor performance, especially if there is a mix of short and long seeks.First Come, First Served (FCFS) is one of the simplest and most intuitive scheduling algorithms used in Operating Systems to manage the execution of processes or tasks in a queue. In FCFS, the process that arrives first is the one that gets executed first. It operates on a firstcome, firstserved basis, just like people waiting in line. Here's an explanation of FCFS with an example:

Example Scenario:

Imagine there are three processes, P1, P2, and P3, that need to be executed by a CPU. These processes arrive in the order P1, P2, and P3. Each process has a specified burst time, which represents how long it needs to execute.

P1 arrives with a burst time of 6 milliseconds.

P2 arrives with a burst time of 4 milliseconds.

P3 arrives with a burst time of 8 milliseconds.

Execution Steps:

Initial State: The CPU is idle.

Execution of P1: Since P1 arrives first, it is allocated the CPU and allowed to execute for its entire burst time of 6 milliseconds.

Execution: P1 (6 ms)

Execution of P2: After P1 completes, P2 is the next process in the queue. It is allocated the CPU and allowed to execute for its entire burst time of 4 milliseconds.

Execution: P1 (6 ms) > P2 (4 ms)

Execution of P3: Finally, after P2 finishes, P3 is the last process in the queue. It is allocated the CPU and allowed to execute for its entire burst time of 8 milliseconds.

Execution: P1 (6 ms) > P2 (4 ms) > P3 (8 ms)

Completion:

Once all processes have executed, the execution sequence in this FCFS example is P1, P2, and P3.

FCFS (Example)

Process	Duration	Oder	Arrival Time
P1	24	1	0
P2	3	2	0
P3	4	3	0

Gantt Chart :

P1 waiting time: 0

P2 waiting time: 24

P3 waiting time: 27

The Average waiting time:

(0+24+27)/3 = 17

Advantages and Disadvantages:

Advantages: FCFS is simple to understand and implement, and it ensures fairness by serving processes in the order they arrive.

Disadvantages: FCFS can suffer from the "convoy effect," where a long process at the front of the queue can delay the execution of shorter processes behind it, potentially leading to inefficient CPU utilization. While FCFS is easy to implement, it may not always be the most efficient scheduling algorithm, especially in scenarios where shorter processes are delayed by longer ones. Other scheduling algorithms, like Shortest Job First (SJF) or Round Robin, address some of FCFS's limitations by considering the execution time of processes.

Shortest Seek Time First (SSTF):

SSTF selects the I/O request that is closest to the current position of the disk's read/write head. It minimizes seek time and is effective in reducing head movement. However, it can lead to starvation of requests that are farther from the current position.

Shortest Seek Time First (SSTF) is a disk scheduling algorithm used in Operating Systems to reduce the seek time when reading or writing data on a disk drive. SSTF selects the I/O request with the shortest seek time (the request that requires the least movement of the disk's read/write head) from the queue of pending requests. This algorithm aims to minimize the time it takes to access data on the disk by prioritizing requests that are physically closer to the current position of the disk head.

QUEUE: 98, 183, 40, 122, 10, 124, 65 HEAD START AT 53 & moves in RIGHT Direction

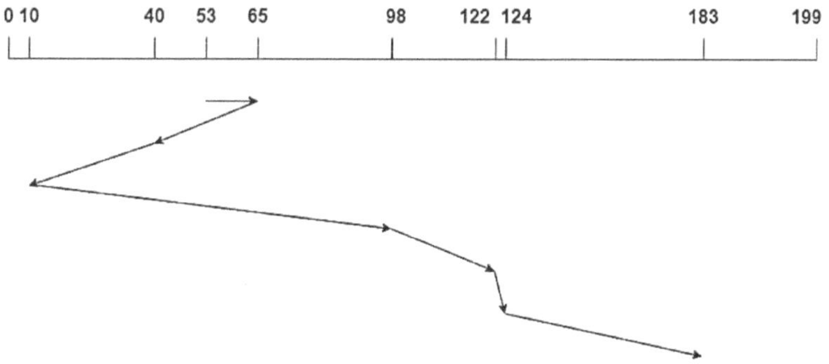

Example Scenario:

Consider a disk with multiple tracks numbered from 0 to 199. The disk read/write head is initially positioned at track 50. There are several pending I/O requests in the queue, each specifying the track number to read from or write to:

Request A: Track 85

Request B: Track 40

Request C: Track 10

Request D: Track 60

Request E: Track 110

Execution Steps:

Initial State: The disk head is at track 50.

Selecting the First Request: Initially, there are multiple pending requests. SSTF selects the request with the shortest seek time from the current head position. In this case, the closest track is track 60 (Request D).

Execution: Request D (Track 60)

Moving the Head: After servicing Request D, the disk head moves to track 60.

Selecting the Next Request: With the disk head at track 60, the next closest request is track 40 (Request B).

Execution: Request D (Track 60) > Request B (Track 40)

Moving the Head: After servicing Request B, the disk head moves to track 40.

Selecting the Next Request: Now, the closest request is track 10 (Request C).

Execution: Request D (Track 60) > Request B (Track 40) > Request C (Track 10)

Moving the Head: After servicing Request C, the disk head moves to track 10.

Selecting the Next Request: The closest request is track 85 (Request A).

Execution: Request D (Track 60) > Request B (Track 40) > Request C (Track 10) > Request A (Track 85)

Moving the Head: After servicing Request A, the disk head moves to track 85.

Selecting the Final Request: The last request remaining is track 110 (Request E).

Execution: Request D (Track 60) > Request B (Track 40) > Request C (Track 10) > Request A (Track 85) > Request E (Track 110)

Completion:

All requests have been serviced in the order: D, B, C, A, E. SSTF minimizes the seek time by selecting requests that require the shortest head movement, resulting in efficient disk I/O.

Advantages:

SSTF minimizes seek time and generally leads to better disk performance compared to some other scheduling algorithms.

Disadvantages:

SSTF may suffer from starvation, where requests far from the current head position are consistently delayed.

It can also experience disk arm movement oscillation if the requests are distributed in a way that causes the head to continuously move back and forth.

C. SCAN (Elevator) Algorithm:

The SCAN Algorithm works like an elevator. The read/write head starts at one end of the disk and moves towards the other end, servicing requests in its path. When it reaches the end, it reverses direction. SCAN helps prevent starvation of requests and provides relatively fair service to all requests.

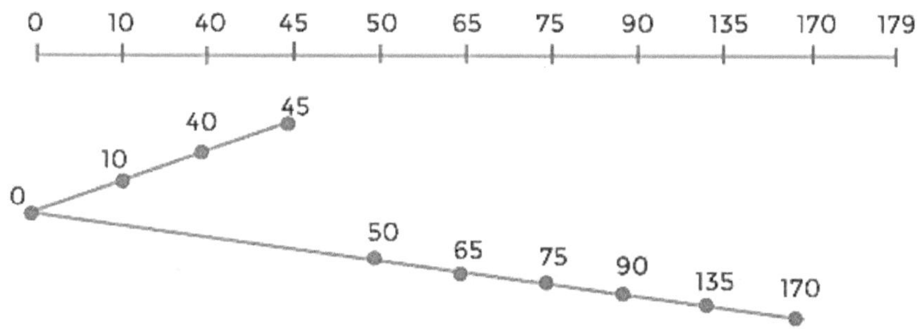

SCAN Disk Scheduling Algorithm

The SCAN Algorithm, often referred to as the "Elevator" algorithm, is a disk scheduling technique used in Operating Systems to manage the order in which I/O requests are serviced on a disk drive. It's named "Elevator" because it mimics the behavior of an elevator: it moves in one direction (up or down) until it reaches the end of the disk and then reverses its direction. SCAN aims to reduce seek time and improve disk I/O performance. Here's an explanation of the SCAN (Elevator) algorithm with an example:

Example Scenario:

Consider a disk with multiple tracks numbered from 0 to 199. The disk read/write head is initially positioned at track 100. There are several pending I/O requests in the queue, each specifying the track number to read from or write to:

Request A: Track 60

Request B: Track 110

Request C: Track 35

Request D: Track 75

Request E: Track 130

Execution Steps:

Initial State: The disk head is at track 100.

Moving in One Direction (Up): Initially, the SCAN algorithm starts by moving the disk head in one direction (upward). It services requests in the path until it reaches the end of the disk.

Execution: Head moves from track 100 to track 199, servicing requests C and D along the way.

Reaching the End of Disk: When the head reaches the end of the disk (track 199), it changes direction to move in the opposite direction (downward).

Servicing Requests in Reverse Direction: Now, the SCAN algorithm services requests in the reverse direction, moving down from track 199 to track 0.

Execution: Head moves from track 199 to track 0, servicing requests E, B, and A along the way.

Completion: All requests have been serviced in the order: C, D, E, B, A.

Advantages:

SCAN (Elevator) minimizes seek time by serving requests in a way that reduces head movement compared to some other scheduling algorithms.

It prevents starvation because eventually, all requests will be serviced.

Disadvantages:

It may lead to delays for requests that are at the extreme ends of the disk, if there are frequent requests closer to the disk's center.

SCAN can cause uneven response times for requests, as requests at the "elevator's" current location are served faster.

CSCAN Algorithm:

CSCAN is a variant of SCAN that only services requests in one direction, moving from one end of the disk to the other. Once it reaches the end, it immediately returns to the beginning without servicing requests in the reverse direction. CSCAN can be more predictable but may not be as fair as SCAN.

QUEUE: 98, 183, 40, 122, 10, 124, 65 HEAD START AT 53 & moves in RIGHT Direction

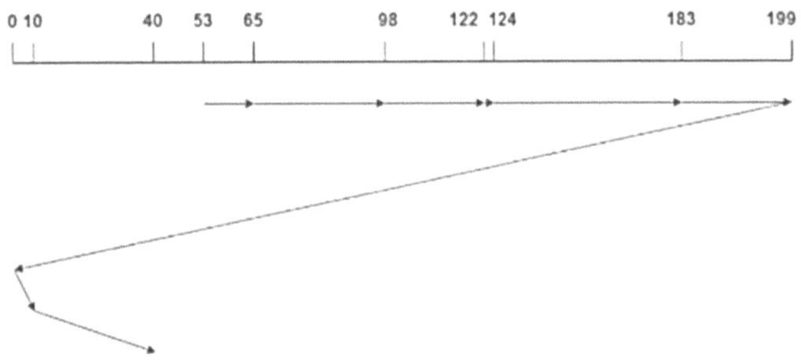

The CSCAN (Circular SCAN) Algorithm is a disk scheduling technique used in Operating Systems to manage the order in which I/O requests are serviced on a disk drive. It's an enhancement of the SCAN (Elevator) algorithm and addresses some of its limitations. CSCAN aims to reduce seek time and improve disk I/O performance by efficiently serving pending I/O requests. Here's an explanation of the CSCAN algorithm with an example:

Example Scenario:

Consider a disk with multiple tracks numbered from 0 to 199. The disk read/write head is initially positioned at track 100. There are several pending I/O requests in the queue, each specifying the track number to read from or write to:

Request A: Track 60

Request B: Track 110

Request C: Track 35

Request D: Track 75

Request E: Track 130

Execution Steps:

Initial State: The disk head is at track 100.

Moving in One Direction (Up): Initially, the CSCAN algorithm starts by moving the disk head in one direction (upward). It services requests in this direction until it reaches the end of the disk (track 199).

Execution: Head moves from track 100 to track 199, servicing request D along the way.

Reaching the End of Disk: When the head reaches the end of the disk (track 199), it doesn't reverse direction immediately, as in SCAN. Instead, it jumps to the opposite end of the disk (track 0) without servicing any requests in the reverse direction.

Moving in Reverse Direction (Down): Now, the CSCAN algorithm services requests in the reverse direction, moving down from track 0 to the original position of the disk head (track 100).

Execution: Head moves from track 0 to track 100, servicing requests E, B, C, and A along the way.

Completion: All requests have been serviced in the order: D, E, B, C, A.

Advantages:

CSCAN minimizes seek time by serving requests in a way that efficiently utilizes the disk's entire surface without excessively favouring either end.

It prevents starvation because eventually, all requests will be serviced.

Disadvantages:

Like SCAN, CSCAN can cause uneven response times for requests, as requests near the current position of the head are served faster.

Requests near the outer or inner edge of the disk may experience longer delays, if there are frequent requests closer to the disk's center.

LOOK Algorithm:

LOOK is similar to SCAN but does not go all the way to the end of the disk in each direction. Instead, it reverses direction when there are no more requests in the current direction. This can reduce unnecessary head movement.

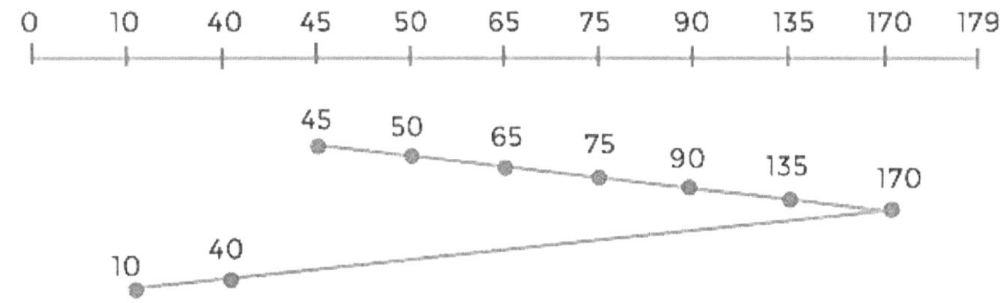

The LOOK Algorithm is a disk scheduling technique used in Operating Systems to manage the order in which I/O requests are serviced on a disk drive. LOOK is an improvement over the SCAN and CSCAN algorithms as it aims to reduce seek time while being fairer to requests that are far from the current head position. It scans the disk in both directions (up and down) but only as far as necessary to serve pending I/O requests. Here's an explanation of the LOOK algorithm with an example:

Example Scenario:

Consider a disk with multiple tracks numbered from 0 to 199. The disk read/write head is initially positioned at track 100. There are several pending I/O requests in the queue, each specifying the track number to read from or write to:

Request A: Track 60

Request B: Track 110

Request C: Track 35

Request D: Track 75

Request E: Track 130

Execution Steps:

Initial State: The disk head is at track 100.

Moving in One Direction (Up): The LOOK algorithm starts by moving the disk head in one direction (upward) to look for requests in that direction.

Execution: The head moves from track 100 to track 110 to service Request B.

Looking for Requests in Reverse Direction (Down): After servicing Request B, the LOOK algorithm reverses direction and moves the head in the opposite direction (downward) to look for requests.

Execution: The head moves from track 110 back to track 75 to service Request D and then further down to track 60 to service Request A.

Looking for Requests in Forward Direction (Up): Once all requests in the downward direction have been serviced, the LOOK algorithm reverses direction again and moves the head back up to look for any remaining requests.

Execution: The head moves from track 60 to track 35 to service Request C.

Completion: All requests have been serviced in the order: B, D, A, C, E.

Advantages:

LOOK reduces seek time by only scanning the disk as far as necessary to service pending requests, which makes it more efficient than SCAN or CSCAN in some scenarios.

It avoids the problem of favoring one end of the disk over the other, leading to more balanced performance.

Disadvantages:

LOOK, like other elevator-based algorithms, may still cause requests at the "elevator's" current location to be serviced faster, potentially leading to uneven response times for requests.

CLOOK Algorithm:

CLOOK is a variant of LOOK that only services requests in one direction, like CSCAN. It is more predictable and can reduce seek time by avoiding unnecessary movement in the reverse direction.

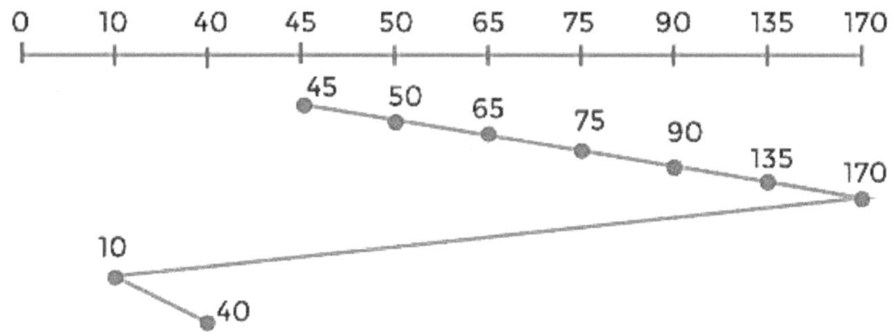

The CLOOK (Circular LOOK) algorithm is a disk scheduling technique used in Operating Systems to manage the order in which I/O requests are serviced on a disk drive. CLOOK is a variation of the LOOK algorithm and aims to reduce seek time while maintaining fairness among I/O requests. It scans the disk in both directions (up and down), but unlike LOOK, it only scans as far as necessary to serve pending I/O requests and doesn't return to the starting point of the disk. Here's an explanation of the CLOOK algorithm with an example:

Example Scenario:

Consider a disk with multiple tracks numbered from 0 to 199. The disk read/write head is initially positioned at track 100. There are several pending I/O requests in the queue, each specifying the track number to read from or write to:

Request A: Track 60

Request B: Track 110

Request C: Track 35

Request D: Track 75

Request E: Track 130

Execution Steps:

Initial State: The disk head is at track 100.

Moving in One Direction (Up): The CLOOK algorithm starts by moving the disk head in one direction (upward) to look for requests in that direction.

Execution: The head moves from track 100 to track 110 to service Request B.

Scanning Upward for Requests (No Requests Found): After servicing Request B, the CLOOK algorithm continues scanning upward for more requests. However, it finds no requests in this direction.

Returning to the Lowest Track with Requests: Since no more requests were found upward, the CLOOK algorithm immediately reverses direction and moves the head to the lowest track number containing a pending request, which is track 35.

Execution: The head moves from track 110 to track 35 to service Request C.

Scanning Downward from the Lowest Track: After servicing Request C, the CLOOK algorithm moves the head in the opposite direction (downward) to scan for requests in this direction.

Execution: The head moves from track 35 to track 60 to service Request A.

Completion: All requests have been serviced in the order: B, C, A.

Advantages:

CLOOK reduces seek time by only scanning the disk as far as necessary to service pending requests, making it more efficient than SCAN or CSCAN in some scenarios.

It maintains fairness by not favouring one end of the disk over the other.

Disadvantages:

CLOOK, like other elevator-based algorithms, may still cause requests at the current head location to be serviced faster, potentially leading to uneven response times for requests.

NStepSCAN Algorithm:

NStepSCAN is a modified version of SCAN that services a fixed number of requests in one direction before reversing direction. This can help improve fairness and reduce latency for some requests.

QUEUE: 98, 183, 40, 122, 10 , 124, 65 HEAD START AT 53 & moves in RIGHT Direction

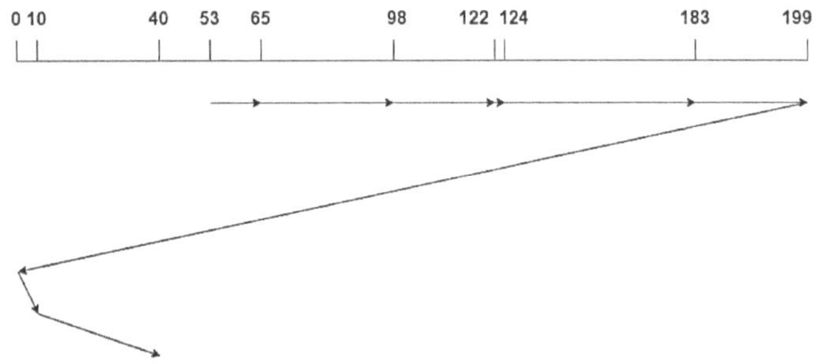

The NStep SCAN Algorithm is a disk scheduling technique used in Operating Systems to manage the order in which I/O requests are serviced on a disk drive. It is an extension of the SCAN (Elevator) algorithm, designed to mitigate some of its limitations. The "N" in NStep SCAN represents the number of tracks that the disk arm moves before changing direction. This algorithm aims to reduce seek time and improve disk I/O performance. Here's an explanation of the NStep SCAN algorithm:

Key Concepts:

Nstep Movement: Unlike traditional SCAN, which moves the disk arm continuously in one direction until it reaches the end, Nstep SCAN moves the arm in steps of "N" tracks at a time.

Execution Steps:

Initial State: The disk head is at its initial position, which is typically the track where the last I/O operation was completed.

Moving in One Direction (Upward): The Nstep SCAN algorithm starts by moving the disk head in one direction (upward) in steps of "N" tracks, looking for requests in that direction. Its services requests in each step, if they are encountered.

Checking for Requests (Upward): At each step, the algorithm checks for pending requests within the range of the current step. If a request is found within the current range, then it is serviced.

Reversing Direction: After completing the upward scan, the algorithm reverses direction and moves the disk head in the opposite direction (downward) in steps of "N," scanning for requests in that direction.

Checking for Requests (Downward): Similar to the upward scan, the algorithm checks for pending requests within the range of the current step while moving downward.

Completion: All requests have been serviced according to the Nstep SCAN algorithm's movement pattern.

Advantages:

Nstep SCAN reduces seek time by moving the disk arm in steps, allowing it to service requests efficiently in both directions.

It prevents starvation because it guarantees that all requests will eventually be serviced.

Disadvantages:

Depending on the value of "N," the algorithm may not provide the most optimal seek time reduction in all scenarios. The choice of "N" affects the trade-off between fairness and efficiency.

Requests near the current head position may still experience shorter delays than those farther away.

FSCAN Algorithm:

FSCAN maintains two request queues: one for pending requests and another for new incoming requests. It services all pending requests before moving to the new queue. This can help prioritize longpending requests.

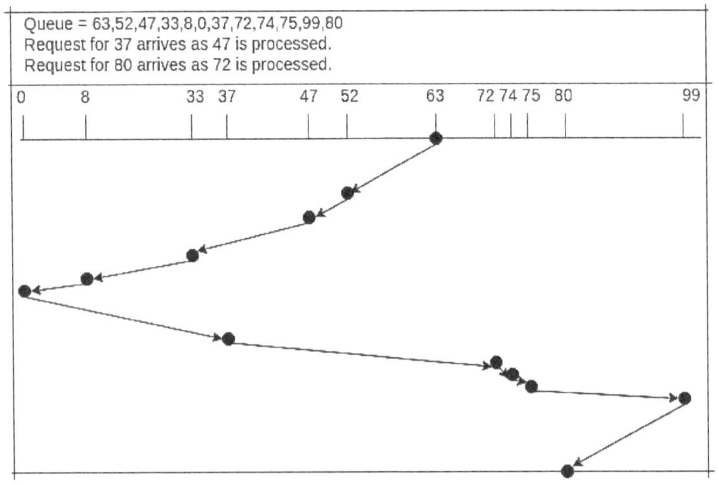

The FSCAN (Fast SCAN) Algorithm is a disk scheduling technique used in Operating Systems to manage the order in which I/O requests are serviced on a disk drive. FSCAN is designed to address some of the limitations of the SCAN and CSCAN algorithms while providing efficient disk I/O performance. It employs two separate queues for I/O requests to achieve fairness and reduce seek time. Here's an explanation of the FSCAN algorithm with an example:

Key Concepts:

Two Queues: FSCAN maintains two separate queues for I/O requests: one for pending requests and another for servicing requests. The servicing queue is empty initially.

Moving in One Direction (Up): FSCAN moves the disk arm in one direction (upward) through the pending request queue until it reaches the end of the disk.

Moving in the Reverse Direction (Down): Once the disk arm reaches the end of the disk, it reverses direction and moves downward through the pending request queue.

Example Scenario:

Consider a disk with multiple tracks numbered from 0 to 199. The disk read/write head is initially positioned at track 100. There are several pending I/O requests in the queue, each specifying the track number to read from or write to:

Request A: Track 60

Request B: Track 110

Request C: Track 35

Request D: Track 75

Request E: Track 130

Execution Steps:

Initial State: The disk head is at track 100. Both the pending request queue and servicing request queue are initially empty.

Moving in One Direction (Upward): The FSCAN algorithm starts by moving the disk head in one direction (upward) to scan through the pending request queue.

Execution: The head moves from track 100 to track 110 to service Request B.

Adding to Servicing Queue: Request B is added to the servicing request queue.

Checking for More Requests (Upward): The algorithm continues scanning upward and encounters Request D at track 75, which is also serviced.

Execution: The head moves to track 75 to service Request D.

Adding to Servicing Queue: Request D is added to the servicing request queue.

Reaching the End of Disk (Upward Scan): When the head reaches the end of the disk (track 199) during the upward scan, it reverses direction to move downward.

Moving in the Reverse Direction (Downward): The algorithm continues scanning downward, looking for pending requests. It encounters Request C at track 35, which is serviced.

Execution: The head moves to track 35 to service Request C.

Adding to Servicing Queue: Request C is added to the servicing request queue.

Checking for More Requests (Downward): The algorithm continues scanning downward and finds Request A at track 60, which is also serviced.

Execution: The head moves to track 60 to service Request A.

Adding to Servicing Queue: Request A is added to the servicing request queue.

Completion: All requests have been serviced in the order: B, D, C, A.

Advantages:

FSCAN provides fairness among requests by maintaining separate queues for pending and servicing requests.

It reduces seek time efficiently by scanning through the pending request queue in both directions.

Disadvantages:

FSCAN may still cause requests near the current head position to be serviced faster, potentially leading to uneven response times for requests. However, it mitigates this issue to some extent compared to SCAN and CSCAN.

SSTF with a Priority Queue:

In this approach, SSTF is combined with a priority queue that allows certain requests to be prioritized over others. This can be used to give higher priority to certain processes or I/O requests.

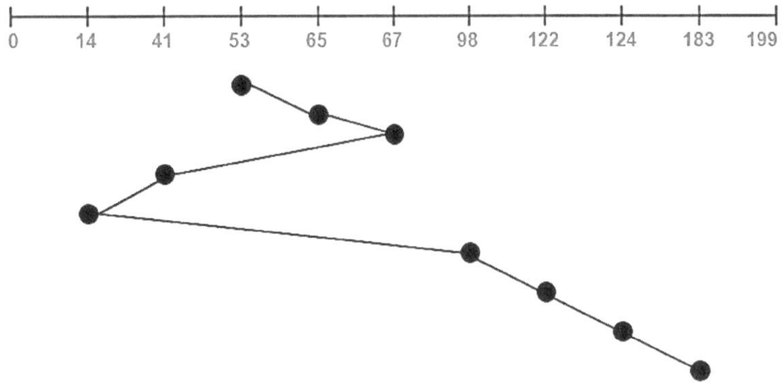

SSTF (Shortest Seek Time First) is a disk scheduling algorithm used in Operating Systems to minimize seek time when accessing data on a disk drive. It prioritizes servicing I/O requests based on the track location that requires the shortest seek time from the current position of the disk read/write head. When implementing SSTF with a priority queue, it becomes more efficient in terms of selecting the next request to be serviced.

Here's how SSTF with a Priority Queue works:

Initial State: The disk head is at a specific track, which we'll call the current position.

Building the Priority Queue:

As I/O requests arrive, each request is added to a priority queue (e.g., a minheap) based on the absolute difference between the track of the request and the current position of the disk head.

The requests in the priority queue are ordered in ascending order of seek time. In other words, the request with the shortest seek time is at the front of the queue.

Servicing Requests:

The disk scheduler selects the request at the front of the priority queue (the one with the shortest seek time) to be serviced next.

After servicing a request, the disk head moves to the track specified by that request.

Updating the Priority Queue:

After servicing a request, it is removed from the priority queue.

As new requests arrive, they are inserted into the priority queue based on their seek time, and the queue is reordered if necessary.

Repeat:

Steps 3 and 4 are repeated until all requests have been serviced.

Example:

Let's consider a simple example with four pending I/O requests and their corresponding track numbers:

Request A: Track 30

Request B: Track 60

Request C: Track 20

Request D: Track 90

Suppose the disk head is initially positioned at track 50.

Execution:

Request C (Track 20) is added to the priority queue, as it has the shortest seek time from the current head position.

The disk head moves to track 20 to service Request C.

Request C is removed from the priority queue.

Now, let's assume that new requests arrive:

Request E: Track 45

Request F: Track 70

Request A (Track 30) is added to the priority queue, as it has the shortest seek time among the remaining requests (A, B, D, E, F).

The disk head moves to track 30 to service Request A.

Request A is removed from the priority queue.

Request E (Track 45) is added to the priority queue.

The disk head moves to track 45 to service Request E.

Request E is removed from the priority queue.

Request B (Track 60) is added to the priority queue.

The disk head moves to track 60 to service Request B.

Request B is removed from the priority queue.

Request F (Track 70) is added to the priority queue.

The disk head moves to track 70 to service Request F.

Request F is removed from the priority queue.

Finally, Request D (Track 90) is added to the priority queue.

The disk head moves to track 90 to service Request D.

Request D is removed from the priority queue.

All requests have been serviced in the order: C, A, E, B, F, D, minimizing seek time.

Deadline Scheduling:

Deadline Scheduling assigns each I/O request a specific deadline by which it must be serviced. The scheduler tries to meet these deadlines while minimizing seek time. This is often used in Real-Time Systems.

The choice of disk scheduling algorithm depends on the specific workload and requirements of the system. There is no onesizefitsall solution, and different algorithms may perform better under different conditions. Some Operating Systems allow users or administrators to choose the scheduling algorithm based on their needs or provide default algorithms that work well in most scenarios.

Deadline Scheduling is a realtime scheduling algorithm used in Operating Systems to manage tasks or processes with specific timing requirements or deadlines. This scheduling algorithm is commonly employed in real-time and embedded systems, where tasks must be completed within predefined time limits to ensure the correct functioning of the system. Deadline scheduling ensures that critical tasks meet their deadlines and maintain system reliability. Here's an explanation of deadline scheduling:

Key Concepts:

Task with a Deadline: In a realtime system, each task or process is associated with a deadline, which is the time by which the task must be completed to achieve the desired functionality.

Priority Assignment: Tasks are assigned priorities based on their deadlines. Tasks with earlier or tighter deadlines typically have higher priorities.

Pre-emption: Tasks with higher priorities can pre-empt (interrupt) the execution of lower priority tasks, ensuring that higher priority tasks are executed first when they become eligible.

Scheduling Decisions: The scheduler makes scheduling decisions to ensure that tasks are executed in a way that meets their deadlines. This may involve selecting the highest priority task for execution.

Operation:

Task Arrival: When a task arrives or becomes eligible for execution, the scheduler assigns it a priority based on its deadline.

Scheduling Decision: The scheduler selects the task with the highest priority to execute. This ensures that tasks with the most imminent deadlines are executed first.

Task Execution: The selected task is allowed to run on the CPU. If a higherpriority task arrives or becomes eligible while another task is executing, then it may pre-empt the currently executing task.

Task Completion: When a task completes its execution before its deadline, it releases the CPU.

Deadline Enforcement: The scheduler monitors task execution and ensures that tasks are completed within their specified deadlines. If a task misses its deadline, then it may lead to system failures or incorrect behavior.

Example:

Consider a realtime system with three tasks:

Task A with a deadline of 10 milliseconds and priority 1.

Task B with a deadline of 15 milliseconds and priority 2.

Task C with a deadline of 5 milliseconds and priority 3.

In this scenario, Task C has the highest priority because it has the tightest deadline. Therefore, it will be executed first whenever it becomes eligible. Task A has the next highest priority, followed by Task B.

If Task C arrives and completes within its deadline, Task A will be executed, followed by Task B. The scheduler ensures that all tasks meet their deadlines, and higher priority tasks pre-empt lower priority tasks if necessary to achieve this.

Deadline Scheduling is crucial in applications where timing requirements are critical, such as aviation systems, industrial automation, and multimedia processing, where missing deadlines can result in severe consequences or degraded system performance.

I/O Device Handling

I/O (Input/Output) Device Handling in an Operating System is a critical component responsible for managing communication between the computer's CPU and various I/O devices, such as keyboards, displays, storage devices, network interfaces, and more. Effective I/O device handling ensures the efficient and reliable transfer of data between applications and hardware devices. Here are the key aspects of I/O device handling in an Operating System:

Device Drivers:

Device Driver: A Device Driver is a software component that acts as an intermediary between the Operating System and a specific hardware device. It provides a standardized interface for the Operating System to communicate with the device.

Driver Development: Device Drivers are typically developed by hardware manufacturers or third-party developers to support a wide range of hardware devices. The Operating System loads and manages these drivers.

Device Abstraction:

Device Abstraction: The Operating System provides a device abstraction layer that abstracts the hardware details of I/O devices. This abstraction allows applications to interact with devices without needing to know the specific hardware details.

Device Enumeration:

Device Enumeration: During system start-up, the Operating System enumerates and identifies connected I/O devices. This process identifies the devices and loads the appropriate device drivers.

I/O Request Handling:

I/O Request: Applications and processes submit I/O requests to the Operating System to perform read, write, or control operations on devices.

Request Queue: The Operating System maintains a request queue to manage pending I/O requests. Requests are queued based on priority and the order in which they are received.

I/O Scheduling:

When multiple I/O requests are pending for a device, the Operating System's I/O scheduler determines the order in which the requests are serviced. Scheduling algorithms optimize disk head movement and minimize latency for various devices.

Buffering:

Buffering involves using memory buffers to temporarily store data between the CPU and I/O devices. It can improve I/O performance by reducing the need for direct interaction with devices.

Direct Memory Access (DMA):

DMA: DMA is a mechanism that allows I/O devices to transfer data directly to and from memory without CPU intervention. It enhances data transfer efficiency and reduces CPU overhead.

Interrupt Handling:

Interrupt Handling: Hardware devices generate interrupts to signal the CPU when they require attention or have completed an operation. The Operating System's interrupt handling routines manage these interrupts and initiate appropriate actions.

I/O Control and Configuration:

I/O Control: The Operating System provides mechanisms for configuring and controlling I/O devices, such as setting parameters, enabling or disabling devices, and managing power states.

Plug and Play (PnP): PnP technology allows the automatic detection and configuration of newly connected hardware devices without requiring user intervention.

Error Handling:

The Operating System manages errors and exceptions that may occur during I/O operations. It provides error codes, logs, and notifications to help diagnose and resolve issues.

I/O Virtualization:

In virtualized environments, I/O virtualization technologies allow multiple virtual machines (VM's) to share and access physical I/O devices while maintaining isolation and security.

Hot Plugging:

Hot Pluggable devices can be connected or disconnected while the computer is running. The Operating System must support hotplugging and handle device addition and removal gracefully.

Power Management:

The Operating System can control the power states of I/O devices to optimize energy consumption and extend battery life in laptops and mobile devices.

Security and Access Control:

Security: The Operating System enforces access control mechanisms to prevent unauthorized access to I/O devices and data. This includes user permissions and authentication.

Effective I/O device handling is crucial for the overall performance, reliability, and usability of a computer system. Operating Systems provide a unified interface and a set of services that allow applications to interact with a wide range of I/O devices seamlessly and efficiently.

Block and Character Devices

In Operating Systems, devices are categorized into two main types: block devices and character devices. These categories describe how data is read from and written to the devices and the nature of the devices themselves.

Block Devices:

Block devices are storage devices that store and retrieve data in fixed size blocks or chunks, typically referred to as sectors or blocks. Each block has a specific size, such as 512 bytes or 4 KB. Block devices are commonly used for non-volatile storage, such as hard disk drives (HDDs), solidstate drives (SSDs), and USB drives. Here are key characteristics of block devices:

Fixed Block Size: Block devices read and write data in fixed size blocks, which are typically multiples of the sector size used by the storage medium. This allows for efficient random access to data.

Random Access: Block devices support random access, meaning that data can be read or written at any block location on the device. This is important for file systems and databases that require fast and random access to data.

Buffering: Block devices often employ buffering mechanisms, where data is temporarily stored in memory buffers before being written to or read from the device. This can improve I/O performance.

File Systems: Block devices are commonly used as the underlying storage for file systems. File systems organize data into files and directories and manage file metadata.

Examples: Hard disk drives (HDDs), solidstate drives (SSDs), USB drives, and RAID arrays are examples of block devices.

Character Devices:

Character Devices are devices that transfer data as a stream of characters or bytes, without organizing it into fixed size blocks. Character devices are typically used for devices that deal with input or output in a continuous stream, such as keyboards, mice, terminals, and serial ports. Here are key characteristics of character devices:

StreamOriented: Character devices operate in a stream-oriented fashion, where data is read and written sequentially, one character or byte at a time. There is no fixed block size.

No Buffering: Character devices may or may not use buffering. Some character devices, like keyboards and mice, often use buffering to store a small amount of input data temporarily.

Sequential Access: Data is processed in a sequential manner, and there is typically no random access to specific data locations within the device.

Examples: Keyboards, mice, serial ports, terminals (e.g., virtual terminals and terminal emulators), and audio devices are examples of character devices.

In summary, Block Devices are used for storage and are characterized by fixed size blocks, random access, and buffering, making them suitable for file systems and storage media. Character devices, on the other hand, deal with data as a stream of characters or bytes and are typically used for input or output devices where sequential data processing is more appropriate. Understanding these device types is essential for developing device drivers and interacting with hardware in an Operating System.

Previous Years Solved Questions

Q 1. What is Scheduling? (RU BCA 2022)

Ans:CPU Scheduling is a process which allows one process to use the CPU while the execution of another process is on hold (in waiting state) due to unavailability of any resource like I/O etc, thereby making full use of CPU. The aim of CPU scheduling is to make the system efficient, fast and fair.

Whenever the CPU becomes idle, the Operating System must select one of the processes in the **ready queue** to be executed. The selection process is carried out by the short-term scheduler (or CPU scheduler). The scheduler selects from among the processes in memory that are ready to execute, and allocates the CPU to one of them.

Types of CPU Scheduling:

The scheduling scheme is non-pre-emptive **otherwise the scheduling scheme is** pre-emptive.

Pre-emptive Scheduling Algorithms:

Round Robin (RR): In RR scheduling, each process is assigned a fixed time slice (time quantum) during which it can execute. After its time slice expires, the process is moved to the back of the ready queue and the next process gets the CPU. This ensures fairness but allows pre-emption.

Priority Scheduling (with Pre-emption): Priority-based scheduling assigns each process a priority, and the process with the highest priority is executed first. If a higher-priority process becomes available, then it pre-empts the currently running process.

Shortest Remaining Time First (SRTF): SRTF is a pre-emptive version of the Shortest Job First (SJF) scheduling algorithm. It selects the process with the shortest remaining execution time whenever a new process arrives or the currently running process completes.

Multilevel Queue (with Pre-emption): Multilevel queue scheduling may have queues with different priorities. Pre-emption can be allowed within the higher-priority queues, and processes can be moved between queues based on their behavior.

Multilevel Feedback Queue (with Pre-emption): This is an extension of multilevel queue scheduling, allowing pre-emption and dynamic queue assignment based on a process's behavior.

Non-Pre-emptive Scheduling Algorithms:

First-Come, First-Served (FCFS): FCFS is a non-pre-emptive scheduling algorithm where processes are executed in the order they arrive in the ready queue. Once a process starts execution, it runs until it completes or voluntarily yields the CPU.

Shortest Job First (SJF): In its non-pre-emptive form, SJF selects the process with the shortest execution time to run next, but it does not pre-empt a running process.

Priority Scheduling (without Pre-emption): In non-pre-emptive priority scheduling, the process with the highest priority is allowed to run until it finishes, without interruption from higher-priority processes.

Non-Pre-emptive Round Robin: In a non-pre-emptive variant of Round Robin, a process runs until its time quantum expires or until it voluntarily yields the CPU. It doesn't get pre-empted by other processes in the same queue.

Exponential Scheduling: This is a non-pre-emptive scheduling algorithm where processes are assigned increasing time quanta, allowing them to execute longer as they remain in the queue.

The choice between pre-emptive and non-pre-emptive scheduling depends on the specific requirements and objectives of a system. Pre-emptiveScheduling is often used in Real-Time Systems or when responsiveness is a priority, while Non-Pre-emptive Scheduling can simplify implementation and avoid context-switching overhead. The choice of a scheduling algorithm, whether pre-emptive or non-pre-emptive, depends on factors such as system characteristics, application requirements, and the desired trade-offs between fairness, throughput, and response time.

Q 2. What are pre-emptive and non-pre-emptive scheduling process? Explain the process state diagram in detail. (RTU B. Tech. Jan 2022)

Ans: Pre-emptive and Non-Pre-emptive Scheduling are two fundamental approaches to process scheduling in Operating Systems. They determine when and how the CPU is allocated to processes in a multitasking environment. Below, I explain both types of scheduling and provide a detailed explanation of the process state diagram:

Pre-emptive Scheduling:

In pre-emptive scheduling, the Operating System has the ability to forcibly interrupt the currently executing process and allocate the CPU to another process. Pre-emption occurs based on priority levels, time slices, or certain events.

Key features of Pre-emptive Scheduling:

Processes can be interrupted while running on the CPU.

The OS can switch between processes at any time, even if the currently running process has not voluntarily released the CPU.

Pre-emptive scheduling is well-suited for time-sharing systems, where multiple users or tasks require fair access to the CPU.

Common pre-emptive scheduling algorithms include Round-Robin, Priority Scheduling, and Multilevel Feedback Queue.

Non-Pre-emptive Scheduling:

In Non-pre-emptiveScheduling (also known as cooperative scheduling), processes are given control of the CPU and hold it until they explicitly release it or voluntarily yield it to the Operating System. The OS cannot forcibly interrupt a running process.

Key features of non-pre-emptive scheduling:

A process runs until it willingly gives up the CPU, enters a waiting state, or completes its execution.

Non-pre-emptive scheduling is simpler to implement and has lower context-switching overhead because processes are not frequently switched.

Non-pre-emptive scheduling is often used in Real-Time Systems, where predictability and determinism are essential.

Process State Diagram:

A Process State Diagram is a visual representation of the various states that a process can transition through during its lifetime. These states represent the current status of a process and indicate what the process is doing at a given point in time. The most common states in a process state diagram include:

New: This is the initial state when a process is first created. In this state, the process is being set up and initialized by the Operating System.

Ready: In the ready state, the process is prepared to run, but the CPU is not currently allocated to it. Processes in this state are waiting to be scheduled for execution.

Running: When a process is in the running state, it is actively executing on the CPU. Only one process can be in the running state at a time on a single CPU core.

Blocked (or Waiting): A process enters the blocked or waiting state when it cannot continue execution due to a specific event, such as waiting for I/O or a resource. The process remains in this state until the event is resolved.

Terminated: The terminated state indicates that the process has completed its execution and is being terminated. It may be removed from memory, and its resources are released.

Suspended: Some process state diagrams include a "suspended" state, which indicates that a process is temporarily removed from memory to free up resources. It can later be resumed.

Transitions between States:

Processes transition between these states based on specific events or actions. For example:

A new process transitions to the ready state once it is initialized.

A process in the ready state transitions to the running state when the CPU becomes available.

A running process can transition to the blocked state when it needs to wait for I/O.

A blocked process transitions back to the ready state when the I/O operation is complete.

A process in the running state may voluntarily yield the CPU and enter the ready state or be pre-empted by another process.

The Process State Diagram provides a clear visualization of how processes move through various states during their lifetime, which is essential for understanding process management in an Operating System and for diagnosing issues such as deadlock or thrashing.

Q 3. Explain the difference between long term, short term and medium-term schedulers. (RTU B. Tech. Jan 2022)

Ans: In Operating Systems, long-term, short-term, and medium-term schedulers are three distinct types of schedulers that play different roles in managing the execution of processes. These schedulers are responsible for various aspects of process management. Here's a breakdown of the differences between them:

Long-Term Scheduler (Job Scheduler):

Role: The long-term scheduler is responsible for selecting processes from the pool of newly created processes and deciding which processes to admit to the ready queue. It determines which processes should be brought into the system from secondary storage (such as the hard disk) to become eligible for execution.

Frequency: Long-term scheduling is infrequent compared to the other types of scheduling. It typically occurs less frequently, as it involves the selection of processes that will become part of the active process pool. This scheduler runs when the system has available resources and space for new processes.

Goal: The primary goal of the long-term scheduler is to maintain an efficient balance between process throughput and system resource utilization. It aims to keep the system fully loaded with processes but not overloaded, avoiding resource contention.

Process State: Processes in the long-term scheduler are in a "new" state, waiting to be brought into the system. They have not yet been allocated CPU time and remain on secondary storage.

Short-Term Scheduler (CPU Scheduler):

Role: The Short-Term Scheduler, also known as the CPU scheduler, is responsible for selecting the next process to execute from the pool of ready processes in main memory. It decides which process should get CPU time for a brief time slice.

Frequency: Short-term Scheduling occurs frequently, often multiple times per second. Its primary goal is to maximize CPU utilization and provide quick response times to processes in the ready queue.

Goal: The primary goal of the short-term scheduler is to efficiently allocate the CPU to processes in the ready queue, ensuring that the CPU is not idle and that processes receive fair and timely access to the CPU.

Process State: Processes in the short-term scheduler are typically in the "ready" state, indicating they are prepared to run and waiting in the ready queue for their turn to execute.

Medium-Term Scheduler:

Role: The Medium-Term Scheduler is responsible for managing processes that are in the ready queue but are not currently executing. It can temporarily remove processes from main memory and place them back in secondary storage. It is involved in swapping processes in and out of main memory.

Frequency: The medium-term scheduler operates when it becomes necessary to alleviate memory congestion or when the system faces memory constraints. This scheduler is less frequent than the short-term scheduler but more frequent than the long-term scheduler.

Goal: The primary goal of the medium-term scheduler is to manage memory efficiently. It helps control the degree of multi-programming in the system, ensuring that the available physical memory is used optimally.

Process State: Processes in the medium-term scheduler are typically in a "blocked" or "suspended" state. They are temporarily removed from main memory but can be brought back into memory when needed.

In summary, long-term, short-term, and medium-term schedulers perform distinct roles in the process management of an Operating System. The long-term scheduler admits new processes into the system, the short-term scheduler selects processes for immediate execution, and the medium-term scheduler manages processes in main memory to optimize memory usage. Each scheduler contributes to the efficient and responsive execution of processes in the Operating System.

Q 4. Explain the Layered Approach of the Operating System. (RTU B. Tech. Jan 2022)

Ans: The Layered Approach in Operating System design is a hierarchical structure or architectural model that organizes the components and functions of an Operating System into distinct layers or levels. Each layer is responsible for specific tasks and provides well-defined interfaces for communication and interaction with the layers above and below it. The layered approach aims to improve modularity, maintainability, and system flexibility. Here's an overview of the typical layers in the layered approach of an Operating System:

Hardware Layer:

The bottom layer represents the actual hardware components of the computer, including the CPU, memory, I/O devices, and storage devices.

This layer interacts directly with the physical hardware and provides low-level services, such as device drivers, memory management, and interrupt handling.

Kernel Layer:

The Kernel is the core component of the Operating System. It is responsible for managing hardware resources and providing essential services to higher layers and user-level applications.

Functions of the kernel include process management, memory management, file system operations, device management, and scheduling of processes.

Device Drivers Layer:

Device Drivers are responsible for enabling communication between the kernel and specific hardware devices, such as printers, disk drives, and network interfaces.

These drivers abstract the hardware details, allowing the kernel and upper layers to interact with devices in a uniform manner.

Operating System Services Layer:

This layer includes various system services and libraries that provide a high-level interface to applications and users.

Services such as file management, network communication, user authentication, and process control are offered here.

System Call Interface Layer:

The System Call interface provides a set of functions and System Calls that allow user-level applications to request services from the Operating System.

These System Calls serve as a bridge between the user-space and the kernel, enabling applications to access OS functionality.

User-Level Applications Layer:

At the topmost layer are user-level applications, including utility programs, graphical user interfaces, compilers, and user applications.

These applications interact with the Operating System primarily through System Calls and libraries provided by the lower layers.

The key advantages of the layered approach in Operating System design include:

Modularity: Each layer has well-defined responsibilities and interfaces, making it easier to develop, test, and maintain the Operating System. Changes or updates to one layer can be made without affecting other layers.

Abstraction: Higher layers are shielded from the complex details of the lower layers. This abstraction simplifies the development of user applications and allows the Operating System to be hardware-independent to some extent.

Scalability: New functionality can be added to the Operating System by introducing new layers or extending existing layers. The layered approach accommodates system growth and adaptation.

Interchangeability: Different implementations of the same layer can be used with minimal impact on other layers. For example, various file systems can be used with the same kernel and applications.

The Layered Approach is a fundamental concept in Operating System design, and it serves as a framework for organizing and managing the complex software components and interactions within an Operating System.

Q 5. Compare the functionalities of **FCFS, SSTF, CSAN** and **CLOOK** disk scheduling algorithms with an example for each. (Anna 2013)

Ans: Let's compare the functionalities of four disk scheduling algorithms: First-Come, First-Served (FCFS), Shortest Seek Time First (SSTF), Circular SCAN (CSCAN), and CLOOK. We'll provide an example for each algorithm.

First-Come, First-Served (FCFS):

Functionality: FCFS schedules disk requests in the order they arrive. It services requests one by one in the order they appear in the request queue.

Example: Consider a disk with the following track requests in the order they arrive: 98, 183, 37, 122, 14, 124, 65, 67. With FCFS, the disk head will service the requests in the same order as they arrive.

Shortest Seek Time First (SSTF):

Functionality: SSTF selects the request that is closest to the current position of the disk head. It minimizes the seek time by selecting the shortest seek time among all pending requests.

Example: Using the same set of requests as in FCFS, suppose the disk head starts at track 53. The SSTF algorithm will first select track 65 since it has the shortest seek time from track 53. After servicing track 65, it will select the next closest track and so on.

Circular SCAN (CSCAN):

Functionality: CSCAN is a variant of the SCAN algorithm that always scans in the same direction, servicing requests as it encounters them. When reaching the end of the disk, it wraps around to the beginning.

Example: Continuing with the same set of requests, suppose the disk head starts at track 53. The CSCAN algorithm will initially service requests in the forward direction until the end of the disk is reached. Then, it will wrap around to the beginning and service requests in the forward direction again.

CLOOK:

Functionality: CLOOK is a variant of the LOOK algorithm that only services requests in one direction (either toward higher or lower track numbers). It scans only until it encounters the last request in that direction before returning to the first request.

Example: Using the same set of requests, suppose the disk head starts at track 53. The CLOOK algorithm will initially service requests in the forward direction until it reaches track 67, the last request in that direction. Then, it will return to track 14, the first request in the forward direction, and service requests until it reaches track 37, the last request in the forward direction.

In summary, each disk scheduling algorithm has its own functionality and behavior, aiming to optimize disk access time based on different criteria such as seek time, fairness, and efficiency. The choice of algorithm depends on the specific requirements and characteristics of the system.

Q 6. Explain various Disk Scheduling Algorithm? (RU BCA 2019)

Ans: Disk Scheduling Algorithms are used to optimize the access and retrieval of data stored on a disk by determining the order in which disk requests are serviced. Here's an explanation of various disk scheduling algorithms:

First-Come, First-Served (FCFS):

Functionality: FCFS schedules disk requests in the order they arrive. It services requests one by one in the order they appear in the request queue.

Advantages: Simple and easy to implement.

Disadvantages: Poor performance for systems with high variation in seek time, as it does not consider the distance between requests.

Shortest Seek Time First (SSTF):

Functionality: SSTF selects the request that is closest to the current position of the disk head. It minimizes the seek time by selecting the shortest seek time among all pending requests.

Advantages: Minimizes seek time and can improve overall disk performance.

Disadvantages: May lead to starvation for requests located far from the current position of the disk head.

SCAN (Elevator):

Functionality: SCAN moves the disk head in one direction (e.g., towards higher track numbers) until it reaches the end of the disk. Then, it reverses direction and services requests in the opposite direction.

Advantages: Ensures fairness by servicing requests in both directions.

Disadvantages: May result in increased average seek time for requests located towards the middle of the disk.

Circular SCAN (CSCAN):

Functionality: CSCAN is a variant of the SCAN algorithm that always scans in the same direction, servicing requests as it encounters them. When reaching the end of the disk, it wraps around to the beginning.

Advantages: Simplifies implementation by avoiding direction reversal.

Disadvantages: May lead to increased waiting time for requests located far from the current position of the disk head.

LOOK:

Functionality: LOOK is similar to SCAN but does not service requests when reversing direction. It scans only until it encounters the last request in that direction before returning to the first request.

Advantages: Reduces unnecessary movement of the disk head, leading to improved performance.

Disadvantages: May lead to starvation for requests located towards the end of the disk.

CLOOK:

Functionality: CLOOK is a variant of the LOOK algorithm that only services requests in one direction (either toward higher or lower track numbers). It scans only until it encounters the last request in that direction before returning to the first request.

Advantages: Further reduces unnecessary movement of the disk head compared to LOOK.

Disadvantages: May lead to increased waiting time for requests located far from the current position of the disk head.

These Disk Scheduling Algorithms offer different trade-offs between seek time, fairness, and efficiency. The choice of algorithm depends on the specific requirements and characteristics of the system.

Q 7. How Operating System control I/O Management?(RU BCA 2018)

Ans: Operating Systems control I/O (Input/Output) Management through various mechanisms and components designed to ensure efficient and reliable communication between the CPU, memory, and I/O devices. Here's how Operating Systems accomplish this task:

Device Drivers: Device Drivers are software components responsible for interfacing with specific I/O devices, such as keyboards, mice, printers, disks, and network adapters. The Operating System communicates with device drivers to initialize, configure, and control I/O devices.

I/O Scheduling: Operating Systems implement I/O scheduling algorithms to optimize the order in which I/O requests are serviced to minimize disk latency and improve system performance. Various scheduling algorithms, such as FCFS (First-Come, First-Served), SSTF (Shortest Seek Time First), and SCAN (Elevator), determine the sequence in which I/O requests are processed.

Buffering: Buffering involves temporarily storing data in memory buffers to smooth out variations in I/O device speeds and improve overall system performance. Operating Systems use different types of buffers, such as input buffers (for incoming data) and output buffers (for outgoing data), to manage I/O operations efficiently.

Caching: Caching involves storing frequently accessed data in a cache memory to reduce the need for repeated disk accesses. Operating Systems use caching techniques to speed up I/O operations by storing frequently accessed disk blocks or file system metadata in memory caches.

Interrupt Handling: I/O devices generate interrupts to signal the CPU when they require attention or have completed an operation. Operating Systems handle interrupts by invoking interrupt service routines (ISRs) to process the interrupt and respond accordingly. Interrupt handling mechanisms ensure timely and efficient communication between the CPU and I/O devices.

Direct Memory Access (DMA): DMA is a mechanism that allows I/O devices to transfer data directly to and from memory without CPU intervention. Operating Systems coordinate DMA operations by configuring DMA controllers and managing memory access permissions to facilitate high-speed data transfers between I/O devices and memory.

Error Handling: Operating Systems implement Error Handling mechanisms to detect, report, and recover from I/O errors or device failures. Error Handling components monitor I/O operations for errors, log error messages, and take appropriate actions, such as retrying failed operations or notifying system administrators.

File Systems: File systems are responsible for organizing and managing data stored on storage devices, such as disks and solid-state drives (SSDs). Operating Systems provide file system services to create, read, write, and delete files, as well as manage file permissions, directories, and file metadata.

Overall, Operating Systems play a crucial role in controlling I/O management by coordinating communication between the CPU, memory, and I/O devices, optimizing I/O operations, and ensuring reliable data transfer between applications and peripheral devices.

Q 8. Explain about the RAID structure in disk management with various RAID levels of organization in details. (Anna 2013)

Ans:RAID (Redundant Array of Independent Disks) is a data storage technology that combines multiple physical disks into a single logical unit to improve performance, reliability, or both. RAID structures use various techniques such as data striping, mirroring, parity, and error correction to achieve these goals. There are several RAID levels, each offering different features and benefits. Let's explore them in detail:

RAID 0 (Striping):

Description: RAID 0 distributes data across multiple disks (at least two) in stripes without redundancy. It offers improved performance by spreading data access across multiple disks, effectively increasing the total bandwidth.

Features:

High performance: RAID 0 offers improved read and write performance since data is striped across multiple disks, allowing parallel access.

No redundancy: There is no data redundancy or fault tolerance. If one disk fails, then all data is lost.

Use Cases: RAID 0 is suitable for applications where performance is critical, such as video editing, gaming, and rendering, but data redundancy is not a concern.

RAID 1 (Mirroring):

Description: RAID 1 mirrors data across two or more disks, creating an exact copy (mirror) of the data on each disk. It provides redundancy and fault tolerance by allowing data to be reconstructed from the mirror, if one disk fails.

Features:

Data redundancy: RAID 1 provides full redundancy since all data is duplicated across multiple disks.

Fault tolerance: If one disk fails, then data can still be accessed from the mirror without interruption.

Use Cases: RAID 1 is commonly used for critical data storage applications where data integrity and reliability are paramount, such as database servers, file servers, and email servers.

RAID 5 (Striping with Distributed Parity):

Description: RAID 5 stripes data across multiple disks and includes distributed parity information. Parity data is spread across all disks, providing fault tolerance and allowing data to be reconstructed in case of disk failure.

Features:

Data Striping: RAID 5 stripes data across multiple disks to improve performance.

Parity Protection: Parity information is distributed across disks, providing fault tolerance and allowing data reconstruction.

Efficient use of Storage: RAID 5 offers a good balance between performance and storage efficiency since it provides redundancy without requiring as much disk space as RAID 1.

Use Cases: RAID 5 is suitable for applications that require a balance between performance, reliability, and storage efficiency, such as file servers, web servers, and virtualization environments.

RAID 6 (Striping with Dual Distributed Parity):

Description: RAID 6 is similar to RAID 5 but uses two parity blocks instead of one. This provides additional fault tolerance by allowing data to be reconstructed even if two disks fail simultaneously.

Features:

Dual Parity Protection: RAID 6 offers higher fault tolerance compared to RAID 5 by using two parity blocks.

Redundancy: RAID 6 provides redundancy and fault tolerance for critical data storage applications.

Use Cases: RAID 6 is recommended for applications that require high levels of fault tolerance and data protection, such as large-scale storage systems, archival storage, and data backup solutions.

RAID 10 (Striping and Mirroring):

Description: RAID 10 combines the features of RAID 0 (striping) and RAID 1 (mirroring). It stripes data across multiple disk pairs and mirrors each pair to provide both performance and redundancy.

Features:

High performance: RAID 10 offers high read and write performance by striping data across multiple disk pairs.

Redundancy: RAID 10 provides full redundancy and fault tolerance by mirroring data within each disk pair.

Use Cases: RAID 10 is ideal for applications that require both high performance and fault tolerance, such as database servers, transaction processing systems, and virtualization platforms.

Each RAID level offers different trade-offs in terms of performance, redundancy, and storage efficiency. The choice of RAID level depends on the specific requirements of the application, including performance needs, data protection requirements, and budget constraints.

Q 9. The following is the sequence of page 10 requests: 1, 3, 2, 5, 4, 2, 1, 5, 3, 2, 4, 3 Assume that there are three frames. How many page faults will occur if the following algorithms are used to replace the pages: (IGNOU June 2013)

FCFS

LRU

OPT

Ans: To determine the number of page faults for each page replacement algorithm (FCFS, LRU, OPT), let's simulate the page replacement process step by step:

Given: Page requests sequence: 1, 3, 2, 5, 4, 2, 1, 5, 3, 2, 4, 3 Number of frames: 3

(i) FCFS (First-Come, First-Served): Page Faults: 8

Sequence of Page Faults:

1 (Page 1)

3 (Page 3)

2 (Page 2)

5 (Page 5)

4 (Page 4)

2 (Page 2) - Replacement: 1 (Page 1)

1 (Page 1) - Replacement: 3 (Page 3)

3 (Page 3) - Replacement: 5 (Page 5)

(ii) LRU (Least Recently Used): Page Faults: 7

Sequence of Page Faults:

1 (Page 1)

3 (Page 3)

2 (Page 2)

5 (Page 5)

4 (Page 4)

2 (Page 2) - Replacement: 1 (Page 1)

1 (Page 1) - Replacement: 3 (Page 3)

(iii) OPT (Optimal): Page Faults: 6

Sequence of Page Faults:

1 (Page 1)

3 (Page 3)

2 (Page 2)

5 (Page 5)

4 (Page 4)

2 (Page 2) - Replacement: 1 (Page 1)

Explanation:

FCFS: Replaces the page that arrived first when there's a page fault.

LRU: Replaces the page that has not been accessed for the longest time.

OPT: Replaces the page that will not be used for the longest time in the future (requires future knowledge, often used for comparison purposes).

In this scenario, FCFS resulted in the highest number of page faults, followed by LRU and then OPT.

Q 10. Suppose the disk queue for the following blocks is created at a time: 50, 91, 150, 42, 130, 18, 140, 70, 60 Assuming the disk head initially at block number 50, explain the disk scheduling for the following algorithms. (IGNOU June 2012)

FCFS

SSTF

Ans: For the given disk queue and starting position of the disk head, let's explain the disk scheduling process for the FCFS (First-Come, First-Served) and SSTF (Shortest Seek Time First) algorithms:

FCFS (First-Come, First-Served):

In FCFS, the disk requests are serviced in the order they arrive in the queue.

Disk Queue: 50, 91, 150, 42, 130, 18, 140, 70, 60

Starting Position of Disk Head: 50

Sequence of Disk Access:

Disk head moves from 50 to 91 (distance: 41)

Disk head moves from 91 to 150 (distance: 59)

Disk head moves from 150 to 42 (distance: 108)

Disk head moves from 42 to 130 (distance: 88)

Disk head moves from 130 to 18 (distance: 112)

Disk head moves from 18 to 140 (distance: 122)

Disk head moves from 140 to 70 (distance: 70)

Disk head moves from 70 to 60 (distance: 10)

Total Seek Distance: 41 + 59 + 108 + 88 + 112 + 122 + 70 + 10 = 610

SSTF (Shortest Seek Time First):

In SSTF, the disk requests are serviced based on the shortest seek time from the current position of the disk head.

Disk Queue: 50, 91, 150, 42, 130, 18, 140, 70, 60

Starting Position of Disk Head: 50

Sequence of Disk Access:

Disk head moves from 50 to 42 (distance: 8)

Disk head moves from 42 to 60 (distance: 18)

Disk head moves from 60 to 70 (distance: 10)

Disk head moves from 70 to 91 (distance: 21)

Disk head moves from 91 to 130 (distance: 39)

Disk head moves from 130 to 140 (distance: 10)

Disk head moves from 140 to 150 (distance: 10)

Disk head moves from 150 to 18 (distance: 132)

Total Seek Distance: 8 + 18 + 10 + 21 + 39 + 10 + 10 + 132 = 248

In summary, for the given disk queue and starting position of the disk head, the FCFS algorithm resulted in a total seek distance of 610, while the SSTF algorithm resulted in a total seek distance of 248. SSTF performs better than FCFS by minimizing the seek time and optimizing disk access.

Previous Year Unsolved Questions

Q 1. For the given five processes arriving at time 10 0, in the order of the length of CPU time in milli second: CPU time

P1	8
P2	4
P3	6
P4	1
P5	5

Consider SJF and FCFS scheduling algorithms for the above processes; which algorithm of the two will give minimum Average Turnaround time and why? (IGNOU 2010)

Q 2. Explain SCAN and LOOK disk scheduling 6 algorithm with suitable diagrams for the given example.

Starting cylinder is 100 in the direction of increasing cylinder number. Cylinder request:

150, 160, 184, 90, 58, 55, 39, 38, 18(IGNOU 2010)

Q 3. Calculate the average waiting time, average turnaround time for the processes given for the following scheduling algorithms: (IGNOU 2010)

SJF

FCFS

RR (quantum = 2)   The list of processes is given as:

Process	Arrival time	Process Time
P1	0	2
P2	1	1
P3	3	3
P4	5	2

Q 4. What do you mean by disk scheduling algorithm? Calculate algorithm for the following block sequence:

91, 150, 42, 130, 18, 70, 60, 128.

Initially the head is at cylinder numbered 0.

Draw suitable diagrams for all.(IGNOU Dec 2010)

Q 5. For the page string(Reference string) as:(IGNOU Dec 2010)

0, 1, 2, 3, 6, 10, 13, 4, 6, 2, 0 and with 3 memory frames calculate member of page faults using OPT and FCFS page replacement algorithms.

Q 6. Consider the set of processes in the given table and the following scheduling algorithms:

FCFS

Shortest Remaining Time First

Round Robin (quantum = 2)

Process id	Arrival Time	Execution Time
A	0	4
B	2	7
C	3	3
D	4	2
E	6	5

Draw the Gantt chart and find the average waiting time and average turnaround time for all the above algorithms. Comment on your result. Which one is better and why? (IGNOU 2015)

Q 7. Draw the Gantt Chart for the FCFS and SJF 10 policy, considering the following set of processes that arrive at time 0, with the length of CPU time given in milliseconds. Also calculate the average waiting and average turn around time.(IGNOU June 2011)

Process	Processing time
P1	13
P2	08
P3	19

Q 8. Implement FCFS, SCAN, LOOK and C LOOK scheduling for the following disk queues: 50, 91, 150, 42, 130, 98, 18, 138, 140. Assume that the disk head is initially at cylinder 50. Calculate the total heat count.(IGNOU June 2011)

Exercise

Exercise 1 – MCQ

1. What is the purpose of a device controller in I/O hardware?

a) To perform arithmetic operations for I/O devices.

b) To manage communication between the CPU and I/O devices.

c) To store data temporarily during I/O operations.

d) To execute System Calls related to I/O.

2. What is the purpose of a buffer in I/O software?

a) To store the final output of I/O operations.

b) To temporarily hold data between the I/O device and the application.

c) To control the flow of interrupts in I/O operations.

d) To act as a secondary storage device.

3. What is the purpose of a disk block in the context of disk structure in Operating Systems?

a) To represent a sector on the disk.

b) To store the file system's metadata.

c) To manage disk access permissions.

d) To store the actual data of files.

4. What is the role of the File Allocation Table (FAT) in disk management?

a) It tracks the allocation status of disk blocks.

b) It encrypts the contents of the disk.

c) It controls the rotational speed of the disk platters.

d) It manages disk formatting operations.

5. Which disk scheduling algorithm is known for minimizing the total movement of the disk arm by selecting the request that is closest to the current position of the arm?

a) First-Come-First-Serve (FCFS)

b) Shortest Seek Time First (SSTF)

c) SCAN

d) C-LOOK

6. In the context of disk scheduling algorithms, what does the term "elevator algorithm" refer to?

a) An algorithm that moves the disk arm towards the center of the disk.

b) An algorithm that simulates the movement of an elevator, scanning in one direction only.

c) An algorithm that uses the Circular LOOK strategy.

d) An algorithm that prioritizes I/O requests based on their arrival time.

7. What is the purpose of a device driver in I/O device handling?

a) To physically connect I/O devices to the computer.

b) To provide an interface for users to interact with I/O devices.

c) To translate generic Operating System commands into specific commands for the I/O device.

d) To control the power supply to I/O devices.

8. Which I/O method allows the CPU to continue its processing tasks while the I/O operation is in progress without waiting for its completion?

a) Programmed I/O

b) Interrupt-Driven I/O

c) Direct Memory Access (DMA)

d) Memory-Mapped I/O

9. What is a characteristic feature of a block device in an Operating System?

a) It transfers data in streams.

b) It treats data as fixed-size blocks.

c) It has a lower data transfer rate compared to character devices.

d) It is primarily used for real-time communication.

10. In the context of character devices, which statement is true?

a) They transfer data in fixed-size blocks.

b) They are always slower than block devices.

c) They are used for storage devices like hard disks.

d) They handle data as a stream of characters.

Exercise 2 – True/ False

1. Polling is a more efficient method of I/O handling than Interrupts.

2. The term "spooling" stands for "Sequential Peripheral Operation On-Line" and is primarily used in mainframe systems for managing I/O operations.

3. Disk formatting is the process of creating a file system on a disk, and it erases all data on the disk.

4. Fragmentation is a common issue in disk management, leading to inefficient disk space utilization.

5. The C-SCAN disk scheduling algorithm always scans the entire disk in both directions, even if there are no pending requests in one direction.

6. The LOOK disk scheduling algorithm may result in starvation for some requests located at the farthest tracks on the disk.

7. Interrupts are a mechanism used in I/O handling to inform the CPU that an I/O operation has been completed.

8. Memory-Mapped I/O allows I/O devices to be treated as if they are part of the computer's memory space, simplifying data transfer between the CPU and devices.

9. Block devices are commonly used for devices that require sequential and continuous data streams, such as keyboards.

10. Block devices are typically faster than character devices for certain operations due to their fixed-size block transfers.

Exercise 3 – Fill in the blanks

1.A ___________ Operating System is optimized for smartphones, tablets, and other mobile devices.

2.RealTimeOperating Systems (RTOS) are designed for systems with strict ___________ requirements, such as robotics and industrial automation.

Answer

Exercise 1 – MCQ

Ans: 1 b, 2 d, 3 d, 4 a, 5 b, 6 b, 7 c, 8 c, 9 b, 10 d

Exercise 2 – True/False

Ans: 1 False, 2 False, 3 True, 4 True, 5 True, 6 False, 7 True, 8 True

Exercise 3 – Fill in The Blanks

Ans: 1 Mobile, 2 Timing or timesensitive

Online Resources

Videos:

MCQ Link:https://youtu.be/Kh4F1vFovR8

QR Code:

True/False Link:https://youtu.be/VYK63a_-h1M

QR Code:

Online Test Paper: https://forms.office.com/r/ckvNPuP2CM

QR Code:

Chapter 7 Distributed Systems

Distributed Operating Systems

Distributed Operating Systems are specialized Operating Systems designed to manage and coordinate resources and tasks across multiple interconnected computers, often referred to as nodes or hosts, in a distributed or networked environment. These systems enable the efficient sharing of computational and storage resources, enhance reliability, and support the development of scalable and fault tolerant applications. Distributed Operating Systems (Distributed OS) represent a specialized area of Operating System design and management where the primary focus is on coordinating and managing the resources and processes of multiple interconnected computers or nodes within a network.

Distributed Operating Systems facilitate the seamless sharing of resources, data, and computation across geographically dispersed machines, enhancing scalability, fault tolerance, and performance. They are instrumental in building largescale systems, such as cloud computing platforms and global data centers, where reliability and efficient resource utilization are paramount.

Key features include process communication and synchronization, distributed file systems, and fault tolerance mechanisms. They enable applications to run concurrently across multiple nodes while abstracting the underlying complexity of network communication and hardware heterogeneity.

Distributed OSs play a pivotal role in modern computing, powering web services, distributed databases, and IoT networks, enabling businesses to efficiently harness the potential of distributed computing resources while ensuring reliability and security in a networked world.

Here are key concepts and characteristics of Distributed Operating Systems:

Resource Sharing: Distributed Operating Systems enable the sharing of hardware resources (such as CPU, memory, and storage) and software resources (such as files, databases, and applications) across the network. This sharing allows multiple users or applications to access and utilize resources on different machines.

Transparency: Distributed OperatingSystems aim to provide transparency to users and applications. Transparency means that users and applications interact with the distributed system as, if it were a single, unified system, hiding the complexities of distributed computing. Types of transparency include location transparency, access transparency, and failure transparency.

Concurrency and Synchronization: Distributed Operating Systems must manage concurrent access to shared resources. They employ synchronization mechanisms to ensure data consistency and avoid conflicts between concurrent processes.

Communication: Communication is a fundamental aspect of Distributed Operating Systems. Distributed Operating Systems provide communication facilities for processes running on different nodes to exchange data and coordinate their activities. Message passing and Remote Procedure Calls (RPCs) are common communication mechanisms.

Fault Tolerance: Distributed OperatingSystems are designed to handle node failures, network failures, and other unexpected events gracefully. Fault tolerance mechanisms, such as redundancy, replication, and error recovery, ensure system reliability and data integrity.

Scalability: Distributed OperatingSystems are scalable by design, meaning they can easily accommodate an increasing number of nodes and users. Horizontal scaling (adding more nodes) and vertical scaling (upgrading existing nodes) are common approaches to scalability.

Load Balancing: To ensure efficient resource utilization and performance, Distributed Operating Systems may employ load balancing algorithms that distribute workloads evenly across nodes in the system.

Security: Security is a critical concern in distributed systems. Distributed Operating Systems provide authentication, authorization, and encryption mechanisms to protect data and resources from unauthorized access and malicious attacks.

Naming and Directory Services: Distributed OperatingSystems often include naming and directory services to provide a consistent and user-friendly way to locate resources across the network. These services map human readable names to network addresses or object references.

Distributed File Systems: Distributed Operating Systems typically include distributed file systems that allow files and data to be stored and accessed across multiple nodes. Examples include NFS (Network File System) and CIFS (Common Internet File System).

Middleware: Middleware is software that sits between the Operating System and applications, providing services like communication, data management, and transaction support for distributed applications. Examples include CORBA (Common Object Request Broker Architecture) and message-oriented middleware (MOM).

Distributed Databases: Distributed Operating Systems often support distributed databases, allowing data to be distributed and replicated across multiple nodes for improved availability and performance. NoSQL databases and NewSQL databases are examples.

Cluster Computing: Distributed Operating Systems are used in cluster computing environments, where a group of interconnected machines works together to perform high-performance computing tasks. Examples include HPC clusters and web server clusters.

Distributed Operating Systems are commonly used in various domains, including cloud computing, data centers, scientific computing, and largescale web applications. They provide the foundation for building scalable and resilient distributed systems, enabling organizations to leverage the power of networked resources efficiently.

Networking Fundamentals

Networking fundamentals in Operating Systems are crucial for enabling communication and data exchange between computers and devices in a networked environment. These fundamentals are essential for modern computing, as they facilitate internet access, file sharing, remote administration, and many other tasks. Networking Fundamentals encompass the essential concepts and principles that underlie computer networks and their operation. It involves the study of data transmission, protocols, network architecture, and the technologies enabling devices to connect and communicate seamlessly. Understanding these fundamentals is crucial in Operating Systems to facilitate network connectivity, data sharing, and communication between devices. Key topics include the OSI model, TCP/IP protocol suite, routing, switching, and network security. Networking Fundamentals are vital in today's interconnected world, supporting the internet, intranets, and various communication technologies, ensuring efficient data exchange and access to resources, making them a cornerstone of modern Operating Systems.Here are two key networking fundamentals in Operating Systems:

Networking Protocols:

Networking Protocols are a set of rules and conventions that define how data is formatted, transmitted, received, and processed in a network. These protocols ensure that devices can communicate effectively, regardless of their hardware or software differences. Some important networking protocols include:

Transmission Control Protocol (TCP): TCP is a reliable, connection-oriented protocol used for transmitting data over networks. It ensures data integrity and delivery confirmation through a series of handshakes and acknowledgments.

Internet Protocol (IP): IP is responsible for addressing and routing packets of data so that they can travel across networks and reach their intended destinations. IPv4 and IPv6 are two versions of the IP protocol.

User Datagram Protocol (UDP): UDP is a connectionless, lightweight protocol that provides faster data transmission but lacks the reliability features of TCP. It is often used for real-time applications like video streaming and online gaming.

Internet Control Message Protocol (ICMP): ICMP is used for network diagnostics and error reporting. Ping and traceroute are examples of tools that rely on ICMP messages.

Hypertext Transfer Protocol (HTTP): HTTP is the protocol used for transferring web pages and other resources on the World Wide Web. It forms the foundation of web communication.

File Transfer Protocol (FTP): FTP is a protocol for transferring files between computers on a network. It provides methods for uploading and downloading files to and from remote servers.

Simple Mail Transfer Protocol (SMTP) and Post Office Protocol (POP3/IMAP): These are protocols used for sending and receiving email, respectively.

Secure Sockets Layer (SSL) and Transport Layer Security (TLS): SSL and TLS protocols provide encryption and authentication mechanisms to secure data transmitted over networks, commonly used in secure web browsing (HTTPS) and email (SMTPS, IMAPS).

Network Architecture and Topology:

Network architecture and topology refer to the physical and logical structures of a network. Understanding these fundamentals is crucial for designing and managing networks efficiently. Key concepts include:

Physical Topology: Physical topology defines how devices are physically connected in a network. Common physical topologies include bus, star, ring, mesh, and hybrid. The choice of topology affects factors like redundancy, scalability, and fault tolerance.

Logical Topology: Logical topology describes how data flows within the network, regardless of its physical layout. Ethernet and WiFi networks often use a logical topology based on the bus or star physical topology.

Network Models: Network models like the OSI (Open Systems Interconnection) model and the TCP/IP model provide a layered framework for understanding network functionality. They divide network tasks into distinct layers, such as physical, data link, network, transport, session, presentation, and application layers.

IP Addressing: IP addressing is a fundamental concept in networking, enabling devices to identify and communicate with each other on a network. IPv4 and IPv6 addresses are used to uniquely identify devices and determine routing.

Subnetting and CIDR: Subnetting involves dividing large IP address ranges into smaller, more manageable subnetworks. CIDR (Classless Interdomain Routing) allows for efficient IP address allocation and routing.

Router and Switch: Routers are devices that interconnect different network segments and make routing decisions based on IP addresses. Switches are used for local network traffic management, forwarding data to specific devices based on MAC addresses.

Firewalls: Firewalls are security devices or software that control and monitor network traffic, enforcing security policies and protecting networks from unauthorized access and threats.

Wireless Networking: Wireless networking technologies, like WiFi (802.11 standards), enable devices to connect to a network without physical cables. Understanding wireless security and access control is crucial for secure wireless networking.

Network Services: Network services include DNS (Domain Name System) for translating domain names to IP addresses, DHCP (Dynamic Host Configuration Protocol) for automatic IP address assignment, and NAT (Network Address Translation) for mapping private IP addresses to a single public IP address.

These networking fundamentals are essential for administrators, developers, and anyone working with computer networks. They form the basis for configuring, troubleshooting, and optimizing networked systems and services in an Operating System environment.

Distributed File Systems

Distributed File Systems (DFS) are a category of file systems designed to distribute and manage files and data across multiple interconnected computers or nodes in a networked environment. These systems enable efficient and reliable file sharing, data access, and storage management in distributed and networked computing environments. Here are some key concepts and characteristics of distributed file systems in Operating Systems:

Transparency:

Distributed File Systems aim to provide transparency to users and applications, hiding the complexities of distributed data storage. Users and applications interact with files as, if they were stored locally, regardless of the physical location of the data.

Location Independence:

DFS abstracts the physical location of files and data. Files can be distributed across multiple servers or nodes, and users access them through a unified file namespace.

Scalability:

Distributed File Systems are designed to be scalable, allowing for the addition of more storage nodes as data storage requirements grow. This scalability can be achieved through horizontal scaling (adding more nodes) or vertical scaling (increasing the capacity of existing nodes).

Redundancy and Fault Tolerance:

Many DFS implementations incorporate redundancy and fault tolerance mechanisms to ensure data availability and reliability. This often involves data replication across multiple nodes, allowing data to be retrieved even, if some nodes fail.

Caching:

Caching is employed in distributed file systems to improve data access performance. Frequently accessed data is cached in memory to reduce the need for disk or network access, resulting in faster retrieval times.

Security:

Security features, such as access control, authentication, and encryption, are integral to DFS to protect data from unauthorized access and ensure data privacy.

Consistency and Coherency:

Distributed File Systems maintain data consistency and coherency, ensuring that all users see a consistent view of the data even when accessed from different locations or nodes.

Namespace Resolution:

DFS provides mechanisms for resolving file and directory names to their corresponding network locations or servers. This includes name resolution services like distributed naming and directory services.

File Locking and Concurrency Control:

To support concurrent access by multiple users and applications, distributed file systems implement file locking and concurrency control mechanisms. These prevent conflicts when multiple users attempt to modify the same file simultaneously.

Backup and Recovery:

Backup and recovery mechanisms are essential for data protection and disaster recovery. DFS often includes features for automated backup and data restoration.

File Access Protocols:

Distributed file systems use various access protocols to enable clients to access files. Common protocols include the Network File System (NFS), Common Internet File System (CIFS/SMB), and Andrew File System (AFS).

Examples of Distributed File Systems:

NFS: NFS is a widely used distributed file system commonly associated with Unix and Linux systems. It allows remote access to files and directories as if they were local.

CIFS/SMB: CIFS (Common Internet File System) and SMB (Server Message Block) are protocols used for file and printer sharing in Windows and cross platform environments.

Hadoop Distributed File System (HDFS): HDFS is designed for storing and managing large volumes of data in a distributed computing environment and is commonly used in big data processing.

Google File System (GFS): GFS is a proprietary distributed file system developed by Google to support its vast data storage needs.

Distributed File Systems play a crucial role in modern computing environments, enabling efficient data sharing and storage management in distributed and networked settings. They are essential for applications ranging from cloud computing and cluster computing to data analytics and content distribution.

Distributed Process Management

Distributed Process Management in Operating Systems refers to the coordination and control of processes (executable programs) that run across multiple interconnected computers or nodes in a distributed or networked environment. This management involves tasks such as process creation, synchronization, communication, load balancing, fault tolerance, and termination. Here are key concepts and components of distributed process management:

Process Creation and Termination:

Distributed systems support the creation of processes across multiple nodes. Processes can be initiated locally or remotely. Termination may involve the graceful shutdown of processes to release resources.

Process Synchronization:

Coordination among distributed processes often requires synchronization mechanisms. Techniques like semaphores, mutexes, and barriers are used to ensure that processes do not interfere with each other's execution.

Communication:

Processes in a distributed system need to communicate to share data and coordinate their activities. Communication mechanisms include message passing, remote procedure calls (RPCs), and interprocess communication (IPC) protocols.

Distributed Shared Memory (DSM):

DSM systems allow processes on different nodes to access a shared memory space, providing a shared data repository. Access to shared memory is coordinated to ensure consistency and synchronization.

Load Balancing:

Load balancing strategies aim to distribute the computational load evenly among distributed processes and nodes. This ensures efficient resource utilization and prevents overloading of specific nodes.

Fault Tolerance:

Distributed systems must handle node failures, network failures, and other unexpected events gracefully. Mechanisms such as redundancy, replication, and error recovery are used to maintain system reliability.

Process Migration:

Process migration involves moving a running process from one node to another. This can be used for load balancing, resource optimization, or fault tolerance.

Distributed Process Coordination:

Coordination protocols and algorithms ensure that distributed processes work together correctly. Examples include leader election, consensus algorithms, and distributed locking mechanisms.

Process Monitoring and Management:

Distributed Process Management includes monitoring the status and performance of processes and nodes. Tools and utilities provide information on process health and resource utilization.

Naming and Directory Services:

Distributed systems often rely on naming and directory services to locate and identify processes and resources across the network. These services map humanreadable names to network addresses or object references.

Security and Access Control:

Security mechanisms, such as authentication, authorization, and encryption, are essential to protect distributed processes and data from unauthorized access and malicious attacks.

Distributed Debugging and Tracing:

Debugging and tracing tools help developers identify and diagnose issues in distributed processes. They provide insights into the flow of messages and events across the network.

Message Queues and PublishSubscribe Models:

Message queuing systems and publishsubscribe models facilitate asynchronous communication between distributed processes. Messages are delivered to subscribers based on topics or queues.

Middleware and Distributed Systems Frameworks:

Middleware platforms and distributed systems frameworks provide highlevel abstractions and services for developing distributed applications. Examples include CORBA, Java RMI, and message-oriented middleware (MOM).

Cluster and Grid Computing:

In cluster and grid computing environments, distributed process management is crucial for coordinating and scheduling computational tasks across a collection of interconnected nodes.

Effective distributed process management is essential for building scalable, reliable, and high-performance distributed systems. It allows applications to harness the power of distributed computing while maintaining the integrity and coherence of data and processes across a networked environment.

Distributed Security

Distributed security in Operating Systems refers to the comprehensive set of measures, policies, and mechanisms used to protect data, resources, and communication in distributed or networked computing environments. Ensuring security in distributed systems is crucial to prevent unauthorized access, data breaches, and other security threats. Here are key concepts and components of distributed security:

Authentication:

Authentication is the process of verifying the identity of users, devices, and processes in a distributed system. Common authentication methods include passwords, multifactor authentication (MFA), digital certificates, and biometric authentication.

Authorization:

Authorization controls what authenticated users and processes are allowed to do within the system. Access Control Lists (ACLs) and Role-Based Access Control (RBAC) are commonly used authorization mechanisms.

Encryption:

Encryption is used to protect data during transmission and storage in distributed systems. Secure communication protocols, such as SSL/TLS, are employed to encrypt data in transit, while disk encryption and file level encryption protect data at rest.

Network Security:

Network security measures include Firewalls, Intrusion Detection Systems (IDS), Intrusion Prevention Systems (IPS), and Virtual Private Networks (VPNs) to safeguard the network infrastructure from unauthorized access and attacks.

Secure Communication Protocols:

Distributed systems use secure communication protocols like HTTPS (secure web browsing), SSH (secure shell for remote access), and IPsec (secure IP communication) to ensure confidentiality and integrity of data exchanged between nodes.

Public Key Infrastructure (PKI):

PKI provides a framework for managing digital certificates and public. private key pairs, which are used for secure authentication and encrypted communication in distributed systems.

Single SignOn (SSO):

SSO solutions enable users to log in once and gain access to multiple distributed systems or services without the need to enter credentials multiple times.

Security Tokens and Tokens Management:

Security tokens, such as JSON Web Tokens (JWTs), are used to authenticate and authorize users and processes in distributed systems. Token management ensures the validity and revocation of tokens.

Secure APIs:

APIs (Application Programming Interfaces) are secured using authentication and authorization mechanisms to control access to resources and services in distributed environments.

Identity Federation:

Identity Federation allows users to access resources in different domains or organizations using their home identity provider (IdP) credentials. It simplifies authentication and access control in cross domain distributed systems.

Secure File and Data Access:

Distributed file systems and databases implement access control, encryption, and auditing features to protect sensitive data from unauthorized access and tampering.

Security Auditing and Logging:

Distributed systems generate logs and audit trails to record security events, access attempts, and system activities. These logs are crucial for monitoring and investigating security incidents.

Security Policies and Compliance:

Security policies define rules and regulations that govern security practices in distributed systems. Compliance with industry standards and regulations, such as HIPAA, GDPR, and PCI DSS, is essential.

Security Patch Management:

Regularly applying security patches and updates to Operating Systems, software, and firmware helps mitigate vulnerabilities and ensures a strong security posture.

Incident Response and Security Monitoring:

Distributed systems should have incident response plans in place to detect, respond to, and recover from security incidents. Security monitoring tools continuously monitor for suspicious activities and threats.

Backup and Disaster Recovery:

Implementing robust backup and disaster recovery strategies ensures data resilience and availability in case of security breaches or system failures.

Security Awareness and Training:

Users and Administrators in distributed systems should receive security awareness training to understand security best practices, recognize threats, and respond effectively to security incidents.

Security in distributed systems is a multifaceted and ongoing process that requires a combination of technical controls, policies, and user awareness. It is essential for safeguarding sensitive information and maintaining the integrity and availability of distributed resources.

Previous Years Solved Questions

Q 1. Explain various authentication and protection mechanism of user files. (RU BCA 2019)

Ans: Authentications is the process of determining whether someone or something is, in fact, who or what it declares itself to be. Authentication technology provides access control for systems by checking to see, if a user's credentials match the credentials in a database of authorized users or in a data authentication server.

Users are usually identified with a user ID, and authentication is accomplished when the user provides a credential, for example a password, that matched with that user Id. Most users ac most familiar with using a password, which as a piece of information that should be known only to the user, is called a knowledge authentication factor. Other authentication factors, and how they are used for two-factor or multifactor authentication (MFA).

During authentication, credentials provided by the user are compared to those on file in a database of authorized users information either on the local Operating System or through an authentication server. If the credentials match, and the authenticated entity is authorized to use the resource, the process is completed sees and the way he can interact with it, including hours of access and other rights such as the amount of resource storage space.

Traditionally, authentication was accomplished by the system or resources being accessed; for example, a server would authenticate users using its own password system, implemented locally, using login Id's (user names) and passwords. Knowledge of the login credentials is assumed to guarantee that the user is authentic.

Each user registers initially (or is registered by someone else, such as a systems and processes can be carried out using machine credentials that work like a user's ID and password, except the credentials are submitted automatically by the device in question. They may also use digital certificated that were issued and verified by a certificate authority as part of a public key infrastructure to authenticate an identity while exchanging information over the internet.

Q 2. Discuss the goal of authentication? (RU BCA 2017)

Ans: Authentication is the process of determiningwhether someone or something is, in fact, who orwhat it is declared to be.

General: Verification of the genuineness of adocument or signature, to make it effective or valid.It usually takes the form of a sealed or stampedcertificate that confirms the authority of a publicofficial (such as judge or a notary public) or Of asignatory.

Computer access: Verification Of the identity of auser through a code such as a password.

Electronic-commerce: Measure employed toensure that the entity requesting access to an onlinesystem is what or who it claims to be, and to counter(by using passwords, authentication certificate, orother identification devices or procedures) anyinappropriate or unauthorized access.

Q 3. Discuss clock synchronization in distributed system of agreement algorithm. (RTU 2016)

Ans: Clock synchronization is a crucial aspect of distributed systems, especially when implementing distributed agreement algorithms like the Paxos or Raft consensus protocols. These algorithms require that all nodes within the distributed system have reasonably synchronized clocks to ensure correct and coordinated decision-making. Clock synchronization addresses issues related to node clock skew, drift, and ensuring that events occur in a logical order across the distributed system.

Let's discuss clock synchronization in the context of distributed agreement algorithms:

Clock Skew and Drift:

Clock Skew: Clock skew refers to the time difference between two clocks that are supposed to be synchronized. In a distributed system, nodes may have different clock speeds due to hardware variations or network latencies, leading to clock skew.

Clock Drift: Clock drift is the rate at which a clock gains or loses time compared to a reference clock. Drift can be caused by imprecise clock hardware or software, which accumulates over time, leading to increasing clock skew.

Logical Clocks:

In distributed systems, logical clocks are often used in place of physical time to order events and achieve consensus. Logical clocks are not tied to wall-clock time but are used to establish a partial order of events. Lamport timestamps and vector clocks are common logical clock implementations used in distributed systems to maintain causality and ordering of events.

Clock Synchronization Protocols:

Distributed systems typically employ clock synchronization protocols to mitigate clock skew and drift. The Network Time Protocol (NTP) and Precision Time Protocol (PTP) are commonly used for this purpose.

NTP relies on a hierarchy of time servers and adjusts a node's clock to synchronize with a reference clock. It can achieve reasonable synchronization accuracy in the sub-millisecond range.

PTP is designed for applications that require high-precision time synchronization, often achieving synchronization in the sub-microsecond range. It's commonly used in industrial automation and financial systems.

Clock Synchronization Challenges:

Clock synchronization is challenging in networks with variable latencies and unpredictable message delivery times.

It can be affected by network congestion, asymmetrical delays, and security threats.

Achieving perfect synchronization is often impractical, but the goal is to keep clock skew and drift within acceptable bounds.

Impact on Distributed Agreement Algorithms:

Clock synchronization is critical in consensus algorithms like Paxos and Raft, as they depend on establishing a consistent order of events across nodes.

Inconsistent or unsynchronized clocks can lead to issues such as split-brain scenarios, where nodes may diverge in their decision-making.

Tolerating Clock Skew:

Some distributed systems are designed to tolerate limited clock skew. For example, in Raft consensus, nodes can operate with clock skew as long as it stays within certain bounds.

Properly designed consensus algorithms can handle clock skew by using logical clocks and quorums.

In summary, clock synchronization in distributed systems is essential to ensure that nodes can coordinate effectively, maintain a consistent order of events, and make reliable decisions. Various clock synchronization protocols and logical clocks are used to address the challenges of clock skew and drift in the context of distributed agreement algorithms like Paxos and Raft.

Q 4. Why NFS protocol is used? (RTU B. Tech)

Ans: The Network File System (NFS) is a protocol used in Operating Systems to enable network-based file sharing and access. NFS allows a computer to access files and directories on remote systems as, if they were local, making it a valuable tool for various purposes. Here are some of the primary reasons why the NFS protocol is used:

File Sharing: NFS simplifies the process of sharing files and directories across a network. It allows multiple computers to access and modify files stored on a remote server as if they were local. This is particularly useful in environments where centralized file storage is needed.

Distributed File Systems: NFS is a key component in building distributed file systems. It allows multiple servers to work together to provide a single, coherent file system that can be accessed by multiple clients.

Cross-Platform Compatibility: NFS is supported by a wide range of Operating Systems, including Unix, Linux, macOS, and some Windows systems with the help of third-party NFS clients. This cross-platform compatibility makes it an excellent choice for heterogeneous environments.

Remote Data Backup: NFS can be used to perform remote data backups. Systems can mount remote directories and back up data to a central server, ensuring data redundancy and disaster recovery.

Diskless Workstations: NFS is used in diskless workstations or thin clients. These machines boot from a network server and rely on NFS to access their file systems. This simplifies system maintenance and reduces hardware requirements for individual workstations.

Cluster Computing: NFS is used in cluster computing environments, where multiple computers work together on a specific task. It allows shared access to data and executable code among cluster nodes, improving performance and resource utilization.
Virtualization: In virtualized environments, NFS can be used to provide shared storage for virtual machines. This enables rapid provisioning and migration of VM's across physical hosts.
Reduced Data Duplication: NFS helps reduce data duplication by allowing multiple clients to access and share the same files. This can save storage space and simplify data management.
Scalability: NFS supports both small-scale and large-scale implementations. It can be used in small office networks as well as in enterprise data centers, making it highly scalable.
Security: While NFS was originally designed with little emphasis on security, modern versions of NFS have added security features such as Kerberos-based authentication and encryption, making it suitable for secure data sharing.
Ease of Management: NFS simplifies the management of data across a network. Administrators can control access permissions and easily maintain and update files on a centralized server.
Performance: NFS is known for its good performance in many scenarios, particularly in environments where low-latency access to remote files is required.

Despite its advantages, it's important to note that NFS has some limitations, such as potential security concerns if not configured properly and the lack of support for some advanced features like distributed locking. However, NFS remains a popular and widely used protocol for network-based file sharing and access in many Operating System environments.

Q 5. What is distributed Operating System? (RU BCA 2019)
Ans: A distributed Operating System is a type of Operating System that runs on multiple interconnected computers or nodes and provides a unified interface for users and applications to access resources and services across the network. In a distributed Operating System, resources such as files, devices, and processing power are distributed across the network, and users can access them transparently regardless of the physical location of the resources.

Key characteristics of a distributed Operating System include:
Transparency: The distributed Operating System provides transparency to users and applications, hiding the complexities of the underlying network and hardware infrastructure. This transparency includes location transparency (users can access resources without knowing their physical location), access

transparency (users can access resources using a uniform interface), and failure transparency (the system can recover from failures without impacting users).

Concurrency: Distributed Operating Systems support concurrent access to resources by multiple users and applications. They provide mechanisms for managing concurrency, such as distributed locking, transactions, and synchronization primitives.

Scalability: Distributed Operating Systems are designed to scale across multiple nodes, allowing them to handle increasing workloads and accommodate growing numbers of users and resources. They use distributed algorithms and protocols to ensure efficient resource utilization and load balancing.

Fault Tolerance: Distributed Operating Systems are resilient to failures and errors, including network failures, node failures, and software errors. They use replication, redundancy, and fault tolerance mechanisms to ensure high availability and reliability.

Interoperability: Distributed Operating Systems support interoperability between heterogeneous hardware and software platforms. They provide standards-based communication protocols and interfaces for seamless integration with different types of systems and devices.

Examples of distributed Operating Systems include Google's distributed Operating System for managing data centers (such as Google File System and MapReduce), Microsoft's Windows Azure, and various open-source distributed Operating Systems like Linux-based clusters and distributed computing frameworks like Apache Hadoop and Apache Spark.

In summary, a distributed Operating System enables the efficient and transparent management of resources and services across a network of interconnected computers, providing scalability, fault tolerance, and interoperability for distributed computing environments.

Previous Years Unsolved Questions

Q 1. How can we implement security and 4 Reliability in Distributed Operating System? (IGNOU 2010)

Q 2. Explain the implementation of RPC in a 5 distributed system.(IGNOU 2010)

Q 3. Explain 'address translation' by direct 5 mapping and associative mapping.(IGNOU 2010)

Q 4. Differentiate between a distributed and networking Operating System with key features.(IGNOU 2010)

Q 5. How can we achieve ordering of events in a distributed OS? Suggest an algorithm and implement an example on it.(IGNOU 2010)

Q 6. How can we ensure authentication in a distributed and Networking Operating System? Suggest two techniques of authentication.(IGNOU Dec 2010)

Q 7. Explain the token based mutual exclusion for distributed Operating System. (IGNOU Dec 2010)

Q 8. Give a short note on mutual exclusion in a distributed system. Explain token based mutual exclusion in the context of it.(IGNOU June 2011)

Q 9. Explain the following in brief: (IGNOU June 2013)

Remote Procedure Call (RPC)

Thrashing

Segmentation

Lock synchronization mechanism

Exercise

Exercise 1 – MCQ

1. What is a key characteristic of a Distributed Operating System (DOS)?

a) Centralized control

b) Single point of failure

c) Limited scalability

d) Decentralized control

2. In a Distributed Operating System, what does the term "transparency" refer to?

a) The ability to see through the system's architecture

b) The seamless integration of hardware and software

c) Hiding the complexity of the distributed environment from users

d) Providing visibility into the network topology

3. Which of the following protocols is used for secure communication over a computer network?

a) HTTP

b) FTP

c) TCP

d) HTTPS

4. What is the function of a switch in a computer network?

a) Connects devices within the same local network

b) Connects devices in different networks

c) Determines the best path for data packets

d) Converts digital data to analog signals

5. What is a characteristic feature of a Distributed File System (DFS)?

a) Centralized storage

b) Single point of access

c) Scalability and fault tolerance

d) Limited file sharing

6. In a Distributed File System, what is the purpose of a metadata server?

a) Manages file storage locations

b) Handles user authentication

c) Encrypts file contents

d) Synchronizes file access

7. What is the purpose of process migration in Distributed Process Management?

a) Load balancing

b) Code optimization

c) Memory allocation

d) File management

8. In a Distributed Process Management system, what is the role of a process coordinator?

a) Allocating CPU time to processes

b) Managing inter-process communication

c) Initiating process migration

d) Handling file I/O operations

9. What is the primary purpose of encryption in Distributed Security?

a) Accelerating data transmission

b) Hiding network topology

c) Securing data against unauthorized access

d) Improving system scalability

10. Which authentication method is commonly used in Distributed Security to verify the identity of users or systems?

a) Public key cryptography

b) MAC (Message Authentication Code)

c) Token-based authentication

d) DNS (Domain Name System)

Exercise 2 – True/ False

1. Fault tolerance is a crucial aspect of Distributed Operating Systems.

2. In a Distributed Operating System, communication between processes is always faster than in a centralized system.

3. A subnet mask is used to divide an IP address into network and host portions.

4. UDP (User Datagram Protocol) provides a connection-oriented communication.

5. One of the advantages of Distributed File Systems is that they eliminate the need for data replication.

6. Consistency in a Distributed File System refers to ensuring that all nodes have the most up-to-date version of a file.

7. In Distributed Process Management, process synchronization is less critical compared to a single-processor system.

8. Fault tolerance is a significant concern in Distributed Process Management, as processes may be distributed across multiple nodes.

9. Role-Based Access Control (RBAC) is a strategy used in Distributed Security to limit access based on a user's role in the organization.

10. Distributed Denial of Service (DDoS) attacks are a less common threat in Distributed Security compared to traditional security models.

Exercise 3 – Fill in the blanks

1. In Distributed Security, the process of verifying the _____________ of users and entities is crucial for maintaining a secure environment.

2. ___________ encryption is a common technique used in Distributed Security to protect data as it travels across networks.

Exercise 4 – Match case

Column A

Process Migration

Load Balancing

Distributed Synchronization

Fault Tolerance

Parallel Processing

Column B

Involves moving a running process from one machine to another.

Distributes computational tasks evenly across multiple machines.

Coordinates activities among processes running on different nodes.

Ensures system reliability and availability in the face of failures.

Simultaneously executing multiple tasks to improve overall performance.

Exercise 5 – One-word

1.What is the primary function of a router in a network?

2. What protocol is commonly used to assign IP addresses automatically on a network?

Exercise 6 – Small answer

1.What is the primary goal of memory hierarchy in an Operating System?

2.What is a file in the context of an Operating System, and how does it differ from a directory?

Exercise 7 – Long answer

1.Can you explain the importance of directory and disk structure in an Operating System, detailing how they organize and manage files and data on storage devices?

2. How do file security and permissions work in an Operating System, and what mechanisms are in place to control and protect access to files and directories?

Answer

Exercise 1 – MCQ

Ans: 1 d, 2 c, 3 d, 4 a, 5 c, 6 a, 7 a, 8 c, 9 c, 10 c

Exercise 2 – True/False

Ans: 1 True, 2 False, 3 True, 4 False, 5 False, 6 True, 7 False, 8 True, 9 True, 10 False

Exercise 3 – Fill in The Blanks

Ans: 1 identity, 2 data

Exercise 4 – Match Case

Ans: 1 b, 2 c,3 d, 4 a, 5 e

Exercise 4 – One-word

Ans: 1 Routing, 2 DHCP (Dynamic Host Configuration Protocol)

Online Resources

Videos:

MCQ Link:https://youtu.be/MIZrAQpGpYY

QR Code:

True/False Link:https://youtu.be/ypnO2xKHZPI

QR Code:

Online Test Paper: https://forms.office.com/r/YHRm7Rrqx0

QR Code:

Chapter 8 Security and Protection

Threats and Security Goals

In Operating Systems and computer security, there are various threats that can compromise the confidentiality, integrity, and availability of data and systems. Security goals are objectives that aim to protect against these threats and ensure a secure computing environment. Here are some common threats and security goals in Operating Systems:

Threats:

Malware: Malicious software, including viruses, worms, Trojans, ransomware, and spyware, can infect and compromise the integrity and functionality of a computer system.

Unauthorized Access:

Unauthorized Access: Unauthorized users gaining access to a system, network, or data can lead to data breaches, theft, or damage.

Brute Force Attacks: Attackers attempt to gain access by trying all possible password combinations.

Password Cracking: Passwords are obtained through various means, such as guessing, dictionary attacks, or rainbow tables.

Privilege Escalation: Unauthorized users exploit vulnerabilities to gain higher level access privileges.

Denial of Service (DoS) and Distributed Denial of Service (DDoS) Attacks:

Attackers flood a system, network, or service with traffic or requests to overwhelm and disrupt its normal operation.

Phishing and Social Engineering:

Phishing emails and Social Engineering techniques trick users into revealing sensitive information like passwords or financial details.

ManintheMiddle (MitM) Attacks:

Attackers intercept and potentially modify communications between two parties without their knowledge.

Insider Threats:

Malicious actions or negligence by authorized users, such as employees or contractors, can pose significant security risks.

Data Leakage and Data Theft:

Sensitive data can be accidentally or intentionally leaked or stolen, leading to data breaches.

Injection Attacks:

Attackers inject malicious code or commands into applications, often exploiting vulnerabilities like SQL injection or cross site scripting (XSS).

Physical Theft and Damage:

Physical theft of devices or infrastructure components can lead to data loss or unauthorized access.

Zero Day Vulnerabilities:

Attackers exploit vulnerabilities that are not yet known to the software vendor or the security community.

Security Goals:

Confidentiality:

Protecting data from unauthorized access or disclosure is a primary security goal. This involves encryption, access controls, and secure data handling practices.

Integrity:

Ensuring data remains unchanged and uncorrupted is essential. Data integrity checks and cryptographic methods help achieve this goal.

Availability:

Systems and data must be available when needed. Measures like redundancy, load balancing, and disaster recovery support availability.

Authentication:

Verifying the identity of users, systems, or processes helps prevent unauthorized access. Strong authentication methods, such as multifactor authentication (MFA), enhance security.

Authorization:

Authorizing users or processes based on their permissions ensures that, they are allowed to access or modify resources.

Audit and Accountability:

Maintaining logs and audit trails helps track and investigate security incidents, providing accountability and transparency.

NonRepudiation:

Nonrepudiation ensures that actions or transactions cannot be denied by the parties involved. Digital signatures and timestamping support nonrepudiation.

Least Privilege:

Users and processes should have the minimum necessary privileges to perform their tasks, reducing the attack surface.

Defense in Depth:

Implementing multiple layers of security controls and measures to protect against various threats is a fundamental approach to security.

Security Awareness:

Training and raising awareness among users and administrators about security risks and best practices can help prevent security incidents.

Patch Management:

Keeping systems, software, and firmware uptodate with security patches helps mitigate vulnerabilities.

Incident Response:

Having an incident response plan and team in place allows for quick detection, response, and recovery from security incidents.

Understanding and addressing these threats and security goals is essential to building and maintaining a secure Operating System and computing environment. Security is an ongoing process that requires continuous monitoring and adaptation to evolving threats and vulnerabilities.

Authentication and Access Control

Authentication and Access Control are fundamental security mechanisms in Operating Systems that help protect resources, data, and the system itself from unauthorized access and potential security threats. These mechanisms ensure that only authorized users and processes can access specific resources and perform certain actions.

Here's an overview of authentication and access control in Operating Systems:

Authentication:

Authentication is the process of verifying the identity of a user, process, or system component to ensure that they are who they claim to be. Common methods of authentication include:

Username and Password: The most common form of authentication, where users provide a unique username and a secret password. Multifactor authentication (MFA) combines this with an additional factor, such as a fingerprint or a onetime code from a mobile app.

Biometric Authentication: This includes fingerprint recognition, iris scanning, facial recognition, and other biometric methods to confirm a person's identity.

Smart Cards and Tokens: Users present physical smart cards or tokens that contain authentication information, such as a cryptographic key, to gain access.

Digital Certificates: Users or devices possess digital certificates issued by a trusted certificate authority. Certificates are used for secure communication and authentication.

Single Segno (SSO): Users authenticate once and gain access to multiple systems or applications without re-entering credentials. SSO is commonly used in enterprise environments.

Kerberos: A network authentication protocol that uses symmetric key cryptography to secure authentication between clients and servers in a distributed network.

Access Control:

Access control defines and enforces the permissions and privileges that determine what actions users, processes, or entities are allowed to perform on specific resources. Access control mechanisms include:

Access Control Lists (ACLs): ACLs are lists associated with objects (files, directories, etc.) that specify which users or groups are granted access and the type of access allowed (e.g., read, write, execute).

Role Based Access Control (RBAC): Users are assigned roles, and permissions are associated with these roles. RBAC simplifies access control management in large organizations.

Mandatory Access Control (MAC): A security model where access is determined by labels and security classifications. Commonly used in government and military environments.

Discretionary Access Control (DAC): Users have discretion over the access controls they set on their resources. It is often used in general-purpose computing environments.

Rule Based Access Control (RBAC): Access decisions are based on predefined rules or policies that consider various factors, including user attributes, time of day, and the resource being accessed.

Attribute Based Access Control (ABAC): Access decisions are made based on attributes associated with users, resources, and environmental conditions.

Role Based Access Control (RBAC): Access permissions are assigned to roles, and users are assigned to roles. This simplifies access management by controlling roles rather than individual users.

File System Permissions: Operating Systems use permissions like read, write, execute, and special permissions (e.g., setuid, setgid) to control access to files and directories.

Access Control Matrix: A comprehensive representation of access rights where rows represent subjects (users or processes), columns represent objects (resources), and cells contain permissions.

Default Deny vs. Default Allow: Access control policies can be based on a default deny or default allow principle. In default deny, all access is denied by default unless explicitly allowed, while default allow allows all access unless explicitly denied.

Effective authentication and access control are crucial for ensuring system security and safeguarding sensitive data. These mechanisms are used in conjunction with other security practices, such as encryption, auditing, and monitoring, to provide comprehensive protection against security threats.

Cryptography

Cryptography plays a crucial role in Operating Systems and computer security by providing mechanisms to protect data confidentiality, integrity, authenticity, and nonrepudiation. It involves the use of mathematical algorithms and cryptographic techniques to secure information and communications.

Here's an overview of cryptography in Operating Systems:

Data Encryption:

Encryption is the process of converting plaintext (readable data) into ciphertext (unreadable data) using encryption algorithms and keys. In Operating Systems, encryption is used to protect sensitive data stored on disks and transmitted over networks. Common encryption algorithms include AES (Advanced Encryption Standard) and RSA (Rivest, Shamir, Adleman).

File and Disk Encryption:

Operating Systems provide tools and features for encrypting entire disks (full disk encryption) or specific files and folders (file level encryption). BitLocker (Windows) and File Vault (macOS) are examples of full disk encryption solutions.

Network Encryption:

Secure communication protocols like SSL/TLS (for web traffic) and IPsec (for network level security) use encryption to protect data during transmission. These protocols are crucial for secure web browsing, email, and virtual private networks (VPNs).

Public Key Infrastructure (PKI):

PKI is a framework that includes digital certificates, public and private keys, and certificate authorities (Cas). It provides a secure way to authenticate and exchange cryptographic keys, ensuring the authenticity and integrity of data and communications.

Digital Signatures:

Digital signatures use asymmetric cryptography to provide authentication and data integrity. They allow the recipient to verify that a message or document was signed by the claimed sender and that it has not been tampered with.

Hash Functions:

Cryptographic hash functions create a fixed length hash value (digest) from input data of any size. Hashes are used to verify data integrity, as even a small change in the input data results in a significantly different hash value. Examples include SHA256 and MD5 (though MD5 is considered weak for security purposes).

Random Number Generation:

Secure random number generation is essential for creating cryptographic keys and initialization vectors (Ivs). Cryptographically secure pseudorandom number generators (CSPRNGs) are used to generate unpredictable and nonrepeating random numbers.

Key Management:

Proper key management is crucial to the security of cryptographic systems. It involves generating, storing, distributing, and securely disposing of cryptographic keys. Hardware security modules (HSMs) are specialized devices for key management.

Authentication Tokens and Smart Cards:

Tokens and smart cards provide a secure means of authentication using cryptographic keys and certificates. They are commonly used in multifactor authentication (MFA) systems.

Secure Boot:

Secure Boot is a feature in modern Operating Systems that ensures the integrity of the boot process by verifying the digital signatures of bootloader and kernel components, preventing the execution of unauthorized or tampered code during startup.

Cryptography Libraries:

Operating Systems provide libraries and APIs (such as OpenSSL and Microsoft CryptoAPI) that developers use to implement cryptographic functionality in applications.

Security Protocols:

Security protocols, such as SSH (Secure Shell), Kerberos, and IPsec, use cryptography to secure network communication and authentication.

Cryptography is a fundamental component of computer security, and its proper implementation is essential for protecting data and communications in Operating Systems. However, it's important to note that cryptographic algorithms and implementations must be regularly updated and monitored to address emerging threats and vulnerabilities.

Malware and Virus Protection

Malware and virus protection in Operating Systems is a critical aspect of computer security. Malware, including viruses, worms, Trojans, ransomware, and other malicious software, poses a significant threat to data, systems, and user privacy.

Here are key strategies and tools for protecting Operating Systems from malware and viruses:

Antivirus Software:

Antivirus software is designed to detect, quarantine, and remove known malware and viruses from a computer. It relies on signature-based detection, analysis, and heuristic methods to identify malicious code.

Antimalware Solutions:

Beyond traditional antivirus software, antimalware solutions offer broader protection against various types of malware, including Trojans, spyware, adware, and rootkits.

Real-time Scanning:

Realtime scanning is a feature of antivirus and antimalware software that continuously monitors file access, downloads, and system activities. When a potentially malicious file or analyses is detected, it is blocked or quarantined.

Regular Updates:

Keeping antivirus and antimalware software up to date is essential to ensure it has the latest virus definitions and security patches to detect and mitigate new threats.

Firewalls:

Firewalls, both software and hardware based, can prevent unauthorized access to a computer or network and block incoming and outgoing malicious traffic.

Operating System Updates:

Regularly applying Operating System updates and security patches is crucial to fixing vulnerabilities that malware can exploit. Enable automatic updates whenever possible.

User Awareness and Training:

Educating users about safe computing practices, such as avoiding suspicious email attachments and links, helps prevent malware infections caused by social engineering attacks.

Email Filtering:

Implement email filtering solutions to scan incoming and outgoing emails for malware, phishing attempts, and malicious attachments.

Web Filtering:

Web filtering tools can block access to malicious websites and prevent drive by downloads of malware.

User Account Control (UAC):

UAC in Windows and similar mechanisms in other Operating Systems prompt users for permission before executing potentially risky actions or installing software, reducing the risk of malware installation.

Least Privilege Principle:

Users and processes should have the minimum necessary permissions and privileges to perform their tasks. This limits the potential impact of malware that may compromise a user account.

Sandboxing and Virtualization:

Sandboxing and virtualization technologies isolate and contain potentially harmful applications or processes, preventing them from affecting the entire system.

Backup and Recovery:

Regularly back up important data and system configurations to offline or secure storage. In the event of a malware infection or data loss, you can restore the system to a clean state.

Remote Desktop and Remote Access Security:

If remote desktop or remote access features are enabled, use strong authentication methods and limit access to authorized users only.

Behavioral Analysis:

Advanced security tools employ behavioral analysis to detect suspicious patterns of activity that may indicate the presence of malware.

Zero Trust Security Model:

Implement a Zero Trust model, where trust is never assumed, and verification is required for all users and devices, regardless of their location within or outside the network.

Security Information and Event Management (SIEM):

SIEM solutions can help monitor and analyse system logs and events for signs of malware activity and security incidents.

Effective malware and virus protection require a combination of these strategies and tools, as no single approach is sufficient to combat all types of threats. Continuous vigilance, security awareness, and a proactive security posture are crucial to maintaining a secure Operating System environment.

Security Policies and Models

Security policies and models are fundamental aspects of computer security in Operating Systems. They define the rules, principles, and guidelines that govern how security is implemented, enforced, and maintained. These policies and models help protect the confidentiality, integrity, and availability of system resources and data.

Here are some key security policies and models in Operating Systems:

Security Policies:

Least Privilege Principle:

The least privilege principle dictates that users and processes should have only the minimum permissions necessary to perform their tasks. This reduces the potential for privilege escalation and limits the impact of security breaches.

Separation of Duties (SoD):

SoD policies prevent a single user or entity from having complete control over a critical system function. It ensures that multiple individuals or roles are involved in sensitive operations, reducing the risk of misuse.

NeedtoKnow Principle:

The needtoknow principle restricts access to information only to those users who require it to perform their job functions. It is often used in environments where sensitive data is involved.

Password Policies:

Password policies define rules for creating, storing, and managing passwords. They typically include requirements for password complexity, expiration, and lockout after multiple failed login attempts.

Data Classification and Handling:

Data classification policies categorize data based on its sensitivity and importance. They specify how data should be handled, stored, transmitted, and disposed of based on its classification.

Remote Access Policies:

Remote access policies govern how users can connect to the network and systems remotely. They include requirements for authentication methods, encryption, and access control.

Acceptable Use Policies (AUP):

AUPs outline acceptable and unacceptable behaviors and actions by users when using company resources, including computers and networks. They often include rules against unauthorized access, data breaches, and misuse of resources.

Incident Response and Reporting:

Incident response policies define the procedures and steps to follow in the event of a security incident or breach. They include guidelines for reporting incidents, assessing damage, and mitigating risks.

Security Models:

BellLaPadula Model (BLP):

BLP is a formal model for mandatory access control that enforces confidentiality by preventing information flow from higher security levels to lower security levels. It uses security labels (e.g., classified, unclassified) and access modes (read, write) to control access.

Biba Model:

The Biba model focuses on integrity and enforces the principle that information should not flow from lower integrity levels to higher integrity levels. It prevents users with lower integrity from corrupting or modifying higher integrity data.

ClarkWilson Model:

This model emphasizes data integrity by ensuring that all updates to data adhere to well-formed transactions and follow a set of integrity rules. It is commonly used in commercial and financial systems.

Role Based Access Control (RBAC):

RBAC is a flexible access control model that assigns permissions to roles rather than individual users. Users are assigned roles, and roles are assigned permissions. This simplifies access management in large organizations.

Discretionary Access Control (DAC):

DAC is a common access control model where the owner of an object (e.g., file) determines who can access it and what level they havean access. It allows users to grant or revoke permissions on their own resources.

Mandatory Access Control (MAC):

MAC enforces access controls based on predefined security labels and classifications. Users have limited control over access, and the system enforces security policies more rigidly.

Attribute Based Access Control (ABAC):

ABAC allows access control decisions to be based on attributes associated with users, resources, and the environment. It provides fine-grained control and dynamic access decisions.

These security policies and models serve as the foundation for building secure Operating Systems and environments. Depending on the organization's security requirements and regulatory compliance, specific policies and models may be adopted and customized. Regular security audits and assessments help ensure that security policies and models are effective and uptodate.

Previous Years Solved Questions

Q 1. What is Process scheduling? What criteria affect the scheduler's performance? (RU BCA 2019)

Ans: The process scheduling is the activity of the process manager that handles the removal ofthe running processfrom the CPU and the selection of another process on the basis of a particular strategy.

Process scheduling is an essential part of a Multiprogramming Operating Systems. Such Operating Systems allow more than one process to be loaded into the executable memory at a tune and the loaded process shares the CPU using time multiplexing.

Various criteria or characteristics that help in designing a good scheduling algorithm arc:

CPU Utilization " A scheduling algorithm should be designed so that CPU remains busy as possible. It should make efficient use of CPU.

Throughput " Throughput is the amount of work completed in a unit oftime in other words throughput is the processes executed to number Of jobs completed in a unit of time. The scheduling algorithm must look to maximize the number of jobs processed per tune unit.

Response time " Response time is the tune taken to Start responding to the request. A scheduler must aim to minimize response time for users

Turnaround time " Turnaround time refers to the time between the moment of submission of a job/ process and the time of Its completion. Thus, how long it takes to execute a process is also an important factor.

Waiting time " It is the time a job waits for resource allocation when several jobs are competing in multiprogramming system is to minimize the waiting time,

Fairness " A good scheduler should make sure that each process gets its fair share 01' the CPU.

Previous Years Unsolved Questions

Q 1. Differentiate between various typesof security models of an Operating System.(IGNOU Dec 2010)

Q 2. What is an Access matrix model of security? Explain with an example.(IGNOU June 2011)

Q 3. Explain Take Grant model for security in an Operating System. Give an example to illustrate the model.(IGNOU June 2011)

Q 4. Differentiate between authorisation and authentication. How can a user choose a good password? (IGNOU June 2011)

Q 5. Explain the following security models: (IGNOU June 2012)

Access Matrix Model

Mandatory Access Control

Discretionry Access Control

Rule Based Access Control

Q 6. Explain any two security models for computer system.(IGNOU Dec 2012)

Q 7. Explain take grant model for security of OS. Also explain three techniques of authentication. (IGNOU June 2013)

Q 8. What is the difference between security policy and security model? Explain the access matrix model. (IGNOU June 2013)

Exercise

Exercise 1 – MCQ

1. What is the primary goal of "Confidentiality" in Operating System security?

a) Preventing unauthorized access

b) Ensuring data integrity

c) Detecting system vulnerabilities

d) Enhancing system performance

2. Which of the following is a common threat to Operating System security?

a) Data encryption

b) Authentication

c) Malware

d) Redundancy

3. What is the purpose of Two-Factor Authentication (2FA) in Operating System security?

a) Simplifying user login processes

b) Enhancing password complexity requirements

c) Adding an extra layer of security by using multiple verification methods

d) Restricting access to specific IP addresses only

4. Which access control model is based on defining permissions assigned to specific users or groups?

a) Mandatory Access Control (MAC)

b) Role-Based Access Control (RBAC)

c) Discretionary Access Control (DAC)

d) Rule-Based Access Control (RBAC)

5. What is the primary purpose of a public key in public key cryptography?

a) Encrypting data

b) Decrypting data

c) Verifying digital signatures

d) Generating random numbers

6. Which cryptographic algorithm is commonly used for secure communication over the internet, providing confidentiality and integrity?

a) AES (Advanced Encryption Standard)

b) RSA (Rivest-Shamir-Adleman)

c) SHA-256 (Secure Hash Algorithm 256-bit)

d) DES (Data Encryption Standard)

7. What is a characteristic of a "Trojan horse" malware?

a) Replicates itself and spreads to other systems

b) Modifies existing programs to perform malicious actions

c) Appears as a legitimate software but performs malicious activities

d) Encrypts files and demands a ransom for decryption

8. Which of the following is a proactive measure against malware that involves analyzing the behavior of programs in a virtual environment?

a) Signature-based detection

b) Heuristic-based detection

c) Behavior-based detection

d) Polymorphic code

9. What is the primary goal of a security policy in an Operating System?

a) Enhancing system performance

b) Ensuring user convenience

c) Protecting system resources and data

d) Facilitating software updates

10. Which security model emphasizes the concept of "need to know" and "least privilege"?

a) Biba Integrity Model

b) Bell-LaPadula Model

c) Clark-Wilson Model

d) Brewer-Nash Model

Exercise 2 – True/ False

1. "Integrity" as a security goal involves ensuring that data is accurate and unaltered.
2. Denial of Service (DoS) attacks are primarily aimed at unauthorized access to sensitive information.
3. Biometric authentication methods, such as fingerprint recognition, fall under the category of something the user knows.
4. Access Control Lists (ACLs) are commonly used in Mandatory Access Control (MAC) to define access permissions.
5. The process of converting plaintext into unreadable ciphertext is known as decryption.
6. One of the key advantages of symmetric key cryptography is its ability to provide secure key exchange over insecure channels.
7. A computer virus is a standalone program that does not require a host program to execute.
8. Anti-virus software primarily relies on detecting and removing malware based on known signatures.
9. Security policies only focus on external threats and do not consider internal risks.
10. The Biba Integrity Model allows information to flow only from higher integrity levels to lower integrity levels.

Exercise 3 – Fill in the blanks

1.A ___________ Operating System is optimized for smartphones, tablets, and other mobile devices.

2.RealTimeOperating Systems (RTOS) are designed for systems with strict __________ requirements, such as robotics and industrial automation.

Answer

Exercise 1 – MCQ

Ans: 1 a, 2 c, 3 c, 4 c, 5 c, 6 a, 7 c, 8 c, 9 c, 10 b

Exercise 2 – True/False

Ans: 1 True, 2 False, 3 False, 4 False, 5 False, 6 False, 7 False, 8 True, 9 False, 10 True

Exercise 3 – Fill in The Blanks

Ans: 1 Mobile, 2 Timing or time sensitive

Online Resources

Videos:

MCQ Link: https://youtu.be/GA4YKELwjCk

QR Code:

True/False Link: https://youtu.be/xvW-dKYv0os

R Code:

Online Test Paper: https://forms.office.com/r/BSinxbH7u7

QR Code:

Chapter 9 Virtualization and Cloud Computing

Virtualization Concepts

Virtualization is a technology that allows multiple virtual instances or environments to run on a single physical computer or server. It abstracts and isolates the underlying hardware, enabling efficient resource utilization, flexibility, and isolation between virtualized environments. Virtualization is widely used in Operating Systems and data centers for various purposes.

Here are key virtualization concepts in Operating Systems:

A. Virtual Machine (VM):

A Virtual Machine is a software-based emulation of a physical computer. It includes a virtual CPU, memory, storage, and network interfaces. Multiple VM's can run concurrently on a single physical host.

B. Hypervisor:

A Hypervisor, also known as a Virtual Machine Monitor (VMM), is a software or hardware layer that manages and monitors multiple VM's running on a physical host. Hypervisors provide resource allocation, isolation, and control over VM's.

C. Type 1 Hypervisor (BareMetal Hypervisor):

Type 1 Hypervisors run directly on the physical hardware without the need for an underlying Operating System. Examples include VMware vSphere/ESXi, Microsoft Hyper-V, and Xen.

D. Type 2 Hypervisor (Hosted Hypervisor):

Type 2 Hypervisors run on top of an existing Operating System and are typically used for desktop virtualization. Examples include VMware Workstation, VirtualBox, and Parallels Desktop.

E. Virtualization Host:

The physical machine that runs one or more virtual machines is called the virtualization host or hypervisor host.

F. Guest Operating System:

Each virtual machine runs its own guest Operating System. These guest OS instances are isolated from each other and from the host OS.

G. Virtualization Resources:

VM's have virtualized resources, including CPU cores, memory, disk storage, and network interfaces. These resources are allocated by the hypervisor from the physical hardware.

H. Virtualization Modes:

VM's can run in various modes, including full virtualization, paravirtualization, and hardware assisted virtualization. These modes impact performance and compatibility.

I. Live Migration:

Live migration, or VM migration, allows a VM to be moved from one physical host to another with minimal downtime. This feature is important for load balancing and maintenance.

J. Snapshot:

VM snapshots capture the state of a VM at a specific point in time. Snapshots can be used for backup, recovery, and testing purposes.

K. Resource Pooling:

Virtualization enables the pooling of physical resources, such as CPU and memory, which can be dynamically allocated to VM's based on demand.

L. Virtual Networking:

Virtual switches and network adapters allow VM's to communicate with each other and with external networks. Network configurations are managed within the virtualization platform.

Templates and Cloning:

VM templates and cloning capabilities simplify the process of creating multiple identical VM instances, saving time and ensuring consistency.

Resource Isolation:

Hypervisors provide strong isolation between VM's, preventing one VM from impacting the performance or security of others. Resource limits and quotas can be set to enforce fair resource sharing.

Application Virtualization:

In addition to server virtualization, application virtualization allows individual applications to run in isolated environments on the same Operating System.

Containerization:

Containerization, often associated with technologies like Docker and Kubernetes, provides a lightweight form of virtualization that isolates applications and their dependencies within containers.

Cloud Virtualization:

Cloud computing relies heavily on virtualization to create and manage virtual instances in a scalable and flexible manner.

Virtualization is a fundamental technology that has transformed how computing resources are utilized, making it possible to achieve higher levels of efficiency, scalability, and resource optimization in Operating Systems and data centers. It has become an integral part of modern IT infrastructure and cloud computing.

Virtual Machines

Virtual machines (VM's) are software-based emulations of physical computers or servers that run on a single physical host or host system. VM's enable multiple independent Operating Systems and environments to coexist and operate concurrently on a single piece of hardware. Each VM functions as if it were a standalone computer with its own CPU, memory, storage, and network interfaces. Here are key aspects of virtual machines in Operating Systems:

Hypervisor:VM's are managed and executed by a hypervisor, also known as a Virtual Machine Monitor (VMM). The hypervisor is responsible for creating, running, monitoring, and managing the virtual machines. It abstracts and allocates physical resources to VM's.

Guest Operating System: Each virtual machine runs its own guest Operating System, which can be different from the host Operating System. The guest OS is isolated from other VM's and the host OS. Common guest OS choices include various versions of Windows, Linux distributions, and other Operating Systems.

Resource Virtualization:VM's have virtualized resources, including virtual CPUs (vCPUs), virtual memory, virtual storage, and virtual network interfaces. These resources are abstracted from the underlying physical hardware and allocated to VM's by the hypervisor.

Isolation:VM's provide strong isolation between themselves and the host system as well as between other VM's. This isolation ensures that one VM cannot directly interfere with or access the resources of another VM or the host system.

Snapshots: VM snapshots capture the state of a VM at a specific point in time. Snapshots can be used for backup, recovery, and testing purposes. They allow VM's to be restored to a previous state.

Templates and Cloning: VM templates and cloning capabilities simplify the process of creating multiple identical VM instances. Templates serve as preconfigured VM images that can be used as a starting point for creating new VM's.

Live Migration: Live migration, or VM migration, allows a running VM to be moved from one physical host to another with minimal downtime. This feature is important for load balancing, resource optimization, and maintenance tasks.

Resource Management: The hypervisor provides resource management features, allowing administrators to allocate CPU, memory, storage, and network resources to VM's based on their needs. Resource allocation can be adjusted dynamically to respond to changing demands.

Networking: Virtual switches and network adapters allow VM's to communicate with each other and with external networks. Networking configurations are managed within the virtualization platform, allowing for custom network topologies.

Security:VM's can be configured with security measures such as firewalls, antivirus software, and encryption to protect against security threats. VM's are isolated, reducing the risk of security breaches affecting other VM's or the host system.

Applications:VM's are used for various purposes, including server virtualization, software testing and development, legacy application support, sandboxing untrusted software, and creating isolated environments for specific tasks.

Cloud Computing: Virtual machines play a pivotal role in cloud computing environments, where they are used to provide scalable and flexible computing resources to users and organizations on demand.

Popular hypervisors for creating and managing virtual machines include VMware vSphere/ESXi, Microsoft HyperV, Oracle VirtualBox, KVM (Kernel based Virtual Machine), and Xen. Virtualization has revolutionized IT infrastructure by increasing resource utilization, simplifying management, and providing flexibility for various computing workloads and environments.

Hypervisors

Hypervisors, also known as Virtual Machine Monitors (VMMs), are software or hardware components that create, manage, and run Virtual Machines (VM's) on a physical computer or server. Hypervisors enable multiple virtualized environments, each with its own Operating System and applications, to coexist and operate independently on the same physical hardware. There are two primary types of hypervisors:

Type 1 Hypervisor (BareMetal Hypervisor):

Type 1 Hypervisors run directly on the physical hardware without the need for an underlying host Operating System. They provide a layer of abstraction between the hardware and VM's. This approach typically offers better performance and security compared to Type 2 Hypervisors.

Examples of Type 1 Hypervisors include:

VMware vSphere/ESXi

Microsoft Hyper-V (when used in a standalone, bare metal configuration)

Xen

KVM (Kernel based Virtual Machine)

Oracle VM Server for SPARC and x86

Type 2 Hypervisor (Hosted Hypervisor):

Type 2 Hypervisors run on top of an existing host Operating System. They are typically used for desktop virtualization and software development/testing scenarios. Type 2 Hypervisors are easier to set up but may introduce some performance overhead.

Examples of Type 2 Hypervisors include:

VMware Workstation

Oracle VirtualBox

Parallels Desktop (for macOS)

Microsoft Virtual PC

Key characteristics and considerations of hypervisors in Operating Systems:

Resource Allocation: Hypervisors allocate physical resources (CPU, memory, storage, network interfaces) to virtual machines. These resources are abstracted and presented as virtualized resources to VM's.

Isolation: Hypervisors provide strong isolation between VM's. Each VM runs independently of others, and there is no direct interaction between VM's at the hardware level. This isolation enhances security and stability.

Resource Management: Hypervisors include resource management features to allocate and control the allocation of resources to VM's. Administrators can allocate CPU shares, memory reservations, and other resources based on VM requirements.

Live Migration: Many hypervisors support live migration, allowing running VM's to be moved from one physical host to another with minimal downtime. This feature is essential for load balancing, resource optimization, and maintenance.

Snapshot and Cloning: Hypervisors typically offer snapshot and cloning capabilities. Snapshots capture the state of a VM at a specific point in time, while cloning allows for the creation of identical VM instances from a template.

Management Interfaces: Hypervisors provide management interfaces (GUI or command line) for configuring, monitoring, and managing VM's, resource allocation, and other aspects of virtualization.

Compatibility: Hypervisors can run various guest Operating Systems, including Windows, Linux, macOS, and others. This flexibility makes them suitable for a wide range of use cases.

Performance: Type 1 Hypervisors often offer better performance compared to Type 2 Hypervisors because they run directly on the hardware. However, the performance impact of virtualization can vary depending on the workload and hardware.

Security: Hypervisors must be secure to prevent vulnerabilities that could compromise the isolation between VM's and the host system. Security is a critical consideration for hypervisor design and implementation.

Licensing: Hypervisors may have different licensing models, including open source, commercial, and enterprise editions with various features and support options.

Hypervisors are fundamental components of virtualization technologies used in data centers, cloud computing, software development, and testing environments. They enable efficient resource utilization, isolation, scalability, and flexibility in managing virtualized workloads.

Cloud Computing Models

Cloud Computing offers various service models that enable users to access and use computing resources over the internet. These cloud computing models provide different levels of control, flexibility, and management for users and organizations. The primary cloud computing models are Infrastructure as a Service (IaaS), Platform as a Service (PaaS), and Software as a Service (SaaS). Here's an overview of each model:

Infrastructure as a Service (IaaS):

In the IaaS model, cloud providers offer virtualized computing resources, including virtual machines (VM's), storage, and networking. Users can provision and manage these resources on demand.

IaaS provides users with the most control over the infrastructure. Users are responsible for managing the Operating System, applications, and data hosted on the virtualized infrastructure.

Examples of IaaS providers include Amazon Web Services (AWS), Microsoft Azure, Google Cloud Platform (GCP), and IBM Cloud.

Key features of IaaS:

Scalable and customizable infrastructure.

Users have full control over VM configurations.

Suitable for deploying and managing virtualized environments.

Platform as a Service (PaaS):

PaaS provides a higher-level cloud computing model that abstracts the underlying infrastructure. It offers a platform and development environment for building, deploying, and managing applications.

Users focus on developing and deploying applications without worrying about the underlying infrastructure, including the Operating System and hardware.

PaaS providers offer tools and services for application development, databases, and middleware.

Examples of PaaS providers include Heroku, Google App Engine, Microsoft Azure App Service, and Red Hat OpenShift.

Key features of PaaS:

Simplified application development and deployment.

Automated infrastructure management.

Ideal for developers and organizations focusing on application development.

Software as a Service (SaaS):

SaaS delivers software applications and services over the internet on a subscription basis. Users access and use the software through web browsers without installingor managing it locally.

SaaS applications cover a wide range of business functions, including email, collaboration, customer relationship management (CRM), and productivity tools.

Users do not have control over the underlying infrastructure, Operating System, or application code.

Examples of SaaS providers include Microsoft 365 (formerly Office 365), Google Workspace, Salesforce, and Dropbox.

Key features of SaaS:

Readytouse software applications accessible from anywhere.

No need for software installation or maintenance.

Simplified software licensing and updates.

Additional cloud computing models and variations include:

Function as a Service (FaaS) or Serverless Computing:

In this model, users focus on writing and deploying individual functions or pieces of code (known as "serverless functions") without managing the underlying infrastructure. The cloud provider automatically scales and manages the execution of functions in response to events.

Examples of FaaS platforms include AWS Lambda, Azure Functions, and Google Cloud Functions.

Containers as a Service (CaaS):

CaaS platforms provide container orchestration and management services for deploying and scaling containerized applications. Users work with containers (e.g., Docker) to package and deploy applications with portability.

Kubernetes is a widely used container orchestration platform that can be considered a CaaS solution.

1

Each cloud computing model has its advantages and use cases, allowing organizations to choose the most suitable model based on their requirements, expertise, and desired level of control over infrastructure and applications. Many cloud providers offer a combination of these models to address diverse customer needs.

Cloud Service Providers

Cloud Service Providers (CSPs) are companies that offer cloud computing services and resources to individuals, businesses, and organizations over the internet. These providers operate largescale data centers with the infrastructure and technology necessary to deliver a wide range of cloud services. Here are some prominent cloud service providers as of my last knowledge update in September 2021:

A. Amazon Web Services (AWS):

AWS is one of the largest and most widely used cloud service providers globally. It offers a vast array of services, including computing, storage, databases, machine learning, analytics, and more.

B. Microsoft Azure:

Microsoft Azure is a cloud platform by Microsoft that provides IaaS, PaaS, and SaaS solutions. It offers services for virtual machines, AI, IoT, and enterprise applications, among others.

C. Google Cloud Platform (GCP):

GCP offers cloud computing services with a strong focus on data analytics, machine learning, and big data. It provides infrastructure, data storage, and developer tools.

D. IBM Cloud:

IBM Cloud offers a range of cloud services, including IaaS, PaaS, and SaaS. It emphasizes hybrid cloud solutions and enterprise grade services.

E. Oracle Cloud:

Oracle Cloud provides cloud infrastructure and application services with a focus on databases, ERP, and other enterprise applications.

F. Alibaba Cloud:

Alibaba Cloud, part of Alibaba Group, is a leading cloud provider in Asia and offers a wide range of cloud services, including computing, storage, and AI.

G. Salesforce (Salesforce.com):

Salesforce is known for its cloud-based customer relationship management (CRM) software. It also offers a variety of cloud-based business applications.

H. Heroku:

Heroku, a subsidiary of Salesforce, provides a cloud platform for developers to build, deploy, and scale web applications and services.

I. Red Hat OpenShift:

OpenShift, by Red Hat (now part of IBM), is a Kubernetesbased container platform that offers container orchestration and management services.

J. Digital Ocean:

DigitalOcean focuses on providing cloud infrastructure and services to developers and small to mediumsized businesses. It offers simplicity and ease of use.

K. VMware Cloud:

VMware offers cloud solutions for virtualization and hybrid cloud deployments, including VMware Cloud on AWS.

L. Tencent Cloud:

Tencent Cloud, part of Tencent Holdings, offers cloud computing services, including virtual servers, databases, and AI.

M. Rackspace Technology:

Rackspace provides cloud management and managed hosting services, helping businesses optimize their cloud environments.

N. SAP Cloud Platform:

SAP Cloud Platform offers cloud-based services for developing, deploying, and managing applications, particularly tailored for SAP software users.

O. Adobe Experience Cloud:

Adobe's cloud platform focuses on digital marketing, advertising, and analytics services.

P. NVIDIA GPU Cloud (NGC):

NGC provides GPUoptimized software containers and libraries for machine learning, AI, and high-performance computing.

These cloud service providers offer a wide range of services, including infrastructure as a service (IaaS), platform as a service (PaaS), software as a service (SaaS), serverless computing, databases, storage, networking, security, and more. Organizations choose a cloud provider based on their specific needs, such as scalability, compliance requirements, geographic regions, and service offerings. It's important to note that the cloud computing landscape evolves, and new providers and services may emerge over time.

Previous Years Solved Questions

Q 1. Describe briefly Virtual Memory Organization and Demand Paging in WINDOWS-10. (IGNOU PGDCA June 2022)

Ans:

Virtual Memory Organization in Windows 10:

Virtual Memory: Virtual Memory is a memory management capability of an Operating System (OS) that uses hardware and software to allow a computer to compensate for physical memory shortages by temporarily transferring data from random access memory (RAM) to disk storage.

Components of Virtual Memory Organization in Windows 10:

Virtual Address Space:

Windows 10 uses a 64-bit virtual address space for each process, providing a vast address range. The virtual address space is divided into user space (for application processes) and kernel space (for the Operating System).

Page Tables:

Page tables are used to map virtual addresses to physical addresses. Windows 10 employs a hierarchical page table structure to efficiently manage large address spaces.

Page Size:

The size of a page in Windows 10 is typically 4 KB, although the Operating System supports larger pages (2 MB and 1 GB) for certain scenarios to improve memory management efficiency.

Page Table Entries (PTE):

Each entry in the page table is a Page Table Entry (PTE), containing information about the corresponding virtual-to-physical address mapping, including status flags.

Memory-Mapped Files:

Windows 10 allows memory-mapped files, enabling the direct mapping of files into virtual memory. This facilitates efficient file I/O operations and supports shared memory mechanisms.

Demand Paging in Windows 10:

Demand Paging: Demand Paging is a virtual memory management scheme where pages are brought into memory only when they are referenced during program execution. It is a technique to reduce the amount of physical memory required to run a process.

Key Features of Demand Paging in Windows 10:

Page Faults:

When a process accesses a page that is not currently in physical memory, a page fault occurs. Windows 10 uses demand paging to handle page faults efficiently.

Lazy Loading:

Windows 10 employs lazy loading, where only the pages that are needed are loaded into memory. This helps minimize the initial loading time of an application and reduces unnecessary disk I/O.

Page Replacement:

If the physical memory becomes full, Windows 10 uses page replacement algorithms (such as Least Recently Used - LRU) to decide which pages to swap out to the disk to make room for new pages.

Working Set:

The working set of a process is the set of pages that are currently resident in physical memory. Windows 10 dynamically adjusts the working set to adapt to changing memory requirements.

Page Prioritization:

Windows 10 prioritizes pages based on their usage patterns. Frequently accessed pages are given higher priority to remain in physical memory, while less frequently used pages may be paged out.

Memory Compression:

Windows 10 includes memory compression techniques to reduce the need for paging to disk. Frequently accessed pages are compressed and stored in memory to improve overall performance.

Page file:

Windows 10 uses a page file on disk to supplement physical memory. When pages are swapped out, they are stored in the page file. The size and location of the page file can be configured by the user.

Demand Paging in Windows 10 is an essential part of the virtual memory system, allowing the Operating System to efficiently manage memory resources by bringing in only the necessary pages as they are required during program execution. This dynamic approach helps optimize system performance and resource utilization.

Q 2. What is Virtual Memory? How is it implemented? Explain its function in detail. (RTU MCA 2022)

Ans: Virtual Memory:

Virtual memory is a memory management technique used by Operating Systems to provide an abstraction of more extensive physical memory than is actually available. It allows programs to use more memory than is physically installed on the system by transparently swapping data between RAM and secondary storage devices, such as hard drives or SSDs.

Implementation:

Virtual memory is implemented using a combination of hardware and software mechanisms. The Operating System manages virtual memory by dividing the address space of each process into fixed-size blocks called pages. These pages are mapped to physical memory or stored on disk as needed. When a process accesses a virtual memory address that is not currently in RAM, a page fault occurs, and the Operating System swaps the required page into memory from disk.

Function:

Increased Memory Capacity: Virtual memory allows programs to use more memory than it is physically available by temporarily storing data on disk, when RAM is full.

Memory Protection: Virtual memory provides memory protection by isolating the address spaces of different processes, preventing one process from accessing the memory of another process.

Memory Sharing: Virtual memory enables memory sharing between processes by mapping the same physical memory pages to multiple processes' virtual address spaces.

Simplified Programming: Virtual memory simplifies programming by providing a uniform memory model to applications, abstracting away the complexities of physical memory management.

Demand Paging: Virtual memory supports demand paging, where pages are only loaded into memory when needed, reducing memory wastage and improving overall system efficiency.

In summary, Virtual Memory allows efficient and flexible use of physical memory resources by providing an abstraction layer between the virtual memory addresses used by programs and the physical memory installed in the system. It enhances system performance, enables memory protection, and simplifies memory management for both the Operating System and applications.

Exercise

Exercise 1 – MCQ

1. What is virtualization in computing?
a) Emulating physical hardware
b) Running software natively
c) Enhancing network security
d) Installing physical servers
2. Which component is responsible for managing and creating virtual machines (VM's) in virtualization?
a) Hypervisor
b) Operating System
c) Compiler
d) Router
3. Which of the following is a type-1 hypervisor?
a) VMware Workstation
b) Microsoft Hyper-V
c) Oracle VirtualBox
d) VMware ESXi
4. What is the primary purpose of a hypervisor?
a) Managing hardware resources
b) Running applications
c) Enhancing user interfaces
d) Handling network traffic
5. In virtualization, what is a snapshot?
a) A photo of the virtual environment
b) A backup of the VM's current state
c) A screenshot of the desktop
d) A security feature for virtual networks

6. What is a cloud computing deployment model where resources are shared among multiple tenants?

a) Public Cloud

b) Private Cloud

c) Hybrid Cloud

d) Community Cloud

7. Which cloud service model provides virtualized computing resources over the internet?

a) Platform as a Service (PaaS)

b) Software as a Service (SaaS)

c) Function as a Service (FaaS)

d) Infrastructure as a Service (IaaS)

8. What is the purpose of a Cloud Service Provider (CSP) in cloud computing?

a) Developing cloud applications

b) Offering virtualization software

c) Providing and managing cloud resources

d) Monitoring network security

9. Which cloud computing model allows users to deploy applications without managing the underlying infrastructure?

a) Infrastructure as a Service (IaaS)

b) Platform as a Service (PaaS)

c) Software as a Service (SaaS)

d) Function as a Service (FaaS)

10. What is a benefit of cloud computing in terms of scalability?

a) Fixed resource allocation

b) Limited network access

c) On-demand resource scaling

d) Offline application deployment

Exercise 2 – True/ False

1. Hypervisors are also known as Virtual Machine Monitors (VMMs).
2. Virtualization allows multiple Operating Systems to run on a single physical machine concurrently.
3. Cloud computing eliminates the need for physical hardware and on-premises infrastructure.
4. Public Cloud is a deployment model suitable for exclusive use by a single organization.
5. Cloud Service Providers (CSPs) are responsible for securing the data and applications in the cloud.

6. Infrastructure as a Service (IaaS) provides ready-to-use software applications over the internet.

7. Virtual Machines (VM's) in virtualization are isolated from each other and share the same Operating System kernel.

8. A snapshot in virtualization captures the state of a virtual machine at a specific point in time.

9. Hybrid Cloud combines aspects of both private and public cloud models.

10.Cloud computing can enhance business agility by providing rapid resource provisioning and scaling.

Answer

Exercise 1 – MCQ

Ans: 1 a, 2 a, 3 d, 4 a, 5 b, 6 a, 7 a, 8 c, 9 b, 10 c

Exercise 2 – True/False

Ans: 1 True, 2 True, 3 True, 4 False, 5 True, 6 False, 7 False, 8 True, 9 True, 10 True

Online Resources

Videos:

MCQ Link:https://youtu.be/YYMaXOOEzZ8

QR Code:

True/False Link:https://youtu.be/uvbLaB8avA0

QR Code:

Online Test Paper: https://forms.office.com/r/KrCjSrYXCh

QR Code:

Chapter 10 Trends and Emerging Technologies

Containerization

Containerization is a lightweight form of virtualization that allows applications and their dependencies to be packaged together in a container image. Containers provide a consistent and isolated runtime environment for applications, ensuring they run consistently across different computing environments, such as development, testing, and production. Here are key concepts and components of containerization:

Container Image:

A Container Image is a standalone package that includes an application, its runtime, libraries, and other dependencies. It is built from a set of instructions defined in a Docker file or a similar configuration file.

Docker:

Docker is one of the most popular containerization platforms. It provides tools for building, distributing, and running container images. Docker also offers a container runtime that manages containers on the host system.

Container Runtime:

The Container Runtime is responsible for executing containers on a host system. Docker's container and container runtimes like runc are examples. They isolate containers from the host and each other, providing resource management and security.

Docker file:

A Docker file is a text-based configuration file used to define the steps and dependencies required to build a container image. It specifies the base image, application code, libraries, environment variables, and more.

Container Registry:

A Container Registry is a repository where container images are stored and distributed. Docker Hub is a popular public container registry, but organizations often use private registries for security and control.

Container Orchestration:

Container Orchestration platforms, such as Kubernetes, Docker Swarm, and Apache Mesos, manage the deployment, scaling, and lifecycle of containers in a distributed environment. They automate tasks like load balancing, self-healing, and rolling updates.

Container Networking:

Containers can communicate with each other and with external systems through container networking. Container orchestration platforms provide networking solutions for connecting containers within clusters.

Isolation and Resource Management:

Containers provide process and file system isolation, allowing multiple containers to run on a single host without interfering with each other. Resource limits can be set to control CPU, memory, and storage usage.

Portability:

Containers are highly portable across different environments, including on-premises data centers, public clouds, and hybrid cloud setups. The consistent runtime environment ensures that applications behave predictably regardless of the underlying infrastructure.

Microservices Architecture:

Containerization aligns well with Microservices Architecture, where applications are decomposed into smaller, independent services. Each microservice can run in its own container, simplifying deployment and scaling.

Security and Isolation:

While containers provide process isolation, they share the same kernel with the host Operating System. Security features like user namespaces and container security policies are used to enhance isolation and security.

Development and DevOps:

Containers streamline the development and deployment process, enabling developers to work in consistent environments and reducing the "it works on my machine" problem. They are a fundamental component of DevOps practices.

Containerization Platforms: Aside from Docker, other containerization platforms include containerd, Podman, and rkt (pronounced "rocket").

Containerization has become a cornerstone of modern software development and deployment, enabling agility, scalability, and consistency in software delivery. It has transformed the way applications are developed, tested, and deployed in various computing environments, including cloud, edge, and on-premises data centers.

Internet of Things (IoT)

The Internet of Things (IoT) is a transformative technological paradigm that interconnects everyday objects and devices to the internet, allowing them to collect, exchange, and act upon data autonomously. It extends the capabilities of the internet beyond traditional computing devices to include a vast array of physical objects, ranging from household appliances and vehicles to industrial machines and wearable gadgets. Operating Systems play a crucial role in managing the complexity and facilitating the communication within IoT ecosystems.

Key Components and Principles:

Devices and Sensors: IoT relies on a multitude of devices equipped with various sensors (e.g., temperature, humidity, motion) to collect data from the physical world. These devices can be anything from smart thermostats in homes to sensors on factory machines.

Connectivity: IoT devices communicate through a range of network technologies, including WiFi, cellular, Bluetooth, Lora WAN, and more. IoT Operating Systems must support multiple communication protocols to enable seamless connectivity.

Data Processing: The data collected by IoT devices is typically processed and analyzed either locally or in the cloud. Operating Systems in IoT devices need to handle data storage, computation, and data transfer efficiently.

Security: IoT presents significant security challenges, as devices may be vulnerable to attacks. IoT Operating Systems must implement robust security measures, such as encryption, authentication, and access controls, to protect data and devices.

Interoperability: IoT encompasses a diverse ecosystem of devices from different manufacturers. To ensure compatibility and interoperability, IoT Operating Systems should adhere to open standards and protocols.

Use Cases and Applications:

IoT has a broad range of applications across various industries:

Smart Homes: IoT enables homeowners to control lighting, heating, security systems, and appliances remotely, enhancing convenience and energy efficiency.

Healthcare: Wearable devices and sensors monitor patients' vital signs, enabling remote patient monitoring and faster response to medical emergencies.

Industrial IoT (IIoT): IoT optimizes manufacturing processes, predictive maintenance, and supply chain management by providing real-time data on machinery and equipment.

Agriculture: IoT sensors and drones assist in precision agriculture, helping farmers monitor soil conditions, crop health, and irrigation needs.

Smart Cities: IoT improves urban infrastructure, including traffic management, waste collection, and public safety, by collecting and analyzing data from various sensors.

Environmental Monitoring: IoT devices track environmental parameters such as air quality, water quality, and weather conditions for research and early warning systems.

Challenges:

Despite its potential, IoT faces challenges, including privacy concerns, scalability issues, and the need for efficient power management in battery-operated devices. Additionally, the sheer volume of data generated by IoT devices necessitates robust data management and analytics capabilities.

In summary, the Internet of Things represents a revolutionary shift in how we interact with and leverage technology. IoT Operating Systems are essential in managing the intricate web of interconnected devices, ensuring they operate reliably, securely, and efficiently within this dynamic and rapidly expanding ecosystem.

Edge Computing

Edge Computing is a distributed computing paradigm that brings computation and data storage closer to the source of data generation or consumption. It aims to reduce latency, enhance real-time processing, improve bandwidth efficiency, and ensure data privacy and security by processing data locally, at the "edge" of the network, rather than relying solely on centralized data centres or the cloud. This approach is particularly relevant in the context of the Internet of Things (IoT) and other applications where immediate or localized processing is critical.

Key Concepts:

Proximity to Data: Edge Computing places computing resources near the data source, which can be IoT devices, sensors, or even end-user devices like smartphones. This proximity reduces the time it takes for data to travel to a remote data centre and back, minimizing latency.

Distributed Architecture: In an Edge Computing ecosystem, Computation and Data Processing are distributed across a network of edge devices or nodes. These nodes can range from edge servers and gateways to IoT devices themselves.

Realtime Processing: Edge Computing enables real-time or nonrealtime data analysis and decision-making. This is crucial for applications where immediate responses are required, such as autonomous vehicles, industrial automation, and augmented reality.

Bandwidth Optimization: By processing data locally, edge computing can reduce the amount of data that needs to be transmitted to central data centres or the cloud. This not only saves bandwidth but also reduces the cost of data transfer.

Use Cases:

Edge computing has diverse applications across various industries:

Industrial IoT (IIoT): In manufacturing, edge devices monitor equipment health, perform predictive maintenance, and optimize production processes.

Smart Cities: Edge computing supports real-time traffic management, public safety systems, and smart grid management, making cities more efficient and responsive.

Telecommunications: For mobile networks, edge computing reduces network latency and improves the quality of services, benefiting applications like augmented reality and online gaming.

Healthcare: Medical devices and wearables with edge processing capabilities enable remote patient monitoring and faster diagnosis.

Retail: Edge Computing can personalize instore shopping experiences, optimize inventory management, and enhance security with real-time analytics.

Autonomous Vehicles: Edge Computing enables autonomous cars to process sensor data and make splitsecond decisions without relying solely on distant data centres.

Challenges:

While Edge Computing offers significant benefits, it also presents challenges:

Security: Edge devices are more vulnerable to physical tampering and cyberattacks. Robust security measures are crucial to protect data and devices at the edge.

Management: Managing a large number of distributed edge devices can be complex. Centralized management tools and orchestration platforms are needed.

Scalability: As edge deployments grow, ensuring scalability and interoperability becomes increasingly important.

In conclusion, Edge Computing is a transformative approach that complements cloud computing by bringing computation closer to where it's needed. Operating Systems for edge devices play a critical role in managing resources, security, and real-time processing, enabling the efficient and reliable operation of edge computing ecosystems across various industries.

Serverless Computing

Serverless computing, often referred to as Function as a Service (FaaS), is a cloud computing model that allows developers to run code in response to events without having to manage traditional server infrastructure explicitly. In this paradigm, developers can focus solely on writing code for specific tasks or functions, while the underlying cloud provider takes care of provisioning and scaling the required resources. Serverless computing is transforming the way applications are developed and deployed, offering benefits such as reduced operational overhead, automatic scaling, and cost optimization.

Key Concepts:

EventDriven: Serverless computing is fundamentally eventdriven. Functions are triggered by events, such as HTTP requests, database changes, file uploads, or timers. Each function is designed to respond to a specific event type.

Stateless: Serverless functions are stateless, meaning they do not maintain information between invocations. This encourages the design of modular and independent functions.

Microservices: Serverless architecture encourages a microservices approach, where applications are decomposed into smaller, loosely coupled components, each handled by a separate function.

Automatic Scaling: Cloud providers automatically scale serverless functions based on demand. Functions are executed in response to events and can scale up or down as needed, ensuring optimal resource utilization.

Advantages:

Reduced Operational Overhead: Serverless computing abstracts away infrastructure management, allowing developers to focus on code development rather than server provisioning, patching, and maintenance.

Scalability: Automatic scaling ensures that functions can handle varying workloads efficiently. Applications can seamlessly accommodate fluctuations in traffic without manual intervention.

Cost Efficiency: With serverless, you only pay for the compute resources used during function execution, making it cost-effective for applications with irregular or unpredictable workloads.

Faster TimetoMarket: Serverless enables rapid development and deployment of individual functions. Developers can iterate quickly, leading to faster application development.

Reduced Vendor LockIn: Many cloud providers offer serverless computing platforms, allowing developers to choose the vendor that best suits their needs and reducing vendor lockin.

Use Cases:

Serverless computing is suitable for various use cases:

Web and Mobile Backends: Serverless can power the backend of web and mobile applications, handling tasks like user authentication, data processing, and content delivery.

Data Processing: Functions can process and analyze data from various sources, making it valuable for data pipelines, ETL (Extract, Transform, Load) processes, and real-time analytics.

IoT (Internet of Things): Serverless can process data generated by IoT devices, enabling Realtimedecision making and control.

Chatbots and AI: Serverless is often used to develop chatbots and AI services, allowing developers to build natural language processing capabilities.

APIs: Serverless functions can serve as APIs, providing access to specific services or data resources.

Challenges:

Cold Starts: Serverless functions may experience latency known as "cold starts" when they are invoked for the first time or after a period of inactivity. This can impact response times for user facing applications.

Resource Limitations: Serverless platforms impose resource limits, such as execution time and memory, which can affect the types of workloads that can be handled.

State Management: Handling application state can be challenging in a stateless environment. Persistent storage or external databases are often required.

Debugging and Testing: Debugging serverless functions can be more complex than traditional applications. Special tools and practices are needed for effective debugging and testing.

In summary, serverless computing is a cloud computing paradigm that simplifies application development and management by abstracting away infrastructure concerns. It is well suited for event driven, scalable, and cost effective applications. Serverless enables rapid development and deployment of functions, making it a valuable approach for modern software development.

Quantum Computing and OS Challenges

Quantum Computing is a revolutionary paradigm that leverages the principles of quantum mechanics to perform computational tasks exponentially faster than classical computers. While quantum computing holds immense promise for solving complex problems, it also poses significant challenges for Operating Systems (OS). In this discussion, we'll explore quantum computing, its potential impact on OS, and the challenges it presents.

Quantum Computing Overview:

Quantum Bits (Qubits): Unlike classical bits that can represent either 0 or 1, qubits can exist in a superposition of states, representing both 0 and 1 simultaneously. This property enables quantum computers to process massive amounts of information in parallel.

Entanglement: Qubits can be entangled, meaning the state of one qubit is dependent on the state of another, even if they are physically separated. This property enables quantum computers to perform complex operations on entangled qubits.

Quantum Gates: Quantum computers use quantum gates to manipulate qubits. Operations like superposition, entanglement, and measurement are performed using quantum gates.

Quantum Supremacy: Quantum computers have demonstrated the ability to solve certain problems much faster than classical computers, achieving "quantum supremacy" in specific domains.

Impact on Operating Systems:

Quantum computing's unique characteristics pose both opportunities and challenges for Operating Systems:

Cryptographic Vulnerabilities:

Challenge: Quantum computers can break commonly used encryption algorithms, threatening the security of data stored and transmitted by traditional systems.

Solution: OS must support postquantum cryptography to secure data against quantum attacks.

New Programming Models:

Challenge: Quantum computing requires a different programming model. OS needs to facilitate the integration of quantum code with classical code.

Solution: OS should provide tools, libraries, and APIs for quantum programming languages.

Hardware Abstraction:

Challenge: Quantum hardware is highly specialized and sensitive to environmental conditions. OS must manage quantum hardware resources efficiently.

Solution: OS should abstract the quantum hardware, providing a unified interface for resource management.

Quantum Resource Allocation:

Challenge: Quantum computing's limited qubits and coherence times require efficient resource allocation.

Solution: OS should schedule quantum tasks optimally, considering hardware constraints.

Error Correction:

Challenge: Quantum computers are prone to errors due to factors like decoherence. Error correction is essential for reliable quantum computations.

Solution: OS should support error correcting codes and quantum fault tolerant algorithms.

Integration with Classical Systems:

Challenge: Quantum and classical systems must work seamlessly together in hybrid computing environments.

Solution: OS should facilitate communication and data exchange between quantum and classical components.

Scalability:

Challenge: Quantum computing systems are evolving rapidly. OS should be scalable to support future quantum hardware developments.

Solution: OS should have a modular architecture to accommodate new quantum technologies.

Quantum Application Management:

Challenge: OS must manage quantum applications alongside classical ones.

Solution: OS should provide tools for monitoring, profiling, and debugging quantum programs.

Security Considerations:

Challenge: Quantum computers could potentially break the security mechanisms of traditional OS.

Solution: OS should implement quantum resistant security measures and adapt to evolving cryptographic standards.

In conclusion, quantum computing represents a ground-breaking technology with the potential to revolutionize computation. Operating Systems play a crucial role in harnessing the power of quantum computing while addressing the unique challenges it presents. Future OS designs will need to be quantum ready, ensuring the seamless integration of quantum and classical computing resources.

Previous Years Solved Questions

Q 1. Write short notes on the following (any four): (IGNOU BCA June 2014)

NTFS

Packet switching

IPsec

EFS services

Firewall

Ans:

NTFS (New Technology File System):

Description:

NTFS is a file system introduced by Microsoft with the Windows NT Operating System.

It is the default file system for Windows Operating Systems from Windows 2000 onwards.

Features:

Security:NTFS supports access control lists (ACLs) and file permissions, allowing for more granular control over file and folder access.

Reliability:NTFS includes features such as journaling, which helps recover the file system quickly after a system failure.

Compression:NTFS supports file and folder compression to save disk space.

Encryption:NTFS provides built-in encryption through the Encrypting File System (EFS) for securing sensitive data.

Limitations:

While NTFS is widely used, it may not be the most suitable file system for cross-platform compatibility as it is primarily designed for Windows environments.

Packet Switching:

Description:

Packet switching is a method of transmitting data in computer networks.

Data is divided into packets, and each packet is transmitted independently through the network.

Unlike circuit-switching, used in traditional telephone networks, packet switching allows shared use of network resources.

Working:

Data is divided into packets, each containing a portion of the original message, along with addressing information.

Packets are sent independently and can take different routes to reach the destination.

At the destination, the packets are reassembled to reconstruct the original data.

Advantages:

Efficient use of network resources as multiple users can share the same communication channel.

Robustness and fault tolerance as packets can take different paths to reach the destination.

Examples:

Internet Protocol (IP) is a widely used packet-switching protocol for data communication.

IPsec (Internet Protocol Security):

Description:

IPsec is a suite of protocols providing secure communication over an Internet Protocol (IP) network.

It ensures the integrity, authenticity, and confidentiality of data transmitted between devices.

Components:

Authentication Header (AH): Provides authentication and integrity but does not encrypt the actual data.

Encapsulating Security Payload (ESP): Encrypts the data and may also provide authentication and integrity.

Use Cases:

Virtual Private Networks (VPNs):IPsec is commonly used to establish secure connections over the internet, creating a private and encrypted tunnel.

Securing Communication:IPsec can be used to secure communication between routers, hosts, and other network devices.

Modes:

Transport Mode: Protects the payload of the data.

Tunnel Mode: Protects the entire packet, including the original IP header.

EFS Services (Encrypting File System):

Description:

EFS is a feature in Windows Operating Systems that provides file-level encryption.

It allows users to encrypt individual files or folders to protect sensitive data from unauthorized access.

Working:

EFS uses asymmetric key cryptography, where a pair of public and private keys is generated.

The public key is used for encryption, while the private key is required for decryption.

Encrypted files can only be accessed by users with the appropriate private key.

Security:

EFS enhances security by encrypting files at the file system level, making it harder for unauthorized users to access sensitive information.

Considerations:

EFS requires careful key management to ensure that encrypted files remain accessible.

Recovery agents, such as designated user accounts, can be configured to access encrypted files in case of key loss.

Firewall:

Description:

A firewall is a network security device or software that monitors and controls incoming and outgoing network traffic based on predetermined security rules.

Functions:

Packet Filtering: Examines data packets and permits or blocks them based on predefined rules.

Stateful Inspection: Monitors the state of active connections and makes decisions based on the context of the traffic.

Proxy Services: Acts as an intermediary between internal and external networks, forwarding requests and responses.

Types:

Network Firewalls: Operate at the network layer and filter traffic based on IP addresses and ports.

Application Layer Firewalls: Operate at the application layer and can understand specific applications and protocols.

Benefits:

Security: Prevents unauthorized access, data exfiltration, and cyberattacks.

Access Control: Controls which network resources are accessible to users and devices.

Monitoring: Logs and analyses network traffic for security events and anomalies.

Q 2. Explain the process of encryption and decryption in symmetric key, asymmetric key crypto systems. (IGNOU BCA Dec 2014)

Ans:

Symmetric Key Cryptography:

Encryption Process:

Key Generation:

A shared secret key is generated and securely shared between the communicating parties.

Plaintext and Encryption Algorithm:

The plaintext message and the shared secret key are input into the encryption algorithm.

Cipher Text:

The encryption algorithm transforms the plaintext into ciphertext, using the shared secret key. The resulting ciphertext is the encrypted message.

Decryption Process:

Key Sharing:

The receiving party also possesses the shared secret key.

Cipher Text and Decryption Algorithm:

The ciphertext and the shared secret key are input into the decryption algorithm.

Recovery of Plaintext:

The decryption algorithmuses the shared secret key to transform the ciphertext back into the original plaintext.

Asymmetric Key Cryptography:

Encryption Process:

Key Pair Generation:

Each user has a pair of keys: a public key and a private key. The public key is shared openly, while the private key is kept secret.

Plaintext and Public Key:

The sender uses the recipient's public key to encrypt the plaintext message.

Cipher Text:

The encryption process generates ciphertext, which is sent to the recipient.

Decryption Process:

Private Key and Cipher Text:

The recipient uses their private key to decrypt the received ciphertext.

Recovery of Plaintext:

The decryption process yields the original plaintext message.

Key Differences:

Key Management:

Symmetric: Both parties share the same secret key, and maintaining the secrecy of the key is crucial.

Asymmetric: Each user has a pair of public and private keys. The public key can be freely shared, but the private key must be kept confidential.

Computational Complexity:

Symmetric: Generally faster and computationally less intensive.

Asymmetric: Slower due to the complexity of mathematical operations involved.

Scalability:

Symmetric: Efficient for large amounts of data but requires secure key distribution.

Asymmetric: Efficient for key exchange but less practical for encrypting large volumes of data.

Use Cases:

Symmetric: Often used for bulk data encryption (e.g., AES).

Asymmetric: Commonly employed for key exchange, digital signatures, and securing communications between parties who have not previously shared a key.

In summary, symmetric key cryptography uses a shared secret key for both encryption and decryption, while asymmetric key cryptography involves a pair of public and private keys, with different keys used for encryptionand decryption.Each system has its advantages and use cases, and often they are combined in hybrid systems to leverage the strengths of both.

Exercise

Exercise 1 – MCQ

1. What is the primary advantage of containerization in software development and deployment?

a) Efficient resource utilization

b) Real-time data processing

c) Hardware virtualization

d) Centralized storage management

2. Which technology enables the interconnection of everyday devices, allowing them to send and receive data?

a) Serverless Computing

b) Internet of Things (IoT)

c) Quantum Computing

d) Edge Computing

3. In the context of Edge Computing, where is data processed and analyzed?

a) Centralized cloud servers

b) On the end-user's device

c) Edge devices near the data source

d) Mainframe computers

4. What is the key characteristic of Serverless Computing architecture?

a) Constant server provisioning

b) Manual resource scaling

c) Pay-as-you-go pricing model

d) Traditional server maintenance

5. Which type of computing leverages the principles of quantum mechanics to perform calculations?

a) Edge Computing

b) Quantum Computing

c) Containerization

d) Serverless Computing

6. What is the fundamental challenge of Operating Systems in the context of Quantum Computing?

a) Inefficient file management

b) Lack of security protocols

c) Handling qubits and quantum states

d) Limited network connectivity

7. Which technology allows developers to write code without worrying about the underlying infrastructure?

a) Internet of Things (IoT)

b) Quantum Computing

c) Serverless Computing

d) Edge Computing

8. What is a common use case for Edge Computing?

a) Large-scale data storage

b) Real-time data processing for IoT devices

c) Quantum encryption algorithms

d) Container orchestration

9. In containerization, what is a container image?

a) A visual representation of data

b) A lightweight, standalone, and executable package

c) A virtual machine snapshot

d) A network protocol for secure communication

10. What is the main advantage of using Quantum Computing for certain applications?

a) Faster execution of traditional algorithms

b) Enhanced data storage capabilities

c) Simultaneous processing of multiple possibilities

d) Improved network latency

Exercise 2 – True/ False

1. Containerization is primarily focused on physical server optimization.
2. Internet of Things (IoT) devices typically have high computing capabilities.
3. Edge Computing involves processing data closer to the source rather than in centralized data centers.
4. Serverless Computing requires users to manage and provision servers manually.
5. Quantum Computing has no impact on Operating Systems.
6. Containerization technology is commonly associated with Docker and Kubernetes.
7. Internet of Things (IoT) devices are often connected to the internet for remote monitoring and control.
8. Edge Computing reduces latency by processing data in distant centralized data centers.
9. Serverless Computing eliminates the need for developers to worry about server management.
10. Quantum Computing poses no challenges to traditional Operating Systems.

Answer

Exercise 1 – MCQ

Ans: 1 a, 2 b, 3 c, 4 c, 5 b, 6 c, 7 c, 8 b, 9 b, 10 c

Exercise 2 – True/False

Ans: 1 False, 2 False, 3 True, 4 False, 5 False, 6 True, 7 True, 8 False, 9 True, 10 False

Online Resources

Videos:
MCQ Link:https://youtu.be/_wIm6WnRPvE

QR Code:

True/False Link:https://youtu.be/2gC0GnSPuLw

QR Code:

Online Test Paper: https://forms.office.com/r/nxr6VkE0GW

QR Code:

Chapter 11 Types of Operating Systems

Linux

Linux is an Opensource, Unixlike Operating SystemKernel that serves as the core component of various Linux distributions or "distros." An Operating System (OS) is software that manages a computer's hardware resources and provides a foundation for running applications and executing tasks. Here's an explanation of Linux as an Operating System:

Kernel: At the heart of Linux is the Linux Kernel, which is responsible for managing the system's hardware resources such as the CPU, memory, disk drives, and input/output devices. It acts as an intermediary between the hardware and software, ensuring that applications can interact with the hardware without having to deal with its complexities directly.

Open Source: Linux is known for its opensource nature, meaning that its source code is freely available to the public, and anyone can view, modify, and distribute it under opensource licenses like the GNU General Public License (GPL). This open approach has led to a large and active community of developers and contributors who continually improve and enhance the Operating System.

Variety of Distributions: Linux is not just a single Operating System but rather a kernel that can be combined with various software packages to create different Linux distributions (distros). Each distribution may include a different set of software, package management tools, desktop environments, and configuration options, making Linux highly customizable. Some popular Linux distributions include Ubuntu, Fedora, CentOS, Debian, and Arch Linux.

MultiUser and MultiTasking: Linux supports multiple users and multitasking, allowing multiple users to log in and run various programs simultaneously. It provides a secure and isolated environment for each user.

File System: Linux uses a hierarchical file system, similar to other Unixlike Operating Systems. Files and directories are organized in a treelike structure, starting from the root directory (/). It supports a wide range of file systems, including ext4, Btrfs, and XFS, among others.

Command Line Interface (CLI): Linux is known for its powerful command line interface (CLI), which allows users to interact with the system using text-based commands. The shell, such as Bash, is a common interface for executing commands, managing files, and automating tasks.

Graphical User Interface (GUI): Many Linux distributions include a graphical desktop environment, such as GNOME, KDE, or Xfce, providing a user-friendly interface for those who prefer a visual environment. These desktop environments make Linux more accessible to a broader range of users.

Software Package Management: Linux distributions typically include package managers like APT (used in Debian based distros), YUM (used in Red Hat based distros), or Pacman (used in Arch Linux), which simplify the installation, updating, and removal of software packages. This helps maintain system integrity and simplifies software management.

Security: Linux is known for its robust security features, including user permissions, access controls, and a strong emphasis on user and group privileges. Regular security updates and patches are actively developed and distributed, making Linux less susceptible to malware and security vulnerabilities.

Server and Embedded Systems: Linux is widely used in server environments due to its stability, scalability, and costeffectiveness. It also powers many embedded systems and devices like smartphones, routers, and IoT devices.

In summary, Linux is an opensource Operating System kernel that forms the basis of numerous Linux distributions. It offers flexibility, security, and a powerful set of tools, making it suitable for a wide range of computing needs, from desktop PCs to servers and embedded systems. Its opensource nature encourages collaboration and innovation within the Linux community, resulting in a versatile and continuously evolving Operating System.

Unix

Unix is a powerful, multiuser, and multitasking Operating System originally developed in the late 1960s at AT&T's Bell Labs. It laid the foundation for many modern Operating Systems and played a pivotal role in the development of the computing industry. Here's an explanation of Unix as an Operating System:

History: Unix was developed by a team of researchers led by Ken Thompson and Dennis Ritchie at Bell Labs in the early 1970s. It was inspired by the Multics project but aimed to be simpler and more practical. Unix was initially written in assembly language and later rewritten in the C programming language, which made it highly portable across different hardware platforms.

Philosophy: Unix follows a set of design principles known as the "Unix Philosophy," which includes concepts such as simplicity, modularity, and the idea that "everything is a file." This philosophy emphasizes building small, single purpose utilities that can be combined to perform complex tasks, promoting efficiency and flexibility.

Multiuser and Multitasking: Unix was one of the first Operating Systems to support multiple users simultaneously. It allows multiple users to log in and work on the same system independently, each with their own user account and workspace. Unix also supports multitasking, enabling users to run multiple processes or programs at the same time.

Hierarchical File System: Unix uses a hierarchical file system where files and directories are organized in a treelike structure. The root directory ("/") serves as the starting point, with subdirectories branching out from it. This structure provides a logical way to organize and access files.

CommandLine Interface (CLI): Unix is renowned for its commandline interface (CLI), where users interact with the system by typing text-based commands. The shell, such as the Bourne shell (sh), Bash, or Zsh, interprets these commands and allows users to perform various tasks, manage files, and automate processes. The CLI is highly flexible and scriptable, making it a powerful tool for experienced users.

Portability: Unix was designed to be highly portable, which means it can run on various hardware architectures with minimal modifications. This portability has contributed to its widespread adoption and longevity.

Networking: Unix was an early pioneer in networking capabilities. It includes built-in support for networking protocols and services, making it wellsuited for both local and remote communication. This aspect of Unix was foundational for the development of the internet.

Security: Unix provides robust security features, including user account management, file permissions, and access control mechanisms. User authentication and authorization are fundamental to Unix's security model, helping to protect the system's integrity and user data.

Variants: Over time, Unix has evolved into several different variants and flavors, including commercial versions like AIX, HPUX, and Solaris, as well as opensource variants such as Linux and the various BSD (Berkeley Software Distribution) Operating Systems. These variants retain many Unix principles while adding their own features and enhancements.

Usage: Unix and its descendants are widely used in various domains, including server environments, scientific research, academia, supercomputing, and embedded systems. It also served as the foundation for the development of Linux, which has become a popular Unixlike Operating System.

In summary, Unix is an influential Operating System known for its design philosophy, multiuser capabilities, commandline interface, and portability. Its legacy lives on in modern Unixlike Operating Systems, and its principles continue to influence the design of software and Operating Systems today.

Shell

A Shell is not an Operating System in itself, but rather a crucial component of an Operating System. It serves as an interface between the user and the kernel (the core part) of the Operating System. The shell is responsible for interpreting and executing commands entered by the user or executed through scripts. Here's an explanation of what a shell is and its role within an Operating System:

Interface: The shell provides a means for users to interact with the Operating System. It acts as a commandline interface (CLI) or, in some cases, a graphical user interface (GUI) for users to give instructions to the computer.

Command Interpretation: When a user enters a command, the shell interprets it, identifies the corresponding program or utility, and executes it. For example, if a user enters "ls" in a Unixlike shell, it triggers the "list" command to display the contents of the current directory.

Scripting: Shells also support scripting, which involves creating and executing sequences of commands stored in script files. These scripts can automate repetitive tasks or perform complex operations, making the shell a powerful tool for automation and system administration.

Customization: Users can customize their shell environments by defining aliases, setting environment variables, and configuring various options. This allows users to tailor the shell to their preferences and needs.

Multiple Shells: Different Operating Systems have various shell options. For example, Unixlike systems often offer shells like Bash, Zsh, or Fish, while Windows has Command Prompt and PowerShell. Users can choose the shell that suits their requirements or switch between them based on the task at hand.

I/O Redirection: Shells support input and output (I/O) redirection, allowing users to control where command input comes from and where command output goes. This includes features like piping, which enables the output of one command to serve as the input for another.

Job Control: Many shells provide job control features, allowing users to manage and manipulate running processes. This includes backgrounding tasks, suspending processes, and managing foreground and background jobs.

History and Command Line Editing: Shells often keep a history of previously executed commands, making it easy for users to recall and rerun commands. They also typically offer command line editing features to improve efficiency and accuracy when entering commands.

Scripting and Automation: Shells are often used for writing shell scripts, which are sequences of shell commands saved in a file. These scripts can automate various tasks, making them particularly valuable for system administrators and programmers.

Security: Shells are crucial for enforcing user access controls and permissions. They ensure that users can only execute commands and access files and resources for which they have the necessary permissions.

In summary, a shell is a vital component of an Operating System that acts as an intermediary between users and the Operating System kernel. It interprets user commands, facilitates automation through scripting, and provides tools and features for efficient commandline interaction. Shells are a fundamental part of the user experience on both Unixlike and Windowsbased Operating Systems.

Windows

The Windows Operating System, commonly referred to as Windows, is a family of proprietary Operating Systems developed and marketed by Microsoft Corporation. It is one of the most widely used Operating

Systems in the world and has a significant presence on personal computers, servers, and various computing devices. Here's an explanation of the Windows Operating System:

Graphical User Interface (GUI): Windows is known for its graphical user interface, which provides a visually intuitive way for users to interact with the computer. The GUI includes features like windows, icons, menus, and a pointing device (usually a mouse) for navigation.

Versions: Microsoft has released numerous versions of the Windows Operating System, with each version having its own features and improvements. Some of the most notable versions include Windows 3.1, Windows 95, Windows XP, Windows 7, Windows 8, Windows 10, and Windows 11 (as of my knowledge cut-off date in September 2021). There are also specialized versions for servers, such as Windows Server editions.

Compatibility: Windows is designed to be compatible with a wide range of hardware and software applications. This compatibility has contributed to its popularity, as users can run a vast array of third-party software and hardware devices on Windows based systems.

File System: Windows typically uses the NTFS (New Technology File System) as its primary file system, which offers features like file and folder permissions, encryption, and support for large file sizes and volumes. In older versions of Windows, FAT (File Allocation Table) file systems were also common.

Multitasking: Windows supports multitasking, allowing users to run multiple applications simultaneously. The Operating System manages the allocation of system resources to these applications to ensure smooth performance.

Networking: Windows includes built-in networking capabilities, making it suitable for both home and business environments. It supports various network protocols and services, allowing users to connect to the internet, share files and printers, and set up remote access.

Security: Security features in Windows have evolved over the years and include user account controls, firewalls, antivirus and antimalware protection, and regular security updates. Windows also introduced features like BitLocker for drive encryption and Windows Defender for real-time protection.

User Account Management: Windows allows for multiple user accounts with different access levels and permissions. Administrators can control and configure user accounts to ensure system security and manage resources effectively.

Updates and Service Packs: Microsoft regularly releases updates, patches, and service packs to address security vulnerabilities, improve system stability, and introduce new features. These updates can be automatically or manually installed by users.

Application Support: Windows has a vast ecosystem of software applications and games, including productivity suites, media players, web browsers, and more. It supports both 32bit and 64bit applications.

Server Capabilities: Windows Server editions are designed for use in server environments, providing features such as Active Directory for user and resource management, web server capabilities, and support for virtualization through Hyper-V.

Cloud Integration: Microsoft has integrated cloud services, such as OneDrive and Azure, into Windows, allowing users to store files and data in the cloud and access them from multiple devices.

Cortana and Virtual Assistants: Some versions of Windows incorporate virtual assistants like Cortana (now integrated into the Windows search function) to provide voiceactivated assistance and perform tasks.

In summary, the Windows Operating System is a family of widely used, user-friendlyOperating Systems developed by Microsoft. It offers a graphical user interface, compatibility with a wide range of software and hardware, security features, networking capabilities, and support for various computing environments. Windows continues to evolve with each new version, adapting to the changing needs of users and businesses.

Previous Years Solved Questions

Q 1. What is Window Server? (RU BCA 2022)

Ans:A Windows Server is a specialized Operating System developed by Microsoft for managing and running networked computer systems. It is designed to provide various server-related services, such as file sharing, user authentication, web hosting, and more. Windows Servers come in various editions tailored to different business needs, from small organizations to large enterprises.Key features of Windows Server include Active Directory for user and resource management, Internet Information Services (IIS) for web hosting, and Hyper-V for virtualization. Windows Servers also support remote administration, ensuring efficient management and maintenance of servers from remote locations.These servers play a vital role in creating and managing a robust IT infrastructure for businesses, enabling them to centralize data storage, enhance security, streamline network management, and deploy various applications and services. Windows Server provides a reliable and scalable platform for businesses to meet their diverse server-related needs.

Q 2. What is PCB? (RU BCA 2020)

Ans:A Process Control Block (PCB) is a data structure in the kernel of an Operating System that contains essential information about a running process or task. The PCB is created and maintained by the Operating System to manage and control processes efficiently. It serves as a repository of process-related information and is essential for process scheduling, resource management, and inter-process communication. Here are the details of what a PCB typically contains and its role in an Operating System:

Contents of a Process Control Block:

Process ID (PID): A unique identifier for each process in the system, which is used for management and tracking.

Process State: Describes the current state of the process, such as running, ready, blocked, or terminated.

Program Counter (PC): Indicates the address of the next instruction to be executed by the CPU when the process resumes.

CPU Registers: The contents of CPU registers, including general-purpose registers, program status registers, and stack pointers. These registers hold the process's execution context.

CPU Scheduling Information: Contains information about the process's scheduling priority, quantum or time slice, and other scheduling-related data.

Memory Management Information: This section includes details about the process's memory allocation, such as the base and limit registers, which define the process's memory boundaries.

Open Files Table: Lists the files and devices opened by the process. Each entry typically includes a file descriptor, file position, and other information required for I/O operations.

Accounting Information: Collects data related to resource usage, such as CPU time, clock time, and memory used by the process.

I/O Status Information: Records information about the I/O operations the process is currently engaged in or waiting for, including device status and pending I/O requests.

Inter-Process Communication (IPC) Information: Holds details about message queues, semaphores, or other synchronization and communication mechanisms being used by the process.

Role of the PCB in an Operating System:

Process Scheduling: The PCB is fundamental for the process scheduling algorithm. It contains information about a process's priority and state, which the scheduler uses to make decisions about which process to execute next.

Context Switching: When a context switch occurs (a process is pre-empted or blocked, and another process is scheduled to run), the contents of the PCB are saved and loaded into the CPU registers. This enables the new process to resume its execution seamlessly.

Resource Management: The PCB tracks various resources allocated to a process, such as memory, open files, and devices. This information is crucial for resource management and allocation.

Inter-Process Communication: Information about IPC mechanisms being used by a process is stored in the PCB. This facilitates communication and synchronization between processes.

Accounting and Monitoring: The PCB helps collect data on resource usage and execution times for accounting and performance monitoring purposes.

Error Handling: In case of errors or exceptions, the PCB can store relevant information, which is helpful for debugging and diagnosing issues.

Process Termination: When a process completes its execution or is terminated, the PCB is updated to reflect the process's termination state and release any allocated resources.

Overall, the PCB is a critical data structure that enables the Operating System to manage and control processes efficiently, ensuring proper allocation of resources, scheduling, and synchronization in a multitasking environment. It plays a central role in the coordination and execution of processes in an Operating System.

Q.3 What is Kernel? (RU B. Tech Jan 2022, RU B. Tech Feb 2021)

Ans: The Kernel is a core component of an Operating System, responsible for managing the system's hardware and providing essential services and abstractions for user-level processes and applications. It serves as an intermediary between software and hardware, allowing applications to interact with hardware resources and ensuring the smooth operation of the computer system. Here's a detailed explanation of the kernel in an Operating System:

Hardware Abstraction:

The Kernel abstracts and simplifies the complexities of hardware interactions. It provides a standardized interface to hardware devices, hiding the low-level details from applications.

Memory Management:

The Kernel manages memory allocation and protection. It ensures that each process has its address space, isolating them from one another to prevent unintended access to memory locations.

Process Management:

The Kernel manages processes (also known as tasks or jobs). It creates, schedules, and terminates processes, providing CPU time and system resources as needed. It enforces process isolation.

File System Management:

The Kernel offers file system services, including file creation, reading, writing, and deletion. It abstracts the file system, allowing users and applications to access files without worrying about the underlying storage device.

Device Drivers:

The Kernel includes device drivers for various hardware components. Device drivers are modules that enable the kernel to communicate with specific hardware, such as disks, network interfaces, and peripherals.

System Calls:

The Kernel provides a set of System Calls that allow user-level applications to request services like I/O, process creation, and memory allocation. System Calls provide a controlled interface for user programs to access kernel functionality.

Task Scheduling:

The Kernel employs scheduling algorithms to allocate CPU time to various processes efficiently. It ensures that each process receives a fair share of the CPU and can make progress.

Inter-Process Communication (IPC):

The Kernel manages IPC mechanisms, such as pipes, message queues, and shared memory, to facilitate communication and data exchange between processes.

Hardware Interaction:

The kernel controls hardware resources like the CPU, memory, disks, network interfaces, and peripheral devices. It allocates these resources, enforces security, and handles exceptions and errors.

Security:

The Kernel is responsible for enforcing security policies and access controls. It ensures that processes do not interfere with one another's memory or resources and enforces file permissions.

Error Handling:

The Kernel detects and handles errors, exceptions, and hardware failures to prevent system crashes and data corruption. It may log errors, generate core dumps, or initiate system recovery procedures.

Bootstrapping:

The Kernel is responsible for bootstrapping the computer system. It loads into memory during the boot process and initializes essential hardware components, eventually starting the first user-level process (usually the init or systemd process).

System Management:

The Kernel allows system administrators to configure and manage system settings, monitor performance, and control system parameters through interfaces like sysctl (in Unix-like systems) or the Windows Registry (in Windows).

In summary, the Kernel is the heart of an Operating System, serving as the bridge between hardware and software. It provides essential services, resource management, and abstraction layers, enabling the execution of user applications and ensuring the stability, security, and efficient operation of the computer system. Different Operating Systems may have different kernel architectures and designs, but the fundamental role of the kernel remains consistent.

Q 4. Differentiate between Windows and Linux based Operating System. (RU B. Tech Jan 2022)

Ans: Windows and Linux are two different families of Operating Systems, each with its own characteristics, design philosophies, and user bases. Here are some key differences between Windows and Linux-based Operating Systems:

Vendor and Licensing:

Windows: Windows is developed and marketed by Microsoft. It is a proprietary Operating System, which means the source code is not publicly available, and users must purchase licenses to use it.

Linux: Linux is a kernel that serves as the foundation for various open-source Operating Systems called distributions (distros). Linux is open-source, which means its source code is freely available, and many Linux distributions are free to use.

Kernel:

Windows: Windows uses the Windows NT kernel, which is designed for both desktop and server environments. Different versions of Windows may use slightly different kernel variants.

Linux: Linux uses the Linux kernel, which is highly modular and can be tailored to different use cases. It is widely used in server environments and as the basis for various Linux distributions for desktop and embedded systems.

User Interface:

Windows: Windows Operating Systems typically feature a graphical user interface (GUI), such as the Windows Desktop, which includes the Start menu and a taskbar.

Linux: Linux distributions often provide a variety of desktop environments, including GNOME, KDE, Xfce, and others. Some Linux servers may operate without a GUI, relying solely on the command-line interface.

Software Ecosystem:

Windows: Windows has a vast software ecosystem, including a wide range of commercial and proprietary applications, games, and utilities. It is the primary platform for many desktop applications and games.

Linux: Linux has a rich open-source software ecosystem, with thousands of free and open-source applications and tools available through package managers. While it has many alternatives, some commercial software and games are also available for Linux.

File System:

Windows: NTFS (New Technology File System) is the primary file system used in Windows. It provides features like journaling, file and folder permissions, and support for large file sizes.

Linux: Linux supports a variety of file systems, including ext4, XFS, and Btrfs. The choice of file system can depend on the specific Linux distribution and use case.

Command-Line Interface:

Windows: Windows provides a command-line interface (CLI) known as the Command Prompt, as well as PowerShell, a more advanced CLI. These are used for system administration and automation.

Linux: Linux has a powerful CLI, and many system administrators and power users prefer it. The default shell is often Bash, but other shells like Zsh are also popular.

Security Model:

Windows: Windows uses a User Account Control (UAC) model, where users often run with limited privileges, and they must elevate permissions for certain tasks. Antivirus software is commonly used for security.

Linux: Linux follows a principle of least privilege, with users running with minimal privileges by default. Security features like sudo and SELinux are commonly used. Linux is often considered more secure due to its open-source nature and the ability to control and audit system components.

Hardware Support:

Windows: Windows is widely supported on a variety of hardware, including PCs, laptops, servers, and embedded systems. Device driver support is usually good.

Linux: Linux is known for its versatility and extensive hardware support. It is commonly used in servers, embedded systems, supercomputers, and IoT devices. Linux distributions may have drivers for a wide range of hardware components.

Update and Release Model:

Windows: Windows has a periodic release model, with new versions (e.g., Windows 10, Windows 11) released every few years. Updates and patches are regularly delivered through Windows Update.

Linux: Linux distributions often have rolling release models (e.g., Arch Linux) or regular release cycles (e.g., Ubuntu LTS, Fedora). Updates are managed using package managers, and system administrators have more control over when and how updates are applied.

Community and Support:

Windows: Microsoft provides official support for Windows. Users can also find third-party support and resources for troubleshooting issues.

Linux: Linux benefits from a large and active open-source community. Users have access to a wealth of documentation, forums, and community-driven support.

These are some of the fundamental differences between Windows and Linux-based Operating Systems. The choice between them often depends on factors such as specific use cases, user preferences, and the need for open-source software or proprietary applications.

Q 5. Describe the function of process scheduler in Linux OS. (RTU B. Tech)

Ans: The process scheduler in a Linux Operating System is a crucial component responsible for managing and allocating system resources to various processes. Its primary function is to determine which process should run on the CPU and for how long, in order to efficiently utilize the system's resources while providing a responsive and fair computing environment. Here are the key functions of the process scheduler in Linux:

Process Scheduling: The scheduler determines the order in which processes are executed on the CPU. It chooses the next process to run from the pool of ready-to-run processes based on certain scheduling policies.

Time Sharing: One of the primary goals of the process scheduler is to provide fair time-sharing among multiple processes running concurrently on the system. This ensures that no single process monopolizes the CPU and that each process gets a fair share of CPU time.

Preemptive Scheduling: Linux uses pre-emptive scheduling, which means that the scheduler can interrupt a running process and switch to another process even if the running process has not completed its execution. This ensures that no process can hog the CPU indefinitely.

Priority Management: Processes in Linux are assigned priorities. The scheduler takes these priorities into account when making scheduling decisions. Higher-priority processes are given preference over lower-priority ones.

Real-time Scheduling: Linux supports real-time processes that have strict timing requirements. The scheduler ensures that real-time processes are given priority and guaranteed CPU time when needed to meet their deadlines.

Multicore and Multiprocessor Support: The scheduler is designed to efficiently distribute processes across multiple CPU cores or processors, takinginto account load balancing and maximizing overall system performance.

Fairness and Load Balancing: The scheduler aims to provide fairness among processes and minimize the chance of system resources being underutilized. It continuously monitors the system's load and redistributes processes as needed.

CPU Affinity: The scheduler can be configured to allow or disallow processes from running on specific CPU cores, which can be beneficial for optimizing performance or ensuring isolation in certain cases.

Scheduling Policies: Linux supports different scheduling policies, such as the Completely Fair Scheduler (CFS), Round Robin, and more. System administrators can choose or configure the appropriate policy based on their specific requirements.

Dynamic Scheduling: The scheduler can adapt to changing conditions, such as CPU load, process priorities, and system resource availability, to make optimal scheduling decisions.

In summary, the process Scheduler in Linux plays a vital role in managing the execution of processes, ensuring fair resource allocation, and optimizing system performance. It uses various scheduling policies and algorithms to achieve these goals, making Linux a versatile and efficient Operating System for both single-user and multi-user environments.

Q 6. Write any two difference between **Unix** and **Linux.** (RTU B. Tech)

Ans:

Aspect	Unix	Linux
Ownership and Licensing	Unix is a family of Operating Systems that are typically proprietary and come from various vendors like IBM (AIX), Oracle (Solaris), and HP (HP-UX). These Operating Systems often require the purchase of a license for use.	Linux is an open-source Operating System kernel that was initially created by Linus Torvalds but has since been developed collaboratively by a global community of volunteers. It is freely available and distributed under open-source licenses (e.g., the GNU General Public License). Various Linux distributions (distros) package the Linux kernel with additional software to create complete Operating Systems. These distros are typically free to use.
Kernel	Unix Operating Systems have different kernels depending on the vendor and version, and they may have proprietary features specific to each variant.	Linux has a single monolithic kernel known as the Linux kernel, which is maintained and distributed independently of specific Linux distributions. The Linux kernel is open source and has a consistent API, making it possible to run the same userland applications on different Linux distributions.

Q 7. Describe the usage and functionality of the command “rm -r*” in UNIX? (RTU B. Tech)

Ans: The command "rm -r*" in UNIX is potentially a dangerous and destructive command that can have unintended and harmful consequences, if used improperly. It is important to clarify the command's usage and functionality while also emphasizing the potential risks associated with it.

Here's an explanation of what the command "rm -r*" does:

Command Components:

rm: This is the command used to remove files and directories in UNIX and Linux.

-r: This is an option that stands for "recursive." When used with **rm**, it instructs the command to remove directories and their contents, including subdirectories and files within them.

*: The asterisk (*) is a wildcard character that typically matches any character or characters in file or directory names. In this context, it represents a placeholder for file and directory names.

Usage:

When you execute the command "rm -r*", you are essentially telling the system to remove all files and directories in the current working directory (where the command is executed) that match the wildcard pattern "*." This means it will attempt to delete everything, recursively.

Risks and Consequences:

Using "rm -r*" without caution can result in the deletion of all files and directories in the current directory, including critical system files, user data, and important configuration files.

If you mistakenly run this command in the wrong directory or with superuser privileges (root), it could potentially damage or render your system unusable.

There is no confirmation or undo mechanism with the "rm" command, so any data deleted with this command is usually irrecoverable.

Safe Alternatives:

If you intend to remove specific files or directories, it is strongly recommended to use more targeted and precise commands. For example, to remove a specific file, use "rm filename," and to remove a directory and its contents, use "rm -r directoryname."

Examples of Safer Usage:

To remove a file named "example.txt": **rm example.txt**

To remove a directory named "myfolder" and its contents: **rm -r myfolder**

In summary, "rm -r*" is a risky command in UNIX, as it attempts to delete everything in the current directory that matches the wildcard pattern. It should be used with extreme caution and is generally discouraged because of the potential for data loss and system instability. Always double-check your command and the current directory to avoid unintended data deletion.

Q 8 (a). Write the steps to configure a Windows 2000 computer to ensure that users can log-on to the server only duringthe specified times. (IGNOU BCA 2014)

Ans: To configure a Windows 2000 computer to restrict user logon times, you can use Group Policy settings. Here are the steps to achieve this:

Step 1: Access Group Policy Editor

Open Group Policy:

Click on the "Start" menu, select "Run," and type gpedit.msc to open the Group Policy Editor.

Step 2: Navigate to User Rights Assignment

Navigate:

In the Group Policy Editor, go to Computer Configuration -> Windows Settings -> Security Settings -> Account Policies -> Logon Hours.

Step 3: Configure Logon Hours

Define Logon Hours:

Double-click on "Logon Hours" to open the properties window.

Configure Logon Hours:

Check the "Define these policy settings" checkbox.

Set the allowed logon hours for each day of the week by specifying the start and end times.

Apply Changes:

Click "OK" to apply the changes.

Step 4: Update Group Policy

Update Group Policy:

Open a command prompt and run the command gpupdate /force to force an immediate update of the Group Policy.

Step 5: Verify Logon Restrictions

Verify Settings:

Log in as a user and check if the logon is allowed only during the specified times.

Note:

These steps apply to the local Group Policy on a standalone Windows 2000 computer. If the computer is part of an Active Directory domain, then these settings may be overridden by domain-level policies.

To enforce logon hour restrictions for users in an Active Directory domain, you can configure this setting in the Group Policy Management Console (GPMC) on a domain controller or through Active Directory Users and Computers.

By following these steps, you can configure logon hours for users on a Windows 2000 computer, ensuring that they can only log in during the specified time frames.

(b). Differentiate the role and responsibilities of user mode and Kernel mode of Windows 2000 system.(IGNOU BCA 2014)

Ans: In the Windows 2000 Operating System, user mode and kernel mode represent two distinct privilege levels, each with specific roles and responsibilities. These modes regulate the access and execution privileges of software components within the system.

User Mode:

Role:

Application Execution:

User mode is where user applications and processes execute.

Common applications like word processors, web browsers, and games run in user mode.

Restricted Access:

Processes in user mode have restricted access to system resources.

They cannot directly access hardware or critical system functions.

User-Space Memory:

Each user-mode process has its own isolated address space.

Processes cannot directly access the memory space of other processes.

System Calls:

User-mode processes request services or resources from the Operating System through System Calls.

System Calls act as an interface for user applications to communicate with the kernel.

Responsibilities:

User Interface:

User interfaces, including graphical user interfaces (GUIs) and command-line interfaces, are managed in user mode.

Application Logic:

The logic and execution of user applications, as well as user interaction, occur in user mode.

File and Network Access:

User mode processes handle file operations, network communication, and other user-level tasks.

Kernel Mode:

Role:

Core System Functions:

Kernel mode is the privileged mode where the core functions of the Operating System execute.

It has direct access to hardware and system resources.

Device Drivers:

Device drivers, which facilitate communication between the Operating System and hardware devices, run in kernel mode.

Drivers have elevated privileges to interact directly with hardware components.

System Services:

Critical system services, such as process scheduling, memory management, and I/O operations, are handled in kernel mode.

Interrupt Handling:

Kernel mode is responsible for handling hardware interrupts, exceptions, and other low-level events.

Responsibilities:

Resource Management:

Allocating and managing system resources, including memory and CPU time, is a kernel mode responsibility.

Security Enforcement:

Enforcing security policies, access controls, and protecting critical system functions from unauthorized access.

Inter-Process Communication:

Kernel mode manages inter-process communication and synchronization between different processes.

System Calls Execution:

Execution of privileged instructions and handling System Calls requested by user-mode processes.

Comparison:

User Mode:

Focus: User applications and user interaction.

Access: Restricted access to system resources.

Responsibility: Application logic, user interfaces, and user-level tasks.

Kernel Mode:

Focus: Core system functions and hardware interaction.

Access: Direct access to hardware and critical system functions.

Responsibility: Resource Management, security enforcement, and core system services.

The differentiation between user mode and kernel mode is crucial for maintaining system stability, security, and efficient resource utilization. User mode ensures that applications run within defined boundaries, while kernel mode provides the necessary privileges for managing system resources and executing critical system functions.

(c). Explain the various file access control mechanisms provided by LINUX Operating System. Also, give the suitable example for each.(IGNOU BCA 2014)

Ans: Linux provides a robust set of file access control mechanisms to regulate access to files and directories. These mechanisms are essential for maintaining the security and integrity of the system. Here are various file access control mechanisms in Linux, along with suitable examples:

File Permissions:

Description: Linux uses a permission system to control access to files and directories. Each file or directory has permissions defined for three categories of users: owner, group, and others.

Example:

$ ls -l file.txt

-rw-r--r-- 1 user1 users 1024 Nov 30 10:00 file.txt

In this example, "user1" is the owner, "users" is the group, and the permissions are set as read and write for the owner, read-only for the group, and read-only for others.

chmod Command:

Description: The chmod command is used to change file permissions. It allows users to add or remove permissions for the owner, group, and others.

Example:

$ chmod +x script.sh

This command adds execute permission to the script.sh file.

chown Command:

Description: The chown command changes the ownership of a file or directory.

Example:

$ chown user2: staff document.txt

This command changes the owner to "user2" and the group to "staff" for the document.txt file.

chgrp Command:

Description: The chgrp command changes the group ownership of a file or directory.

Example:

```
$ chgrp developers project_folder
```

This command changes the group ownership of the project_folder directory to the "developers" group.

Access Control Lists (ACLs):

Description:ACLs provide a more granular level of control by allowing users to set specific permissions for multiple users or groups on a file or directory.

Example:

```
$ setfacl -m u:john:rw file.txt
```

This command adds read and write permissions for the user "john" on the file.txt file.

umask:

Description: The umask command sets the default permissions for newly created files and directories.

Example:

```
$ umask 007
```

This command sets the default permissions to read and write for the owner and group, and no permissions for others.

Sticky Bit:

Description: The sticky bit is a permission that can be applied to directories. It restricts the deletion of files within a directory to only the file owner.

Example:

```
$ chmod +t shared_folder
```

This command adds the sticky bit to the shared_folder directory.

SELinux (Security-Enhanced Linux):

Description:SELinux is a security mechanism that enhances Linux security by enforcing mandatory access controls (MAC).

Example:

$ getenforce

This command checks the SELinux enforcement status.

These file access control mechanisms collectively ensure that users and processes have the appropriate permissions to access and modify files and directories, contributing to the overall security and integrity of the Linux system.

(d). List the important components of domain name server. Also, explain how the domain name server is configured in LINUX Operating System.(IGNOU BCA 2014)

Ans:

Important Components of Domain Name Server (DNS):

DNS Server Software:

DNS server software is the core component responsible for handling DNS queries, resolving domain names to IP addresses, and providing authoritative responses.

Zone Files:

Zone files contain the mapping between domain names and corresponding IP addresses. Different types of records, such as A, CNAME, MX, and NS, are defined in zone files.

Resolver:

The resolver is a component in the client's Operating System or DNS client software responsible for sending DNS queries to DNS servers. It translates human-readable domain names into IP addresses.

Root Name Servers:

Root name servers are the top-level DNS servers that maintain information about top-level domains (TLDs) and their authoritative DNS servers.

Authoritative DNS Servers:

Authoritative DNS servers hold the authoritative information for a specific domain. They provide responses to DNS queries based on the data in their zone files.

Forwarders:

DNS forwarders are servers configured to forward DNS queries to another DNS server, usually a higher-level DNS server. This can improve DNS resolution efficiency.

Cache:

DNS servers maintain a cache of recently resolved domain names and their corresponding IP addresses. Caching helps in speeding up subsequent DNS queries for the same domain.

Configuration of DNS in LINUX Operating System:

Configuring a DNS server in Linux involves setting up DNS server software, defining zone files, and configuring server settings. Here are the general steps using BIND (Berkeley Internet Name Domain), a popular DNS serversoftware:

Install BIND:

Use the package manager to install BIND on your Linux system. For example, on a Debian-based system:

```
$ sudo apt-get install bind9
```

Configure BIND:

Edit the BIND configuration file, typically located at /etc/bind/named.conf. Define the options, such as listening IP addresses, access control, and logging.

Create Zone Files:

Create zone files for the domains you want to host. Zone files contain resource records (RR) that map domain names to IP addresses. Example for a forward zone:

```
$TTL 1D
@  IN  SOA ns1.example.com. admin.example.com. (
2023112101 ; Serial
8H ; Refresh
2H ; Retry
4W ; Expire
1D ; Minimum TTL
)

@     IN  NS  ns1.example.com.
@     IN  NS  ns2.example.com.
@     IN  A   192.168.1.1
www   IN  A   192.168.1.2
```

Configure Named.conf.local:

Add references to the zone files in the named.conf.local file.

```
zone "example.com" {
type master;
file "/etc/bind/db.example.com";
};
```

Restart BIND:

After making changes, restart the BIND service to apply the configuration.

```
$ sudo service bind9 restart
```

Set DNS Server IP in Clients:

Configure client machines to use the Linux DNS server by setting its IP address in the network configuration or DHCP settings.

Test DNS Resolution:

Test DNS resolution using tools like dig or nslookup to ensure that the DNS server is functioning correctly.

```
$ dig www.example.com
```

Configuring a DNS server in Linux involves careful management of zone files, configuration files, and ensuring proper communication between DNS servers. It's crucial to periodically review logs and monitor DNS server performance for optimal functionality.

(e). How is print server configured in Windows 2000? Also, explain the importance of print queue management.(IGNOU BCA 2014)

Ans:

Configuring a Print Server in Windows 2000:

Configuring a print server in Windows 2000 involves setting up a computer or server to manage and share printers on a network. Here are the general steps:

Install Print Services:

Open the "Control Panel" and go to "Add/Remove Programs."

Select "Add/Remove Windows Components" and choose "Print Services for Windows."

Click "Next" and follow the prompts to install the print services.

Add Printers:

After installation, open the "Printers" folder in the "Control Panel."

Right-click in the "Printers" window and select "Add Printer."

Follow the wizard to add printers connected to the print server.

Share Printers:

Right-click on a printer and select "Sharing."

Enable printer sharing and provide a share name for network users to access.

Configure Printer Properties:

Adjust printer properties, such as paper size, print quality, and sharing permissions, to meet the needs of users.

Manage Print Queue:

Open the "Printers" folder, right-click on a printer, and select "Open."

In the printer window, view the print queue and manage print jobs.

Access Control:

Set access control and permissions to restrict or allow specific users or groups to print to certain printers.

Test Print:

Print a test page to ensure that the printer is configured correctly.

Monitor Printers:

Monitor the printers using the "Printers" folder to check for errors, low toner, or other issues.

Importance of Print Queue Management:

Job Prioritization:

Print Queue Management allows administrators to prioritize print jobs. Urgent or critical print jobs can be moved to the top of the queue.

Resource Optimization:

Efficient print Queue Management helps optimize printer resources by preventing the queue from being overloaded with numerous print jobs.

Avoiding Print Delays:

By managing the print queue, administrators can identify and address print jobs causing delays, ensuring a smoother printing process.

Error Handling:

Print Queue Management facilitates the identification and resolution of errors. Failed print jobs can be addressed promptly to prevent disruptions.

Monitoring Print Usage:

Administrators can monitor print usage patterns and identify printers with high demand. This information can be used for resource planning and optimization.

Access Control:

Print Queue Management allows administrators to control who can print to specific printers. Access permissions can be configured to ensure only authorized users can submit print jobs.

Efficient Printer Utilization:

By managing the print queue, administrators can ensure that each printer is efficiently utilized, preventing bottlenecks and maximizing throughput.

User Accountability:

Print Queue Management helps in tracking and managing user print activities. This can be useful for assessing resource usage and assigning costs to print jobs for accounting purposes.

Troubleshooting:

Print Queue Management provides tools for troubleshooting printer-related issues. Administrators can view the status of print jobs, identify errors, and take corrective actions.

Effectively managing the print queue is crucial for maintaining a smooth and efficient printing environment in a Windows 2000 network. It contributes to resource optimization, timely print job execution, and overall user satisfaction.

(f). What is Kerberos? Explain the complete process of client authentication through Kerberos.(IGNOU BCA 2014)

Ans:

Kerberos:

Kerberos is a network authentication protocol designed to provide secure authentication for client-server applications by using secret-key cryptography. It is widely used in environments where users and services need to authenticate across a potentially insecure network, such as in a corporate or organizational setting.

Process of Client Authentication through Kerberos:

The Kerberos Authentication Process involves several steps to ensure secure and mutual authentication between the client and the server. Here is a step-by-step explanation of the client authentication process through Kerberos:

Registration:

The client and server must be registered with the Kerberos Key Distribution Center (KDC). The KDC consists of two components: the Authentication Server (AS) and the Ticket Granting Server (TGS).

User Authentication (Initial Ticket Request):

When a user (client) wants to access a service, they first authenticate themselves to the AS.

The client sends a request to the AS, providing their username and a timestamp (nonce).

The AS verifies the user's identity and generates a session key (TGT - Ticket Granting Ticket) encrypted with the user's password.

TGT Response:

The AS sends back the TGT to the client. The TGT is a temporary credential that can be used to request additional tickets from the TGS without re-entering the password.

Ticket Granting Server (TGS) Request:

The client wants to access a specific service, so it sends a request to the TGS.

The request includes the TGT and the name of the target service.

TGS Authentication:

The TGS decrypts the TGT using its own secret key and verifies the client's identity.

If authentication is successful, the TGS generates a new session key and creates a service ticket (TGS ticket) for the requested service.

Service Ticket Response:

The TGS sends back the service ticket to the client. The service ticket is encrypted with the service's secret key and includes the client's new session key.

Service Request:

The client sends the service ticket to the service along with a timestamp and other necessary information.

The client also includes an authenticator, which is encrypted with the session key obtained from the TGS.

Service Authentication:

The service decrypts the service ticket using its secret key.

The service verifies the client's identity by decrypting the authenticator using the session key.

If the client's identity is confirmed, the service provides the requested service to the client.

Session Key Usage:

The client and service now share a session key that was securely negotiated through the Kerberos authentication process.

This session key is used for subsequent communication between the client and the service.

Advantages of Kerberos:

Mutual Authentication:

Both the client and the service authenticate each other, preventing impersonation.

Secure Key Distribution:

Keys are distributed securely through trusted third parties (AS and TGS), reducing the risk of interception.

Single Sign-On:

Users can obtain multiple tickets with a single login, facilitating single sign-on capabilities.

Session Key Usage:

Session keys provide a secure means for encrypting communication between the client and the service.

Ticket Expiry:

Tickets have a limited validity period, reducing the risk of unauthorized access.

Kerberos provides a robust and trusted mechanism for client-server authentication, ensuring the confidentiality and integrity of communications in networked environments.

Q 9. Describe the concept and advantages of using EFS services in Windows 2000. (IGNOU BCA Dec 2014)

Ans:

Encrypting File System (EFS) Services in Windows 2000:

Concept of EFS: Encrypting File System (EFS) is a feature in Windows Operating Systems, including Windows 2000, that provides file-level encryption to protect sensitive data stored on NTFS (New Technology File System) volumes. EFS uses public key cryptography to secure files and folders, ensuring that only authorized users can access the encrypted content.

Advantages of EFS Services in Windows 2000:

Data Confidentiality:

EFS ensures the confidentiality of data by encrypting files and folders. Even if unauthorized users gain physical access to the storage media, they cannot read the encrypted content without the appropriate encryption keys.

User-Level Encryption:

EFS operates at the user level, allowing individual users to encrypt their own files. Each user has a unique set of encryption keys, providing a personalized security layer.

Seamless Integration with NTFS:

EFS seamlessly integrates with the NTFS file system, making it a native and efficient solution for securing files. Users can enable encryption on specific files or folders through the file properties in Windows Explorer.

Transparent Encryption and Decryption:

Once a user encrypts a file, EFS transparently encrypts and decrypts the file on the fly during read and write operations. Users don't need to manually decrypt files before accessing them; the process is seamless and automatic.

Scalability:

EFS is designed to scale with the needs of the organization. It can be implemented on individual workstations or across enterprise networks, providing flexibility in securing data at various levels.

Integration with Active Directory:

In a domain environment, EFS integrates with Active Directory, allowing administrators to manage encryption policies centrally. This enables efficient key recovery and simplifies the administration of EFS across a network.

Recovery of Encrypted Files:

Windows 2000 provides a mechanism for recovering encrypted files in case a user loses access to their private key. Authorized recovery agents can assist in recovering encrypted data, ensuring data accessibility in critical scenarios.

Selective Encryption:

EFS allows users to selectively encrypt specific files or folders based on their sensitivity. This granular control ensures that only the necessary data is encrypted, minimizing the impact on system performance.

Secure Key Storage:

EFS securely stores users' private encryption keys. These keys are protected with the user's logon credentials, ensuring that only authorized users can access their encrypted data.

File and Folder Sharing:

EFS supports secure sharing of encrypted files and folders among authorized users. As long as the recipient has the necessary permissions, they can access and work with the encrypted content.

Compliance and Regulation:

EFS helps organizations comply with security regulations and standards that mandate the protection of sensitive data. It provides a robust solution for encrypting data to meet legal and regulatory requirements.

EFS services in Windows 2000 offer a powerful and flexible solution for securing sensitive data at the file level. By leveraging encryption and key management, EFS enhances data confidentiality and provides administrators with the tools needed to implement and manage encryption policies across Windows networks.

Q 10. What is the responsibility of Kernel in LINUX Operating System?(Anna University 2013)

Ans: In Linux, the Kernel is the core component of the Operating System responsible for managing system resources, providing essential services to higher-level software, and facilitating communication between hardware and software components. Its responsibilities include:

Process Management: The Kernel manages processes, allocating resources such as CPU time and memory to each process, scheduling their execution, and handling process creation, termination, and synchronization.

Memory Management: It allocates and deallocates memory for processes, manages virtual memory, implements memory protection mechanisms, and handles memory paging and swapping.

Device Management: The Kernel interacts with hardware devices such as disk drives, network interfaces, and peripherals, providing device drivers to abstract hardware-specific details and manage device I/O operations.

File System Management: It manages file systems, including reading and writing files, directory operations, file permissions, and file system caching.

Network Management: The Kernel implements networking protocols, manages network connections, handles packet routing, and facilitates communication between different networked devices.

Security: It enforces security policies, manages user permissions, and provides mechanisms for access control, authentication, and encryption.

System Calls: The Kernel provides an interface for user-space programs to interact with system resources through System Calls, allowing applications to request services from the kernel.

Interrupt Handling: It handles hardware interrupts generated by devices, servicing them in a timely manner to ensure responsive system behavior.

Overall, the Kernel acts as the bridge between hardware and software, providing a layer of abstraction that enables the efficient and reliable operation of the Linux Operating System.

Q 11. Explain Following:(RU BCA 2019)

Linux

Unix

Window Server

Ans:

Linux:

Definition: Linux is a free and open-source Operating SystemKernel initially developed by Linus Torvalds in 1991. It is based on the Unix Operating System and is widely used in various computing environments, including servers, desktops, mobile devices, embedded systems, and supercomputers.

Features:

Open Source: Linux is distributed under the GNU General Public License (GPL), allowing users to view, modify, and distribute the source code freely.

Multi-Platform Support: Linux supports multiple hardware architectures, including x86, ARM, PowerPC, and MIPS, making it versatile and adaptable to diverse computing environments.

Stability and Reliability: Linux is known for its stability, robustness, and reliability, making it a popular choice for mission-critical applications and server environments.

Security: Linux offers strong security features, including access controls, permissions, encryption, and auditing mechanisms, to protect against security threats and unauthorized access.

Scalability: Linux scales efficiently from embedded devices to high-performance servers, supporting large-scale deployments and resource-intensive workloads.

Rich Software Ecosystem: Linux provides access to a vast ecosystem of open-source software and development tools, including libraries, compilers, scripting languages, and application frameworks.

Examples: Popular Linux distributions (distros) include Ubuntu, Debian, Fedora, CentOS, and Arch Linux, each offering different features, package managers, and user interfaces to cater to various user preferences and requirements.

Unix:

Definition: Unix is a family of multitasking, multi-user Operating Systems developed in the late 1960s and 1970s at AT&T Bell Labs. It is characterized by its modular design, portability, and support for a wide range of programming languages.

Features:

Multi-User and Multitasking: Unix supports multiple users and concurrent execution of multiple processes, allowing efficient resource sharing and utilization.

Hierarchical File System: Unix organizes files and directories in a hierarchical tree-like structure, providing a flexible and intuitive way to manage data and storage.

Shell and Command-Line Interface: Unix systems feature a command-line interface (CLI) and shell environment, allowing users to interact with the Operating System using commands and scripts.

Networking Capabilities: Unix includes built-in networking support, enabling seamless communication and collaboration across distributed systems and networks.

Portability and Compatibility: Unix systems are designed to be portable across different hardware platforms, facilitating software development and deployment in diverse computing environments.

Standards Compliance: Unix adheres to various standards, including POSIX (Portable Operating System Interface) and Single UNIX Specification, ensuring compatibility and interoperability among Unix-based systems.

Examples: Historic Unix variants include AT&T Unix, BSD (Berkeley Software Distribution), and System V Unix. Modern Unix-like Operating Systems include Linux, macOS (formerly OS X), and various BSD distributions.

Windows Server:

Definition: Windows Server is a series of server Operating Systems developed by Microsoft Corporation. It is designed to provide a reliable, scalable, and secure platform for running network services, business applications, and web services in enterprise environments.

Features:

Active Directory: Windows Server includes Active Directory (AD), a directory service that centralizes network management and authentication, enabling administrators to manage users, groups, and resources centrally.

Role-Based Services: Windows Server offers role-based installation options, allowing administrators to install and configure server roles such as file services, web services, domain controllers, and database services based on specific requirements.

Virtualization Support: Windows Server includes built-in support for virtualization through Hyper-V, Microsoft's hypervisor technology, allowing administrators to create and manage virtual machines (VM's) efficiently.

Security Enhancements: Windows Server implements various security features, including access controls, encryption, authentication mechanisms, and security auditing, to protect against security threats and unauthorized access.

Scalability and High Availability: Windows Server supports scalability and high availability features such as failover clustering, load balancing, and automatic recovery, ensuring continuous operation and minimizing downtime for critical services.

Integration with Microsoft Ecosystem: Windows Server integrates seamlessly with other Microsoft products and services, including Microsoft Azure, Office 365, Exchange Server, and SharePoint, providing a comprehensive enterprise solution.

Versions: Windows Server has evolved through multiple versions, including Windows Server 2003, 2008, 2012, 2016, and 2019, each offering new features, improvements, and enhancements to meet evolving business needs and technology trends.

Previous Years Unsolved Questions

Q 1. Explain file management in UNIX OS, in comparison with WINDOWS OS filemanagement.(IGNOU 2014, 2018)

Q 2. Explain the following commands/utilities of (IGNOU 2021)

Pipes and Filters

Redirecting Input and Output

Q 3. Discuss the working of Remote ProcedureCall (RPC) with the help of a flow (activity)diagram. (IGNOU 2021)

Q 4. Write short notes on the following (IGNOU June 2022)

Pipes and Filters in Unix Operating System

Network Operating System

File Management in WINDOWS 2000

Fault Tolerance in Distributed Operating System

Q 5. Explain the structure of Unix Operating System along with its components. (IGNOU 2021)

Q 6. Compare and contrast the architecture of 8 WINDOWS OS with UNIX OS. (IGNOU 2021)

Q 7. Explain memory organisation in UNIX. 5 Draw appropriate diagrams.(IGNOU 2021)

Q 8. How is booting done in WINDOWS 2000 10 Operating System? Explain windows process and threads with the help of a suitable diagram. (IGNOU 2010)

Q 9. Explain Pipes and Filters in Unix Operating System. (IGNOU 2010)

Q 10. Explain (with diagram) the WINDOWS 2000 OS structure. (IGNOU Dec 2010)

Q 11. Give Short note on: (IGNOU Dec 2010)

Fault tolerance in Distributed OS.

UNIX structure.

A cyclic graph directory

PCB/TCB

Q 12. Compare FileManagement in UNIX with WINDOWS. Give diagrams in support of the answer.(IGNOU Dec 2010)

Q 13. Explain howMemory Management is done in Windows 2000 OS. (IGNOU Dec 2014)

Q 14. Discuss the linked and index file allocation schemes. Which allocation scheme is used in UNIX OS? (IGNOU Dec 2015)

Q 15. Explain pipes and filters in UNIX 5 (with examples). (IGNOU June 2011)

Q 16. Explain the structure of UNIX and Windows Operating Systems. (IGNOU June 2012)

Q 17. Explain the booting process of windows 10 2000 Operating System.(IGNOU Dec 2012)

Q 18. Illustrate and discuss interprocess 5 communication features in windows 2000 Operating System.(IGNOU June 2013)

Q 19. What are different kinds of file systems in 10 Unix? Explain in brief.(IGNOU June 2013)

Q 21. Write short notes on the Linux network services. (Anna University 2013)

Q 22. Discuss about the steps involved in the installation of a Linux Multifunction server. (Anna University 2013)

Q 23. Briefly discuss about the requirements to become a Linux System Administrator.(Anna University 2013)

Q 24. Explain the significance and steps involved in setting up Xen, VMware software on Linux Host for successful virtualization in detail.(Anna University 2013)

Exercise

Exercise 1 – MCQ

1. Which of the following is an open-source Operating System?

a) Unix

b) Windows

c) macOS

d) Linux

2. Which Operating System is known for its command-line interface called Terminal?

a) Windows

b) macOS

c) Linux

d) Unix

3. Which Operating System is NOT based on Unix?

a) macOS

b) Linux

c) Windows

d) Unix

4. Which of the following Operating Systems is widely used in servers and supercomputers?

a) macOS

b) Windows

c) Linux

d) Unix

5. Which Operating System is developed by Microsoft Corporation?

a) Unix

b) macOS

c) Linux

d) Windows

6. What is the primary programming language used to develop the Linux kernel?

a) Java

b) C++

c) Python

d) C

7. Which Operating System is commonly used in academic and research institutions?

a) macOS

b) Windows

c) Linux

d) Unix

8. Which Operating System is the foundation for Apple's desktop and laptop computers?

a) macOS

b) Linux

c) Windows

d) Unix

9. Which Operating System is NOT POSIX-compliant?

a) Linux

b) Unix

c) macOS

d) Windows

10. Which Operating System provides multiple shell options like Bash, Zsh, and Fish?

a) Windows

b) macOS

c) Linux

d) Unix

Exercise 2 – True/ False

1. Linux is based on Unix.

2. Windows is an Open-Source Operating System.

3. macOS is exclusively designed for Apple hardware.

4. Unix Operating System is primarily used in personal computers.

5. Shell is an Operating System.

6. Windows Operating System is known for its command-line interface called Terminal.

7. Linux is only used in server environments.

8. Windows Operating System is POSIX-compliant.

9. Unix Operating System is not customizable.

10. macOS is built on top of the Linux kernel.

Answer

Exercise 1 – MCQ

Ans: 1 d, 2 b, 3 c, 4 c, 5 d, 6 d, 7 c, 8 a, 9 d, 10 c

Exercise 2 – True/False

Ans: 1 True, 2 False, 3 True, 4 False, 5, False, 6

Online Resources

Videos:

MCQ Link:https://youtu.be/Wg_wCTdnyBY

QR Code:

True/False Link:https://youtu.be/AuKqCQhZ3a0

QR Code:

Online Test Paper: https://forms.office.com/r/YfwBVKpm8M

QR Code:

Miscellaneous Questions

1. Explain Chaining and Indexing disk 10 allocation schemes with the help of a suitable example.(IGNOU 2010)

Ans: Chaining and Indexing are two different disk allocation schemes used in Operating Systems to manage the allocation of disk space for files. These schemes help keep track of the locations of file data on the disk. Let's explain both with suitable examples:

Chaining Allocation Scheme:

Chaining is a simple and straightforward method of disk allocation. In this scheme, each file is divided into blocks or clusters of a fixed size. Each block contains a pointer to the next block in the file. The last block in the file has a pointer to indicate the end of the file. This creates a linked list of blocks that make up the file. Free space on the disk is managed separately.

Example:

Suppose you have a disk with five blocks, and you want to store a file of 10 blocks using the chaining allocation scheme. Here's how it might look:

Disk Blocks:

1 -> 2 -> 3 -> 4 -> 5

File A:

Block 1 -> Block 2 -> Block 3 -> Block 4 -> Block 5

In this example, each block contains a pointer to the next block. Block 5 contains a special pointer indicating the end of the file. The file "A" is stored as a linked list of blocks on the disk.

Advantages of Chaining:

It's easy to implement.

Files can grow or shrink without much overhead.

Disadvantages of Chaining:

Retrieving data is slow as it involves traversing the linked list.

It can lead to fragmentation.

Indexing Allocation Scheme:

In the indexing allocation scheme, each file has its own index block that contains pointers to the actual data blocks on the disk. The index block acts as a table of contents for the file. The index block can be a separate block on the disk or a part of the file's metadata.

Example:

Suppose you have a disk with five blocks and want to store a file of 10 blocks using the indexing allocation scheme. Here's how it might look:

Disk Blocks:

2 3 4 5

File A:

Index Block -> Block 2 -> Block 4 -> Block 5

In this example, the index block for file "A" contains pointers to the data blocks used by the file. Block 2, Block 4, and Block 5 are the actual data blocks containing the file's content.

Advantages of Indexing:

Fast access to data because you can directly access data blocks using the index.

Minimal fragmentation.

Disadvantages of Indexing:

Overhead of maintaining the index blocks for each file.

Limited by the size of the index block (number of pointers).

In summary, chaining uses a linked list structure to allocate disk space for files, while indexing uses an index block to point to data blocks. Each has its own set of advantages and disadvantages, and the choice of allocation scheme depends on the specific requirements of the Operating System and the use case.

2. Discuss two alternative forms of authentication.(IGNOU 2010)

Ans: Alternative forms of Authentication in Operating Systems are important for enhancing security and ensuring that only authorized users gain access to system resources. Here are two common alternative authentication methods:

Biometric Authentication:

Biometric authentication relies on unique physical or behavioral characteristics of individuals to verify their identity. This method is increasingly popular due to its accuracy and convenience. Some common forms of biometric authentication include:

Fingerprint Recognition: Users are authenticated by scanning and matching their fingerprint patterns with stored templates.

Retina or Iris Scanning: This involves scanning the unique patterns in a person's retina or iris to verify their identity.

Facial Recognition: Facial features, such as the geometry of a person's face, are captured and compared to stored data.

Voice Recognition: The user's voice characteristics, including pitch and tone, are analyzed for authentication.

Hand Geometry: This method measures the size and shape of a person's hand, including the lengths of fingers.

Behavioural Biometrics: Typing patterns, mouse movements, and other behavioral traits are analysed for authentication.

Biometric authentication is highly secure because it is difficult to fake or share these unique characteristics. However, it may not be fool proof, and it can be costly to implement due to specialized hardware and software requirements.

Two-Factor Authentication (2FA) or Multi-Factor Authentication (MFA):

Two-factor authentication and multi-factor authentication require users to provide multiple forms of verification to access a system. This enhances security by ensuring that even if one form of authentication is compromised, there is an additional layer of protection. Common factors for 2FA and MFA include:

Something You Know: This is typically a password or PIN that the user must enter.

Something You Have: Users may need to provide a physical token, such as a smart card, key fob, or mobile device, which generates one-time passcodes (OTP).

Something You Are: This factor can involve biometric authentication methods, as discussed earlier.

Something You Do: Behavioral factors, like keystroke dynamics or gesture patterns, can be used for authentication.

For example, a common form of 2FA involves combining a password (something you know) with a time-based OTP generated by a mobile app (something you have). To gain access, a user must provide both the password and the current OTP.

2FA and MFA are highly effective in preventing unauthorized access, even if a password is compromised. They are widely used for online services, banking, and secure access to corporate networks.

In summary, biometric authentication leverages unique physical or behavioral traits, while two-factor authentication and multi-factor authentication require users to provide multiple forms of verification. These alternative authentication methods enhance security and help protect systems and data from unauthorized access.

3. How can we achieve Ordering of events in a distributed OS? Suggest an algorithm and implement an example on it.(IGNOU Dec 2010)

Ans: Achieving the ordering of events in a distributed Operating System is essential to ensure that various processes or nodes in the system can coordinate and synchronize their actions. To achieve event ordering, you can use a Lamport timestamp or vector clock algorithm. I'll explain the Lamport timestamp algorithm and provide a simple example.

Lamport Timestamp Algorithm:

The Lamport timestamp algorithm, developed by Leslie Lamport, assigns a logical timestamp to each event in a distributed system. These timestamps are used to establish a partial ordering of events. The algorithm ensures that if event A happened before event B, their timestamps will reflect this order.

Algorithm Steps:

Each process or node maintains a counter, initially set to 0.

When an event occurs at a process, it increments its counter and assigns the incremented value as the timestamp for that event.

When a process sends a message, it includes its timestamp in the message.

When a process receives a message, it compares the timestamp in the received message with its own timestamp:

If the received timestamp is greater, the process updates its own timestamp to be the maximum of its current timestamp and the received timestamp plus one.

If the received timestamp is less than the process's timestamp, the process does nothing.

If the received timestamp is equal to the process's timestamp, the process increments its timestamp by one.

Example:

Let's illustrate the Lamport timestamp algorithm with a simple example involving two processes, P1 and P2, and a few events:

P1 sends a message to P2.

P2 receives the message.

P1 receives a response from P2.

P1 sends another message to P2.

Initially, both P1 and P2 have their counters set to 0.

Event 1 (P1 sending a message): P1 increments its counter to 1 and assigns a timestamp of 1 to this event.

Event 2 (P2 receiving the message from P1): P2 increments its counter to 1 and assigns a timestamp of 1 to this event.

Event 3 (P1 receiving a response from P2): P1 increments its counter to 2 and assigns a timestamp of 2 to this event.

Event 4 (P1 sending another message): P1 increments its counter to 3 and assigns a timestamp of 3 to this event.

Now, let's consider the ordering of these events based on their Lamport timestamps:

Event 1 (P1 sending a message) - Timestamp 1

Event 2 (P2 receiving the message from P1) - Timestamp 1

Event 3 (P1 receiving a response from P2) - Timestamp 2

Event 4 (P1 sending another message) - Timestamp 3

The LamportTimestamps correctly order the events according to their causality, even in a distributed environment.

By using this algorithm, distributed systems can ensure the ordering of events and maintain logical consistency when coordinating various processes or nodes. It is crucial for tasks like distributed databases, distributed file systems, and distributed consensus algorithms like the Raft or Paxos protocols.

4. Explain the Hardware Support for Segmentation with an example.(IGNOU Dec 2010)

Ans: Hardware Support for Segmentation in Operating Systems typically involves memory management units (MMUs) that are capable of implementing segmentation. Segmentation is a memory management technique that divides the logical address space of a process into various segments, each with its own permissions and characteristics. Segmentation is distinct from paging, which divides memory into fixed-size pages.

The key components of hardware support for segmentation include segment registers and segment tables. Here's a basic overview with an example:

Hardware Components:

Segment Registers: The CPU typically has special registers known as segment registers. These registers hold information about the location and size of segments. Common segment registers include Code Segment (CS), Data Segment (DS), Stack Segment (SS), and Extra Segment (ES).

Segment Table: A segment table is a data structure that resides in memory and is used to map logical addresses to physical addresses. Each entry in the segment table corresponds to a segment and contains information about the segment's base address and its limit (size). The segment table is managed by the Operating System and is typically stored in system memory.

Example:

Let's consider a simple example where we have a program with two segments: a code segment and a data segment.

Code Segment: This segment contains the executable instructions of the program.

Data Segment: This segment contains the program's data, such as variables.

Assuming that the code segment starts at address 0x1000 and has a size of 0x2000 bytes, and the data segment starts at address 0x3000 and has a size of 0x1000 bytes, the segment table would look something like this:

Segment Table:

Segment	Base Address	Limit
Code	0x1000	0x2000
Data	0x3000	0x1000

Now, when a program executes, it uses segment registers to access its segments. For example, the CS register would point to the code segment, and the DS register would point to the data segment.

Suppose the program tries to access a location within the code segment, say address 0x1200. The hardware, with the help of the CS register and the segment table, translates this logical address to the physical address by adding the base address of the code segment:

Logical Address: 0x1200 (within the code segment)

Physical Address: 0x1000 (base address of the code segment) + 0x1200 (offset) = 0x2200

The hardware ensures that the program can only access addresses within the segment's limit, thus providing memory protection.

Segmentation is valuable because it allows for more fine-grained control over memory protection and sharing. However, it does have its limitations, such as external fragmentation, which can be mitigated by combining segmentation with paging (known as segmentation with paging or segmentation and paging). This hybrid approach is used in many modern Operating Systems to manage memory efficiently.

5. Explain physical and logical clocks. Explain Lamport's scheme of ordering of events.(IGNOU June 2011)

Ans: Physical and logical clocks are concepts used in distributed systems to establish a notion of time and to order events. These concepts play a crucial role in maintaining consistency and coordination among processes in a distributed environment.

Physical Clocks:

Physical clocks refer to real-time clocks based on the physical time of a system or a device.

They are typically maintained by hardware components, like the motherboard's real-time clock.

Physical clocks provide a globally agreed-upon time that is synchronized across all devices.

Examples include wall clocks, atomic clocks, and GPS time.

Logical Clocks:

Logical clocks are not based on real-world time but are used to order events in a distributed system.

Logical clocks are typically implemented in software and are often used to maintain causality among events.

Logical clocks do not require synchronization across all devices; they are local to individual processes.

Logical clocks are typically implemented using algorithms like Lamport's logical clocks.

Lamport's Scheme of Ordering of Events: Leslie Lamport introduced a logical clock algorithm to order events in a distributed system. The Lamport timestamp algorithm is a simple and widely used method to establish a partial ordering of events based on causality. This algorithm is used to ensure that events occurring in different processes can be correctly ordered, even if they have different physical timestamps.

Key Features of Lamport's Algorithm:

Timestamps: Each event in a distributed system is associated with a Lamport timestamp, which is an integer value. These timestamps are initially set to zero.

Event and Message Timestamping:

When an event occurs in a process, it increments the process's LamportTimestamp.

When a process sends a message, it includes its current LamportTimestamp with the message.

Event and Message Comparison:

When a process receives a message, it compares the timestamp in the message with its own timestamp.

The process then sets its timestamp to the maximum of its current timestamp and the received timestamp (plus one, to ensure causality).

If the received timestamp is smaller than the process's timestamp, the process updates its timestamp by taking the maximum of its current timestamp and the received timestamp (plus one).

Example:

Let's consider a simple example involving two processes, P1 and P2, and two events:

P1 sends a message to P2.

P2 receives the message.

Initially, both P1 and P2 have their timestamps set to 0.

Event 1 (P1 sending a message): P1 increments its timestamp to 1 and assigns this value to the message.

Event 2 (P2 receiving the message): P2 increments its timestamp to 1 because it receives a message with a timestamp of 1.

In this example, the timestamps correctly order the events according to their causality. LamportTimestamps allow us to reason about the relative ordering of events in a distributed system, ensuring that events that causally depend on one another are correctly ordered.

Q 6. What is Thrashing? Give a solution to this problem.(IGNOU June 2011)

Ans:Thrashing is a phenomenon in Operating Systems where a system becomes overwhelmed by excessive paging or swapping, leading to a significant decrease in overall system performance. When thrashing occurs, the system spends more time moving data between main memory (RAM) and secondary storage (e.g., a hard disk) than it does actually performing useful computations. This results in a severe degradation of system responsiveness and can lead to system unresponsiveness or even crashes.

Thrashing typically happens when the system is overcommitted regarding the amount of virtual memory it can effectively manage. Overcommitment occurs when there is not enough physical RAM to satisfy the memory demands of running processes, and the system relies heavily on paging or swapping to maintain the illusion of abundant memory.

Causes of Thrashing:

Running too many processes concurrently, each with high memory demands.

Inadequate physical RAM to accommodate the working set of active processes.

Poor memory management and inefficient page replacement algorithms.

Solutions to the Thrashing Problem:

Add More Physical RAM:

The most straightforward solution is to increase the amount of physical RAM in the system. With more RAM, the system can better accommodate the working set of active processes, reducing the need for frequent paging or swapping.

Optimize System Resources:

Reduce the number of running processes or lower the memory demands of active processes. Close unnecessary applications or services to free up memory.

Use efficient algorithms and data structures to minimize memory usage within your software applications.

Adjust Virtual Memory Settings:

You can fine-tune Virtual Memory Settings to improve system performance. For example, you can adjust the size of the page file or swap space to match your system's requirements better.

Ensure that the swapping and paging areas are on fast storage devices to minimize the impact of I/O operations on system performance.

Implement Efficient Page Replacement Algorithms:

Utilize Page Replacement Algorithms that minimize thrashing. The most common algorithms are LRU (Least Recently Used), LFU (Least Frequently Used), or working set-based algorithms.

Page Replacement Algorithms aim to keep the most frequently used pages in physical memory to reduce the need for frequent page swaps.

Use System Monitoring and Profiling:

Monitor system performance regularly to detect signs of thrashing, such as a high page fault rate or excessive disk I/O.

Profiling tools can help identify memory-hungry processes and memory leaks, allowing you to take appropriate actions.

Dynamically Adjust the Number of Processes:

Some Operating Systems or resource management tools can dynamically adjust the number of active processes based on system load. This can help prevent overcommitment and thrashing.

Prioritize Processes:

Use process prioritization to give higher priority to essential processes or those with real-time requirements to avoid thrashing in critical applications.

In summary, Thrashing is a performance issue that arises when the system is overwhelmed by excessive paging or swapping. The solutions to thrashing involve optimizing memory resources, adding more physical RAM, implementing efficient memory management strategies, and monitoring system performance to detect and prevent thrashing when it occurs.

Q 7. How is Overlay different from Swapping? Explain.(IGNOU June 2011)

Ans: Overlay and Swapping are both techniques used in memory management, but they operate differently and serve different purposes.

Overlay:

Purpose: Overlay is a technique used to overcome the limitations of limited memory space in a system, particularly in early computing systems with small memory capacities.

Functionality: In overlay technique, a program is divided into multiple sections or overlays. Only one overlay is loaded into memory at a time, and when a different section of the program is needed, the current overlay is swapped out of memory, and the new overlay is loaded in its place.

Usage: Overlay techniques were commonly used in systems where the entire program could not fit into memory at once, so different parts of the program were loaded and unloaded as needed during execution.

Swapping:

Purpose: Swapping is a technique used to manage processes in memory by temporarily moving them between main memory (RAM) and secondary storage (usually a hard disk).

Functionality: When a process is moved out of main memory to free up space for other processes, it's stored in a swap file on the disk. Later, when the process is needed again, it can be swapped back into memory from the swap file.

Usage: Swapping is used to maximize the utilization of available memory by moving less frequently used processes out of memory temporarily to make room for other processes.

Key Differences:

Purpose: Overlay is primarily used to run programs that are too large to fit entirely into memory, while swapping is used to manage memory resources efficiently by moving processes in and out of memory as needed.

Granularity: Overlay operates at a finer granularity, swapping out specific sections or overlays of a program, whereas swapping operates at a coarser granularity, moving entire processes in and out of memory.

Storage Medium: Overlay typically involves swapping data between main memory and other parts of main memory, while swapping involves moving data between main memory and secondary storage.

Time Complexity: Overlay involves more frequent swapping operations as different parts of the program are loaded and unloaded, whereas swapping involves less frequent but larger transfers of entire processes.

In summary, while both overlay and swapping techniques involve moving data in and out of memory, overlay is primarily used for managing program execution in systems with limited memory, whereas swapping is used for efficient management of memory resources in modern Operating Systems.

Q 8. Give short notes on: (IGNOU June 2011)

Disk Organisation in UNIX.

DOS and NOS.

Multiprocessor Interconnection.

Macintosh OS.

Ans:

Disk Organization in UNIX:

UNIX-based Operating Systems, including Linux, use a hierarchical file system structure.

The file system is organized as a tree with a root directory (represented by "/").

Files and directories are arranged in a tree-like structure, where directories can contain subdirectories and files.

UNIX file systems support various file types, such as regular files, directories, symbolic links, device files, and special files.

In UNIX, devices and files are treated, as if they are part of the file system, allowing easy access to hardware devices.

(ii) DOS and NOS (Disk Operating System and Network Operating System):

DOS (Disk Operating System) refers to a family of Operating Systems, including MS-DOS and PC-DOS, which were widely used on personal computers in the 1980s and early 1990s.

DOS was primarily a single-user, single-tasking Operating System with a command-line interface.

NOS (Network Operating System) refers to an Operating System designed for networked environments.

NOS typically includes features for managing network resources, user authentication, and file sharing, making it suitable for multi-user and multi-computer environments.

(iii) Multiprocessor Interconnection:

Multiprocessor interconnection refers to the ways in which multiple processors or CPU cores are connected in a multiprocessor system.

Common interconnection topologies include shared memory systems, where all processors share a single, large memory pool, and distributed memory systems, where each processor has its own memory.

Interconnection can be achieved through various topologies like buses, crossbar switches, mesh networks, or hypercube networks, depending on the architecture of the multiprocessor system.

Effective interconnection is crucial for achieving good parallel processing performance in multi-core or multi-processor systems.

(iv) Macintosh OS:

The Macintosh Operating System, also known as macOS (formerly OS X), is the Operating System developed by Apple Inc. for their Macintosh line of computers.

macOS is known for its user-friendly graphical user interface and is built on a Unix-based foundation.

It includes features like the Aqua user interface, robust multimedia support, and compatibility with a wide range of software applications.

macOS also provides advanced features for developers, including support for multiple programming languages and extensive development tools.

Please note that the specifics and features of these topics may have evolved over time, and the information provided here is based on knowledge available as of September 2021.

Q 9. Explain Single and Multiple Partition Systems with reference to memory. Give suitable examples.(IGNOU June 2012)

Ans: Single and Multiple Partition Systems are memory allocation schemes used in Operating Systems to manage memory resources efficiently. These schemes determine how memory is divided and allocated to different processes. Let's explore each of them with suitable examples:

Single Partition System:

In a Single Partition System, the entire physical memory (RAM) is used as a single, continuous block, and this block is allocated to a single process at a time. When one process completes its execution, the entirememory becomesavailable for the next process. This approach is simple but has several limitations, such as inefficient utilization of memory and lack of support for concurrent execution of multiple processes.

Example:

Consider an early computer system with 1 GB of RAM. In a Single Partition System, if Process A is running and occupies the entire 1 GB of RAM, no other process can execute concurrently. Only when Process A finishes its execution can the memory be allocated to another process like Process B.

Multiple Partition System:

A Multiple Partition System divides the physical memory into multiple fixed-sized or variable-sized partitions. Each partition can be allocated to a single process. This approach allows concurrent execution of multiple processes, making better use of available memory. However, it may still suffer from fragmentation issues, such as internal and external fragmentation.

Example:

Suppose you have 2 GB of physical memory, and you divide it into four equal partitions, each with 512 MB. In this Multiple Partition System, you can simultaneously run up to four processes, with each process allocatedone of the four partitions. This enables better utilization of memory resources, as multiple processes can run concurrently.

Advantages and Disadvantages:

Single Partition System:

Advantages:

Simple and easy to implement.

No fragmentation issues.

Disadvantages:

Inefficient memory utilization, as only one process can run at a time.

Limited support for concurrent execution.

Multiple Partition System:

Advantages:

Allows concurrent execution of multiple processes.

Better memory utilization.

Disadvantages:

Fragmentation issues can occur. External fragmentation arises when free memory is split into small, non-contiguous blocks. Internal fragmentation occurs when allocated memory is larger than what is required, leading to wasted space.

In modern Operating Systems, Multiple Partition Systems have largely replaced Single Partition Systems because they offer better support for multitasking and efficient utilization of memory resources. However, to address fragmentation concerns, Advanced Memory Management Techniques like Paging and Segmentation are often used in conjunction with multiple partition systems.

Q 10. Explain the Crossbar and Fly BeranbeMulti-ProcessorInterconnection Network.(IGNOU June 2012)

Ans: The Crossbar and Flattened Butterfly (also known as "Fly Beranek") are two different interconnection network topologies used in multiprocessor systems to connect multiple processors or nodes. These topologies play a crucial role in determining the communication and data transfer efficiency of the system. Let's discuss both of these interconnection networks:

Crossbar Interconnection Network:

Structure: A Crossbar network is essentially a grid of horizontal and vertical wires that intersect like a grid, forming a matrix. Each wire intersection represents a switch. Processors or nodes are connected to the inputs and outputs of the matrix.

scalability: Crossbars can be used to build large-scale multiprocessor systems. However, their size and complexity increase with the number of processors, making them expensive and difficult to scale to very large numbers of nodes.

Advantages:

High Bandwidth and Low Latency: Crossbars offer a direct and simultaneous connection between any input and output, providing high bandwidth and low latency communication.

Non-blocking: In ideal conditions, a Crossbar is non-blocking, meaning that any input can communicate with any output simultaneously without contention.

Disadvantages:

Cost and Complexity: Building large Crossbar networks can be expensive and complex.

Scalability Limitations: It becomes impractical to build very large Crossbars with a large number of processors.

Use Case: Crossbars are often used in smaller-scale multiprocessor systems, such as symmetric multiprocessing (SMP) systems, to provide high-speed, low-latency communication between processors.

Flattened Butterfly (Fly Beranek) Interconnection Network:

Structure: The Flattened Butterfly network is a variant of the Butterfly network and is typically organized in multiple stages or levels. Each stage is constructed using butterfly switches, and processors or nodes are connected to the inputs and outputs of these switches. The connections between switches are designed to allow efficient communication between nodes at different levels.

Scalability: Flattened Butterfly networks are more scalable than Crossbars, making them suitable for larger multiprocessor systems, including high-performance computing clusters.

Advantages:

Scalability: Flattened Butterfly networks can efficiently accommodate a large number of nodes while maintaining manageable complexity.

Fault tolerance: They offer fault tolerance, as multiple paths exist for communication between nodes, reducing the impact of a single link or switch failure.

Disadvantages:

Slightly higher latency: Communication in Flattened Butterfly networks may involve more hops compared to Crossbars, resulting in slightly higher latency.

Use Case: Flattened Butterfly networks are commonly used in high-performance computing clusters and large multiprocessor systems where scalability and fault tolerance are critical.

In summary, the Crossbar and Flattened Butterfly (Fly Beranek) are two different Multiprocessor Interconnection Network topologies. Crossbars provide high bandwidth and low latency but are less scalable and cost-effective for large systems. Flattened Butterfly networks, on the other hand, are more scalable andsuitable for larger multiprocessor systemswhilemaintaining fault tolerance, though they may have slightly higher latency. The choice of the interconnection network depends on the specific requirements and constraints of the multiprocessor system being designed.

Q 11. Explain the concepts of shared memory, distributed memory and distributed shared memory.(IGNOU June 2012)

Ans: In the context of Operating Systems and parallel computing, three important memory models are often discussed: Shared Memory, Distributed Memory, and Distributed Shared Memory. Each of these models defines how multiple processes or nodes in a parallel or distributed computing environment access and share memory. Let's explain each concept:

Shared Memory:

In a shared memory model, multiple processes or threads within the same system or computer can access a common, shared memory space.

This shared memory region is typically part of the physical RAM and is accessible by all processes running on the same machine.

Processes can read from and write to this shared memory, allowing for easy and efficient communication and data sharing between processes.

Shared memory is commonly used in symmetric multiprocessing (SMP) systems where multiple CPU cores share access to a single, large memory pool.

It is relatively easy to implement and provides efficient communication between processes.

Example: In a multi-threaded program, threads can share data by accessing the same memory locations, which is possible due to the shared memory model.

Distributed Memory:

In a Distributed Memory model, multiple processes or nodes in a distributed computing environment have their own separate memory spaces. They do not share a common memory pool.
Communication between processes in this model is typically achieved through message passing, where processes explicitly send and receive data over a network or interconnect.
Distributed memory systems are commonly used in cluster computing or supercomputing environments where each node has its own local memory and resources.
Scalability is a significant advantage of distributed memory systems, as they can easily accommodate a large number of nodes.
Example: In a cluster of computers, each node has its own memory, and communication between nodes occurs through message passing, such as using the Message Passing Interface (MPI) standard.

Distributed Shared Memory (DSM):
Distributed Shared Memory is a hybrid model that combines elements of both shared memory and distributed memory.
In a DSM system, each node or process has its own local memory, but a software layer provides the abstraction of shared memory.
Processes can access this shared memory abstraction, and the DSM system takes care of data distribution and coherence behind the scenes.
This model allows for more straightforward programming and code portability while still leveraging the advantages of distributed memory systems.
However, it may introduce performance overhead due to the need for data synchronization and coherence management.

Example: In a DSM system, processes on different nodes can access a shared memory space even though their actual memory is distributed. The DSM system ensures that data access and coherence are maintained correctly.
The choice of memory model depends on the specific requirements and characteristics of the computing environment. Shared memory is suitable for tightly coupled multi-core systems, while distributed memory is used in loosely coupled distributed computing clusters. Distributed shared memory aims to strike a balance between ease of programming and scalability, making it a practical choice for some parallel and distributed computing applications.

Q 12. What is the difference between a Loosely Coupled and Tightly Coupled System? Give suitable examples.(IGNOU Dec 2012)

Ans: Loosely coupled and tightly coupled systems refer to different levels of integration and communication between system components in a computing environment. These terms are commonly used to describe the degree of interdependence and interaction between hardware or software elements in a system. Let's explore the differences between loosely coupled and tightly coupled systems and provide suitable examples:

Loosely Coupled System:

Definition: In a Loosely Coupled System, components are relatively independent and have limited knowledge of each other. They communicate through well-defined interfaces or protocols, and the coordination between components is minimal.

Characteristics:

Components can operate independently.

Communication between components often occurs through message passing or network protocols.

Components may run on separate machines and may even be heterogeneous in nature.

Failures in one component typically do not lead to the failure of the entire system.

Examples:

Cluster of Computers: In a Cluster, each node operates independently, and communication happens over a network. Nodes can be running different Operating Systems or software.

Web Services: Web Services communicate through standard protocols like HTTP. Different web services can be hosted on various servers, and they interact through well-defined interfaces.

Distributed Databases: Distributed Databases may consist of multiple database instances running on different servers. They communicate through standardized database protocols.

Tightly Coupled System:

Definition: In a Tightly Coupled System, components are highly integrated and interdependent. They share resources and have in-depth knowledge of each other's operation, which enables fast and efficient communication.

Characteristics:

Components are closely interconnected and often share a common memory space or hardware resources.

Communication between components is usually faster, often through direct function or method calls.

Tightly coupled systems typically achieve higher performance but may be less fault-tolerant.

Examples:

Symmetric Multiprocessing (SMP) Systems: In SMP systems, multiple processors or CPU cores share a single memory space and are closely interconnected. This allows for parallel execution of processes and threads and efficient data sharing. Examples include multi-core CPUs in modern computers.

Tightly Coupled Cluster: In some high-performance computing clusters, nodes may be interconnected through high-speed interconnects like InfiniBand, providing a level of coupling that enables efficient message passing and shared-memory programming models.

Mainframes: Mainframe computers have tightly integrated hardware components and share common memory, making them well-suited for high-performance and reliable transaction processing.

Comparison:

Loosely coupled systems are more flexible and can be easier to scale, making them suitable for distributed and heterogeneous environments.

Tightly coupled systems often provide higher performance and are well-suited for applications where low latency and efficient resource sharing are critical.

The choice between loosely coupled and tightly coupled systems depends on the specific requirements of the application and the desired trade-offs between performance, fault tolerance, and flexibility.

Q 13. Explain all types of Multi-Processor Operating Systems.(IGNOU Dec 2012)

Ans: Multiprocessor Operating Systems, also known as multiprocessor OS or multiprocessing Operating Systems, are designed to manage and coordinate multiple CPUs (Central Processing Units) or processor cores within a single computer system. These multiprocessor systems are typically categorized into four main types based on their architecture and resource sharing approaches:

Symmetric Multiprocessing (SMP):

In an SMP system, all processors are treated equally and have equal access to shared system resources, such as memory and I/O devices.

Characteristics:

All processors have uniform access to memory and other system resources.

Load balancing is achieved through task scheduling.

High availability and fault tolerance can be challenging to implement.

Example: Modern multi-core CPUs in desktop and server computers are typically SMP systems.

Asymmetric Multiprocessing (AMP):

In an AMP system, one processor, known as the master processor, is responsible for system management tasks, while other processors, known as slave processors, perform application-specific tasks.

Characteristics:

The master processor is responsible for managing system resources and can reassign tasks to slave processors.

Load balancing and task assignment are determined by the master processor.

Provides better fault isolation and easier resource management.

Example: Some embedded systems, such as those used in consumer electronics or automotive applications, use AMP to manage system resources.

Clustered Multiprocessing:

In a clustered multiprocessing system, multiple independent computer systems (nodes) are interconnected in a cluster, and each node can be an SMP system in itself.

Characteristics:

Each node in the cluster operates independently with its own Operating System.

Nodes communicate over a network, and tasks may be distributed among them.

High availability and fault tolerance can be achieved by distributing tasks across nodes.

Example: High-performance computing clusters, web server farms, and cloud computing infrastructure often use clustered multiprocessing.

Non-Uniform Memory Access (NUMA):

In a NUMA system, multiple processors or processor cores are organized into nodes, and each node has its own memory. While processors can access their local memory with low latency, access to remote memory nodes may incur higher latency.

Characteristics:

Provides a compromise between SMP and clustered multiprocessing.

Load balancing and memory access policies consider the locality of data to minimize remote memory access.

Suitable for systems with multiple processors and large memory capacities.

Example: Enterprise servers and high-end workstations often use NUMA architecture to balance the trade-off between memory capacity and access latency.

These types of multiprocessor Operating Systems cater to various requirements, from high-performance computing clusters and data centers to consumer electronics and embedded systems. The choice of the most suitable multiprocessor OS depends on factors like system architecture, application workload, performance goals, and fault tolerance requirements.

Q 14. System has instances of a resource. Resource requirement of 3 processes are given as below:

P1 P2 P3

Max. Requirement 8 7 5

Current Allocation 3 1 3

Is the current allocation in a safe state? If the new requirement from process P1of 1 instance arrives, whether the state will remain in same state? Apply Banker's algorithm to answer this question.(IGNOU Dec 2012)

Ans: To determine if the current allocation is in a safe state and whether the state will remain the same after the new requirement from process P1 arrives, we can apply the Banker's algorithm.

Banker's Algorithm works by simulating the allocation of resources to processes and checking, if there exists a safe sequence in which all processes can complete their execution without causing a deadlock.

Given:

Max Requirement:

P1: 8

P2: 7

P3: 5

Current Allocation:

P1: 3

P2: 1

P3: 3

Let's calculate the available resources and the need matrix:

Available Resources = Total Resources - Current Allocation:

Available Resources = (8, 7, 5) - (3, 1, 3) = (5, 6, 2)

Need Matrix = Max Requirement - Current Allocation:

Need Matrix:

P1: (8 - 3) = 5

P2: (7 - 1) = 6

P3: (5 - 3) = 2

Next, let's check if the system is in a safe state:

Start with the Available Resources:

Available Resources = (5, 6, 2)

Check, if there exists a process whose resource needs can be satisfied with the available resources:

Process P3 can run since its resource needs (2) are less than or equal to the available resources (5, 6, 2).

After P3 runs, it releases its resources, updating the available resources:

Available Resources = (5, 6, 2) + (3, 3, 0) = (8, 9, 2)

Now, check if there exists another process whose resource needs can be satisfied:

Both P1 and P2 can run since their resource needs (5 and 6, respectively) are less than or equal to the available resources (8, 9, 2).

After both P1 and P2 run and release their resources, updating the available resources:

Available Resources = (8, 9, 2) + (3, 1, 3) + (5, 7, 0) = (16, 17, 5)

Since all processes can complete their execution in this sequence without causing a deadlock, the system is in a safe state.

Now, let's consider the new requirement from process P1 of 1 instance:

New Requirement from P1: 1

If the new requirement from process P1 of 1 instance arrives, we need to check if the system remains in a safe state. Let's recalculate the Available Resources:

Available Resources = (16, 17, 5) - (1, 0, 0) = (15, 17, 5)

We repeat the Banker's algorithm steps to check if there exists a safe sequence:

Process P2 can run since its resource needs (6) are less than or equal to the available resources (15, 17, 5).

After P2 runs, it releases its resources, updating the available resources:

Available Resources = (15, 17, 5) + (0, 1, 0) = (15, 18, 5)

Now, check if there exists another process whose resource needs can be satisfied:

Both P1 and P3 can run since their resource needs (5 and 2, respectively) are less than or equal to the available resources (15, 18, 5).

After both P1 and P3 run and release their resources, updating the available resources:

Available Resources = (15, 18, 5) + (3, 0, 3) + (5, 0, 0) = (23, 18, 8)

Since all processes can complete their execution in this sequence without causing a deadlock, the system remains in a safe state after the new requirement from process P1 arrives.

Q 15. Write Bakery's Algorithm for handling critical section problem for n processor.(IGNOU Dec 2012)

Ans: The Bakery Algorithm is a simple and elegant solution to the critical section problem for n processors (where n is any finite number). It provides a mechanism to ensure that multiple processors or threads cansafely enter a critical section without conflicting with one another. The algorithm uses a ticket system, assigning each processor a unique ticket based on their request to enter the critical section. Here's a detailed explanation of the Bakery Algorithm:

The Bakery Algorithm

Initialization:

Each processor maintains two variables: `choosing` and `number`.

`choosing` is a boolean variable that signifies a processor's intention to enter the critical section.

`number` is an array with an element for each processor, initialized to zero.

Request Entry:

When a processor wants to enter the critical section, it first sets its `choosing` flag to true and simultaneously finds the maximum ticket number issued to any other processor.

It then increments its own ticket number to one greater than the maximum ticket number.

choosing[i] = true;

number[i] = max(number[0], number[1], ..., number[n-1]) + 1;

choosing[i] = false;

Waiting:

After obtaining its ticket number, the processor must wait until it is its turn to enter the critical section.

It does this by checking the `number` of all other processors and waiting until their ticket numbers are either smaller or equal but with a lower processor ID (in case of a tie).

```
for (j = 0; j < n; j++) {
// Wait until all processors with smaller or equal ticket numbers finish.
while (choosing[j]);
while ((number[j] != 0) && (number[j], j) < (number[i], i));
}
```

Critical Section:

Once a processor determines that it has the smallest ticket number and all other processors have either higher ticket numbers or lower processor IDs, it enters the critical section to execute the protected code.

Exit Critical Section:

After completing its critical section, the processor sets its ticket number back to zero (indicating it is done with the critical section), allowing other processors to enter.

number[i] = 0;

Explanation:

The Bakery Algorithm guarantees that processors enter the critical section in increasing order of their ticket numbers.

The `choosing` flag prevents processors from both issuing a new ticket and entering the critical section simultaneously.

The waiting process ensures fairness, as processors with lower ticket numbers get to enter the critical section first.

The use of the `choosing` and `number` variables helps avoid race conditions in the critical section.

The Bakery Algorithm is relatively simple and easy to understand but may not be the most efficient choice for high contention scenarios. In practice, more advanced algorithms like Peterson's Algorithm, Dekker's Algorithm, or hardware-based solutions like atomic instructions and locks are often preferred for managing critical sections in modern Operating Systems.

Q 16. Explain Multilevel, Acyclic Graph and General Graph Directory Structure.(IGNOU Dec 2012)

Ans: Directory Structures are an essential component of file systems in Operating Systems, and they define how files and directories are organized and accessed. Three commonly used directory structures are Multilevel Directory Structure, Acyclic Graph Directory Structure, and General Graph Directory Structure.

Multilevel Directory Structure:

Definition: In a multilevel directory structure, directories are organized hierarchically, creating a tree-like structure. Each directory can contain files and subdirectories.

Features:

Directories can be nested within each other.

A parent directory can contain multiple subdirectories, and each subdirectory can contain its own set of files and subdirectories.

Allows for a logical and organized organization of files and directories.

Example: In a Unix-like file system, the root directory ("/") contains subdirectories like "/home," "/var," and "/usr." The "/home" directory, in turn, can have subdirectories for individual user accounts.

Acyclic Graph Directory Structure:

Definition: An acyclic graph directory structure represents directories as nodes and the relationships between them as edges. However, this structure prohibits cycles (loops) in the graph, ensuring that a directory cannot be its ancestor or descendant.

Features:

Offers flexibility in organizing directories and files.

Provides the ability to create symbolic links and shortcuts between directories without creating circular references.

Example: In Windows, symbolic links or junctions allow you to create references to directories in different locations without creating a cycle in the directory structure.

General Graph Directory Structure:

Definition: In a general graph directory structure, directories and their relationships form a graph, which means cycles are allowed. This structure allows for more complex and interconnected directory relationships.

Features:

Allows directories to be interconnected in various ways, potentially creating loops in the directory structure.

Provides advanced flexibility in directory organization.

Can be useful in certain specialized use cases.

Example: A hypothetical use case could involve a directory structure where specific directories are linked to multiple parent directories, creating more complex interconnections.

In-depth Explanation:

Multilevel Directory Structure: This is the most common and intuitive type of directory structure. It is hierarchical and allows for easy navigation and organization. Each directory level represents a deeper layer of organization, such as a directory for user accounts that contains subdirectories for each user.

Acyclic Graph Directory Structure: In this structure, symbolic links and shortcuts are often used to create references to directories in other locations. These references provide a convenient way to access directories without duplicating content. The absence of cycles ensures that there is a clear, one-way relationship between directories.

General Graph Directory Structure: This is the most flexible but potentially complex structure. It allows for various relationships between directories, including loops, and can be useful when advanced directory interconnections are required. However, managing such a structure can be challenging due to the potential for loops, which might lead to ambiguity or unexpected behavior.

The choice of directory structure depends on the specific needs of the Operating System and its users. Multilevel directory structures are the most common and user-friendly, while acyclic and general graph structures provide more flexibility and power for advanced use cases.

Q 17. Consider the following set of processes, with the length of the CPU burst time given in milliseconds. Process Burst time P1 12 P2 5 P3 27 P4 3 P5 15 (IGNOU June 2013)
All five processes arrive at time 0, in the order given. Draw Gantt charts illustrating the execution of the processes using FCFS, SJF and RR (quantum =1) scheduling. What is the turnaround time of each process for each of the scheduling algorithms? Also find the average waiting time for each algorithm.
Ans:solve this step by step for each scheduling algorithm:

FCFS (First-Come, First-Served):

The processes execute in the order they arrive.
Gantt Chart:

| P1 | P2 | P3 | P4 | P5 |

Turnaround Time:

P1: 12 ms

P2: 17 ms

P3: 44 ms

P4: 47 ms

P5: 62 ms

Average Waiting Time:

(0 + 12 + 17 + 44 + 47) / 5 = 24 ms

SJF (Shortest Job First):

The process with the shortest burst time runs first.
Gantt Chart:

| P4 | P2 | P5 | P1 | P3 |

Turnaround Time:

P1: 37 ms

P2: 22 ms

P3: 69 ms

P4: 3 ms

P5: 47 ms

Average Waiting Time:

(0 + 3 + 22 + 37 + 47) / 5 = 21.8 ms

RR (Round Robin with quantum = 1):

Each process runs for 1 ms in a round-robin fashion until completion.

Gantt Chart:

| P1 | P2 | P3 | P4 | P5 | P1 | P3 | P5 | P1 | P5 | P1 |

Turnaround Time:

P1: 49 ms

P2: 19 ms

P3: 63 ms

P4: 15 ms

P5: 57 ms

Average Waiting Time:

(11 + 0 + 36 + 12 + 42) / 5 = 20.2 ms

In summary:

For FCFS, the average waiting time is 24 ms.

For SJF, the average waiting time is 21.8 ms.

For RR with quantum = 1, the average waiting time is 20.2 ms.

Q 18. Illustrate a 3-dimensional Hypercube System and describe its features.(IGNOU June 2013)

Ans: A 3-dimensional Hypercube, often referred to as a 3D hypercube or cube-connected cycles (C3), is a specific type of interconnection network used in parallel and distributed computing systems. It is a three-dimensional analogy of the more well-known binary hypercube, which is commonly used in high-performance computing environments. A 3D hypercube has unique properties and features that make it suitable for certain types of applications. Let's illustrate a 3D hypercube system and describe its features in detail.

Illustration of a 3D Hypercube:

A 3D hypercube can be visualized as a cube with each vertex of the cube representing a processing element (PE) or node. Each edge of the cube represents a direct communication link between two PEs. The 3D hypercube is structured in such a way that each PE is connected to exactly three other PEs, forming a cube shape. This network structure extends in three dimensions (x, y, z), creating a grid of interconnected nodes.

Here's a simplified representation of a 3D hypercube:

In this representation, each number (0-7) corresponds to a processing element (PE). The edges represent communication links between PEs.

Features of a 3D Hypercube:

Deterministic Routing: A 3D hypercube has Deterministic Routing, meaning that there is a unique path between any pair of PEs. This makes it predictable and easy to manage.

Scalability: The 3D hypercube can be extended by adding more PEs and dimensions. You can have a 4D, 5D, or higher-dimensional hypercube, but the complexity increases with dimension.

Fault Tolerance: A 3D hypercube has some fault tolerance built in. If a link or a node fails, there are typically alternative routes for communication.

Regular Structure: The 3D hypercube has a highly regular structure, making it easier to understand and analyze. This regularity simplifies both hardware and software design.

Parallelism: It's well-suited for parallel computing and distributed processing tasks. Each PE can work on different tasks, and communication between PEs is efficient due to the regular topology.

Communication Efficiency: The 3D hypercube minimizes the number of hops required for communication, reducing latency and improving overall system performance.

Message Passing: In a 3D hypercube system, communication between PEs is typically implemented using a message-passing model, where PEs send messages to each other.

Applications: The 3D hypercube is used in various parallel computing applications, including scientific simulations, data analysis, and parallel algorithm development.

It's important to note that as the dimension of the hypercube increases, its complexity and the number of connections grow exponentially. While this structure offers numerous advantages, it's important to carefully consider the trade-offs, especially in terms of hardware complexity and scalability, when designing systems based on 3D hypercube interconnections.

Q 18. What is meant by Context Switch? Explain the overhead incurred due to context switching on process and thread.(IGNOU June 2013)

Ans: Context Switching is a fundamental concept in Operating Systems. It refers to the process of saving and restoring the state of a CPU so that it can execute multiple processes or threads in a multitasking or multi-threaded environment. During context switching, the Operating System saves the context (state) of the currently executing process or thread and loads the context of another process or thread, allowing it to continue execution.

The context of a process or thread typically includes the following information:

Program Counter (PC): The memory address of the next instruction to be executed.

CPU registers: The contents of the processor registers, including general-purpose registers, stack pointers, and program status registers.

Memory Management Information: Information about memory boundaries, such as base and limit registers.

Stack Pointers: Pointers to the top of the process's or thread's stack.

State Information: Information about whether the process or thread is in running, ready, or blocked state.

Context switching occurs for several reasons, including when:

The CPU scheduler decides to switch to another process or thread.

A process or thread voluntarily yields the CPU, such as when it performs an I/O operation and becomes blocked.

A hardware interrupt or exception occurs, forcing the Operating System to switch to a different context.

Overhead Incurred Due to Context Switching:

Context switching introduces several types of overhead:

Time Overhead: Each context switch takes time to save the state of one process or thread and load the state of another. This time overhead can reduce the overall system performance and throughput.

Memory Overhead: Storing and managing the context information for each process or thread requires memory. The more processes and threads that are active, the more memory is needed for context information.

Cache Overhead: Context Switching can disrupt the cache behavior. When a new process or thread is loaded, it may not have the data and code that was in the cache when the previous process or thread was executing, leading to cache misses and degraded performance.

Complexity Overhead: Context Switching is a complex operation that involves a significant amount of code and data structures to manage context information and state transitions. This complexity can lead to increased code size, making the Operating System more complex and potentially error-prone.

Synchronization Overhead: Context Switches often involve synchronization mechanisms, such as locking and unlocking data structures to protect them from concurrent access. This adds additional overhead, especially when multiple threads are involved.

Interrupt Latency: In a system with frequent context switches, the response time to hardware interrupts may increase, as the CPU may be busy performing context switches.

Efficient management of context switching overhead is essential for optimizing the performance and responsiveness of a multitasking or multi-threaded system. This includes minimizing the frequency of context switches, optimizing the context switch code, and efficiently managing memory and cache to reduce overhead. Additionally, hardware and Operating System design can impact context switching efficiency, and many techniques are used to mitigate these overheads in modern computing systems.

Q 19. Why API's need to be used rather than System Calls?(Anna University 2013)

Ans: APIs (Application Programming Interfaces) are an essential layer in modern software development, especially in Operating Systems. While System Calls are the low-level interface that allows applications to interact with the Operating System kernel directly, there are several reasons why APIs should be used instead of making direct System Calls:

Abstraction and Portability:

APIs provide an abstraction layer that shields application developers from the underlying complexity of the Operating System. This abstraction allows developers to write code that is more portable across different platforms.

System Calls, on the other hand, are specific to an Operating System, and direct use of System Calls can lead to non-portable code. By using APIs, developers can write code that is less dependent on the underlying OS, making it easier to maintain and migrate to other platforms.

Consistency:

APIs offer a standardized and consistent way to access Operating System functionality. This standardization ensures that applications work consistently across different versions of the same OS and across different OSs.

System Calls, while consistent within a particular OS, can vary significantly between different Operating Systems. APIs provide a unified interface that abstracts away these differences.

Ease of Use:

APIs are designed to be user-friendly and developer-friendly. They often include well-documented functions and data structures, which can simplify application development.

System Calls typically require a deep understanding of the OS internals, which can be complex and error-prone for application developers. APIs provide a higher level of abstraction, making it easier for developers to work with the Operating System.

Security and Sandboxing:

Many modern Operating Systems employ security mechanisms that restrict direct access to System Calls to prevent unauthorized or malicious operations. APIs are typically designed to work within these security constraints and provide a safer way for applications to interact with the system.

By using APIs, applications can take advantage of the OS's security features, which may not be accessible through direct System Calls.

Resource Management:

APIs often handle resource management, such as memory allocation and deallocation, more efficiently and with less risk of resource leaks or errors. Using APIs can improve resource management in applications.

System Calls may require developers to manage resources manually, which can lead to resource leaks or other issues,if not handled correctly.

Error Handling and Reporting:

APIs typically include well-defined error handling mechanisms, making it easier for applications to detect and respond to errors in a consistent manner.

System Calls may not provide the same level of error handling and reporting, leading to less robust applications.

Compatibility and Versioning:

APIs often have versioning mechanisms that allow developers to maintain compatibility with older versions of the API, even as the OS evolves.

Direct System Calls may not offer the same versioning support, which can lead to compatibility issues when the OS is updated.

In summary, while System Calls are a fundamental way for applications to interact with the Operating System, using APIs offers numerous benefits in terms of abstraction, portability, consistency, ease of use, security, resource management, error handling, and compatibility. APIs provide a higher-level, user-friendly interface that simplifies application development and makes it easier to create robust, cross-platform software.

Q 20. Define the term 'Dispatch Latency'.(Anna University 2013)

Ans: Dispatch Latency is a term used in the context of Operating Systems and computer systems to describe the time delay that occurs when a process is selected to run on the CPU (Central Processing Unit) after being dispatched from the ready queue. This latency can impact the overall responsiveness and performance of a multitasking system. Let's dive into the details of dispatch latency:

Selection from Ready Queue:

In a multitasking Operating System, multiple processes are typically ready to execute but must wait for their turn on the CPU.

When the Operating System scheduler selects a process from the ready queue for execution, this is the point at which the dispatch latency starts.

Save and Restore Context:

The dispatcher (a component of the Operating System) is responsible for saving the context of the currently running process. This context includes the program counter, CPU registers, and other relevant data.

The saved context is stored in a data structure known as the process control block (PCB).

Load New Process Context:

Once the context of the currently running process is saved, the dispatcher loads the context of the selected process (the one being dispatched) from its PCB.

Loading the context involves setting the program counter, CPU registers, and other relevant state to the values saved in the PCB of the new process.

Overhead and Time Delay:

The activities involved in saving and restoring the context, as well as switching the CPU to the new process, introduce overhead and time delay. This overhead is the dispatch latency.

Dispatch latency includes not only the time taken for saving and loading context but also any additional activities like memory management and scheduling bookkeeping.

Impact on System Performance:

Dispatch latency can have a significant impact on system performance and responsiveness, especially in real-time and time-sensitive applications.

Long dispatch latencies can lead to delayed response times, which may not be acceptable for tasks like multimedia processing, real-time control systems, and gaming.

Reducing Dispatch Latency:

Operating Systems are designed to minimize dispatch latency through efficient context-switching mechanisms. Techniques like quick context switchers, which optimize the saving and loading of context, are used to reduce latency.

Hardware support, such as the use of multi-core processors and specialized instructions, can also help reduce dispatch latency.

Frequency of Dispatches:

The frequency of context switches can impact dispatch latency. Systems with more frequent context switches may experience higher dispatch latency, while systems with longer time slices between context switches may have lower dispatch latency.

In summary, Dispatch Latency is the time delay incurred when switching from one process to another in a multitasking Operating System. It includes the time needed to save and restore the context of processes and can affect system responsiveness and performance. Operating Systems aim to minimize dispatch latency through efficient context-switching mechanisms and hardware support to ensure the smooth execution of multiple processes.

Q 21. Write short notes on Free Space Management.(Anna University 2013)

Ans: Free Space Management is a critical component of a file system in an Operating System. It involves the organization and tracking of available storage space on storage devices, such as hard drives and solid-state drives. Effective free space management is essential for optimizing storage utilization, performance, and reliability. Here are some key points in short notes on free space management:

Data Blocks and Free Space:

In a file system, data is stored in blocks or clusters. These blocks can vary in size but are typically a fixed size.

To store new files or data, the file system must allocate one or more free blocks from the storage medium.

Allocation Methods:

File systems employ various allocation methods to manage free space. The common methods include:

Contiguous Allocation: Files are stored as contiguous blocks. Free space is managed as a single block or a group of contiguous blocks.

Linked Allocation: Each block contains a pointer to the next free block, creating a linked list of free blocks.

Indexed Allocation: An index or allocation table is used to manage free space. It provides quick access to available blocks.

Fragmentation:

Fragmentation refers to the division of free space into small, non-contiguous segments. Two types of fragmentation exist:

Internal Fragmentation: Space within allocated blocks that remains unused. It occurs when a block is not fully occupied by a file.

External Fragmentation: Unallocated space scattered throughout the storage medium. It results from a collection of non-contiguous free blocks.

File System Performance:

Effective free space management impacts the performance of the file system. Contiguous allocation can minimize file fragmentation but might lead to disk fragmentation. Linked or indexed allocation can minimize disk fragmentation but might result in file fragmentation.

Defragmentation:

To address fragmentation issues, file systems often employ defragmentation tools. These tools reorganize files and free space to reduce fragmentation and improve storage efficiency.

File System Efficiency:

Efficient free space management is crucial for maintaining high storage utilization. It helps prevent wasted space and ensures that available storage is used optimally.

Dynamic Allocation:

Some file systems use dynamic allocation strategies to adapt to changing storage requirements. This involves adjusting the allocation method and block sizes dynamically to accommodate different file sizes.

Reliability and Data Recovery:

Effective free space management is essential for ensuring data integrity and recovery. It helps prevent data corruption and loss by minimizing the risk of overwriting or allocating storage blocks that contain valuable data.

File Deletion:

When a file is deleted, its associated storage blocks become free. The file system must update its free space management structures to reflect the newly available space.

In conclusion, Free Space Management is a core aspect of file system design in Operating Systems. It involves allocating and tracking available storage space, selecting appropriate allocation methods, addressing fragmentation, and ensuring efficient storage utilization. Effective Free Space Management contributes to system reliability, performance, and data integrity.

Q 22. Briefly discuss about the various Directory Structure.(Anna University 2013)

Ans: Directory structures are an essential component of file systems in Operating Systems. They determine how files and directories are organized, accessed, and managed. There are several types of directory structures, each with its characteristics and use cases. Here's a brief overview of some of the common directory structures:

Single-Level Directory:

In a Single-Level Directory structure, all files are located in a single directory, making it a straightforward but limited organization. Each file must have a unique name.

This structure is rarely used in modern Operating Systems because it lacks the ability to organize files and manage access efficiently.

Two-Level Directory:

A Two-Level Directory structure introduces the concept of user directories. Each user has a directory at the second level, allowing users to organize their files without name conflicts.

This structure is simple and provides better organization than a single-level directory.

Tree-Structured Directory:

In a Tree-Structured Directory, directories can contain subdirectories, creating a hierarchical tree. Users can create a more extensive and organized file structure.

This is the most common type of directory structure in modern file systems like Windows and Unix-like systems.

Acyclic-Graph Directory:

Acyclic-Graph Directories allow for directories to contain subdirectories and form a directed acyclic graph (DAG). Cycles (loops) are not allowed in this structure.

It provides flexibility in organizing files and directories, with symbolic links and shortcuts often used to create references between directories.

General-Graph Directory:

In a General-Graph Directory structure, directories can form a graph, which means cycles are allowed. This structure can create complex directory interconnections.

It offers significant flexibility but can also become more challenging to manage and navigate.

Mount Point Directory:

In systems with Multiple Storage Devices, mount points are used to attach secondary storage devices to specific directory locations. Each device can appear as part of the overall directory structure.

This structure allows for the seamless integration of various storage devices.

Distributed Directory:

Distributed Directory structures are used in networked or distributed file systems, where files and directories can be located on different servers or nodes.

They allow users to access and manage files across a network of interconnected systems.

Virtual Directory:

Virtual Directories are not physical directories on the storage device but are logical or virtual views of the file system. They can be used to aggregate files from multiple locations into a single, user-friendly view. The choice of directory structure depends on the specific requirements of the Operating System, the complexity of the file organization, and the desired user experience. In practice, hierarchical tree-structured directories are the most common, offering a balance between organization and accessibility. However, other structures are used when specific needs or constraints dictate alternative approaches.

Q 23. Write short notes on Memory Mapped Files.(Anna University 2013)

Ans: Memory-Mapped Files are a mechanism used in Operating Systems that allows files to be directly mapped into a process's virtual memory space. This enables processes to read and write data in a file as if it were an array in memory, making it a powerful and efficient method for file I/O. Here are some key points in short notes about memory-mapped files:

Mapping File into Memory:

In a Memory-Mapped File, a section of a file is mapped into a process's virtual address space. This allows the process to access the file's data as if it were an array in memory.

Efficient I/O Operations:

Memory-Mapped Files provide efficient file I/O operations by reducing the need for explicit read and write System Calls. Instead, data can be accessed through memory operations, which can be faster.

Shared Memory and IPC:

Memory-Mapped Files can be used for inter-process communication (IPC) in multi-processing or multi-threading environments. Multiple processes or threads can map the same file into memory, allowing them to share data and communicate efficiently.

Mapping Modes:

Memory-Mapped Files can be mapped with different modes, including read-only, read-write, and copy-on-write. These modes determine whether the data can be modified in memory and how changes are reflected back to the file.

Advantages:

Memory-Mapped Files simplify file I/O, particularly for large files. They eliminate the need for explicit read and write operations, reducing code complexity.

They allow for efficient random access to data within a file because data is already in memory.

In some cases, memory-mapped files can provide performance advantages over traditional file I/O methods.

Disadvantages:

Memory-Mapped Files require careful management of memory, especially when working with large files, to prevent excessive memory consumption.

Changes made to memory-mapped files must be explicitly synchronized with the file on disk to ensure data consistency.

Operating System Support:

Memory-Mapped Files are supported by most modern Operating Systems, including Unix-based systems (Linux, macOS) and Windows.

Common Use Cases:

Memory-Mapped Files are used in various scenarios, including database systems (to map database files), memory-mapped I/O in databases, shared memory segments for inter-process communication, and optimizing large data processing tasks.

Security Implications:

Care must be taken when using Memory-Mapped Files, especially when mapping user-provided data into memory. Improper use can lead to security vulnerabilities, such as buffer overflows.

APIs:

Operating Systems provide APIs to work with Memory-Mapped Files, such as `mmap()` in Unix-based systems and `MapViewOfFile()` in Windows.

In summary, Memory-Mapped Files provide an efficient and powerful method for working with files in an Operating System. They are particularly useful for scenarios that involve large files, inter-process communication, and optimized data access. However, they require careful management and synchronization to ensure data consistency and to avoid memory-related issues.

Q 24. What are the advantages of Peer to Peer systems over client server systems?(Anna University 2017)

Ans: Peer-to-Peer (P2P) systems and client-server systems are two different network architectures, each with its own set of advantages and disadvantages. While client-server systems are prevalent and suitable for many applications, P2P systems offer several advantages in specific use cases. Here, we'll explain in detail the advantages of P2P systems over client-server systems in the context of Operating Systems:

Decentralization:

Advantage of P2P: P2P systems are inherently decentralized. In a P2P network, there is no central server or point of failure. Instead, each node (or peer) can communicate directly with other peers.

In Client-Server: In client-server systems, the server is a central point of control and administration. If the server goes down, it can disrupt the entire network.

Scalability:

Advantage of P2P: P2P systems can be highly scalable because new peers can join the network without a central authority's approval or intervention. As the network grows, it becomes more robust and can handle increasing loads.

In Client-Server: Scalability in Client-Server Systems often requires significant investments in server hardware and infrastructure, making it more challenging to scale rapidly.

Resource Sharing:

Advantage of P2P: P2P networks excel in Resource Sharing. Users can share their own resources, such as files, processing power, and bandwidth, with other peers. This can be highly efficient for distributing content and load balancing.

In Client-Server: Resource Sharing in client-server systems is more limited and typically controlled by the server, making it less efficient for peer-to-peer resource exchange.

Redundancy and Fault Tolerance:

Advantage of P2P: P2P networks can be highly fault-tolerant because data and services are distributed across multiple peers. If one peer fails, the network can often continue functioning.

In Client-Server: In Client-Server Systems, fault tolerance often relies on backup servers and redundancy, which can be complex and costly to set up.

Cost Efficiency:

Advantage of P2P: P2P systems can be more cost-effective as they utilize resources available on individual devices. This reduces the need for extensive server infrastructure, making it suitable for resource-constrained environments.

In Client-Server: Setting up and maintaining client-server infrastructure can be expensive due to hardware and operational costs.

Data Privacy and Security:

Advantage of P2P: P2P systems can offer better data privacy and security because data is distributed, and peers have more control over their own resources.

In Client-Server: Client-Server Systems may be vulnerable to centralized attacks, and data privacy can be challenging to enforce, especially when data is stored on central servers.

Distributed Processing:

Advantage of P2P: P2P networks can leverage distributed processing by utilizing the computational power of multiple peers for tasks like distributed computing and data processing.

In Client-Server: While Client-Server Systems can distribute some processing tasks, true distributed processing often requires complex coordination and load balancing mechanisms.

Content Availability:

Advantage of P2P: P2P systems can provide better content availability, as content is distributed across multiple peers. Popular content can be replicated and accessed from multiple sources.

In Client-Server: Content availability in client-server systems relies on the server's uptime and accessibility.

Content Delivery:

Advantage of P2P: P2P systems can optimize content delivery by sourcing data from multiple peers, reducing the load on central servers and improving content access speed.

In Client-Server: In Client-Server Systems, content delivery speed depends on server capacity and network latency.

Resistance to Censorship:

Advantage of P2P: P2P systems can be more resistant to censorship or content blocking, as they lack a central point of control. Data can be distributed across the network, making it harder to target specific servers.

It's important to note that while P2P systems have these advantages, they also come with challenges, such as coordination, security concerns, and the potential for misuse. The choice between P2P and client-server architecture should be based on the specific requirements and constraints of the application or network in question.

Q 25. Differentiate between Hard Real Time Systems and Soft Real Time Systems.(Anna University 2017)

Ans: Real-Time Systems are a class of computer systems designed to perform tasks within specified timing constraints. They are commonly used in applications where timing and predictability are critical. Real-Time Systems can be categorized into two main types: hard Real-Time Systems and soft Real-Time Systems. These categories are differentiated by the strictness of their timing requirements and how they handle missed deadlines. Here, we'll explain in detail the differences between hard Real-Time Systems and soft Real-Time Systems in the context of Operating Systems:

Hard Real-Time Systems:

Timing Constraints:

Strict Timing Constraints: Hard Real-Time Systems have strict and deterministic timing constraints. Tasks in a hard real-time system must meet their deadlines without exception.

Task Prioritization:

Fixed Priority Scheduling: Hard Real-Time Systems typically use fixed-priority scheduling algorithms. Tasks are assigned priorities, and higher-priority tasks pre-empt lower-priority tasks to ensure that they meet their deadlines.

Consequences of Missing Deadlines:

Unacceptable: Missing a deadline in a hard real-time system is unacceptable and can lead to catastrophic consequences. The system is designed to ensure that deadlines are always met.

Examples:

Aircraft Control Systems: Flight control systems in airplanes are examples of hard Real-Time Systems. Failure to respond within a strict time frame could result in a crash.

Operating System Support:

Specialized Real-Time OS: Hard Real-Time Systems often use specialized real-time Operating Systems with low and deterministic interrupt latencies.

Resource Allocation:

Resource Reservation: Hard Real-Time Systems may employ resource reservation mechanisms to guarantee resources (CPU time, memory) for critical tasks.

Trade-offs:

Performance Predictability: Hard Real-Time Systems prioritize performance predictability over resource utilization efficiency. They sacrifice resource sharing to guarantee task deadlines.

Soft Real-Time Systems:

Timing Constraints:

Relaxed Timing Constraints: Soft Real-Time Systems have timing constraints that are more relaxed compared to hard Real-Time Systems. They aim to meet deadlines whenever possible but can tolerate occasional misses.

Task Prioritization:

Dynamic Priority Scheduling: Soft Real-Time Systems often use dynamic priority scheduling. Task priorities may change based on the system's current state and the urgency of tasks.

Consequences of Missing Deadlines:

Tolerable: Missing a deadline in a soft real-time system is tolerable as long as it does not occur too frequently. Soft Real-Time Systems aim to optimize overall system performance while still meeting most deadlines.

Examples:

Streaming Services: Online Video Streaming Platforms like Netflix or YouTube use soft Real-Time Systems. A minor buffer underflow causing a momentary pause in video playback is acceptable.

Operating System Support:

General-Purpose OS with Real-Time Extensions: Soft Real-Time Systems often use General-Purpose Operating Systems with real-time extensions or features.

Resource Allocation:

Resource Sharing: Soft Real-Time Systems focus on efficient resource sharing among tasks. They balance the need for meeting deadlines with maximizing resource utilization.

Trade-offs:

Resource Utilization: Soft Real-Time Systems prioritize resource utilization efficiency and system throughput over strict deadline adherence. They aim to meet deadlines most of the time but accept occasional deviations for better overall system performance.

In summary, the key differentiation between hard Real-Time Systems and soft Real-Time Systems lies in the strictness of their timing constraints and how they handle missed deadlines. Hard Real-Time Systems have non-negotiable, strict timing requirements, while soft Real-Time Systems have more flexible constraints and can tolerate occasional deviations. The choice between these types of Real-Time Systems depends on the specific application's requirements and the trade-offs between strict timing and system efficiency.

Q 26. Tabulate the different Interrupt Classes.(Anna University 2017)

Ans: Interrupts are essential mechanisms in Operating Systems and computer architecture that allow the Operating System to respond to various events and requests from both hardware and software. Interrupts are categorized into different classes based on their sources and functions. Here's a tabulation of the different interrupt classes:

Interrupt Class	**Description**
Hardware Interrupts	These interrupts are triggered by external hardware devices or events and are usually asynchronous in nature.
1. External Interrupts	Generated by external devices, such as keyboards, mice, network cards, and timers.
2. Internal Interrupts	Triggered by internal hardware events, such as arithmetic errors, hardware malfunctions, or thermal issues.
3. Non-Maskable Interrupts (NMI)	Critical hardware events that cannot be masked or disabled by the CPU. Often used for system failure detection.
Software Interrupts	These interrupts are generated by software and are typically used for System Calls, exceptions, and program control.
1. System Calls (Syscalls)	Invoked by programs to request services from the Operating System, such as file operations or memory management.
2. Exceptions and Traps	Raised in response to exceptional conditions, such as divide-by-zero, page faults, or illegal instructions.
3. Software Interrupt Instructions	Some CPUs provide explicit instructions (e.g., INT in x86) for triggering software interrupts.
Machine Check Interrupts (MCI)	These are hardware interrupts that signal CPU and system-level errors, such as cache errors or data corruption.
Inter-Processor Interrupts (IPI)	Used in multiprocessor systems to allow one processor to communicate with or interrupt another processor.
Spurious Interrupts	Unexpected or unexplained interrupts that occur for various reasons, such as electrical noise or glitches.
Timer Interrupts	Generated by the system's timer or clock hardware at regular intervals for time-keeping and scheduling purposes.
Network Interrupts	Specific to network interface controllers (NICs), these interrupts are triggered when data is received or sent.
I/O Interrupts	Associated with input and output operations, such as disk I/O, interrupting the CPU when data is ready to be read or written.
Performance Monitoring Interrupts (PMIs)	Used for monitoring and profiling system performance and gathering statistics.

These Interrupt Classes play a crucial role in maintaining system stability, enabling multitasking, handling exceptions, and facilitating efficient communication between software and hardware components in an Operating System.

Q 27. What is Thread?(RU B. Tech. Jan 2022)

Ans:A Thread is the smallest unit of a CPU's execution, and it represents an independent path of execution within a process. Threads are a fundamental concept in Operating Systems and are used to achieve concurrent and parallel execution of tasks. Here's a detailed explanation of threads in the context of Operating Systems:

Thread vs. Process:

In a traditional Operating System, a process is an independent program with its memory space and resources. Processes are heavy-weight entities. In contrast, a thread is a subunit of a process and shares the same memory space and resources with other threads in the same process. Threads are lightweight compared to processes.

Thread Attributes:

Threads have their attributes, including a unique identifier (Thread ID), program counter, register set, and stack. However, they share other resources, such as the process's memory, file descriptors, and global variables.

Benefits of Threads:

Concurrency: Threads allow multiple tasks to be executed in parallel, utilizing the available CPU cores efficiently.

Responsiveness: Multi-Threaded applications remain responsive, as one thread can continue executing even, if another is blocked, waiting for I/O or other resources.

Resource Sharing: Threads within the same process can easily share data and communicate, making it easier to implement inter-thread communication and synchronization.

Scalability: Threads can enhance system performance on multi-core CPUs, as multiple threads can run in parallel.

Types of Threads:

User-level threads (ULTs): Managed by a user-level thread library and are not visible to the kernel. ULTs offer flexibility but may not take full advantage of multi-core systems.

Kernel-level threads (KLTs): Managed by the Operating System's kernel. KLTs are more efficient and can be scheduled independently on multiple CPU cores. Most modern Operating Systems use KLTs.

Thread States:

Threads can be in various states, including:

Running: Currently executing on a CPU core.

Ready: Ready to run but waiting for CPU time.

Blocked: Waiting for some event or resource to become available.

Terminated: Finished executing.

Thread Scheduling:

Thread Scheduling is the process of determining which thread to execute next on a CPU core. Scheduling Algorithms, like round-robin or priority-based scheduling, are used to make this decision.

Thread Communication:

Threads can communicate and synchronize through shared memory or synchronization primitives like semaphores, mutexes, and condition variables. This inter-thread communication is essential for avoiding data races and ensuring data consistency.

Thread Safety:

Multithreaded programming can introduce race conditions and data inconsistencies. Ensuring thread safety through proper synchronization mechanisms is critical in multithreaded applications.

Use Cases:

Threads are commonly used in applications where parallelism and concurrency are required, such as web servers, database management systems, scientific simulations, and multimedia applications.

Challenges:

Multithreaded programming introduces challenges, such as synchronization, deadlock prevention, and debugging, which must be carefully addressed.

In summary, threads are a fundamental concept in Operating Systems that enable concurrent and parallel execution of tasks within a process. They offer advantages in terms of concurrency, responsiveness, resource sharing, and scalability. Properly managing and synchronizing threads is crucial to avoid issues like data races and ensure the correctness of multithreaded applications.

Q 28. What are Context Switches? (RU B. Tech. Jan 2022)

Ans:A Context Switch is a fundamental operation in the management of processes in an Operating System. It involves saving the current state of a process and loading the saved state of another process, allowing the CPU to switch from executing one process to another. Context switches are essential for multitasking and time-sharing systems, enabling the efficient sharing of CPU resources among multiple processes or threads. Here's a detailed explanation of context switches in Operating Systems:

Process States:

Processes in an Operating System can be in various states, such as running, ready, blocked, or terminated. The running state indicates that the process is currently executing on the CPU.

Need for Context Switches:

Context Switches are necessary for several reasons:

Multitasking: In a Multitasking environment, multiple processes or threads compete for CPU time. The Operating System must switch between them to provide each with a fair share of processing time.

Blocking and Unblocking: Processes may block, for example, when waiting for I/O operations to complete. The CPU must be allocated to other ready processes while a blocked process is waiting.

Interrupt Handling: When an Interrupt occurs (e.g., a timer interrupt or hardware interrupt), the CPU switches from executing user code to handling the interrupt. After the interrupt is processed, the CPU must return to the previous process.

Time Sharing: In time-Sharing systems, each process is allocated a small time slice (quantum) for execution. Context switches occur when a time slice expires to allow other processes to run.

Context Information:

Context Information includes the state of the process that needs to be saved and later restored. This information typically consists of:

CPU registers, including the Program Counter (PC), stack pointer, and general-purpose registers.

Process Control Block (PCB) data, which includes the process's program and data pointers, process state, scheduling information, and other relevant data.

Memory Management Data, such as page tables and memory allocation information.

Context Switch Sequence:

When a Context Switch occurs, the following sequence of operations typically takes place:

The Operating System scheduler selects the next process to run from the ready queue.

The current process's context information is saved, including its CPU registers, PCB data, and memory management data.

The saved context information is stored in the process's PCB.

The scheduler loads the context information of the selected process from its PCB into the CPU registers.

The CPU resumes execution from the point where the selected process was previously interrupted.

Overhead and Performance Impact:

Context Switches have associated overhead, as they require saving and restoring process states. Excessive context switching can reduce system performance. Therefore, it's important to minimize unnecessary context switches.

Priority and Scheduling:

The Scheduling Algorithm used by the Operating System determines the order and frequency of context switches. Different scheduling policies, such as round-robin, priority-based, or multi-level feedback queues, affect context switch behavior.

Pre-emption:

Pre-emption occurs when the Operating System forcibly interrupts the currently running process to allow another process to run. Preemptive scheduling policies, like time-sharing systems, often result in frequent context switches.

In summary, Context Switches are a vital mechanism in Operating Systems that facilitate multitasking, process scheduling, and system responsiveness. They allow the Operating System to efficiently allocate CPU time to multiple processes, enabling users to run multiple applications concurrently and share system resources. Proper management of context switches is essential for maintaining system performance and responsiveness.

Q 29. What criteria should be adopted for choosing types of File Organization?(RTU B. Tech. Jan 2022)

Ans: Choosing the right File Organization method for your data depends on various factors, including your specific needs, the nature of the data, and the intended use of the files. Here are some criteria to consider when selecting a file organization method:

Access Patterns:

Consider how frequently and in what manner data will be accessed. If you need quick and efficient access, you might choose a different organization method than if access is infrequent or sequential.

Data Structure:

Analyze the structure of your data. Is it hierarchical, networked, or relational? Different file organization methods are better suited for different data structures.

Retrieval Speed:

Evaluate the performance requirements for data retrieval. Some methods provide faster access, while others are slower but can handle larger datasets.

Insertion and Deletion:

Consider how often you will need to add or remove data from your files. Some methods are better suited for frequent updates, while others are more suitable for static data.

Storage Efficiency:

Assess the space requirements for storing your data. Some methods are more space-efficient than others, which can be critical for large datasets.

Simplicity:

Think about the complexity of the file organization method. Simpler methods are easier to implement and maintain, while more complex methods may offer performance advantages but require more effort.

Scalability:

Consider whether your data storage needs will grow over time. Choose a method that can scale with your requirements without significant performance degradation.

Data Integrity:

Evaluate the need for data integrity and data validation. Some file organization methods offer better data consistency and integrity than others.

Security:

If data security is a concern, choose a file organization method that supports encryption, access controls, and other security features.

Compatibility:

Ensure that the chosen file organization method is compatible with your existing software and hardware infrastructure.

Industry Standards:

Check, if there are industry-specific standards or best practices that recommend specific file organization methods for your type of data.

Cost:

Consider the cost associated with implementing and maintaining the chosen file organization method, including hardware, software, and personnel.

Redundancy and Backup:

Think about the need for redundancy and backup. Some file organization methods inherently provide redundancy and data recovery options.

Metadata and Search:

Assess the need for metadata and search capabilities. Some file organization methods allow for easier indexing and searching of data.

Common file organization methods include sequential, indexed, hashed, and B-tree. The choice will ultimately depend on a balance of these criteria, tailored to your specific use case and data requirements. It's important to thoroughly analyze your needs and constraints to make an informed decision.

Q 30. Define C-Shell.(RTU B. Tech)

Ans: The C Shell, often abbreviated as "csh," is a Unix-based command-line shell or shell program. It is a type of command interpreter that provides a text-based interface for users to interact with the Unix or Unix-like Operating Systems, such as Linux. The C shell is so named because its syntax and some of its features were inspired by the C programming language.

Key characteristics and features of the C shell include:

Syntax: The C shell has a C-like syntax, which means it uses constructs and symbols that are similar to the C programming language. This includes features like semicolons to separate commands and C-style control structures.

Interactive Shell: The C shell is primarily used as an interactive shell for users to enter commands directly. Users can type commands at the command prompt, and the C shell will interpret and execute them.

Scripting: Like other Unix shells, the C shell can also be used for scripting. Users can create shell scripts by writing a series of commands in a text file, which can then be executed as a program or batch file.

History Mechanism: The C shell maintains a command history that allows users to recall and reuse previously executed commands. This can be helpful for efficiency and error correction.

Job Control: The C shell provides job control features that allow users to manage and control processes and tasks running in the background or foreground. This includes commands for backgrounding processes, bringing them to the foreground, and controlling their execution.

Aliases: Users can define command aliases in the C shell, which are custom shortcuts or abbreviations for longer commands. This can simplify and streamline command entry.

Customization: Users can customize the C shell environment, including defining environment variables and modifying the shell's behavior to suit their preferences.

It's important to note that while the C shell was historically one of the default shells on Unix systems, it has largely been replaced by other shells like the Bourne shell (sh), Bourne-Again shell (bash), and others. These newer shells offer enhanced features, better compatibility, and a more consistent syntax. Nonetheless, some users and administrators may still choose to use the C shell due to familiarity or specific requirements.

Linux Operating System Interview Questions and Answer

What is Linux, and how does it differ from other Operating Systems?

Answer: Linux is an open-source, Unix-like Operating System kernel that serves as the foundation for many Linux distributions. It differs from other Operating Systems in that it is free, open-source, and highly customizable.

Who is the creator of Linux, and when was it first released?

Answer: Linux was created by Linus Torvalds in 1991. He released the first version of the Linux kernel in August of that year.

What is the significance of the GNU Project in the context of Linux?

Answer: The GNU Project, initiated by Richard Stallman, aimed to develop a free and open-source Unix-like Operating System. Linux became a key component, providing the kernel, while the GNU Project contributed user-level utilities, forming the basis of many Linux distributions.

What are Linux distributions, and can you name a few popular ones?

Answer: Linux distributions, often called "distros," are complete Operating Systems built around the Linux kernel. Popular examples include Ubuntu, CentOS, Debian, Fedora, and Red Hat Enterprise Linux.

Explain the concept of open source in Linux and how it impacts its development and distribution.

Answer: Open source means that the source code of Linux is freely available for anyone to view, modify, and distribute. This encourages collaborative development, rapid bug fixing, and a wide variety of distributions tailored to different needs.

What is the Linux shell, and why is it important in Linux administration?

Answer: The Linux shell is a command-line interface that allows users to interact with the Operating System. It is vital in Linux administration because it provides powerful tools for system management, automation, and scripting.

What is the difference between a Linux server and a Linux desktop distribution, and how are they typically used?

Answer: A Linux server distribution is optimized for server tasks, emphasizing stability and performance. A Linux desktop distribution is tailored for use on personal computers, focusing on a graphical user interface and user-friendly applications.

What is the Linux file system hierarchy, and how does it differ from the Windows file system structure?

Answer: The Linux file system hierarchy is a tree structure starting from the root directory ("/"). It differs from Windows with a more organized and case-sensitive layout, and it doesn't use drive letters like "C:" or "D:."

What is the role of package management in Linux, and how does it simplify software installation and updates?

Answer: Package management in Linux allows users to install, update, and remove software in a consistent and controlled manner. It simplifies software management by handling dependencies and providing centralized repositories.

What are the primary advantages of using Linux over other Operating Systems, and in what scenarios is Linux most suitable?

Answer: Linux offers advantages such as cost-effectiveness, flexibility, security, and a vast ecosystem of open-source software. It is suitable for a wide range of scenarios, including server hosting, web development, embedded systems, and scientific computing.

What is the Linux terminal, and why is it important for system administrators?

Answer: The Linux terminal is a text-based interface where users can interact with the Operating System by entering commands. It is crucial for system administrators as it provides direct access to system functions, troubleshooting tools, and automation capabilities.

Can you explain the concept of "root" in Linux and why it should be used with caution?

Answer: In Linux, "root" refers to the superuser with complete control over the system. It should be used with caution because mistakes made as the root user can have severe consequences, including data loss or system instability.

What is the difference between a process and a thread in the context of Linux?

Answer: In Linux, a process is an independent program with its own memory space, while a thread is a lightweight unit of execution within a process. Multiple threads can run within a single process and share resources, making them more efficient for certain tasks.

How does Linux handle file permissions, and what are the main components of file permissions?

Answer: Linux uses a permission system based on three components: user (owner), group, and others. Each component has read, write, and execute permissions, allowing fine-grained control over who can access and modify files.

What is the role of the Linux init system, and can you name some common init systems used in Linux distributions?

Answer: The init system in Linux is responsible for initializing and managing system processes. Common init systems include systemd, SysVinit, and Upstart. systemd is widely adopted in modern Linux distributions.

What is the purpose of the Linux swap space, and how does it affect system performance?

Answer: The Linux swap space is a dedicated area on the storage device used as virtual memory when physical RAM is exhausted. It helps prevent system crashes due to memory overload but can slow down performance when heavily used.

Explain the importance of the /etc/fstab file in Linux and how it relates to disk mounting.

Answer: The /etc/fstab file is a configuration file that defines how and where storage devices are mounted in the system. It ensures consistent mounting of disks at boot and specifies options like read/write permissions and file system types.

What is the significance of the "cron" utility in Linux, and how is it used for job scheduling?

Answer: "cron" is a time-based job scheduler in Linux. It allows users to schedule tasks or scripts to run automatically at specified intervals, making it essential for automating system maintenance and repetitive tasks.

What is SELinux (Security-Enhanced Linux), and how does it enhance security in Linux systems?

Answer:SELinux is a security framework for Linux that enforces mandatory access control policies. It enhances security by defining fine-grained permissions for system resources and preventing unauthorized access and privilege escalation.

How does Linux handle network configuration, and can you explain the role of tools like "ifconfig" and "ip"?

Answer: Linux manages network configuration using tools like "ifconfig" and "ip." "ifconfig" is used for legacy purposes, while "ip" is more modern and versatile, providing comprehensive control over network interfaces, routing, and addressing.

Can you describe a scenario where you successfully mitigated a security vulnerability in a Linux environment, and what measures did you take?

Answer: In a previous role, I identified a critical security vulnerability in a web server. I promptly applied the relevant patches, configured a robust firewall, and conducted a thorough security audit to ensure there were no residual vulnerabilities.

Explain the role of a Linux firewall, and how do you configure it to enhance system security?

Answer: A Linux firewall controls incoming and outgoing network traffic. I configure it using tools like iptables or firewall to define rules that allow or deny specific connections based on port numbers, IP addresses, and protocols, thereby enhancing system security.

Can you discuss your experience with Linux containers and container orchestration tools like Docker and Kubernetes?

Answer: In a containerized environment, I have used Docker for container creation and management. Additionally, I have experience with Kubernetes for orchestrating and scaling containerized applications, ensuring efficient deployment and resource utilization.

How do you approach system monitoring in a Linux environment, and what tools do you use for performance analysis?

Answer: I employ tools like Nagios, Zabbix, or Prometheus for real-time system monitoring. These tools help me track system metrics, identify performance bottlenecks, and proactively address issues to ensure optimal system performance.

Can you discuss your strategy for ensuring high availability in a Linux server cluster?

Answer: I implement high availability using techniques such as load balancing, failover clustering, and redundant storage. This ensures that if one server fails, traffic is seamlessly redirected to others, minimizing downtime.

Unix Operating System Interview Questions & Answers

What is Unix, and how would you describe its core principles?

Answer: Unix is a multiuser, multitasking Operating System designed for stability and portability. Its core principles include simplicity, modularity, and the idea that **"everything is a file."**

Can you explain the concept of "everything is a file" in Unix?

Answer: In Unix, devices, directories, and even certain system resources are represented as files. This simplifies interaction with various components, as they can be read from or written to like regular files.

Describe the client-server model in Unix.

Answer: Unix follows a client-server model, where server processes provide services, and client processes request these services. Communication between them often occurs through sockets.

What is the significance of the shell in Unix?

Answer: The shell is the command-line interpreter that facilitates interaction between the user and the Operating System. It interprets user commands and executes them.

Explain the role of the kernel in Unix.

Answer: The kernel is the core of the Unix Operating System, managing resources, providing essential services, and acting as an interface between hardware and user-level applications.

How does Unix handle file permissions, and what are the permission types?

Answer: Unix uses a three-tiered permission system: read, write, and execute for owner, group, and others. Permissions are managed using chmod, chown, and chgrp commands.

What is an Inode in Unix file systems?

Answer: An Inode is a data structure that stores information about a file or directory, excluding its name and actual data. It includes metadata such as permissions, owner, size, and timestamps.

How do you identify the current working directory in Unix?

Answer: The pwd command is used to print the current working directory in Unix.

Explain the purpose of the PATH environment variable.

Answer: The PATH variable contains a list of directories where the shell looks for executable files. It simplifies command execution by allowing users to run programs without specifying their full paths.

What is a symbolic link in Unix, and how does it differ from a hard link?

Answer:A symbolic link is a pointer to a file or directory. It differs from a hard link in that it can span file systems and points to the file's pathname rather than its inode.

Describe the differences between a process and a thread in Unix.

Answer:A process is an independent program with its own memory space, while a thread is a lightweight, independent sequence of execution within a process that shares the same memory space.

How does Unix manage system time and date?

Answer: Unix uses the date command to display and set system date and time. The /etc/timezone file and the tzselect command are used to set the time zone.

What is a shell script, and how does it differ from a regular program?

Answer: A shell script is a series of Unix commands written in a file. It is interpreted by the shell. Unlike regular programs, shell scripts don't need compilation and are executed line by line.

Explain the purpose of the umask command in Unix.

Answer: The umask command sets the default file permissions for newly created files. It masks out the permissions that the user does not want to grant by default.

How does Unix handle inter-process communication (IPC)?

Answer: Unix provides several mechanisms for IPC, including pipes, sockets, message queues, and shared memory, allowing processes to communicate and synchronize with each other.

What are the different run levels in Unix, and how do they affect system behavior?

Answer: Run levels in Unix represent different system states. Common run levels include 0 (halt), 1 (single-user mode), 3 (multi-user mode), and 6 (reboot). The default run level is specified in the /etc/inittab file.

Explain the purpose of the ps command in Unix.

Answer: The ps command is used to display information about active processes. It provides details such as process ID (PID), terminal, status, and resource utilization.

What is the purpose of the /etc/passwd file in Unix?

Answer: The /etc/passwd file stores user account information, including usernames, encrypted passwords, user IDs, group IDs, home directories, and login shells.

Describe the differences between soft limits and hard limits in Unix resource management.

Answer: Soft limits define the current resource limits for a user, while hard limits represent the maximum values that a user can set for their soft limits using the ulimit command.

How does Unix handle signals, and can you provide examples of common signals?

Answer: Signals are software interrupts used by processes to communicate with each other. Examples include SIGKILL (terminate), SIGTERM (terminate gracefully), and SIGUSR1 (user-defined signal).

What is the purpose of the cron and at commands in Unix?

Answer: The cron command is used for scheduling recurring tasks, while the at command is used for one-time job scheduling.

How does Unix manage swap space, and what is its significance?

Answer: Swap space is used as virtual memory when physical memory is insufficient. The swapon and swapoff commands are used to enable and disable swap space.

Explain the purpose of the /etc/fstab file in Unix.

Answer: The /etc/fstab file contains information about disk drives and partitions, specifying how they should be mounted and with what options during system boot.

What is the role of the tar command in Unix, and how is it used?

Answer: The tar command is used for archiving files and creating tape backups. It can compress and decompress files, and it is often used in conjunction with other commands like gzip and find.

How does Unix handle environment variables, and can you provide examples of commonly used variables?

Answer: Environment variables are used to store information about the environment. Examples include PATH, HOME, USER, and PS1 (shell prompt).

Explain the concept of fork() System Call in Unix.

Answer: The fork()System Call creates a new process (child process) that is an exact copy of the calling process (parent process). The child process has its own unique process ID.

What is the purpose of the grep command in Unix?

Answer: The grep command is used for searching text patterns within files. It is a powerful tool for pattern matching and text processing.

Describe the purpose of the kill command in Unix.

Answer: The kill command is used to send signals to processes, allowing you to terminate or modify their behavior. The default signal is SIGTERM, but SIGKILL can be used for a forceful termination.

How does Unix handle environment initialization during user login?

Answer: When a user logs in, the system reads configuration files like .bash_profile and .bashrc to initialize the user's environment, setting variables, aliases, and other preferences.

Explain the purpose of the /etc/hosts file in Unix networking.

Answer: The /etc/hosts file maps IP addresses to hostnames, providing a local mechanism for resolving hostnames before querying DNS.

What is the significance of the passwd command in Unix?

Answer: The passwd command is used to change a user's password. It updates the encrypted password in the /etc/shadow file.

How does Unix handle shared libraries, and why are they important?

Answer: Shared libraries contain code that multiple programs can use simultaneously. They reduce disk space usage and memory requirements, promoting code reusability.

Explain the purpose of the chroot command in Unix.

Answer: The chroot command changes the root directory for a specified command or shell, restricting access to a limited portion of the file system.

What is the role of the mount command in Unix, and how is it used?

Answer: The mount command attaches a file system to the directory tree, allowing access to its contents. It is crucial for mounting external devices and network file systems.

Describe the purpose of the strace command in Unix.

Answer: The strace command is used for tracing System Calls made by a process. It helps in debugging and understanding the interactions between a program and the kernel.

mac OS Interview Questions & Answers

What is the core philosophy behind mac OS design?

Answer: mac OS follows the principle of simplicity, user-friendly interfaces, and seamless integration of hardware and software.

Explain the role of Finder in mac OS.

Answer: Finder is the file management application that allows users to browse files, manage documents, and organize their system on mac OS.

How does Time Machine work, and why is it important for mac OS users?

Answer: Time Machine is a backup feature that automatically backs up the entire system. It's crucial for data recovery and system restoration in case of failures.

Describe the key features of mac OS Dock.

Answer: The Dock provides quick access to applications, documents, and features. It includes the Trash, frequently used apps, and system preferences.

What is Spotlight Search, and how does it enhance user productivity?

Answer: Spotlight is a search feature that allows users to find files, launch applications, and perform calculations quickly, enhancing overall system navigation.

Explain the concept of Gatekeeper in mac OS.

Answer: Gatekeeper is a security feature that ensures only trusted software is installed on a Mac, providing a layer of protection against malware.

How does File Vault contribute to mac OS security, and what are its benefits?

Answer: File Vault is disk encryption that secures data on the start-up disk. It protects sensitive information, ensuring confidentiality and integrity.

Describe the role of Terminal in mac OS and its significance for advanced users.

Answer: Terminal is a command-line interface for mac OS, providing advanced users with direct access to the Unix-based system for scripting and customization.

What is iCloud, and how does it integrate with mac OS?

Answer: iCloud is Apple's cloud service. It integrates with mac OS, allowing seamless synchronization of data, such as photos, documents, and settings, across devices.

How can you troubleshoot common network connectivity issues on mac OS?

Answer: Troubleshooting may involve checking network settings, renewing DHCP leases, resetting Wi-Fi configurations, and examining system logs for clues.

Explain the role of Launchpad in mac OS and its relationship with the App Store.

Answer: Launchpad provides a visual representation of installed applications, akin to iOS. It complements the App Store for app management and installations.

Discuss the significance of system logs in mac OS for system administrators.

Answer: System logs, available in the Console app, provide detailed information on system events, errors, and processes, aiding in troubleshooting and monitoring.

How does mac OS manage hardware resources, and what are the tools available for performance tuning?

Answer: mac OS utilizes technologies like Grand Central Dispatch and Instruments for efficient resource management. Tools like Activity Monitor assist in performance tuning.

Describe the steps involved in configuring Time Machine for network backups.

Answer: Configuring Time Machine for network backups involves selecting a network drive, ensuring proper permissions, and configuring backup intervals in System Preferences.

Can you explain the role of Terminal profiles in customization and improving productivity?

Answer: Terminal profiles allow users to customize the appearance and behavior of the Terminal, providing a personalized and efficient command-line experience.

Can you provide an overview of the major milestones in the evolution of mac OS over the past 15 years?

Answer: Certainly. Mac OS has undergone significant changes, including transitions from PowerPC to Intel architecture, the introduction of Mac OS X, and subsequent mac OS releases with advancements in performance, design, and features.

How has the user interface of Mac OS evolved over the years, and what impact has it had on user experience?

Answer: The user interface has evolved from Aqua in Mac OS X to the modern flat design in recent mac OS versions. These changes aim to enhance user experience, providing a more intuitive and visually appealing interface.

Can you discuss the transition from mac OS versions using big cat names (e.g., Snow Leopard) to mac OS versions named after California landmarks (e.g., Yosemite)?

Answer: The transition was symbolic, representing a shift from a focus on internal improvements to external features and enhancements. It also aligned with Apple's California-centric approach to product naming.

How has Apple's integration of iOS features into mac OS, such as iCloud and continuity, influenced the evolution of the Operating System?

Answer: The integration has led to a seamless user experience across Apple devices. Features like Handoff and iCloud Drive enhance productivity and create a unified ecosystem for users.

Explain the significance of the transition from PowerPC to Intel processors in the evolution of Mac OS.

Answer: The transition to Intel processors in 2006 marked a major shift, allowing for increased performance, better power efficiency, and the ability to run Windows applications through Boot Camp.

Discuss the role of the UNIX-based foundation in mac OS and how it contributes to the stability and security of the Operating System.

Answer: The UNIX foundation provides a robust and secure platform. It supports features like Terminal, and the permission system enhances security by restricting access to critical system files.

How has the evolution of Mac OS contributed to advancements in graphics and multimedia capabilities, especially considering the introduction of Metal?

Answer: Metal, introduced in mac OS El Capitan, significantly improved graphics performance by providing lower-level access to the GPU. This has benefited gaming, video editing, and other graphics-intensive applications.

Explain the significance of the transition to Apple Silicon, and how it has impacted the performance and efficiency of Mac computers.

Answer: The transition to Apple Silicon, starting with M1, marked a shift to custom-designed ARM-based processors. This has resulted in significant performance gains, improved energy efficiency, and a unified architecture across Apple's product line.

How has the evolution of Xcode and developer tools influenced the mac OS development ecosystem?

Answer: Xcode improvements, including enhanced debugging tools and interface builders, have streamlined the development process. Swift, introduced in 2014, has become a powerful language for mac OS development.

Discuss the impact of the Mac App Store on software distribution and the mac OS application ecosystem.

Answer: The Mac App Store has provided a centralized platform for software distribution, making it easier for users to discover and install applications. However, it has also faced challenges with app discoverability.

How has the introduction of Catalyst affected the development of cross-platform applications for both mac OS and iOS?

Answer: Catalyst allows developers to create apps that run on both mac OS and iOS with a shared codebase. It streamlines development and encourages consistency in user experience across different devices.

Discuss the evolution of security features in mac OS, including technologies like Gatekeeper and FileVault.

Answer: Gatekeeper ensures only trusted software runs on a Mac, while FileVault provides full-disk encryption. These features, along with regular security updates, contribute to mac OS's reputation for strong security.

How has Apple addressed user privacy concerns in recent mac OS updates, such as App Tracking Transparency and Privacy Labels in the App Store?

Answer: Apple has taken a proactive approach to user privacy by introducing features like App Tracking Transparency, giving users more control over their data. Privacy Labels in the App Store provide transparency about how apps handle user data.

Discuss the role of Dark Mode in recent mac OS versions and its impact on user experience.

Answer: Dark Mode provides users with an alternative visual style, reducing eye strain in low-light environments. It's a design choice that enhances user comfort and personalization.

How has the evolution of Mac OS contributed to accessibility features, such as VoiceOver and Dynamic Type, and their impact on inclusivity?

Answer: Accessibility features have been integral to mac OS, making the Operating System usable by individuals with different abilities. Voice Over and Dynamic Type are examples of features that enhance inclusivity.

Discuss the integration of collaboration features like Continuity Camera and Handoff and their impact on user productivity across Apple devices.

Answer: These features seamlessly connect Macs, iPhones, and iPads, allowing users to start an activity on one device and continue on another. It enhances productivity and provides a cohesive user experience.

How has the evolution of mac OS contributed to advancements in virtual collaboration tools, especially in response to changing work trends?

Answer:mac OS has adapted to the increasing demand for virtual collaboration tools, integrating with popular platforms and optimizing performance for remote work scenarios

Windows Operating System Interview Questions & Answers

What is Windows OS?

Answer: Windows is an Operating System developed by Microsoft that provides a graphical user interface (GUI) for personal computers and servers.

What are the different versions of Windows for desktop computers?

Answer: Some popular versions include Windows 10, Windows 8.1, Windows 7, and Windows Vista.

How does Windows differ from other Operating Systems like Linux or macOS?

Answer: Windows is known for its user-friendly GUI, while Linux is open-source and offers more flexibility. macOS is designed for Apple hardware and is Unix-based.

What is the Windows Registry, and what is its purpose?

Answer: The Windows Registry is a hierarchical database that stores configuration settings and options for the Operating System and installed applications.

How do you access the Task Manager in Windows, and what is its main purpose?

Answer: You can access Task Manager by pressing Ctrl+Shift+Esc or Ctrl+Alt+Delete and selecting it. It is used to manage running processes and applications and monitor system performance.

Explain the Windows File System (NTFS).

Answer: NTFS (New Technology File System) is the default file system for Windows, known for its security features, file compression, and support for large file sizes.

What is the purpose of the Windows System Restore feature?

Answer: System Restore allows users to revert the system's configuration and settings to a previous state, helping to recover from system issues or software conflicts.

What is the Windows Control Panel used for?

Answer: The Control Panel provides a centralized location for configuring and managing various system settings, including hardware, software, and user accounts.

How do you create a user account in Windows, and what are the different types of user accounts?

Answer: User accounts can be created through the Control Panel or Settings app. Windows supports three main types of user accounts: Administrator, Standard, and Guest.

What is the purpose of the Windows Event Viewer?

Answer: Event Viewer is a tool that records system, security, and application events, helping users and administrators diagnose system issues and monitor system health.

What is the Windows Update service, and why is it essential?

Answer: Windows Update is responsible for delivering security updates, bug fixes, and feature enhancements to keep the Operating System secure and up to date.

How can you troubleshoot network connectivity issues in Windows?

Answer: Troubleshooting network issues involves checking network settings, resetting network adapters, and using built-in tools like Ping, ipconfig, and tracert.

Explain the concept of BitLocker in Windows.

Answer: BitLocker is a disk encryption program that helps protect data on Windows devices by encrypting the entire drive.

What is the Windows Task Scheduler, and how can it be used?

Answer: Task Scheduler allows users to automate the execution of tasks or programs at specific times or in response to events, helping to streamline system management.

What is the Blue Screen of Death (BSOD), and how can you troubleshoot it?

Answer: BSOD is an error screen that appears when Windows encounters a critical error. To troubleshoot it, note the error code, check for recent hardware or software changes, and use online resources.

What is Windows PowerShell, and how does it differ from the Command Prompt?

Answer: PowerShell is a more powerful scripting and automation tool compared to the Command Prompt. It uses a more versatile scripting language and cmdlets for system management.

What is the purpose of Windows Defender, and how does it protect the system?

Answer: Windows Defender is an integrated antivirus and antimalware program that helps protect the system from threats by providing real-time scanning and threat detection.

How can you create a backup of files and folders in Windows, and what tools can you use?

Answer: You can create backups using tools like File History, Backup and Restore, or third-party backup software. These tools help protect data from accidental loss.

Explain the difference between 32-bit and 64-bit versions of Windows.

Answer: 32-bit Windows can address up to 4GB of RAM, while 64-bit Windows supports larger memory and is more efficient for modern hardware.

How can you enable Remote Desktop in Windows, and what is it used for?

Answer: To enable Remote Desktop, go to System Properties and enable the feature. Remote Desktop allows users to access and control a Windows system remotely, which is useful for remote administration and support.

When was the first version of Windows released, and what was it called?

Answer: The first version of Windows, Windows 1.0, was released on November 20, 1985.

What was the primary purpose of Windows 1.0, and how did it differ from MS-DOS?

Answer: Windows 1.0 introduced a graphical user interface (GUI) to MS-DOS-based systems, making it easier for users to interact with their computers using a mouse and windows.

What was the first 32-bit version of Windows, and when was it released?

Answer: Windows 95 was the first 32-bit version of Windows, and it was released on August 24, 1995.

What was the significance of Windows 3.1 in the evolution of Windows?

Answer: Windows 3.1 was the first widely successful version of Windows and introduced features like TrueType fonts, multimedia support, and improved performance.

Which version of Windows introduced the Start menu, and in what year?

Answer: The Start menu was introduced in Windows 95, released in 1995.

When did Microsoft release Windows 98, and what were some of its key features?

Answer: Windows 98 was released on June 25, 1998. It featured improved hardware support, the Windows Driver Model (WDM), and the ability to browse the web using Internet Explorer.

What was Windows Me (Windows Millennium Edition), and why was it not well-received?

Answer: Windows Me was released in 2000 and was intended for home users. It was criticized for its instability and lack of significant improvements.

What was the major change introduced in Windows 2000, and in which year was it released?

Answer: Windows 2000, released in 2000, was a significant release as it merged the consumer and business lines of Windows, providing a more stable and secure platform.

Which Windows version replaced Windows 9x and was based on the Windows NT kernel?

Answer: Windows XP replaced Windows 9x and was based on the Windows NT kernel. It was released in 2001.

What is the significance of Windows Vista, and when was it released?

Answer: Windows Vista, released in 2007, introduced a new GUI, enhanced security features, and improvements in search functionality.

What is the Windows Aero user interface, and which version of Windows introduced it?

Answer: Windows Aero is a graphical user interface introduced in Windows Vista, featuring translucent windows, live thumbnails, and visual effects.

When was Windows 7 released, and what made it popular among users?

Answer: Windows 7 was released in 2009 and gained popularity due to its improved performance, stability, and user-friendly features.

What was Windows 8 known for, and how did it differ from previous versions?

Answer: Windows 8, released in 2012, featured a touch-optimized interface with live tiles but received criticism for its departure from the traditional Start menu.

What is the Windows NT family of Operating Systems, and how did it contribute to Windows' evolution?Answer: The Windows NT family includes versions like Windows NT 4.0, 2000, XP, and later. It brought stability, security, and support for multiple processors to the Windows platform.

When was Windows 10 released, and what are some of its key features?

Answer: Windows 10 was released in 2015 and introduced a unified platform for PCs, tablets, and smartphones, along with the return of the Start menu.

sOnline Resources

Videos:https://www.youtube.com/playlist?list=PLzlh_31VWEFoZUJQ_f2U6gaug4W_KGRm1